A·N·N·U·A·L E·D·I·T·I·O·N·S

American History Volume II

15th Edition

Reconstruction through the Present

EDITOR

Robert James Maddox
Pennsylvania State University
University Park

Robert James Maddox, distinguished historian and professor of American history at Pennsylvania State University, received a B.S. from Fairleigh Dickinson University in 1957, an M.S. from the University of Wisconsin in 1958, and a Ph.D. from Rutgers in 1964. He has written, reviewed, and lectured extensively, and is widely respected for his interpretations of presidential character and policy.

Dushkin/McGraw-Hill
Sluice Dock, Guilford, Connecticut 06437

Visit us on the Internet
http://www.dushkin.com/annualeditions/

Credits

1. Reconstruction and the Gilded Age
Facing overview—Nebraska State Historical Society.
2. The Emergence of Modern America
Facing overview—Photo from the Library of Congress.
3. From Progressivism to the 1920s
Facing overview—Photo from the Library of Congress.
4. From the Great Depression to World War II
Facing overview—Photo from the Library of Congress.
110—Museum of American Financial History, UPI/Corbis-Bettmann.
113, 114—State Historical Society of Iowa—Des Moines.
5. From the Cold War to the 1990s
Facing overview—AP/Wide World photo.
6. New Directions for American History
Facing overview—Bay Area Rapid Transit Photo.

Copyright

Cataloging in Publication Data
Main entry under title: Annual Editions: American history, vol. two: Reconstruction through the present. 15/E.
1. United States—History—Periodicals. 2. United States—Historiography—Periodicals. 3. United States—Civilization—Periodicals. I. Title: American history, vol. two: Reconstruction through the present.
ISBN 0–697–39379–8   973′.05   75–20755   ISSN 0733–3560

Fifteenth Edition

Cover image © 1999 PhotoDisc, Inc.

Printed in the United States of America   12334567890BAHBAH901234098   Printed on Recycled Paper

Members of the Advisory Board are instrumental in the final selection of articles for each edition of ANNUAL EDITIONS. Their review of articles for content, level, currentness, and appropriateness provides critical direction to the editor and staff. We think that you will find their careful consideration well reflected in this volume.

Editors/Advisory Board

Staff

To the Reader

In publishing ANNUAL EDITIONS we recognize the enormous role played by the magazines, newspapers, and journals of the public press in providing current, first-rate educational information in a broad spectrum of interest areas. Many of these articles are appropriate for students, researchers, and professionals seeking accurate, current material to help bridge the gap between principles and theories and the real world. These articles, however, become more useful for study when those of lasting value are carefully collected, organized, indexed, and reproduced in a low-cost format, which provides easy and permanent access when the material is needed. That is the role played by ANNUAL EDITIONS.

New to ANNUAL EDITIONS is the inclusion of related World Wide Web sites. These sites have been selected by our editorial staff to represent some of the best resources found on the World Wide Web today. Through our carefully developed topic guide, we have linked these Web resources to the articles covered in this ANNUAL EDITIONS reader. We think that you will find this volume useful, and we hope that you will take a moment to visit us on the Web at *http://www.dushkin.com/* to tell us what you think.

Some scholars have pointed out how much the "velocity of history" has speeded up. If one were to go back in the past to the year 1800, conditions would not have changed all that much from what they had been 100 or 150 years earlier. People wore much the same clothing, ate the same foods cooked in the same way, traveled overland on foot or horseback, and relied on the same remedies for illnesses. In the 140 years since the end of the Civil War, however, revolutionary changes have taken place in virtually all areas. Following the development of automobiles, people were able to travel in just hours distances that would have taken days. Airplanes have put any place on the globe within reach. Radio, television, and computers have vastly changed the transmission of knowledge, earlier restricted to word of mouth or the printed page. Still, many of the issues we confront today have echoes in the past: race relations, gender roles, domestic terrorism, and environmental problems, to name just a few. We can all profit from studying history, not to get "answers" to our problems but perhaps to discover in the past some guidelines for our own time.

The study of history has changed over the years. Early scholars mostly wrote about "chaps," usually prominent white men of achievement. Now virtually everything that has happened is considered fair game. Books and articles tell us about the lives of ordinary people, about groups previously ignored or mentioned only in passing, and about subjects previously considered too trivial or commonplace to warrant examination. History "from the bottom up," once considered innovative, has become commonplace.

New approaches to the study of history complement, but do not replace, the more traditional emphasis upon people who made large differences as *individuals*. Presidents such as Woodrow Wilson and Franklin D. Roosevelt had to make decisions that affected tens of thousands if not millions of lives. The Reverend Martin Luther King Jr. provided inspiration through his oratory and presence that people of lesser gifts could not have hoped to achieve. Margaret Sanger and Eleanor Roosevelt, though never holding official positions of power, nonetheless excercised influence over the ways that people perceived a number of issues.

This fifteenth edition of *Annual Editions: American History, Volume II*, constitutes an effort to provide a balanced collection of articles that deal with great leaders and great decisions as well as with ordinary people at work, at leisure, and at war. Practically everyone who uses the volume will think of one or more articles that he or she thinks would have been preferable to the ones included. Some readers will wish more attention had been paid to one or another subject; others will regret the attention devoted to matters that seem marginal to themselves. That is why we encourage teachers and students to let us know what they believe to be the strengths and weaknesses of this edition.

Annual Editions: American History, Volume II, contains a number of features designed to make the volume "user friendly." These include the *table of contents*, which summarizes each article with key concepts in boldface; a *topic guide* to help locate articles on specific individuals or subjects; and a comprehensive *index*.

New to this edition are *World Wide Web* sites that can be used to further explore the topics. These sites will be cross-referenced by number in the *topic guide*.

Articles are organized into six units. Each unit is preceded by an overview that provides background for informed reading of the articles, briefly introduces each one, and presents key points to consider. World Wide Web sites are also listed to match the unit's theme. Please let us know if you have any suggestions for improving the format.

There will be a new edition of *Annual Editions: American History, Volume II*, in 2 years, with approximately half the readings being replaced by new ones. By completing and mailing the postpaid article rating form included in the back of the book, you will help us judge which articles should be retained and which should be dropped. You can also help to improve the next edition by recommending (or better yet, sending along a copy of) articles that you think should be included. A number of essays included in this edition have come to our attention in this way.

Robert James Maddox

Robert James Maddox
Editor

Contents

UNIT 1

Reconstruction and the Gilded Age

Seven articles examine the development of the United States after the Civil War. Society was changed enormously by Western expansion and technology.

The concepts in bold italics are developed in the article. For further expansion please refer to the Topic Guide and the Index.

UNIT 2

The Emergence of Modern America

Six articles review the beginnings of modern America. Key issues of this period are examined, including terrorism on U.S. soil, turn-of-the century lifestyles, poverty, and military conflicts.

The concepts in bold italics are developed in the article. For further expansion please refer to the Topic Guide and the Index.

UNIT 3

From Progressivism to the 1920s

Seven articles examine American culture in the early twentieth century. The economy began to reap the benefits of technology, women gained the right to vote, and Henry Ford ushered in mass production. Featured are taxation, racial issues, women's liberation and alcohol and drug abuse.

The concepts in bold italics are developed in the article. For further expansion please refer to the Topic Guide and the Index.

vii

UNIT 4

From the Great Depression to World War II

Six selections discuss the severe economic and social trials of the Great Depression of the thirties, the slow recovery process, and the enormous impact of World War II on America's domestic and foreign social consciousness.

The concepts in bold italics are developed in the article. For further expansion please refer to the Topic Guide and the Index.

UNIT 5

From the
Cold War to
the 1990s

Nine articles that cover the
post–World War II period address
the G.I. Bill, racial equality, Korean
War, space technology, radicalism,
and Watergate.

The concepts in bold italics are developed in the article. For further expansion please refer to the Topic Guide and the Index.

ix

UNIT 6

**New Directions
for American
History**

Six articles discuss the current state
of American society and the role the
United States plays in the world.

The concepts in bold italics are developed in the article. For further expansion please refer to the Topic Guide and the Index.

The concepts in bold italics are developed in the article. For further expansion please refer to the Topic Guide and the Index.

Topic Guide

This topic guide suggests how the selections and World Wide Web sites found in the next section of this book relate to topics of traditional concern to American history students and professionals. It is useful for locating interrelated articles and Web sites for reading and research. The guide is arranged alphabetically according to topic.

The relevant Web sites, which are numbered and annotated on pages 4 and 5, are easily identified by the Web icon (◎) under the topic articles. By linking the articles and the Web sites by topic, this ANNUAL EDITIONS reader becomes a powerful learning and research tool.

TOPIC AREA	TREATED IN	TOPIC AREA	TREATED IN
African Americans	1. New View of Reconstruction 20. When White Hoods Were in Flower 28. Baseball's Noble Experiment 32. Martin Luther King's Half-Forgotten Dream 33. Scenes from the '60s 38. American Apartheid? ◎ *1, 3, 5, 8, 9, 20, 27, 30*		39. Revolution in Indian Country ◎ *3, 5, 15, 20, 22, 27, 29, 30, 32*
		Depression, Great	21. Bang! Went the Doors of Every Bank in America ◎ *1, 2, 3, 5, 17, 20, 21*
Anti-Semitism	16. Fate of Leo Frank ◎ *15, 27, 29*	**Diplomacy**	10. Meaning of '98 11. Our First Southeast Asian War 29. From Plan to Practice ◎ *26, 27, 28, 32*
Asians	5. 'Chinese Must Go' 11. Our First Southeast Asian War 30. Echoes of a Distant War ◎ *18, 27, 29, 30*	**Environment**	13. Theodore Roosevelt 41. Our Century . . . and the Next One ◎ *21, 28*
Atomic Bomb	26. Biggest Decision ◎ *25, 26, 28*	**Fitzgerald, F. Scott**	19. F. Scott Fitzgerald
Business	6. Nickel and Dime Empire 21. Bang! Went the Doors of Every Bank in America ◎ *1, 2, 3, 27*	**Frank, Leo**	16. Fate of Leo Frank ◎ *15, 27, 29*
Central Intelligence Agency	37. Can't Anybody Here Play This Game? ◎ *21, 26*	**Government**	1. New View of Reconstruction 3. First Chapter of Children's Rights 4. Stolen Election 9. Electing the President, 1896 13. Theodore Roosevelt 14. Woodrow Wilson, Politician 15. Burden of Taxation 21. Bang! Went the Doors of Every Bank in America 22. Monumental Man 27. G. I. Bill 34. Legacy of Watergate 37. Can't Anybody Here Play This Game? 40. America after the Long War ◎ *1, 2, 3, 4, 6, 7, 12, 13, 18, 19, 20, 21, 24, 25, 26, 27, 28, 29, 31*
Children	3., First Chapter of Children's Rights ◎ *3, 5, 6, 7, 31*		
Cold War	29. From Plan to Practice 30. Echoes of a Distant War 31. Sputnik 37. Can't Anybody Here Play This Game? 40. American after the Long War ◎ *21, 22, 25, 26*		
Culture	7. Iron John in the Gilded Age 17. Margaret Sanger 18. Alcohol in American History 19. F. Scott Fitzgerald 20. When White Hoods Were in Flower 24. Home Front 27. G. I. Bill 28. Baseball's Noble Experiment 31. Sputnik 32. Martin Luther King's Half-Forgotten Dream 33. Scenes from the '60s 35. How the Seventies Changed America 36. Near-Myth of Our Failing Schools 38. American Apartheid?	**Immigrants**	5. 'Chinese Must Go' ◎ *29*
		King, Martin L., Jr.	32. Martin Luther King's Half-Forgotten Dream ◎ *1, 3, 4, 5, 8, 27*
		Korean War	30. Echoes of a Distant War ◎ *26*
		Labor	8. Terrorism Revisited
		Native Americans	39. Revolution in Indian Country ◎ *3, 5*
		Nixon, Richard	34. Legacy of Watergate ◎ *1, 3, 7*

2

◉ AE: American History, Volume II

The following World Wide Web sites have been carefully researched and selected to support the articles found in this reader. If you are interested in learning more about specific topics found in this book, these Web sites are a good place to start. The sites are cross-referenced by number and appear in the topic guide on the previous two pages. Also, you can link to these Web sites through our DUSHKIN ONLINE support site at *http://www.dushkin.com/online/*.

The following sites were available at the time of publication. Visit our Web site—we update DUSHKIN ONLINE regularly to reflect any changes.

General Sources

1. American Historical Association
http://chnm.gmu.edu/aha/
This is the logical first visitation site for someone interested in virtually any topic in American history. All affiliated societies and publications are noted, and AHA and its links on this site present material related to myriad fields of history and having to do with different levels of education.

2. Harvard University/John F. Kennedy School of Government
http://www.ksg.harvard.edu/
Starting from this home page, you will be able to click on a huge variety of links to information about American history, ranging from data about political parties to general debates of enduring issues.

3. History Net
http://www.thehistorynet.com/THNarchives/AmericanHistory/
Supported by the National Historical Society, this site provides information on a wide range of topics. The articles are of excellent quality, and the site has book reviews and even special interviews. It is also frequently updated.

4. Library of Congress
http://www.loc.gov/
Examine this extensive Web site to learn about the extensive resource tools, library services/resources, exhibitions, and databases available through the Library of Congress in many different subfields related to American history.

5. Smithsonian Institution
http://www.si.edu/
This site provides access to the enormous resources of the Smithsonian, which holds some 140 million artifacts and specimens in its trust for "the increase and diffusion of knowledge." Here you can learn about American social, cultural, economic, and political history from a variety of viewpoints.

6. U.S. Founding Documents/Emory University
http://www.law.emory.edu/FEDERAL/
Through this site you can view scanned originals ot the Declaration of Independence, the Constitution, and the Bill of Rights. The transcribed texts are also available, as are *The Federalist Papers.*

7. The White House
http://www.whitehouse.gov/WH/Welcome.html
Visit the home page of the White House for direct access to information about commonly requested federal services, the White House Briefing Room, and the presidents and vice presidents. The "Virtual Library" allows you to search White House documents, listen to speeches, and view photos.

Reconstruction and the Gilded Age

8. Anacostia Museum/Smithsonian Institution
http://www.si.edu/organiza/museums/anacost/

This is the home page of the Center for African American History and Culture of the Smithsonian Institution. Explore its many avenues. This is expected to become a major repository of information.

9. Civil War
http://www.access.digex.net/~bdboyle/cw.html
This useful site provides dozens of links to Civil War sites on the Internet as well as topics having to do with Reconstruction.

10. Jim Zwick/Syracuse University
http://home.ican.net/~fjzwick/
Jim Zwick's home page explores the often-forgotten Filipino revolt against U.S. acquisition of the Philippines after the Spanish-American War. Zwick also discusses anti-imperialist crusades within the United States during the Gilded Age.

The Emergence of Modern America

11. Chicago Historical Society/Northwestern University
http://www.chicagohs.org/fire/
This site, created by the Academic Technologies unit of Northwestern University and the Chicago Historical Society, is interesting and well constructed. Besides discussing the Great Chicago Fire at length, the materials provide insight into the era in which the event took place.

12. Jim Zwick/Syracuse University
http://home.ican.net/~fjzwick/ail98-35.html
Jim Zwick created this interesting site exploring American imperialism from the Spanish-American War years to 1935. It provides valuable primary resources in a variety of related topics.

13. Ohio State University/Department of History
http://www.cohums.ohio-state.edu/history/projects/McKinley/
Browse through this site for insight into the era of William McKinley, including discussion of the Spanish-American War.

14. Small Planet Communications/"The Age of Imperialism"
http://www.smplanet.com/imperialism/toc.html
During the late nineteenth and early twentieth centuries, the United States pursued an aggressive policy of expansionism, extending its political and economic influence around the globe. That pivotal era in the nation's history of is the subject of this interactive site. Maps and photographs are provided.

From Progressivism to the 1920s

15. International Channel
http://www.i-channel.com/features/
Visit this interesting site to experience the memories, sounds, even tastes of Ellis Island. Hear immigrants describe in their own words their experiences entering the gateway to America. It shows the immigrants who helped to create modern America.

16. Mike Iavarone
http://www.worldwar1.com/
This interesting site supplies extensive resources about the Great War and is the appropriate place to begin exploration of this topic as regards the American experience in

World War I. The creator provides "virtual tours" on certain topics, such as "Life on the Homefront."

17. World Wide Web Virtual Library
http://www.iisg.nl/~w3vl/
This site, part of the WWW Virtual Library, focuses on labor and business history. As an index site, this is a good place to start exploring these two vast topics.

From the Great Depression to World War II

18. C John Yu
http://www.geocities.com/Athens/8420/main.html
Created by John Yu, this site, which focuses on the Japanese American internment during World War II, is especially useful for links to other related sites.

19. Miami University
http://www.lib.muohio.edu/inet/subj/history/wwii/general.html
Visit this site as a starting point to find research links for World War II, including topics specific to the United States' participation and the impact on the country.

20. Works Progress Administration/Folklore Project
http://lcweb2.loc.gov/ammem/wpaintro/wpalife.html
Open this home page of the Folklore Project of the Works Progress Administration (WPA) Federal Writers' Project to gain access to thousands of documents on the life histories of ordinary Americans from all walks of life during the Great Depression.

From the Cold War to the 1990s

21. The Federal Web Locator
http://www.law.vill.edu/Fed-Agency/fedwebloc.html
Use this handy site as a launching pad for the Web sites of federal U.S. agencies, departments, and organizations. It is well organized and easy to use for informational and research purposes.

22. The Gallup Organization
http://www.gallup.com/
Open this Gallup Organization home page for links to an extensive archive of public opinion poll results and special reports on a huge variety of topics related to American society, politics, and government.

23. George Mason University
http://mason.gmu.edu/~mgoldste/index.federalism.html
Federalism versus states' rights has always been a spirited debate in American government. Visit this site, "Federalism: Relationship between Local and National Governments," for links to many articles and reports on the subject.

24. STAT-USA
http://www.stat-usa.gov/stat-usa.html
This essential site, a service of the Department of Commerce, contains daily economic news, frequently requested statistical releases, information on export and international trade, domestic economic news and statistical series, and databases.

25. University of California at San Diego
http://ac.acusd.edu/history/20th/coldwar0.html

This superb site presents U.S. government policies during the cold war, listed year by year from 1945 through 1991. It is extensive, with Web links to many other sites.

26. U.S. Department of State
http://www.state.gov/
View this site for understanding into the workings of what has become a major U.S. executive branch department. Links explain what exactly the Department does, what services it provides, what it says about U.S. interests around the world, and much more information.

New Directions for American History

27. American Studies Web
http://www.georgetown.edu/crossroads/asw/
This eclectic site provides links to a wealth of Internet resources for research in American studies, from agriculture and rural development, to history and government, to race and ethnicity.

28. National Center for Policy Analysis
http://www.public-policy.org/~ncpa/pd/pdindex.html
Through this site, you can click onto links to read discussions of an array of topics that are of major interest in the study of American history, from regulatory policy and privatization to economy and income.

29. The National Network for Immigrant and Refugee Rights
http://www.nnirr.org/
The NNIRR serves as a forum to share information and analysis, to educate communities and the general public, and to develop and coordinate plans of action on important immigrant and refugee issues. Visit this site and its many links to explore these issues.

30. STANDARDS: An International Journal of Multicultural Studies
http://stripe.colorado.edu/~standard/
This fascinating site provides access to the *Standards* archives and a seemingly infinite number of links to topics of interest in the study of cultural pluralism.

31. Supreme Court/Legal Information Institute
http://supct.law.cornell.edu/supct/index.html
Open this site for current and historical information about the Supreme Court. The archive contains many opinions issued since May 1990 as well as a collection of nearly 600 of the most historic decisions of the Court.

32. U.S. Information Agency
http://www.usia.gov/usis.html
This interesting and wide-ranging home page of the USIA provides definitions, related documentation, and a discussion of topics of concern to students of American history and government. It addresses today's "Hot Topics" as well as ongoing issues. Many Web links are provided.

We highly recommend that you review our Web site for expanded information and our other product lines. We are continually updating and adding links to our Web site in order to offer you the most usable and useful information that will support and expand the value of your Annual Editions. You can reach us at: *http://www.dushkin.com/annualeditions/*.

www.dushkin.com/online/

Unit 1

Unit Selections

1. **The New View of Reconstruction,** Eric Foner
2. **Miriam Leslie: Belle of the Boardroom,** Donald Dale Jackson
3. **The First Chapter of Children's Rights,** Peter Stevens and Marian Eide
4. **The Stolen Election,** Bernard A. Weisberger
5. **'The Chinese Must Go,'** Bernard A. Weisberger
6. **The Nickel and Dime Empire,** Joseph Gustaitis
7. **Iron John in the Gilded Age,** Mark Carnes

Key Points to Consider

❖ Radical Reconstruction was an attempt to ensure full citizenship to freed people in a society that for centuries had embraced slavery. In view of such fierce resistance by white Southerners, could this attempt have succeeded? How?

❖ Who is to decide what constitutes acceptable discipline and what constitutes child abuse? What rights do parents or guardians have against the intrusion of government into family situations?

❖ How do those who want to exclude members of another race from the society justify their position? Discuss the similarities between the anti-Chinese sentiment of the late nineteenth century and present day opposition to immigration from Asia and Latino countries.

❖ What purposes do exclusionary rituals serve for those who participate in them? Can these rituals be beneficial to individuals or groups who share experiences?

 **Links**   **www.dushkin.com/online/**

8. **Anacostia Museum/Smithsonian Institution**
   http://www.si.edu/organiza/museums/anacost/
9. **Civil War**
   http://www.access.digex.net/~bdboyle/cw.html
10. **Jim Zwick/Syracuse University**
    http://home.ican.net/~fjzwick/

These sites are annotated on pages 4 and 5.

The Civil War destroyed the institution of slavery but left the status of freed peoples undefined. Northern "Radical" Republicans wished to use the power of the federal government, including force if necessary, to ensure that former slaves enjoyed full civil and legal rights. These Republicans had their way, after a grueling struggle with the moderate president Andrew Johnson, and the South was divided into five military districts. White Southerners used every means possible to keep blacks "in their place," including terroristic organizations such as the Ku Klux Klan. Eric Foner's article, "The New View of Reconstruction," tells how Radical Reconstruction failed to achieve its goals in the short run but provided what he calls an "enduring vision." In "The Stolen Election," Bernard Weisberger explains how the disputed presidential election of 1876 ended Reconstruction in the last three Southern states.

Donald Dale Jackson, in "Miriam Leslie: Belle of the Boardroom," reviews the life and times of an exceptional late-1800s businesswoman. Miriam Leslie was an actress, an early feminist, and a successful CEO of a publishing empire.

No one defends child abuse, but who defines what it is and what steps can be taken to remedy a specific situation? The report "The First Chapter of Children's Rights" describes how in 1874 a church caseworker sought legal help to get little Mary Ellen McCormack away from an abusive environment. Citing a seldom-invoked legislative act, the attorneys who took the case persuaded a judge of the New York Supreme Court to rule that Mary Ellen be removed from the hovel in which she lived. Authors Peter Stevens and Marian Eide point out, however,

that there are still disagreements over the role of government and its right to intervene in a family situation. Child abuse continues to haunt society.

Racial prejudice has always been with us. It was particularly virulent on the west coast with regard to Asians during the latter part of the nineteenth century. The essay "The Chinese Must Go" describes how the Chinese population of San Francisco became the target of mob violence in 1877. Author Bernard Weisberger tells us that anti-Chinese sentiment continued to grow, and in 1882 resulted in a ban on all Chinese immigration for 10 years.

During the years following the Civil War, new types of enterprise were developed to take advantage of the population movement from farms to towns and cities. In "The Nickel and Dime Empire," Joseph Gustaitis tells how F. W. Woolworth made available to customers a bewildering variety of inexpensive goods in his five-and-dime stores. The idea caught on, and his chain of stores spread from coast to coast. The demise of the Woolworth empire marked the end of an era.

The rise of feminism and the increased questioning of gender roles has caused some men to question their identities. In 1990 the publication of Robert Bly's Iron John: A Book about Men influenced a number of males to undertake experiences in order to "get in touch" with their masculinity. These included rituals such as chanting and dancing around campfires or imitating the grunts and howls of various animals. "Iron John in the Gilded Age" describes earlier rituals that millions of men periodically performed from which women were excluded.

The New View of Reconstruction

Whatever you were taught or thought you knew about the post–Civil War era is probably wrong in the light of recent study

Eric Foner

Eric Forner is Professor of History at Columbia University and author of Nothing but Freedom: Emancipation and Its Legacy.

In the past twenty years, no period of American history has been the subject of a more thoroughgoing reevaluation than Reconstruction—the violent, dramatic, and still controversial era following the Civil War. Race relations, politics, social life, and economic change during Reconstruction have all been reinterpreted in the light of changed attitudes toward the place of blacks within American society. If historians have not yet forged a fully satisfying portrait of Reconstruction as a whole, the traditional interpretation that dominated historical writing for much of this century has irrevocably been laid to rest.

Anyone who attended high school before 1960 learned that Reconstruction was a era of unrelieved sordidness in American political and social life. The martyred Lincoln, according to this view, had planned a quick and painless readmission of the Southern states as equal members of the national family. President Andrew Johnson, his successor, attempted to carry out Lincoln's policies but was foiled by the Radical Republicans (also known as Vindictives or Jacobins). Motivated by an irrational hatred of Rebels or by ties with Northern capitalists out to plunder the South, the Radicals swept aside Johnson's lenient program and fastened black supremacy upon the defeated Confederacy. An orgy of corruption followed, presided over by unscrupulous carpetbaggers (Northerners who ventured south to reap the spoils of office), traitorous scalawags (Southern whites who cooperated with the new governments for personal gain), and the ignorant and childlike freedmen, who were incapable of properly exercising the political power that had been thrust upon them. After much needless suffering, the white community of the South banded together to overthrow these "black" governments and restore home rule (their euphemism for white supremacy). All told, Reconstruction was just about the darkest page in the American saga.

Originating in anti-Reconstruction propaganda of Southern Democrats during the 1870s, this traditional interpretation achieved scholarly legitimacy around the turn of the century through the work of William Dunning and his students at Columbia University. It reached the larger public through films like *Birth of a Nation* and *Gone With the Wind* and that best-selling work of myth-making masquerading as history, *The Tragic Era* by Claude G. Bowers. In language as exaggerated as it was colorful, Bowers told how Andrew Johnson "fought the bravest battle for constitutional liberty and for the preservation of our institutions ever waged by an Executive" but was overwhelmed by the "poisonous propaganda" of the Radicals. Southern whites, as a result, "literally were put to the torture" by "emissaries of hate" who manipulated the "simple-minded" freedmen, inflaming the negroes' "egotism" and even inspiring "lustful assaults" by blacks upon white womanhood.

In a discipline that sometimes seems to pride itself on the rapid rise and fall of historical interpretations, this traditional portrait of Reconstruction enjoyed remarkable staying power. The long reign of the old interpretation is not difficult to explain. It presented a set of easily identifiable heroes and villains. It enjoyed the imprimatur of the nation's leading scholars. And it accorded with the political and social realities of the first half of this century. This image of Reconstruction helped freeze the mind of the white South in unalterable opposition to any movement for breaching the ascendancy of the Democratic party, eliminating segregation, or readmitting disfranchised blacks to the vote.

Nevertheless, the demise of the traditional interpretation was inevitable, for it ignored the testimony of the central participant in the drama of Reconstruction—the black freedman. Furthermore, it was grounded in the conviction that blacks were unfit to share in political power. As Dunning's Columbia colleague John W. Burgess put it, "A black skin means membership in a race of men which has never of itself succeeded in subjecting passion to reason, has never, therefore, created any civilization of any kind." Once objective scholarship and modern experience rendered that assumption untenable, the entire edifice was bound to fall.

The work of "revising" the history of Reconstruction began with the writings of a handful of survivors of the era, such as John R. Lynch, who had served as a black congressman from Mississippi af-

---

Black initiative established as many schools as did Northern religious societies and the Freedmen's Bureau. The right to vote was not simply thrust upon them by meddling outsiders, since blacks began agitating for the suffrage as soon as they were freed.

---

ter the Civil War. In the 1930s white scholars like Francis Simkins and Robert Woody carried the task forward. Then, in 1935, the black historian and activist W. E. B. Du Bois produced *Black Reconstruction in America,* a monumental revaluation that closed with an irrefutable indictment of a historical profession that had sacrificed scholarly objectivity on the altar of racial bias. "One fact and one alone," he wrote, "explains the attitude of most recent writers toward Reconstruction; they cannot conceive of Negroes as men." Du Bois's work, however, was ignored by most historians.

It was not until the 1960s that the full force of the revisionist wave broke over the field. Then, in rapid succession, virtu-

ally every assumption of the traditional viewpoint was systematically dismantled. A drastically different portrait emerged to take its place. President Lincoln did not have a coherent "plan" for Reconstruction, but at the time of his assassination he had been cautiously contemplating black suffrage. Andrew Johnson was a stubborn, racist politician who lacked the ability to compromise. By isolating himself from the broad currents of public opinion that had nourished Lincoln's career, Johnson created an impasse with Congress that Lincoln would certainly have avoided, thus throwing away his political power and destroying his own plans for reconstructing the South.

The Radicals in Congress were acquitted of both vindictive motives and the charge of serving as the stalking-horses of Northern capitalism. They emerged instead as idealists in the best nineteenth-century reform tradition. Radical leaders like Charles Sumner and Thaddeus Stevens had worked for the rights of blacks long before any conceivable political advantage flowed from such a commitment. Stevens refused to sign the Pennsylvania Constitution of 1838 because it disfranchised the state's black citizens; Sumner led a fight in the 1850s to integrate Boston's public schools. Their Reconstruction policies were based on principle, not petty po-

litical advantage, for the central issue dividing Johnson and these Radical Republicans was the civil rights of freedmen. Studies of congressional policy-making, such as Eric L. McKitrick's *Andrew Johnson and Reconstruction,* also revealed that Reconstruction legislation, ranging from the Civil Rights Act of 1866 to the Fourteenth and Fifteenth Amendments, enjoyed broad support from moderate and conservative Republicans. It was not simply the work of a narrow radical faction.

Even more startling was the revised portrait of Reconstruction in the South itself. Imbued with the spirit of the civil rights movement and rejecting entirely the racial assumptions that had underpinned the traditional interpretation, these historians evaluated Reconstruction from the black point of view. Works like Joel Williamson's *After Slavery* portrayed the period as a time of extraordinary political, social, and economic progress for blacks. The establishment of public school systems, the granting of equal citizenship to blacks, the effort to restore the devastated Southern economy, the attempt to construct an interracial political democracy from the ashes of slavery, all these were commendable achievements, not the elements of Bowers's "tragic era."

Until recently, Thaddeus Stevens had been viewed as motivated by irrational hatred of the Rebels (left). Now he has emerged as an idealist in the best reform tradition.

EDWARD S ELLIS, *The History of Our Country*, VOL. 5, 1900

SCHOMBERG CENTER, NEW YORK PUBLIC LIBRARY

Reconstruction governments were portrayed as disastrous failures (left) because elected blacks were ignorant or corrupt. In fact, postwar corruption cannot be blamed on former slaves.

Unlike earlier writers, the revisionists stressed the active role of the freedmen in shaping Reconstruction. Black initiative established as many schools as did Northern religious societies and the Freedmen's Bureau. The right to vote was not simply thrust upon them by meddling outsiders, since blacks began agitating for the suffrage as soon as they were freed. In 1865 black conventions throughout the South issued eloquent, though unheeded, appeals for equal civil and political rights.

With the advent of Radical Reconstruction in 1867, the freedmen did enjoy a real measure of political power. But black supremacy never existed. In most states blacks held only a small fraction of political offices, and even in South Carolina, where they comprised a majority of the state legislature's lower house, effective power remained in white hands. As for corruption, moral standards in both government and private enterprise were at low ebb throughout the nation in the postwar years—the era of Boss Tweed, the Credit Mobilier scandal, and the Whiskey Ring. Southern corruption could hardly be blamed on former slaves.

Other actors in the Reconstruction drama also came in for reevaluation. Most carpetbaggers were former Union soldiers seeking economic opportunity in the postwar South, not unscrupulous adventurers. Their motives, a typically American amalgam of humanitarianism and the pursuit of profit, were no more insidious than those of Western pioneers. Scalawags, previously seen as traitors to the white race, now emerged as "Old Line" Whig Unionists who had

opposed secession in the first place or as poor whites who had long resented planters' domination of Southern life and who saw in Reconstruction a chance to recast Southern society along more democratic lines. Strongholds of Southern white Republicanism like east Tennessee and western North Carolina had been the scene of resistance to Confederate rule throughout the civil War; now,

Under slavery most blacks had lived in nuclear family units, although they faced the constant threat of separation from loved ones by sale. Reconstruction provided the opportunity for blacks to solidify their preexisting family ties.

as one scalawag newspaper put it, the choice was "between salvation at the hand of the Negro or destruction at the hand of the rebels."

At the same time, the Ku Klux Klan and kindred groups, whose campaign of violence against black and white Repub-

licans had been minimized or excused in older writings, were portrayed as they really were. Earlier scholars had conveyed the impression that the Klan intimidated blacks mainly by dressing as ghosts and playing on the freedmen's superstitions. In fact, black fears were all too real: the Klan was a terrorist organization that beat and killed its political opponents to deprive blacks of their newly won rights. The complicity of the Democratic party and the silence of prominent whites in the face of such outrages stood as an indictment of the moral code the South had inherited from the days of slavery.

By the end of the 1960s, then, the old interpretation had been completely reversed. Southern freedmen were the heroes, the "Redeemers" who overthrew Reconstruction were the villains, and if the era was "tragic," it was because change did not go far enough. Reconstruction had been a time of real progress and its failure a lost opportunity for the South and the nation. But the legacy of Reconstruction—the Fourteenth and Fifteenth Amendments—endured to inspire future efforts for civil rights. As Kenneth Stampp wrote in *The Era of Reconstruction,* a superb summary of revisionist findings published in 1965, "if it was worth four years of civil war to save the Union, it was worth a few years of radical reconstruction to give the American Negro the ultimate promise of equal civil and political rights."

As Stampp's statement suggests, the reevaluation of the first Reconstruction was inspired in large measure by the impact of the second—the modern civil rights movement. And with the waning of that movement in recent years, writing on Reconstruction has undergone still another transformation. Instead of seeing the Civil War and its aftermath as a second American Revolution (as Charles Beard had), a regression into barbarism (as Bowers argued), or a golden opportunity squandered (as the revisionists saw it), recent writers argue that Radical Reconstruction was not really very radical. Since land was not distributed to the former slaves, they remained economically dependent upon their former owners. The planter class survived both the war and Reconstruction with its property (apart from slaves) and prestige more or less intact.

Not only changing times but also the changing concerns of historians have contributed to this latest reassessment of Reconstruction. The hallmark of the past decade's historical writing has been an emphasis upon "social history"—the evocation of the past lives of ordinary Americans—and the downplaying of strictly political events. When applied to Reconstruction, this concern with the "social" suggested that black suffrage and officeholding, once seen as the most radical departures of the Reconstruction era, were relatively insignificant.

Recent historians have focused their investigations not upon the politics of Reconstruction but upon the social and economic aspects of the transition from slavery to freedom. Herbert Gutman's influential study of the black family during and after slavery found little change in family structure or relations between men and women resulting from emancipation. Under slavery most blacks had lived in nuclear family units, although they faced the constant threat of separation from loved ones by sale. Reconstruction provided the opportunity for blacks to solidify their preexisting family ties. Conflicts over whether black women should work in the cotton fields (planters said yes, many black families said no) and over white attempts to "apprentice" black children revealed that the autonomy of family life was a major preoccupation of the freedmen. Indeed, whether manifested in their withdrawal from churches controlled by whites, in the blossoming of black fraternal, be-

nevolent, and self-improvement organizations, or in the demise of the slave quarters and their replacement by small tenant farms occupied by individual families, the quest for independence from white authority and control over their own day-to-day lives shaped the black response to emancipation.

In the post–Civil War South the surest guarantee of economic autonomy, blacks believed, was land. To the freedmen the justice of a claim to land based on their years of unrequited labor appeared self-evident. As an Alabama black convention put it, "The property which they [the planters] hold was nearly all earned by the sweat of *our* brows." As Leon Litwack showed in *Been in the Storm So Long,* a Pulitzer Prize–winning account of the black response to emancipation, many freedmen in 1865 and 1866 refused to sign labor contracts, expecting the federal government to give them land. In some localities, as one Alabama overseer reported, they "set up claims to the plantation and all on it."

The Civil War raised the decisive questions of American's national existence: the relations between local and national authority, the definition of citizenship, the balance between force and consent in generating obedience to authority.

In the end, of course, the vast majority of Southern blacks remained propertyless and poor. But exactly why the South, and especially its black population, suffered from dire poverty and economic retardation in the decades following the Civil War is a matter of

much dispute. In *One Kind of Freedom* economists Roger Ransom and Richard Sutch indicted country merchants for monopolizing credit and charging usurious interest rates, forcing black tenants into debt and locking the South into a dependence on cotton production that impoverished the entire region. But Jonathan Wiener, in his study of postwar Alabama, argued that planters used their political power to compel blacks to remain on the plantations. Planters succeeded in stabilizing the plantation system, but only by blocking the growth of alternative enterprises, like factories, that might draw off black laborers, thus locking the region into a pattern of economic backwardness.

If the trust of recent writing has emphasized the social and economic aspects of Reconstruction, politics has not been entirely neglected. But political studies have also reflected the postrevisionist mood summarized by C. Vann Woodward when he observed "how essentially nonrevolutionary and conservative Reconstruction really was." Recent writers, unlike their revisionist predecessors, have found little to praise in federal policy toward the emancipated blacks.

A new sensitivity to the strength of prejudice and laissez-faire ideas in the nineteenth-century North has led many historians to doubt whether the Republican party ever made a genuine commitment to racial justice in the South. The granting of black suffrage was an alternative to a long-term federal responsibility for protecting the rights of the former slaves. Once enfranchised, blacks could be left to fend for themselves. With the exception of a few Radicals like Thaddeus Stevens, nearly all Northern policy-makers and educators are criticized today for assuming that, so long as the unfettered operations of the marketplace afforded blacks the opportunity to advance through diligent labor, federal efforts to assist them in acquiring land were unnecessary.

Probably the most innovative recent writing on Reconstruction politics has centered on a broad reassessment of black Republicanism, largely undertaken by a new generation of black historians. Scholars like Thomas Holt and

Some scholars exalted the motives of the Ku Klux Klan (left). Actually, its members were part of a terrorist organization that beat and killed its political opponents to deprive blacks of their rights.

Nell Painter insist that Reconstruction was not simply a matter of black and white. Conflicts within the black community, no less than divisions among whites, shaped Reconstruction politics. Where revisionist scholars, both black and white, had celebrated the accomplishments of black political leaders, Holt, Painter, and others charge that they failed to address the economic plight of the black masses. Painter criticized "representative colored men," as national black leaders were called, for failing to provide ordinary freedmen with effective political leadership. Holt found that black officeholders in South Carolina most emerged from the old free mulatto class of Charleston, which shared many assumptions with prominent whites. "Basically bourgeois in their origins and orientation," he wrote, they "failed to act in the interest of black peasants."

In emphasizing the persistence from slavery of divisions between free blacks and slaves, these writers reflect the increasing concern with continuity and conservatism in Reconstruction. Their work reflects a startling extension of revisionist premises. If, as has been argued for the past twenty years, blacks were active agents rather than mere victims of manipulation, then they could not be absolved of blame for the ultimate failure of Reconstruction.

Despite the excellence of recent writings and the continual expansion of our knowledge of the period, historians of

Reconstruction today face a unique dilemma. An old interpretation has been overthrown, but a coherent new synthesis has yet to take its place. The revisionists of the 1960s effectively established a series of negative points: the Reconstruction governments were not as bad as had been portrayed, black supremacy was a myth, the Radicals were not cynical manipulators of the freedmen. Yet no convincing overall portrait of the quality of political and social life emerged from their writings. More recent historians have rightly pointed to elements of continuity that spanned the nineteenth-century Southern experience, especially the survival, in modified form, of the plantation system. Nevertheless, by denying the real changes that did occur, they have failed to provide a convincing portrait of an era characterized above all by drama, turmoil, and social change.

Building upon the findings of the past twenty years of scholarship, a new portrait of Reconstruction ought to begin by viewing it not as a specific time period, bounded by the years 1865 and 1877, but as an episode in a prolonged historical process—American society's adjustment to the consequences of the Civil War and emancipation. The Civil War, of course, raised the decisive questions of America's national existence: the relations between local and national authority, the definition of citizenship, the balance between force and consent

in generating obedience to authority. The war and Reconstruction, as Allan Nevins observed over fifty years ago, marked the "emergence of modern America." This was the era of the completion of the national railroad network, the creation of the modern steel industry, the conquest of the West and final subduing of the Indians, and the expansion of the mining frontier. Lincoln's America—the world of the small farm and artisan shop—gave way to a rapidly industrializing economy. The issues that galvanized postwar Northern politics—from the question of the greenback currency to the mode of paying holders of the national debt—arose from the economic changes unleased by the Civil War.

Above all, the war irrevocably abolished slavery. Since 1619, when "twenty negars" disembarked from a Dutch ship in Virginia, racial injustice had haunted American life, mocking its professed ideals even as tobacco and cotton, the products of slave labor, helped finance the nation's economic development. Now the implications of the black presence could no longer be ignored. The Civil War resolved the problem of slavery but, as the Philadelphia diarist Sydney George Fisher observed in June 1865, it opened an even more intractable problem: "What shall we do with the Negro?" Indeed, he went on, this was a problem "*incapable* of any solution that will satisfy both North and South."

As Fisher realized, the focal point of Reconstruction was the social revolution known as emancipation. Plantation slavery was simultaneously a system of labor, a form of racial domination, and the foundation upon which arose a distinctive ruling class within the South. Its demise threw open the most fundamental questions of economy, society, and politics. A new system of labor, social, racial, and political relations had to be created to replace slavery.

The United States was not the only nation to experience emancipation in the nineteenth century. Neither plantation slavery nor abolition were unique to the United States. But Reconstruction was. In a comparative perspective Radical Reconstruction stands as a remarkable experiment, the only effort of a society experiencing abolition to bring the former slaves within the umbrella of equal citizenship. Because the Radicals did not achieve everything they wanted, historians have lately tended to play down the stunning departure represented by black suffrage and officeholding. Former slaves, most fewer than two years removed from bondage, debated the fundamental questions of the polity: what is a republican form of government? Should the state provide equal education for all? How could political equality be reconciled with a society in which property was so unequally distributed? There was something inspiring in the way such men met the challenge of Reconstruction. "I knew nothing more than to obey my master," James K. Greene, an Alabama black politician later recalled. "But the tocsin of freedom sounded and knocked at the door and we walked out like free men and we met the exigencies as they grew up, and shouldered the responsibilities."

You never saw a people more excited on the subject of politics than are the negroes of the south," one planter observed in 1867. And there were more than a few Southern whites as well who in these years shook off the prejudices of the past to embrace the revision of a new South dedicated to the principles of equal citizenship and social justice. One ordinary South Carolinian expressed the new sense of possibility in 1868 to the Republican governor of the state: "I am sorry that I cannot write an elegant stiled letter to your excellency. But I rejoice to think that God almighty has given to the poor of S.C. a Gov. to hear to feel to protect the humble poor without distinction to race or color. . . . I am a native borned S.C. a poor man never owned a Negro in my life nor my father before me. . . . Remember the true and loyal are the poor of the whites and blacks, outside of these you can find none loyal."

Few modern scholars believe the Reconstruction governments established in the South in 1867 and 1868 fulfilled the aspirations of their humble constituents. While their achievements in such realms as education, civil rights, and the economic rebuilding of the South are now widely appreciated, historians today believe they failed to affect either the economic plight of the emancipated slave or the ongoing transformation of independent white farmers into cotton tenants. Yet their opponents did perceive the Reconstruction governments in precisely this way—as representatives of a revolution that had put the bottom rail, both racial and economic, on top. This perception helps explain the ferocity of the attacks leveled against them and the pervasiveness of violence in the postemancipation South.

The spectacle of black men voting and holding office was anathema to large numbers of Southern whites. Even more disturbing, at least in the view of those who still controlled the plantation regions of the South, was the emergence of local officials, black and white, who sympathized with the plight of the black laborer. Alabama's vagrancy law was a "dead letter" in 1870, "because those who are charged with its enforcement are indebted to the vagrant vote for their offices and emoluments." Political debates over the level and incidence of taxation, the control of crops, and the resolution of contract disputes revealed that a primary issue of Reconstruction was the role of government in a plantation society. During presidential Reconstruction, and after "Redemption," with planters and their allies in control of politics, the law emerged as a means of stabilizing and promoting the plantation system. If Radical Reconstruction failed to redistribute the land of the South, the ouster of the planter class from control of politics as least ensured that the sanctions of the criminal law would not be employed to discipline the black labor force.

An understanding of this fundamental conflict over the relation between government and society helps explain the pervasive complaints concerning corruption and "extravagance" during Radical Reconstruction. Corruption there was aplenty; tax rates did rise sharply. More significant than the rate of taxation, however, was the change in its incidence. For the first time, planters and white farmers had to pay a significant portion of their income to the government, while propertyless blacks often escaped scot-free. Several states, moreover, enacted heavy taxes on uncultivated land to discourage land speculation and force land onto the market, benefiting, it was hoped, the freedmen.

In the end neither the abolition of slavery nor Reconstruction succeeded in resolving the debate over the meaning of freedom in American life.

As time passed, complaints about the "extravagance" and corruption of Southern governments found a sympathetic audience among influential Northerners. The Democratic charge that universal suffrage in the South was responsible for high taxes and governmental extravagance coincided with a rising conviction among the urban middle classes of the North that city government had to be taken out o the hands of the immigrant poor and returned to the "best men"—the educated, professional, financially independent citizens unable to exert much political influence at a time of mass parties and machine politics. Increasingly the "respectable" middle classes began to retreat from the very notion of universal suffrage. The poor were not longer perceived as honest producers, the backbone of the social order; now they became the "dangerous classes," the "mob." As the historian Francis Parkman put it, too much power rested with "masses of imported ignorance and hereditary ineptitude." To Parkman the Irish of the Northern cities and the blacks of the South were equally incapable of utilizing the ballot: "Witness the municipal corruptions of New York, and the monstrosities of negro rule in South Carolina." Such attitudes helped to justify Northern inaction as, one by one, the Reconstruction regimes of the South were overthrown by political violence.

In the end, then, neither the abolition of slavery nor Reconstruction succeeded in resolving the debate over the meaning of freedom in American life. Twenty years before the American Civil War, writing about the prospect of abolition in France's colonies, Alexis de Tocqueville had written, "If the Negroes have the right to become free, the [planters] have the incontestable right not to be ruined by the Negroes' freedom." And in the United States, as in nearly every plantation society that experienced the end of slavery, a rigid social and political dichotomy between former master and former slave, an ideology of racism, and a dependent labor force with limited economic opportunities all survived abolition. Unless one means by freedom the simple fact of not being a slave, emancipation thrust blacks into a kind of no-man's land, a partial freedom that made a mockery of the American ideal of equal citizenship.

Yet by the same token the ultimate outcome underscores the uniqueness of Reconstruction itself. Alone among the societies that abolished slavery in the nineteenth century, the United States, for a moment, offered the freedmen a measure of political control over their own destinies. However brief its sway, Reconstruction allowed scope for a remarkable political and social mobilization of the black community. It opened doors of opportunity that could never be completely closed. Reconstruction transformed the lives of Southern blacks in ways unmeasurable by statistics and unreachable by law. It raised their expectations and aspirations, redefined their status in relation to the larger society, and allowed space for the creation of institutions that enabled them to survive the repression that followed. And it established constitutional principles of civil and political equality that, while flagrantly violated after Redemption, planted the seeds of future struggle.

Certainly, it terms of the sense of possibility with which it opened, Reconstruction failed. But as Du Bois observed, it was a "splendid failure." For its animating vision—a society in which social advancement would be open to all on the basis of individual merit, not inherited caste distinctions—is as old as America itself and remains relevant to a nation still grappling with the unresolved legacy of emancipation.

Miriam Leslie

Belle of the Boardroom

By Donald Dale Jackson

First and always she was a great beauty, the "belle of the ball" at Abraham Lincoln's first inaugural and a diamond-bedecked dazzler well into her 60s. But Miriam Leslie was much more than a pretty face amid swirling copper-colored hair. She was a writer who produced one very good travel book and truckloads of essays on life and love; a reporter with the moxie to debate polygamy with Brigham Young on his home turf; an editor with enough talent and drive to rescue a failing publishing empire and turn it around—twice; an accomplished linguist and translator; an early feminist who championed women's rights and bequeathed the bulk of her $2 million estate to the cause; and, finally, but by no means incidentally, a much-married, oft-entangled, ever-beguiling and flirtatious convention-flouter and social rule breaker, a woman whom small minds might call a home wrecker. Reaching for a late 20th-century parallel to this phenomenon of the late 19th is a formidable stretch, but think of a combination of Ann Landers, Gloria Steinem, Katharine Graham and Elizabeth Taylor, with Clare Boothe Luce and Pamela Harriman thrown in for good measure.

The succession of names she bore is an outline of her vivid career. She began as Miriam Florence Follin of New Orleans, did a brief, cloudy and later suppressed stint as Mrs. David Peacock of New York, then took a turn on stage as Minnie Montez, sister of the world-renowned actress Lola, before the Civil War. She emerged next as Miriam Squier, wife of an archaeologist/diplo-

Overseeing a publishing empire that pioneered illustrated coverage, she became a legendary CEO

mat/journalist, an identity that persisted through considerable stress and storm until it metamorphosed into Mrs. Frank Leslie, spouse of a publishing tycoon and a journalistic powerhouse in her own right.

After Leslie died she actually *became* Frank Leslie, legally changing her name so she could hold the contracts (and debts) that had been his. When she married for the fourth time she was Mrs. Willie Wilde (he was Oscar Wilde's brother), though the world—and most of the world knew her by then—still called her Frank Leslie. In a final spasm of vanity she declared in her dowager years that she merited a title as a descendant of French nobility, and when she died at age 78 (though the hoodwinked *New York Times* thought she was 63), she exited, with due grandeur, as the Baroness de Bazus.

Miriam Leslie (to settle on one name for convenience) was in the end more and less than she seemed. She had the good editor's gift for staying ahead, but not too far ahead, of her audience, but as a writer she lapsed too often into mauve-tinted self-indulgence. She was a remarkably successful businesswoman, perhaps her most notable achievement, in an age when executives in silk dresses were rarely taken seriously. The feminism she professed seems quaint by today's sterner standards—women should be credited for their brainpower, she argued, but also cherished, on occasion, as charmingly helpless. With Miriam there was often an impulse to have it both ways; she believed, she wrote, in clothing an iron hand in a velvet glove. She was an unabashed snob with the prejudices of a plutocrat, but she could also argue for fairer treatment of the cruelly persecuted Chinese in California. Her life was singular, as different from that of most American women of her time as that of a queen, and her life was her legacy.

Her early years were both an apprenticeship in refinement and a series of narrowly averted wrong turns. She was born in New Orleans' French Quarter in 1836 to parents who, it seems, never bothered to marry, though they remained more or less together. Her father, descended from French Huguenot nobility, raised her to appreciate literature and culture, tutoring her not just in French but in Italian, Spanish, German and Latin as well. The family moved to Cincinnati and then, when she was 11, to New York. When she was 17, Miriam,

During the Leslies' tour of the West, Miriam met with Mormon leader Brigham Young; predictably, her views on women did not accord with his polygamist stance.

already a knockout, made her first detour from the straight and narrow. The man's name was David Peacock, and it was doubtless no coincidence, given what would become her lifelong obsession with diamonds, that he worked as a jewelry clerk. The untidy details, surfacing two decades later in the most awkward possible way, showed that Miriam's mother found out about her affair with Peacock and threatened him with jail unless he married her. The outflanked clerk obliged on the understanding that he wouldn't have to support her, nor would they live together, and two years later the marital charade was annulled.

Single again and not quite 20, Miriam turned up next on the stage, billed as Minnie, the younger sister and partner of Lola Montez, one of the most famous and flamboyant stars of the 1850s and the onetime mistress of King Ludwig of Bavaria. The two teamed up

in a series of perishable comedies with titles like *The Cabin Boy* and *Plot and Passion,* performing in various Eastern cities and receiving polite notices but no thunderous mandate to carry on. Miriam soon retired from the boards after keeping company, temporarily, with a wealthy (and married) former congressman from Tennessee.

She was beginning to move in the loftier social strata her father had envisioned for her. Charming, radiant and intelligent, she captivated the accomplished archaeologist and Central America expert Ephraim G. Squier at their first meeting. Miriam and the multi-talented Squier—he was a diplomat, businessman, writer and scholar, and 15 years her senior—were married in October 1857. For a while they made a handsome and happy couple. They traveled to Europe, she helped him with a Spanish-language newspaper he published in New York, and his background

in diplomacy earned them an invitation to Lincoln's first inaugural in March 1861, where the 24-year-old Miriam had her first whirl in the society spotlight.

"This lady's personal attractions, youth and graceful manner, made her the acknowledged belle of the ball," a newspaper account said, "while her sprightly and intellectual conversation, and her knowledge of various languages, placed all who came within her sphere perfectly at their ease. Her dress alone—a vision in cherry satin, flounces and puffed sleeves—rated several sentences.

This description appeared in *Frank Leslie's Illustrated Newspaper,* which was significant because publisher Leslie, the reigning king of pictorial journalism in America, would in short order emerge as, first, Squier and Miriam's tenant in their Manhattan house, next as their employer and then—but that would be getting ahead of the story.

Leslie was a dynamo, an earthy, generous and talented engraver-entrepreneur who had emigrated from England and launched a series of illustrated journals that adhered to his motto, "Never shoot over the heads of the people." His weeklies and monthlies aimed instead at all members of the family, combining high-quality illustrations with a zest for the sensational and a folksy, down-home flavor. Miriam would before long leave her own stamp on the Leslie product, but first the domestic drama had to play out.

Leslie hired Squier as a writer and editor for his *Illustrated Newspaper* in late 1861. The publisher, Squier had learned, was unhappily married and seeking separate lodging, so that same year Squier had invited him to board with him and Miriam, an offer he may have rued for the rest of his life. Miriam charmed Leslie from the beginning, and she soon became an editor of *Frank Leslie's Lady's Magazine*. The Squiers and Leslie presented a contented threesome at first, but before long Frank and Miriam were clearly showing interest in each other.

In 1867 the trio visited Europe, but Squier didn't enjoy the trip quite as much as the other two. Leslie arranged to have him jailed for a debt he owed in Britain, freeing the publisher and his fellow litterateur to enjoy two weeks in London together before they bailed him out. Back home in New York, rumors had scudded for years around Leslie headquarters about the sleeping arrangements in the Squier home, and which doors were open and which closed. Leslie's wife fought his efforts to get a divorce for several years before she finally acquiesced in 1872.

Getting rid of Squier, who by this time was drinking heavily, was more complicated. Miriam arranged for him to attend a party where he drunkenly cavorted with a prostitute while friends of Leslie's watched as potential witnesses in a divorce action. Squier didn't contest the divorce, and Leslie and Miriam married in 1874. Less than a month after their wedding, Squier was adjudged insane in a New York court and confined to the Sanford Hall Asylum in Flushing.

Miriam had by this time evolved into a capable and productive journalist. She was editing three of the Leslie papers, the *Lady's Magazine, Frank Leslie's Lady's Journal* and a family weekly called *Frank Leslie's Chimney Corner,* which she had planned and launched and which soon was earning $72,000 a year on a circulation of 80,000. *Chimney Corner* billed itself as "high-toned and pure, combining entertainment with instructive features." A normal issue contained fiction, a story about an exotic place or custom, a sketch of a "self-made man of our times," an item on a natural wonder, poetry, a joke page and an essay by the editor. She held forth on topics ranging from "Broken Hearts" to "Social Tyrants" and "Ennui" to "Useless Men," dispensing common-sense advice and observations in a somewhat arch but often engaging style. An essay on middle age asked forgiveness for any number of encroaching infirmities—including an "inability to waltz with distinction" and a "tendency" for the hair "to thin." Another, on children (which Miriam lacked), expressed surprise that anyone could cherish a "scratching, kicking, struggling little creature that chiefly occupies its waking hours in making the most extraordinary grimaces and smiling feebly at those who temporarily become imbecile for its amusement."

The mid-1870s were golden years for the Leslies. The pretense and circumspection were over. They lived in a house on Fifth Avenue once owned by the notorious Boss Tweed and had a 12-room lakeside cottage at Saratoga where they idled away vacations amid the stables, the esplanade, the sunken croquet lawn, the steam launch at their private dock. There were guests such as Gen. Ulysses S. Grant and Emperor Dom Pedro of Brazil, elegant soirees and nights at the opera. Ever partial to diamonds, Miriam donned $70,000 worth of diamond jewelry for an 1875 reception in honor of Samuel Tilden, the governor of New York. "Money is the all in all of our existence," she had once advised the unfortunate Squier, and she knew how to enjoy the all in all.

The Leslies' appetite for extravagance culminated in a luxurious and carefully planned coast-to-coast railroad trip in 1877, a grand tour that yielded an enlightening close-up confrontation between the most refined of Eastern sophisticates and the still untamed and unruly West, where Custer's cavalrymen had made their stand at Little Bighorn only a year earlier. The trip was a brilliant stroke: the railroads picked up the tab for their opulent palace car, with its oversize roaster oven and plush furnishings, in exchange for the publicity; artists and writers traveling with them (the party totaled 12, plus Miriam's Skye terrier, Follette) sent dispatches back to the Leslie periodicals, while Miriam took notes for a book that would prove to be her most impressive literary legacy.

LIBRARY OF CONGRESS

Years before Miriam met Frank Leslie, she appeared in one of his publications: in 1857, she and actress Lola Montez were shown crossing an icy Hudson on their way to perform.

The Leslies and the West got their first look at each other when the train rattled onto the Great Plains after stops at Niagara Falls and Chicago. Outside Omaha, Miriam peered out at a lonely band of Indians riding into a storm on the "apparently illimitable" tawny-colored plain. Few if any other tourists could have compared the appeal of buffalo grass for grazing animals to the way "a gourmand accepts fresh truffles." In Cheyenne they visited a theater and noted a sign above the bar reading "Gents, be liberal." In Colorado Springs they learned how to circumvent local prohibition laws: the thirsty party, Miriam wrote, "approaches [a] window, beside which there is a slit in the wall, and, passing through this latter ten or twenty-five cents . . . sighs audibly: 'How I wish I had a glass of ale,' and presto! the window shelf is turned by some mysterious hand, and presently on it rests a mug of foaming ale. . . ."

They lingered longest in San Francisco, savoring the comforts of the Palace Hotel, touring Chinatown and looking in on an opium den in the company of a detective, and hobnobbing with millionaires Leland Stanford and William Sharon. Miriam, alluding to the free and easy style that has always characterized San Francisco, observed that "the climate, like the society, like the morals, and like the social habits . . . is a little mixed." She was both fascinated and repelled by the Chinese. She was distressed to see an Asian girl who had been sold into slavery, but she marveled at a Chinese drama when a dozen men "turned somersaults across the stage . . . each one flinging himself fully six feet in [the] air and spinning round like a wheel. . . ." Miriam deplored the pervasive persecution of the Chinese, praising their work habits and defending their right to "that freedom and manly self-government we are so justly proud of."

A side trip by stage to Yosemite gave the Leslie party and four friends an unscheduled glimpse of how most Westerners really lived. A storm forced the 16 of them to spend the night in a three-room stage station already occupied by two women and three children. Miriam appointed herself cook, improvising a meal from the minimal victuals on hand

before bedding down on a table with a bag of salt for a pillow. As her biographer Madeleine Stern put it, Miriam brought "not only her fashion but her fortitude to the West."

Eastbound again, they paused in the bonanza town of Virginia City, Nevada. While Frank was fascinated by the underground silver mines and mills, Miriam was contemptuous of Virginia City, dismissing it in a few haughty lines that would come back to hurt her in a way she never could have imagined. "To call a place dreary, desolate, homeless, uncomfortable, and wicked is a good deal," she wrote, "but to call it God-forsaken is a good deal more, and . . . we never found a place better deserving the title." She complained that every other house was a casino or saloon, adding a gratuitous slam at the women in the town where Mark Twain once worked as a newspaperman: "The population is largely masculine, very few women, except of the worst class."

The journalistic highlight of the trip was the Mormon capital, Salt Lake City. Miriam, married to her third husband (even if the third didn't know about the first), was no admirer of a religion whose leader had between 19 and 27 wives, but she marshaled charm enough to get a revealing interview with 76-year-old Brigham Young. They began with pleasantries about the weather, but Miriam was having none of that. "Do you suppose, Mr. President, that I came all the way to Salt Lake City to hear that it was a fine day?" she said. The courtly Young replied that he was sure she didn't, "for it must be fine weather wherever you are."

Maintaining the offensive, she wondered, "What religion can make a woman happy in seeing the husband whom she loves devoted to another wife . . . ? Any woman, I should think, would spend all her strength . . . to attract and retain his love." Young, cocking an eyebrow and allowing that she looked "like just the woman to do that sort of thing," replied that Mormon women were content and accepted church teachings. Miriam then asked whether Mormon husbands felt no preferences among their wives. "Well, perhaps," the patriarch replied. "Human nature is frail, but

our religion teaches us to control and conceal those preferences . . . and we do—we do."

Miriam's book about the trip, *California: A Pleasure Trip from Gotham to the Golden Gate,* was out before the end of the year. In a coy preface she tried to derail criticism by calling the book the "vapory visions of a woman's memory and "not so much a book as a long gossipy letter to one's friends," but she needed no extra help. The book succeeded as a lively, perceptive narrative by a sensitive if insulated traveler. The *New York Herald* found it a "pleasantly written" history, while the *Sun* lauded her "happy faculty of description."

The trip and the travel book were in retrospect the zenith of the good times for the Leslies as a couple; after that the pendulum swung the other way. The first blast of bad news was Frank's financial collapse. He had been spending more than he earned for some time, and the economic crisis of 1877 sent him deeper into debt, as did overexpansion of his press empire and the Leslies' lavish lifestyle. A news item in late 1877 listed debts of $324,825. His property was assigned to another publisher, with

NEW YORK PUBLIC LIBRARY

Miriam Leslie scooped her competitors in coverage of an assassin's attack on President Garfield in 1881; circulation soared.

At her empire's Fifth Avenue headquarters, Miriam's office possessed an imposing aura. A bust of her late husband stood on the mantle; a stuffed eagle soared overhead.

use the name in the publications. The problem now was repaying the widow and reclaiming the stones.

Her professionalism saved her—and the Leslie empire. When an assassin gravely wounded President James Garfield on Saturday, July 2, 1881, Miriam immediately sent two artists to Washington, summoned the entire staff to work on Sunday and produced an issue of the *Illustrated Newspaper* with full coverage of the shooting by Tuesday; she put out an extra edition that Friday and published the regular edition the following Tuesday, all with double-page engravings. Issuing three editions of a pictorial in one week was unprecedented, and so were the rewards—an explosion in the paper's circulation from 30,000 to 200,000 and a chorus of praise for the enterprising editor.

Having seized the initiative on the biggest story she had ever encountered, she doggedly held on to it. *Leslie's* ran dozens of pictures of the stricken President, his family and the assassin, Charles Guiteau, while Garfield lingered for more than two months before finally succumbing on September 19. When he died that Monday night after the paper had gone to press, Miriam ordered the pressrun halted and hastily put together a new edition that appeared on Wednesday. She pulled off another coup by reaching the streets a day early with coverage of the funeral. Miriam would never again be relegated to the women's and family journals: she was a hardnews star, saluted as the "Empress of Journalism" and a commercial Joan of Arc." Almost incidentally, she repaid the $50,000 loan and retrieved her diamonds.

She demonstrated business savvy as well as editorial acumen, reorganizing staffs, cutting back the number of periodicals that Leslie had so zealously increased, until by 1885 there remained only two weeklies and four monthlies. By then she was earning $100,000 annually while meeting a payroll for as many as 400 employees. The talk about crime and licentiousness had subsided, replaced by requests for interviews, speeches and articles. She still churned out essays and an occasional book, employing this forum to ponder relation-

Frank, as general manager, to receive only 20 percent of his publications' profits.

The most devastating blow fell in July 1878. A Virginia City newspaper, the *Territorial Enterprise,* and a simultaneously issued 24-page pamphlet unleashed a vicious—but overwhelmingly accurate—attack on Miriam Leslie. "OUR FEMALE SLANDERER," the headline blared. "MRS. FRANK LESLIE'S BOOK SCANDALIZING THE FAMILIES OF VIRGINIA CITY. THE HISTORY OF THE AUTHORESS—A LIFE DRAMA OF CRIME AND LICENTIOUSNESS." Readers learned about her illegitimacy, her short-lived marriage to the jewelry clerk Peacock, the ex-congressman who briefly kept her, and most of all her adulterous affair with Frank Leslie, culminating in the sordid scheme to disgrace and divorce Squier. "They have set aside all the laws of God and man," the anonymous writer charged. "Their own selfish ends have been their only thoughts. . . ." Leslie compiled a list of several suspects as the conduit to the Nevada paper while he tried to buy up all available copies of the issue, but there was only one candidate with the requisite knowledge—and

spite: E. G. Squier, who would spend his life in and out of the asylum, finally had his revenge. Miriam, meanwhile, seems to have reacted by not reacting. If she said or wrote anything in response to the attack, no record of it survives.

Frank, struggling to salvage his business amid the buzz, negotiated a 50 percent settlement of his debts, but before he could finish repaying them he died of throat cancer, in January 1880. Miriam, widowed at 43, inherited the debt along with the papers. Dramatic as always, she vowed never to dance or to wear color again. Alone now, with a deflated bank account and a muddied reputation—she spoke later of being reduced to living in a "carpetless flat"—she was in fact on the brink of her finest hour.

After fending off a flurry of lawsuits contesting Frank's will, Miriam confronted a pay-in-ten-days ultimatum from a group of creditors. She made the $50,000 payment with the aid of what she called "a little romance"—a young artist Leslie had befriended persuaded a wealthy widow to loan her the money, with Miriam's diamonds as collateral. She next had her name legally changed to Frank Leslie so she could continue to ships and argue for equality between the sexes.

In the late 1880s and the 1890s Miriam moved effortlessly into a role she had seemingly been preparing for all her life—the gracious, bespangled grande dame, hostess of a weekly salon where the rich and accomplished mingled with the merely rich. Like many of New York's upper crust, she had a taste for European royalty. She was engaged for a while to a French-English marquis of no known distinction, abandoning him in favor of a Russian prince. An ugly scene erupted in London's Hyde Park when the marquis spotted her on a carriage jaunt with the prince, nearly precipitating a duel—and this when the object of all this aristocratic attention had already crested 50.

She settled, mistakenly as it turned out, for the witty if notoriously bibulous William C. K. W. Wilde, brother of author-playwright Oscar Wilde. Their hasty 1891 marriage lasted only two years, most of which Wilde spent drinking on Miriam's tab. When told of his wife's complaint, that he spent his waking hours at his club, he replied, "What of it? . . . Don't I spend her money there too? It's an even thing between us."

Miriam eased out of publishing in stages. She sold the remaining Leslie weeklies in 1889, allowing her to concentrate on the *Popular Monthly.* In 1895, nearing 60 (though never admitting it), she leased the three surviving monthlies and the annual almanacs to a syndicate, but three years later the company was mired in such financial trouble that they asked her to return as president and editor-in-chief of the *Popular Monthly.* She promptly streamlined and livened up the magazine while cutting its price, and within a few months the circulation was again on the rise along with the profits; she still had the touch. Two years after that she was forced out in a power struggle, this time for good.

In 1901 she announced on her return from one of her frequent voyages to Europe that she had discovered she was a baroness, by virtue of her descent from Philippe Picot, the first Baron de Bazus, whose family had emigrated to Louisiana. In retirement she continued to write and travel, and even accumulated one more titled lover, a Spanish count who died before they could marry. She increased the fortune she had earned in publishing through investments in Manhattan real estate. At her death in 1914 she was worth close to $2 million.

With no children and only a few relatives, she left most of her estate to the activist Carrie Chapman Catt for "the furtherance of the cause of Woman's Suffrage," a cause that would succeed, with Miriam's help, six years later. Fittingly, she departed as she had lived—on her own terms, with a velvet-gloved gesture of defiance.

Donald Dale Jackson, a frequent contributor, has written on a wide range of historical subjects for SMITHSONIAN.

The First Chapter of Children's Rights

*More than a century ago an abused child began a battle
that is still being fought today*

Peter Stevens and Marian Eide

In the quiet New York courtroom, the little girl began to speak. "My name is Mary Ellen McCormack. I don't know how old am.... I have never had but one pair of shoes, but can't recollect when that was. I have had no shoes or stockings on this winter.... I have never had on a particle of flannel. My bed at night is only a piece of carpet, stretched on the floor underneath a window, and I sleep in my little undergarment, with a quilt over me. I am never allowed to play with any children or have any company whatever. Mamma has been in the habit of whipping and beating me almost every day. She used to whip me with a twisted whip, a raw hide. The whip always left black and blue marks on my body. I have now on my head two black and blue marks which were made by mamma with the whip, and a cut on the left side of my forehead which was made by a pair of scissors in mamma's hand. she struck me with the scissors and cut me. I have no recollection of ever having been kissed, and have never been kissed by mamma. I have never been taken on my mamma's lap, or caressed or petted. I never dared to speak to anybody, because if I did I

would get whipped.... Whenever mamma went out I was locked up in the bedroom.... I have no recollection of ever being in the street in my life."

At the beginning of 1874 there were no legal means in the United States to save a child from abuse. Mary Ellen's eloquent testimony changed that, changed our legal system's view of the rights of the child.

Yet more than a century later the concerns that arose from Mary Ellen's case are still being battled over in the courts. The classic dilemmas of just how deeply into the domestic realm the governmental arm can reach and what the obligations of public government are to the private individual take on particular urgency in considering child abuse.

Early in 1989, in the case of *DeShaney* v. *Winnebago County,* the Supreme Court declared that the government is not obligated to protect its citizens against harm inflicted by private individuals. DeShaney brought the case before the court in a suit against county social service agencies that had failed to intervene when her estranged husband abused their son, Joshua, who, as a result of his father's brutality, suffered

permanent brain damage. The father was convicted, but his former wife believes that fault also lies with the agencies, whose failure to intercede violated her son's Fourteenth Amendment right not to be deprived of life or liberty without due process of the law. Chief Justice William H. Rehnquist wrote that intervening officials are often charged with "improperly intruding into the parent-child relationship." Justice William J. Brennan, Jr., dissenting, wrote: "Inaction can be every bit as abusive of power as action, [and] oppression can result when a State undertakes a vital duty and then ignores it."

The difficulty in bringing Mary Ellen McCormack into the New York Supreme Court in 1874 grew from similar controversy over the role of government in family matters, and Mary Ellen's sad history is not so different from Joshua DeShaney's.

When Mary Ellen's mother, Frances Connor, immigrated to the United States from England in 1858, she took a job at the St. Nicholas Hotel in New York City as a laundress. There she met an Irishman named Thomas Wilson who worked in the hotel kitchen shucking oysters. They were married in April 1862, shortly after Wilson had been drafted into the 69th New York, a regiment in the famous Irish Brigade. Early in 1864 she gave birth to their daughter, whom she named Mary after her mother and Ellen after her sister.

The birth of her daughter seems to have heralded the beginning of Frances Wilson's own decline. Her husband was killed that same year in the brutal fighting at Cold Harbor, Virginia, and with a diminished income she found it necessary to look for a job. In May 1864, unable to pay someone to watch the baby while she was at work, she gave Mary Ellen over to the care of a woman named Mary Score for two dollars a week, the whole of her widow's pension. Child farming was a common practice at that time, and many women made a living taking in unwanted children just as others took in laundry. Score lived in a tenement in the infamous warrens of Mulberry Bend, where thousands of immigrants crowded into small, airless rooms, and it is likely that providing foster care was her only means of income.

Finally Frances Wilson Became unable to pay for the upkeep of her child; three weeks after the payments ceased, Score turned Mary Ellen over to the Department of Charities. The little girl—whose mother was never to see her again—was sent to Blackwells Island in July 1865. Her third home was certainly no more pleasant than Mulberry Bend. Mary Ellen was among a group of sick and hungry foundlings; fully two-thirds of them would die before reaching maturity.

The same slum-bred diseases that ravaged the children on Blackwells Island had also claimed all three children of a couple named Thomas and Mary McCormack. So when Thomas frequently bragged of the three children he had fathered by another woman, his wife was more receptive to the idea of adopting them than she might otherwise have been. Those children, he told her, were still alive, though their mother had turned them over to the care of the city. On January 2, 1866, the McCormacks went to the Department of Chari-

ties to reclaim one of the children Thomas's mistress had abandoned. The child they chose as their own was Mary Ellen Wilson. Because the McCormacks were not asked to provide any proof of relation to the child and gave only the reference of their family doctor, there is no evidence that Thomas was in any way related to the child he brought home that day. More than a month later an indenture was filed for Mary Ellen in which the McCormacks promised to report on her condition each year. There were no other requirements.

Shortly after bringing the child home, Thomas McCormack died, and his widow married a man named Francis Connolly. Little more than that is known of the early childhood of Mary Ellen. She came to her new home in a flannel petticoat, and when her clothing was removed from Connolly's home as evidence six years later, there was barely enough to fill a tiny suitcase. She was beaten, set to work, deprived of daylight, and locked in closets for days at a time; she was rarely bathed, never kissed, and never addressed with a gentle word. During the six years she lived with Connolly, only two reports on her progress were filed with the Commissioners of Charities and Correction.

Late in 1873 Etta Angell Wheeler, a Methodist caseworker serving in the tenements of New York City, received a disturbing report. It came from Margaret Bingham, a landlord in Hell's Kitchen, and told of a terrible case of child abuse. The child's parents had been tenants of Bingham for about four years, and almost immediately after they moved in, Bingham began to observe how cruelly they treated their child, Mary Ellen. They confined her in close quarters during hot weather, kept her severely underdressed in cold, beat her daily, and left her unattended for hours at a time. On several occasions Bingham tried to intervene; each time the child's mother said she would call upon the fullest resources of the law before she would allow any interference in her home. Finally Bingham resorted to threat: The beatings and ill treatment would have to stop, or the family would be evicted. When her plan backfired and the family left, Bingham, in a last-ditch effort, sent

for Etta Wheeler. In order to observe Mary Ellen's predicament, Wheeler went to the Connollys' neighbor, an ailing tubercular woman named Mary Smitt. Enlisting Smitt's aid, she proposed that Mary Ellen be sent over each day to check on the patient. Smitt reluctantly agreed, and on the pretext of inquiring about this sick neighbor, Wheeler knocked on Mary Connolly's door.

Inside she saw a "pale, thin child, bare-foot, in a thin, scanty dress so tattered that I could see she wore but one garment besides.

"It was December and the weather bitterly cold. She was a tiny mite, the size of five years, though, as afterward appeared, she was then nine. From a pan set upon a low stool she stood washing dishes, struggling with a frying pan about as heavy as herself. Across the table lay a brutal whip of twisted leather strands and the child's meager arms and legs bore many marks of its use. But the saddest part of her story was written on her face in its look of suppression and misery, the face of a child unloved, of a child that had seen only the fearsome side of life.... I never saw her again until the day of her rescue, three months later.... "

The child belonged to the animal kingdom; perhaps the Society for Prevention of Cruelty to Animals could save her.

Though social workers often witnessed scenes of cruelty, poverty, and grief, Wheeler found Mary Ellen's plight especially horrifying. She went first to the police; they told her she must be able to furnish proof of assault in order for them to act. Charitable institutions she approached offered to care for the child, but first she must be brought to them through legal means. There were none. Every effort Wheeler made proved fruitless. Though there were laws to protect children—laws, in fact, to prevent assault and battery to any person—

there were no means available for intervention in a child's home.

Finally Wheeler's niece had an idea. The child, she said, was a member of the animal kingdom; surely Henry Bergh, the founder of the American Society for the Prevention of Cruelty to Animals, who was famous for his dramatic rescue of mistreated horses in the streets of New York, might be willing to intervene. Within the hour Wheeler had arranged a meeting with Bergh. Despite its apparent strangeness, this sort of appeal was not new to Bergh. Once before he had tried to intervene in a case of child abuse and had failed. This time he was more cautious.

"Very definite testimony is needed to warrant interference between a child and those claiming guardianship," Bergh told Wheeler. "Will you not send me a written statement that, at my leisure, I may judge the weight of the evidence and may also have time to consider if this society should interfere? I promise to consider the case carefully."

Wheeler provided a statement immediately, including in it the observations of neighbors to whom she had spoken. Bergh was convinced. "No time is to be lost," he wrote his lawyer, Elbridge T. Gerry. "Instruct me how to proceed."

The next day Wheeler again visited the sick woman in Hell's Kitchen and found in her room a young man who, on hearing Wheeler's name, said, "I was sent to take the census in this house. I have been in every room." Wheeler then knew him to be a detective for Bergh.

On the basis of the detective's observations and the testimony provided by Etta Wheeler, Bergh's lawyers, Gerry and Ambrose Monell, appeared before Judge Abraham R. Lawrence of the New York Supreme Court to present a petition on behalf of Mary Ellen. They showed that Mary Ellen was held illegally by the Connollys, who were neither her natural parents nor her lawful custodians, and went on to describe the physical abuse Mary Ellen endured, the marks and bruises on her body, and the general state of deprivation that characterized her existence. They offered a list of witnesses willing to testify on behalf

of the child and concluded by stating that there was ample evidence to indicate that she was in clear danger of being maimed or even killed. The lawyers requested that a warrant be issued, the child removed from her home and placed in protective custody, and her parents brought to trial.

Bergh testified that his efforts on behalf of the child were in no way connected to his work with abused animals and that they did not make use of the special legal provisions set up for that purpose. Because of Bergh's association with animal rescue, to this day the case is often described as having originated in his conviction that the child was a member of the animal kingdom. Bergh, however, insisted that his actions were merely those of any humane citizen and that he intended to prevent cruelties inflicted on children through any legal means available.

Judge Lawrence issued a warrant under Section 65 of the Habeas Corpus Act as requested. This provision read in part: "Whenever it shall appear by satisfactory proof that any one is held in illegal confinement or custody, and that there is good reason to believe that he will . . . suffer some irreparable injury, before he can be relieved by the issuing of a *habeas corpus* or *certiorari,* any court or officer authorized to issue such writs, may issue a warrant . . . [and] bring him before such court or officer, to be dealt with according to law."

The press of the day hailed Gerry's use of Section 65 of the Habeas Corpus Act as brilliant. The act was rarely invoked, and the legal means for removing a child from its home were nonexistent. In using the little-known law, Gerry created a new method for intervention.

That same day, April 9, 1874, Mary Ellen was taken from her home and brought into Judge Lawrence's court. Having no adequate clothing of her own, the child had been wrapped in a carriage blanket by the policemen who held her in custody. A reporter on the scene described her as "a bright little girl, with features indicating unusual mental capacity, but with a care-worn, stunted, and prematurely old look. . . . no change

of custody or condition could be much for the worse."

Jacob Riis "saw a child brought in at the sight of which men wept aloud, and heard the story that roused the conscience of a world."

The reporter Jacob Riis was present in the court. "I saw a child brought in . . . at the sight of which men wept aloud, and I heard the story of little Mary Ellen told . . . that stirred the soul of a city and roused the conscience of a world that had forgotten, and as I looked, I knew I was where the first chapter of children's rights was being written." Her body and face were terribly bruised; her hands and feet "showed the plain marks of great exposure." And in what almost instantly seemed to condemn Mrs. Connolly before the court, the child's face bore a fresh gash through her eyebrow and across her left cheek that barely missed the eye itself. Mary Ellen was to carry this scar throughout her life.

Interestingly, there is no further mention in the ample reports surrounding Mary Ellen's case of her foster father, Francis Connolly. He was never brought into court, never spoke publicly concerning the child. All her life Mary Ellen exhibited a frightened timidity around men, yet it was against her foster mother that she testified.

On the evening of her detention, Mary Ellen was turned over to the temporary custody of the matron of police headquarters. The next day, April 10, the grand jury read five indictments against Mary Connolly for assault and battery, felonious assault, assault with intent to do bodily harm, assault with intent to kill, and assault with intent to maim. Once the stepmother had been brought into the legal system, there were ample means to punish her.

Mary Ellen herself was brought in to testify against the woman she had called her mother. On her second appearance in court she seemed almost wholly altered. She was clothed in a new suit, and her pale face reflected the kindness that surrounded her. She carried with her a new picture book, probably the first she had ever owned. She acted open and uninhibited with strangers, and interestingly, seemed to show no great fear of her mother or any apparent enmity toward her.

The lawyers Gerry and Monell gathered several witnesses against Mary Connolly, among them neighbors, Wheeler, and Mary Ellen herself. Margaret Bingham said she had seen the child locked up in a room and had told other neighbors, but they said there was no point in interfering since the police would do nothing. Bingham had tried to open the window of the child's room to let in some air, but it would not lift more than an inch. As a constant presence and reminder, a cowhide whip was locked in the room with the child. Wheeler recounted her first visit to Mary Ellen, during which the child washed dishes that seemed twice her size and was apparently oblivious of the visitor's presence. The whip lay on the table next to her. The next day, when Wheeler came by again, the child was sewing, and the whip lay on a chair near her.

Then it was the mother's turn to testify. On the witness stand Mary Connolly showed herself to be a woman of some spirit. Despite her treatment of the child, there is something compelling in Connolly's strength and humor. At one point the prosecutor asked if she had an occupation beyond housekeeping. "Well," she said, "I sleep with the boss." As the trial wore on, she became enraged at Gerry's prodding questions; finally she accused him of being "ignorant of the difficulties of bringing up and governing children." Yet she admitted that contrary to regulations, in the six years she had Mary Ellen in her custody, she had reported on her condition to the Commissioners of Charities and Correction only twice.

Two indictments were brought against Connolly, the first for her assault on the child with scissors on April 7, the second for the continual assaults inflicted on the child throughout the years 1873

and 1874. After twenty minutes of deliberation the jury returned a verdict of guilty of assault and battery. Connolly was sentenced to one year of hard labor in the city penitentiary, then known as the Tombs. In handing down this sentence, the judge defined it not only as a punishment to Connolly but also as a statement of precedence in child-abuse cases.

Mary Ellen never returned to the Connollys' home. In the ensuing months the publicity that her case received brought in many claims of relation. But on investigating, her guardian, Judge Lawrence, discovered the stories were fictions, and he finally placed the child in the Sheltering Arms, a home for grown girls; soon after, she was moved to the Women's Aid Society and Home for Friendless Girls. This mirrors another critical problem in the system's treatment of minors. All juveniles were handled by the Department of Charities and Correction, and whether they were orphaned or delinquent, their treatment was the same. And so it was that the ten-year-old Mary Ellen was placed in a home with mostly delinquent adolescents.

Etta Wheeler knew this was wrong for Mary Ellen, and she expressed her hesitations to Judge Lawrence. He, in turn, consulted with Henry Bergh, and eventually they agreed to turn the girl over to Etta Wheeler herself. Unable to imagine giving up her work in the slums of New York City but believing that Mary Ellen deserved a better environment, Wheeler brought the child to her mother in North Chili, New York. Wheeler's mother became ill shortly afterward, and Mary Ellen was raised mostly by Wheeler's sister.

Here began a new life," Wheeler wrote. "The child was an interesting study, so long shut within four walls and now in a new world. Woods, fields, 'green things growing,' were all strange to her, she had not known them. She had to learn, as a baby does, to walk upon the ground,—she had walked only upon floors, and her eye told her nothing of uneven surfaces. . . . But in this home there were other children and they taught her as children alone can teach each other. They taught her to

play, to be unafraid, to know her rights and to claim them. She shared their happy, busy life from the making of mud pies up to charming birthday parties and was fast becoming a normal child."

The happiness of her years in the upstate New York countryside lies in stark contrast to her early childhood. And indeed, as Wheeler wrote, she learned by example the ways of normal childhood. She grew up strong and well, learning how to read and playing with friends and pet kittens. In 1875 Wheeler reported to Gerry that Mary Ellen was growing up as a normal child. "She has some faults that are of the graver sort. She tells fibs and sticks to them bravely, steals lumps of sugar & cookies and only confesses when the crumbs are found in her pocket—in short she is very much like other children, loving—responding to kindness & praise, hating a task unless there be a play, or a reward thereof, and inevitably 'forgetting' what she does not wish to remember—what children do not do some or all of these forbidden things! She is a favorite with nearly all the people who have come to know her."

When she was twenty-four, Mary Ellen married a widower named Louis Schutt and with him had two children, Etta—named after the woman who had rescued her—and Florence. She adopted a third, orphaned child, Eunice. She also raised Louis Schutt's three children from his first wife.

In 1911 Wheeler visited her protégé in her home, "finding her well and happy. . . . The family income is small, but Mary Ellen is a prudent housewife & they are comfortable. The two daughters are promising girls." The eldest daughter, Etta, worked industriously through that summer, finished high school, and became a teacher. Florence followed her sister's path, teaching first grade for thirty-eight years. When she retired, the elementary school in North Chili was renamed in her honor. Eunice earned a business degree, married, and raised two sons.

Florence remembers her mother as a solemn woman who came alive whenever she listened to Irish jigs and especially to "The Irish Washerwoman." She was unfailingly generous with her time and her affection. Her years in North Chili had saved her from the vicious cycle abused children often suffer of becoming abusers themselves. According

---

Mary Ellen was survived by three daughters—and by a movement that would help avert tragedies like hers.

---

to Florence her mother was capable of sternness and certainly willing to punish her daughters, but the terrible experiences of her early childhood never spilled into her own child rearing. As Etta Wheeler wrote, "To her children, two bright, dutiful daughters, it has been her joy to give a happy childhood in sharp contrast to her own."

Etta and Florence often asked their mother about the Connollys, but Mary Ellen was reluctant to speak of her early years. She did show her daughters the scars on her arms where she had been burned with a hot iron, and of course they could see the scissors scar across her face. Florence distinctly recalls that in the few times they spoke of her mother's years in New York City, she never mentioned a woman inflicting her injuries; it was always a man.

In October of 1913 Mary Ellen Schutt attended a meeting of the American Humane Society in Rochester. She was accompanied by Etta Wheeler, who was there to present a paper entitled "The Finding of Mary Ellen." The paper concluded: "If the memory of her earliest years is sad, there is this comfort that the cry of her wrongs awoke the world to the need of organized relief for neglected and abused children."

Mary Ellen died on October 30, 1956, at the age of ninety-two. She was survived by her two daughters, her adopted daughter, three stepchildren, three grandchildren, and five great-grandchildren. More important, she was

survived by the beginning of a movement to prevent the repetition of tragedies like her own. On December 15, 1874, Henry Bergh, Elbridge Gerry, and James Wright founded the New York Society for the Prevention of Cruelty to Children (SPCC) with the ample assistance of Cornelius Vanderbilt. It was the first organization of its kind in America. At the outset of their work the founders signed a statement of purpose: "The undersigned, desirous of rescuing the unprotected children of this city and State from the cruelty and demoralization which neglect and abandonment engender, hereby engage to aid, with their sympathy and support, the organization and working of a Children's Protective Society, having in view the realization of so important a purpose."

The SPCC saw its role essentially as a legal one. As an agent or friend of the court, the society endeavored to intervene on the behalf of children, enforcing the laws that were in existence to prevent cruelty toward them and at the same time introducing new legislation on their behalf.

At the first meeting of the SPCC on December 16, 1874, Gerry stressed the fact that the most crucial role of the society lay in the rescue of children from abusive situations. From there, he pointed out, there were many excellent groups available to care for and shelter children and many state laws to punish parents. He went on to predict that as soon as abusers learned that the law could reach them, there would be few cases like that of Mary Ellen.

Bergh was less optimistic. At the same meeting, he pointed out that neglected and abused children were to become the mothers and fathers of the country and that unless their interests were defended, the interests of society in general would suffer.

In its first years the SPCC investigated more than three hundred cases of child abuse. Many people felt threatened by the intrusion of the government into their private lives; discipline, they believed, was a family issue, and outside influence was not only unwelcome but perhaps even unconstitutional. When, with the aid of a state senator, James W. Booth, Gerry introduced in the New

York legislature a law entitled "An Act to Prevent and Punish Wrongs to Children," the proposal was immediately and vigorously attacked. The New York *World* wrote that Bergh was to be authorized to "break into the garrets of the poor and carry off their children upon the suspicion of spanking." According to the *World,* the law would give Bergh "power to discipline all the naughty children of New York.... We sincerely hope that it may not be finally kicked out of the legislature, as it richly deserves to be, until the public mind shall have had time to get itself thoroughly enlightened as to the state of things in which it has become possible for such a person as Mr. Bergh to bring the Legislature to the point of seriously entertaining such an impudently senseless measure. This bill is a bill to supersede the common law in favor of Mr. Bergh, and the established tribunals of justice in favor of an irresponsible private corporation." The bill was passed in 1876, however, and became the foundation upon which the SPCC performed its work.

From its initial concentration on preventing abuse in the home, the society broadened its franchise to battle neglect, abandonment, and the exploitation of children for economic gain. In 1885, after considerable effort by the SPCC and in the face of yet more opposition, Gerry secured passage of a bill that made labor by children under the age of fourteen illegal.

As the explosive story of the death of Lisa Steinberg in the home of her adoptive parents revealed to the nation in 1987, abuse still haunts American society. There are still legal difficulties in removing a child from an abusive situation. In 1987 the House Select Committee on Children, Youth, and Families reported that the incidence of child abuse, particularly sexual abuse and neglect, is rising; in 1985 alone almost two million children were referred to protective agencies. In part, the committee said, this increase was due to a greater awareness of the issue, and there has also been an increased effort to educate children themselves about situations that constitute abuse or molestation and about ways to get help.

Despite a plethora of programs designed to address abuse, the committee concluded that not enough is being done. The most effective programs were found to be those that worked to prevent the occurrence of abuse at the outset through education in parenting techniques, through intervention in high-risk situations, such as unwanted pregnancies, and through screening for mental and emotional difficulties. However, funding for public welfare programs has fallen far below the demands, and what funding there is must frequently be diverted to intervene in more and more sensational and hopeless cases.

If there is still much hard, sad work ahead, there is also much that has been accomplished. And all of it began when Mary Ellen McCormack spoke and, in speaking, freed herself and thousands of other children from torment.

Peter Stevens, who lives in Quincy, Massachusetts, writes frequently on historical themes. Marian Eide is a graduate student in the Comparative Literature and Critical Theory Program at the University of Pennsylvania. We would like to thank Dr. Stephen Lazoritz for his contributions to the research of this article. Lazoritz, a pediatrician specializing in child-abuse cases, first became interested in Mary Ellen's history when, preparing for a lecture on child abuse, he read "The Great Meddler," Gerald Carson's profile of Henry Bergh in the December 1967 issue of American Heritage. Lazoritz was fascinated by the child and traced her history through a trail of documents and newspaper articles. In the story of Mary Ellen's childhood he found the roots of a movement to prevent child abuse in which he is very much involved today. Lazoritz's youngest daughter was born during his pursuit of the case. Her name is Mary Ellen. Thanks, too, to the New York Society for the Prevention of Cruelty to Children, whose archives contain full documentation of the Mary Ellen case.

The Stolen Election

By Bernard A. Weisberger

Last February the White House was jubilant over the outcome of the election held in Nicaragua, where voters turned out the governing Sandinista National Liberation Front, which has run the country since 1979, as well as its president, Daniel Ortega. The new president is Violeta Chamorro, the candidate of the National Opposition Union (UNO), a coalition of anti-Sandinista parties backed by Washington as part of its long war against what the Bush and Reagan administrations styled a Marxist-Leninist dictatorship. In the days just after the results were published, however, conservative commentators expressed anxiety over whether or not there could be an orderly transfer of power.

In fact, such a peaceful transfer is rare. This country ought to know; we almost failed at it 113 years ago. And whereas in Nicaragua, in 1990, there was no doubt about the legitimate winner of the election, it was not certain who was going to become President of the United States on March 4, 1877, until 4:00 A.M. on March 2.

It happens that I was in Nicaragua this year as an election observer—a senior historian rejoicing in the chance for a close-up view of a bit of history in the making. I was fascinated by what I saw, and in my opinion any direct comparison between the Sandinista regime and totalitarian Stalinist states is simplistic at best. But that's not my story here. History is my beat, so let us return to 1877.

That year, in three Southern states, conservatives recaptured power after nearly ten years of enforced racial and social revolution. They did so in a climate of electoral fraud, fear, and plain murder. And because the electoral votes of the three states would be the decisive ones in the presidential election, local disputes about who won state campaigns

ELLIOTT BANFIELD

ripened into a national constitutional and political crisis that some thought might start a new civil war.

The country was approaching the end of the experiment that history knows as Reconstruction. Florida, Louisiana, and South Carolina were the last states in which Republican regimes survived, based heavily on the votes of blacks. In 1867 Congress had decreed that the former Confederate states (with Tennessee a lone exception) would lose their autonomy and become occupied territory until they installed new governments from which all supporters of the former Confederacy were excluded and in which the ex-slaves would be included.

At varying speeds the garrisoned states complied. Not surprisingly the newly elected officials were Republicans, representing classes previously excluded from power. As Southern folk speech put it, "the bottom rail was on the top." Like most one-party regimes, they waxed in corruption the longer they held power, though not much beyond the average for the Gilded Age. And like most political organizations catering to lesser folk, they also did a great deal of yeoman work in the areas of education, social welfare, economic development, and the equalizing of tax burdens. They even gradually lifted the restrictions on ex-Confederates, hoping to broaden their support base.

In vain. Most Southern whites were unappeased and unrelenting in their denunciation of local white Republicans as "scalawags" and "carpetbaggers." For the blacks their hate was unbounded. And gradually they began to take back power. They did so partly by frightening black voters away from the polls through terrorism.

One by one, conservative white Democrats "redeemed" their states. A Southern revolution imposed by Republicans in Washington could last only as long as there was Republican unity. But in 1872 came a secession of "Liberal Republicans" protesting Grant-era corruption. In 1873 a gigantic depression hit the country. In 1874 the Democrats won a majority in the House of Representatives. And then came 1876.

On election night the Democratic presidential candidate, Samuel Tilden of New York, beat the Republican Rutherford B. Hayes of Ohio in the popular votes—4,288,546 to 4,034,311 to be exact. But Tilden had only 184 electoral votes for certain, and 185 were needed to win. Hayes definitely had 165. There were 19 out there in Florida, Louisiana, and South Carolina, the final Southern

From *American Heritage*, July 1990, pp. 18, 20. © 1990 by Forbes, Inc. Reprinted by permission of *American Heritage* magazine, a division of Forbes, Inc.

Republican strongholds. In the latter two the state campaigns had been especially dirty and bloody. The Republican incumbents were dutifully proclaiming victory, while the Democrats were insisting that *they* had won and been cheated in the count. In the three state capitals there were two sets of self-proclaimed "lawful" governors, legislators—and presidential electors.

In addition, one electoral vote from Oregon was disputed on a technicality. If Hayes got that one, plus the other 19, he would have the 185 needed to take the inaugural oath. But which set of electoral votes would actually be counted? And by whom?

The Constitution was ambiguous. It says that the incumbent state officials shall send their electoral votes to the president of the Senate, who shall open them "in the presence of the Senate and House of Representatives," whereupon "the votes shall then be counted." Was it the president of the Senate who was to do the counting and decide which ones to count? If so, he was part of a Republican Senate majority and would accept the votes sent in by Republicans. But if disputed votes were *not* counted, then neither candidate had a majority, and the election would go into the House of Representatives, which was Democratic. To add a twist, if no decision was reached by March 4, then the Vice-President was to become acting president—but there was no Vice-President: Henry Wilson had died while holding the office.

Hayes and the Republicans argued that the votes certified by the sitting regimes in the disputed states had to be taken at face value and that Congress wasn't authorized to go behind the results. If it had done so, it would have found Republican fraud balanced against Democratic intimidation, with the *provable* evidence probably in the Democrats' favor. So the Democrats insisted on just such a scrutiny. Otherwise why would the Constitution provide for the ballot count under the eyes of House and Senate? The Democrats would not recognize a President chosen without such a review. And the Republicans would recognize no other.

Dangerous murmurs circulated in the deadlock. Some Democrats talked of having the House declare Tilden President if the Senate counted in Hayes—so there would be two Presidents trying to seize the keys to the White House. Some Republicans believed that if the issue was not settled by March 4, and there was no Vice-President, then Grant, backed by the Army, should simply remain in office. Slogans like Tilden or Blood were allegedly uttered. Ex-generals on both sides offered to raise armies of veterans and march on Washington.

Many a Democrat went to his grave grumbling about the election and complaining about "His Fraudulency" Rutherford B. Hayes.

In the end a curious, cumbersome compromise was reached. It was engineered by the businessmen of both parties, quintessential conservatives, who did not want the already struggling economy hit with political paralysis or renewed warfare. The votes would be reviewed by a special fifteen-member electoral commission of five representatives (two Republicans, three Democrats), five senators (two Democrats, three Republicans), and five justices of the Supreme Court (two Republicans, two Democrats, and one, Davis, considered to be an independent). Commission decisions would be binding unless rejected by both House and Senate.

But before the commission could begin to hear what one candidate called "the great lawsuit," the Illinois legislature elected Justice David Davis to the Senate. The other four justices voted to fill his place with Justice Joseph Bradley, a known Republican, considered to be fairminded. Perhaps he was. But as each set of Republican returns was presented to the commission during February, he voted with his fellow Republicans to accept

them. By a straight 8 to 7 party-line vote, every disputed electoral vote went to Hayes to give him the needed 185.

A few outraged Democrats mounted a filibuster in the House to prevent final acceptance of the result before the relentlessly approaching March 4 deadline. But a majority of their colleagues deserted them, thanks to more dollar-conscious "unofficial" bargaining.

The final terms, secret but understood by the key players, were these: Hayes would not support the remaining Southern Republican machines with troops, so that they would soon collapse. A Southern Democrat would become Postmaster General in Hayes's cabinet. Votes would be found on both sides of the aisle for more federal subsidies to the South. In a word, Southern Democrats, even more than Northern, had accepted national industrialization and wanted their cut of it. And the party of Lincoln was ready to call off the struggle for equality.

The final vote was reached at a bleary-eyed middle-of-the-night session on Friday, March 2. Hayes took the oath formally on Monday, the fifth, but for safety's sake was privately sworn in on Saturday night. Some Democrats boycotted the public inauguration, and many a Democrat went to his grave grumbling about the "stolen election" and condemning "His Fraudulency" Rutherford B. Hayes.

So the revolution ended, and the transition to conservative rule took place. It was not violent on the national level. It was very much so within the states. It seemed a vindication of the American pattern of compromise, and so it was—among white Americans, who had finally decided that peace should take priority. The genuine political consensus without which elections are a meaningless form had finally been reached. But over the ensuing years the unconsulted Southern blacks paid the price.

One final irony is noted by the historian James P. Shenton. In 1860 a wrenching era began with the Southern refusal to accept the legitimate election of Abraham Lincoln. In 1877 it ended when the South surrendered what was very likely a legitimate mandate for Samuel Tilden.

'The Chinese Must Go'

By Bernard A. Weisberger

One splendid morning during a recent West Coast vacation, I was turning the pages of a San Francisco newspaper over my coffee when I came upon a headline that clouded my cheerful mood: GERMAN POLL FINDS SENTIMENT AGAINST FOREIGNERS RUNS DEEP. According to the story below it, one-quarter of a group of Germans polled in a survey agreed entirely or partly with the slogan "Germany for the Germans," which right-wing extremists had been chanting during several weeks of rampages against foreign refugees. Included in the atrocities were the rock-throwing attacks on refugee shelters and the torching of foreigners' homes. "Shades of the 1930s," I thought with the automatic shudder that any possible neo-Nazi activity sends through me—in Germany or anywhere else.

Then I thought a bit longer. Something tickled my memory, and it flashed a new message: "Shades of the 1870s too. And not in Europe but in San Francisco, California!" I remembered that San Francisco had been seized, in 1877, by a violent spasm of antiforeign, specifically anti-Chinese, feeling that broke into murderous riots against innocents of the "wrong" ancestry. The fever started among working-class whites, but before it ran its full course, it infected the governments of both California and the United States, with long-lasting results.

Please understand that I have no intention of drawing farfetched comparisons, or of calling Americans of the 1870s neo-Nazis—quite the contrary. Nor do I aim to exonerate the 1990s neo-Nazis by trite reminders that they are not the first, last, or only haters to sully history's pages with brutality. Still, one of the best things about *good* history is its power to reduce national arrogance and to promote reflection and caution. So this story needs telling.

Xenophobia wasn't new in the United States a century and a quarter ago. A strong nativist movement before the Civil War had been responsible for discrimination and occasional violence against foreign-born Catholics. In the 1850s the Protestant crusade went political in the shape of the American (or "Know-Nothing") party and scored some short-term gains. But California's nativism in 1877 was especially sharp after four years of a bitter depression that had begun in 1873. (Economic pain will do that every time; the 1992 wave of German antiforeignism is strongest in formerly Communist East Germany, where unemployment is high and living standards low.)

America in 1877 was hurting all over, but as is often the case, the situation was special in California, particularly in San Francisco. It was less than thirty years since the gold rush had filled the city with brazen fortune seekers. The giddiness of their expectations was now offset by brutal reality, and most of them were facing the fact that they would spend their lives in a post-boom economy. Gold and silver production was down, and unemployment now hovered around 20 percent. Where land had been plentiful, the best acreage was being concentrated into great estates.

Where San Francisco grocers had made fortunes selling infrequent ships loads of coveted goods, they now faced tough competition in a national market created by the newly completed transcontinental railroad line. And that same railroad, once hailed as the salvation of California, had become a monster monopoly that was charged with gouging the state's shippers and buying exemption from the law by bribing and lobbying.

The Big Four who built and owned the Southern Pacific Railroad—Mark Hopkins, Charles Crocker, Collis P. Huntington, and Leland Stanford—typified the widening social chasm. Basically storekeepers who had struck it rich by their timely investment in the rails, they and other new millionaires built, on San Francisco's Nob Hill, gingerbread mansions tended by liveried servants. Thus the social cast of San Francisco included a restless down-at-the-heels population, a class of power-flaunting neo-aristocrats, a supervillain in the shape of a railroad monopoly—and, finally, a set of scapegoats in the Chinese.

There were between twelve thousand and twenty-two thousand of them in the city, all recent immigrants and visibly, achingly different in their Manchu pigtails and their "bizarre" customs. They had been run out of the mining camps by discriminatory state laws and vigilante violence and settled in the cities to cook and wash for the Anglo-Saxons. Then the Big Four had discovered that they made wonderful railroad-construction workers—patient, diligent, and, above all, vulnerable and therefore cheap. Crocker imported thousands of them. So did other employers through wholesale contracts with Chinese labor agents. The Chinese composed perhaps only 15 percent of the San Francisco labor force, but they were blamed and hated by apparently every unemployed or underemployed white San Franciscan.

On July 23, 1877, the trigger on violence was pulled by news from the East. Between July 14 and 26 striking rail workers had clashed with militia in Pittsburgh, Baltimore, Chicago, and Martinsburg, West Virginia. At least seventy people had been murdered in the tumult. A meeting in support of the strikers was called in an empty downtown sandlot in San Francisco by sympathizers associated with the ten-year-old Marxist International Association of Workingmen. The crowd shouted its approval of anticapitalist resolutions. Then, inevitably, someone cried, "On to Chinatown," and the mob boiled out to look for victims. Twenty laundries were burned that night. On the next, there was an attack on a woolen mill employing many Chinese workers. At that the city fathers, alarmed about threats to property, formed a Committee of Safety and called out the militia. On the third night the rioters attacked the docks of the Pacific Steamship Company and set fire to a lumberyard. Police charged their ranks; four rioters were killed and fourteen wounded. That was the end of the collective violence.

But not of the anti-Chinese revolt. Two months later the crowd found a leader in a thirty-year-old Irish-born small businessman named Denis Kearney. Self-made and self-educated, Kearney was the guiding spirit in creating a new organization, the Workingmen's Party of California (WPC). Night after night he held forth to sandlot crowds in speeches full of political brimstone, like his pro-

nouncement that "the dignity of labor must be sustained, even if we have to kill every wretch that opposes it." He frightened the city fathers enough to have him arrested in November, but since his threats were always vaguely conditional rather than immediate, he was acquitted. Actually, he mainly urged his audiences to vote for delegates to a forthcoming state constitutional convention that he hoped would empower "the people" by tightly regulating corporations and their lobbyists and subsidies. But his most powerful attention-getter was a demand for an end to the immigration and hiring of Chinese. "We intend to try and vote the Chinamen out, to frighten him out, and if this won't do, to kill him out. . . . The heathen slaves must leave this coast." He boiled it down to a sledgehammer four-word cry: "The Chinese must go!"

The evil that Denis Kearney's anti-Chinese movement did lived after him. The virus of xenophobia is never really extinguished.

Kearney touched on worker anxieties with his hints of a scheme by the rich to bring feudalism to the United States through the replacement of American workingmen with "coolies" who would neither expect nor receive a living wage or democratic rights.

He enjoyed fleeting political success. The Workingmen's Party of California won many local and state offices in 1878 and named fifty-two delegates to the convention, which did include some of their proposals in the new Constitution of 1879. But the anti-business strictures were gradually eviscerated by the courts and by lack of implementation, and the WPC faded away, though Kearney himself lived on until 1907. Kearney's legislative influence was brief, but the evil that he did to the Chinese lived after him.

That was because "The Chinese must go" had more than local impact. It struck powerful echoes in a time of social Darwinist racism. The Chinese were almost universally disdained by the "advanced" Americans. The newspaper baron James Gordon Bennett discouraged their immigration with the comment that only "on the Caucasian element can we hope to build up such an empire as the world has never seen." Other opinion makers, lumping all classes and conditions of Chinese together, labeled them "ignorant of civilized life" or "listless, stagnant [and] unprogressive." In the popular image they were criminals, gamblers, prostitutes, and opium smokers. In Far Western towns Chinese storekeepers were often beaten and robbed by drunken miners and cowboys, or at a minimum tormented by teen-age hoodlums. And in 1885 twenty-eight Chinese were massacred in Rock Springs, Wyoming.

Therefore, legal exclusion was easily enacted. California in 1880 virtually shut the door on the importation and use of Chinese labor. The Congress of the United States followed suit with the Exclusion Act of 1882, barring all Chinese immigration for ten years. Renewed and renewed, the exclusion policy remained in force until World War II, when it began to be modified gradually until it was finally dropped, after eighty-six years, in a 1968 overhaul of immigration legislation.

It would be possible and pleasant to conclude this column on an upbeat note. Anti-Asian prejudice in the United States is only a glimmer of its former self, and the Chinese are even considered a "model minority," held up for others' emulation. That is certainly a credit to American pluralism. But the virus of xenophobia is never really extinguished in any multiethnic body politic. It merely becomes temporarily inactive. And as for racism—enough said. Human beings have an inextinguishable capacity to be cruel to one another, particularly in groups. It takes constant self-reminders of how bad things can get to keep alive the energy to make them better.

The Nickel & Dime Empire

When F. W. Woolworth opened his first five-and-ten in 1879, he never dreamed that his business would become a monument of American marketing.

By Joseph Gustaitis

July 1997 was a melancholy month for admirers of a vanishing American way of life—the era of family values, corner grocery stores, day baseball, unlocked front doors, and twice-a-day mail delivery.

On July 3 the nation's newspapers reported the death of film star Jimmy Stewart, and obituaries paid tribute to his folksiness and the way he captured the core of American individualism—characteristics people like to associate with a time that was less frantic, more diffident, and more concerned with the folks next door than the celebrities on television.

Two weeks later an equally woeful event transpired. The Woolworth Corporation announced that it was closing its 400 remaining five-and-ten-cent stores. Once again, the media cranked up the nostalgia machine as reporters fanned out across the country to assess this latest left hook to the national psyche. "It's the passing of an era," a real estate executive in San Francisco said. "They've been on Main Street forever," echoed one shopper in Denver, "I'm sure we're going to feel this loss." New York's *Daily News* pretty much summed it up with the words, "We aren't just losing stores. We're losing pieces of Americana."

Like many retail empires, this one started small. Frank Winfield Woolworth was born in Rodman, New York, just south of Watertown, on April 13, 1852. He grew up on a 108-acre farm near Great Bend that his father managed, but young Frank couldn't wait to escape the agrarian life and its relentless labor. He later recalled that his parents "worked hard to make ends meet. My father would think nothing of getting up at four in the morning and work till eight at night in the summertime at hard manual labor. Everything that came into farm labor I had experience in, and my mother would break me into housework, too. I got both ends of the stick."

For a lad with no financial advantages and a modest education, the position of store clerk sounded like a ticket to emancipation, so the 20-year-old presented himself eagerly to William Harvey Moore, part owner of the dry goods firm of Augsbury & Moore—later to become Moore & Smith—in the heart of Watertown. Moore took him on for a six-month trial.

F. W. Woolworth started at the bottom, cleaning cuspidors, delivering packages, and washing windows. He received no salary at all for the first three months, after which he earned $3.50 a week. Although he was a rather ineffective sales clerk, Woolworth showed a talent for window dressing, which then became a part of his job. He also made himself useful in the stock room and soon was considered a valued employee, earning the respectable weekly salary of $10.00. That enabled him to propose to Jennie Creighton, a 23-year-old seamstress from Canada. The couple was married on June 11, 1876.

Around 1878, when Moore & Smith found itself groaning under the burden of surplus inventory, a traveling salesman told the store's management of an interesting experiment conducted by a shop in Michigan. The proprietors had set up a display, affixed a sign to it reading, "Any Article on This Counter, 5¢," and sold the goods at a dizzy pace. The idea seemed to be worth a try and Moore told Woolworth to erect a similar counter and tack up a similar sign. Sure enough, as Frank later recalled, "Like magic, the goods on the 5¢ counter faded away and money flowed into the cash drawer."

From *American History*, March 1998, pp. 40-46, 71. © 1998 by Cowles Magazine, Inc. Reprinted through the courtesy of Cowles Magazines, publishers of *American History*.

BROWN BROTHERS

Woolworth's store in Lancaster, Pennsylvania, was the first of his many stores that were filled with a mass of five-and-ten-cent goods.

For Woolworth, it was as if he had seen his future. The young man was convinced that an entire store dedicated to selling items for a nickel could be a success. Frank's employers were willing to back their ambitious employee, lending him $315.41 so that he could purchase the notions needed to stock his proposed emporium.

Woolworth chose Utica, New York, as the site of his enterprise. He distributed handbills and opened the doors of his store on February 22, 1879. Frank's first customer was a woman who wanted to buy one of his advertised 5-cent fire shovels. Many years later, Woolworth reminisced, "She was my first customer and had I dreamed of the things that were destined to happen to me in subsequent years, I most certainly would have taken her name and kept that first money. As it is, I don't even know who she was."

The "Great 5¢ Store" was a success at first, and Woolworth paid off his loan, but then business began to decline. Still, he remained confident; the problem, he concluded, was his location on a poorly traveled side street. When a friend gave him a glowing account of business in Lancaster, Pennsylvania, the young entrepreneur wasted no time in relocating south. He unveiled a much grander outlet in Lancaster on June 21, 1879. This store had a comer location, three show windows, seven clerks, and a rent bill of $30 a month.

Woolworth's new store was a hit from the start, and soon the merchandise was moving so swiftly that he was faced with supply problems. Lacking the purchasing power to buy five-cent items in bulk, he added a new tier of higher-priced merchandise, making his 5¢ store into a five-and-ten.

Woolworth also opened stores in the Pennsylvania cities of York and Harrisburg, but these outlets flamed brightly and then burned out. In November 1880, however, Woolworth scored with a store in Scranton. "By the end of 1880," Woolworth later recalled, "I was so rich that I decided to take the first vacation I had ever enjoyed. I was worth $2,000, which looked bigger to me than $20,000,000 would now. In fact, I felt quite as rich then as I do now because I had the consciousness and the satisfaction of having made a success in business." Woolworth's holiday was not especially ambitious. The once impecunious youth succumbed to the temptation to show off, and he took his wife, all decked out in a new dress and a feather-trimmed hat, back to Watertown, where old acquaintances admired the local man who had done so well.

F W. Woolworth, of course, was just beginning. But as he looked to the future he vowed that he would never go into debt again. It was a vow he never broke. Instead of borrowing, Woolworth sought entrepreneurs who would put up the cash to become partners in new stores. His first collaborators were his younger brother Charles Sumner, his cousin Seymour Horace Knox, and his former employer, W. H. Moore. Another businessman, Fred Kirby, also became a partner.

From then on, the Woolworth phenomenon grew. In addition to a lengthening list of Pennsylvania stores, he had locations in Trenton, New Jersey, and Elmira, New York, by late 1886. Even the emporium of Moore & Smith transformed itself into a five-and-ten in 1885.

In order to move into the big time, however, Woolworth had to conquer the citadel of commerce, New York City. And so, in 1886 he and his family moved to a new home in Brooklyn, and F. W. opened an office on Chambers Street in Manhattan. Two years later he moved to the Stewart Building at 280 Broadway, where he remained until he opened his own building 25 years later. By this time Woolworth no longer needed partners and so became the sole

owner of all new Woolworth stores. His four associates opened up retail chains of their own, but all remained on friendly terms.

In 1890, Woolworth decided to go to Europe after a business associate told him about inexpensive merchandise there. In Germany he found dolls reasonably priced but was appalled that women and children toiled cruelly making them "while the men drink beer." In one town he found a good source of glass marbles and Christmas tree ornaments. He passed through Vienna and Bohemia, inspecting the vases and glassware, then he journeyed to the Leipzig Fair and to Berlin before spending a week in Paris. Shortly after Woolworth's return to the United States, customers began finding imported goods on his store shelves. By 1907, Woolworth was annually importing more than $2 million worth of European merchandise.

Soon after his homecoming, Woolworth sent the following message to his managers: "I have been looking over a census of the United States and I am convinced that there are one hundred cities and towns where we can locate five-and-ten-cent stores and we can sell a million dollars' worth of goods a year!"

It has often been remarked that when bad times assail a nation's economy some businesses—like shoe repair, used cars, and relocation services—flourish. When the Panic of 1893, the worst depression the nation had experienced up to that time, struck the United States, F. W. Woolworth easily rode out the storm. True to his vow he incurred no debts, and when wholesale prices dropped he was able to snap up merchandise cheaper than ever. Besides, his low prices seemed even more of a bargain to hard-pressed consumers.

Between 1895 and 1897, Woolworth opened major emporia in Washington, D.C., Brooklyn, Philadelphia, and Boston. Then, on the last day of October 1896, he unveiled his grandest achievement—a store in Manhattan itself. The outlet, at 17th Street and 6th Avenue, was such a hit that four years later he opened an even larger store on 14th Street. This "world's largest five-and-ten" boasted a pipe organ and 12,000

square feet of space; it sold everything from candy and jewelry to toys, perfume, hardware, knitted goods, stationery frames, and novels.

In 1901 the Woolworth family moved into a 30-room mansion on 5th Avenue and 80th Street in Manhattan—the so-called "Millionaire's Row"—which he had built to impress members of New York Society, who to this point had ignored the man they considered nothing more than an upstart tradesman. Later, when his three daughters, Helena, Edna, and Jessie, were wed, F. W. purchased lots further down East 80th Street and built houses for all of them.

Life was good for the retail magnate. On May 25, 1907, his company conducted a census of the 170 stores it had in 23 states and the District of Columbia and found that 1,137,449 customers entered the establishments on that day—82 percent of whom made purchases. Two years later, Woolworth expanded overseas to Britain, where his outlets were called "Three-and-Sixpence" stores.

That same year the Woolworth store in Philadelphia opened a small food counter, and three years later, customers were welcomed at the first of the true Woolworth lunch counters at the 14th Street store in Manhattan. It began a tradition of grilled cheese sandwiches, malted milk, the 60¢ turkey dinner, hot dogs on a rotating cooker, cream pie, and coffee that became as much a part of Woolworth's stores as the merchandise.

With companies such as J. G. McCrory and S. S. Kresge offering competition, Woolworth merged his chain in 1912 with five others—four owned by his former partners, plus a chain west of the Rocky Mountains owned by Earle Perry Charlton—and created an empire, the F. W. Woolworth Company with 596 stores and annual sales of more than $50 million.

On his trips to Europe, Woolworth did more than ferret out merchandise. He enjoyed attending the opera, and he gamely tried to master both the French and German languages. Architecture also enthralled him. He found the Gothic Revival Houses of Parliament in London very impressive, and

CORBIS-BETTMANN

The Woolworth Building still ranks as one of the world's most distinguished structures.

when he began planning a new building for his headquarters he selected the same style.

The architect Woolworth chose to design the building was Cass Gilbert, who had already made a name for himself with his brilliant designs for the Minnesota State Capitol and the New York Customs House. When Gilbert asked his employer how tall the new building should be, Woolworth told him, "750 feet." "Am I limited to that?" the architect queried. "That's the minimum," Woolworth answered.

Woolworth's new building on Broadway at Park Place in Manhattan was completed in 1913. It topped out at 792 feet, the tallest building in the world, until the 1,046-foot-high Chrysler Building was completed in 1930. Although the

Woolworth Building had only 60 stories, each floor averaged more than 13 feet in height. The lowest ceiling was 11 feet, and some were as high as 20 feet. With its soaring lines, sumptuous mosaic lobby and flamboyant Gothic spire, the Woolworth Building was, and still is, a landmark in New York City

True to his promise never to borrow money, Woolworth carried no mortgage on his tower, paying for it in cash—$13.5 million. Yet, for all the building's grandeur, there's one indication that Woolworth didn't see himself as an Ozymandian figure. In one of the upper corners of the lobby there is a gargoyle of F. W. himself, clutching the nickels and dimes that built his kingdom.

World War I put a dent in Woolworth's European supply chain, but by

then the company was too big to let even a war put a stop to it. In 1916 alone, 115 stores opened their doors, and sales were solid even in war-torn Britain. At the same time, sadness began to shadow the empire. The spring of 1915 brought the deaths of Carson Peck, Woolworth's general manager for 25 years, and Woolworth's cousin Seymour Knox.

The retail magnate's own health was declining, as was his wife's mental capacities (her symptoms bore the signs of Alzheimer's disease). In 1916, Woolworth's first employer and friend of many years, W. H. Moore, died of a stroke. Two years later Woolworth's second daughter Edna (Hutton) died at age 35. The coroner's verdict was mastoiditis, which "had caused contraction of the tongue muscles and consequent suffocation." Others were suspicious that her death could have been suicide by poisoning.

Moore had had the majority of his teeth removed shortly before he died. Woolworth thought the action had contributed to his friend's death, so he vowed to refuse dental care for his own teeth, which were in poor condition. He began to have increasing problems with them and could eat only soft foods, his favorite being overripe bananas. Despite warnings from his physicians that septic poisoning would set in, Woolworth would not visit a dentist. On April 4, 1919, Woolworth began to run a high fever. Doctors diagnosed his condition as gallstones and uremic and septic poisoning, and he died on April 8, just five days short of his 67th birthday.

Woolworth had built a personal fortune estimated at $65 million, which he left to his wife. She was by that time totally incompetent and, without knowing it, had become one of the richest people in America. When Jennie died five years later, the estate went in equal parts to their surviving daughters, Helena and Jessie, and to Barbara Hutton, the only child of Woolworth's deceased daughter, Edna.

The Woolworth Empire, however, had many years to live. By its 50th anniversary in 1929, the company had 2,247 stores in the United States, Canada, Cuba, England, and Germany. The directors had managed for a remarkably long time to hold the maximum price of merchandise to a dime, but by the early 1930s, although the term "five-and-ten" was still used, it was an anachronism, as many items were going for 20¢ and more.

After World War II, the great migration to the suburbs began, eventually gutting American downtown areas as buyers shifted to the malls. The situation deteriorated rapidly for the company and its 1953 earnings hit a five-year low of $29.8 million. A series of presidents addressed some of the problems, but the company was still not growing at the rate of its competitors. By 1996, Woolworth stores were selling items that a customer could find elsewhere, and usually at a lower price. The newer chains, such as Wal-Mart and Target, were offering a wider range of merchandise at a bigger discount, while franchise specialty stores and a host of supersized drugstores were providing a greater variety of the same type of merchandise.

To make matters worse, the Woolworth stores themselves had deteriorated, offering poor service, uninspiring displays, unappealing merchandise, and a general air of shabbiness. Customers got the feeling that the company had lost interest. One analyst put it this way: "F. W. Woolworth and the entire variety-store concept became defunct 20 years ago and began to decline 35 years ago. It was a company that had completely lost its reason for being. It died many years ago, but it just wasn't buried."

Yet Woolworth Corporation survives as the owner of several profitable divisions—Foot Locker and Kinney Shoes among them. And it may get stronger now that it has shed its biggest liability. It could be taken as a lamentable sign of the unsentimental, bottom-line view of the modern economy, but after the Woolworth Corporation announced the closings of its five-and-tens, company stock went up ten percent.

New York writer Joseph Gustaitis is a frequent contributor to American History *magazine.*

Iron John in the Gilded Age

Behind the yelps and toms-toms of the current men's movement stretches an immense fraternal tradition in which American men once spent as much on initiation rites as their government did on defense

by Mark Carnes

"The Almighty dollar," Washington Irving wrote, was the "great object of universal devotion" among Americans. Tocqueville described moneymaking as the "prevailing passion." And though the object of their craving sometimes changed, Tocqueville noticed that the emotional intensity persisted. This was why tightfisted Yankee merchants would break down in penitential tears and convert to Christ, why sober Ohio farmers would abandon their homesteads and join utopian communes. Because Americans were so bound up in the struggle to get ahead, Tocqueville concluded, they rushed "unrestrained beyond the range of common sense" when cut loose. Thus did a materialistic nation beget so many "strange sects," each striking out on such "extraordinary paths to eternal happiness."

Yet even Tocqueville might have flinched at the spectacle of thousands of adult men, most of them well-to-do and college-educated, chanting before bonfires and pounding on drums, growling and cavorting in imitation of foxes and bears, plunging naked into baptismal mudholes, and smudging their faces with ashes—all of them following a path blazed by the poet Robert Bly in the final decade of the twentieth century.

What set them in motion was Bly's 1990 *Iron John: A Book About Men.* Manhood had seldom been of much interest to general readers, and the book's odd amalgam of romantic poetry, esoteric philosophy, and popular psychology, all bolted to a little-known myth by the Grimm brothers, seemed unlikely to appeal to the masses. But *Iron John* clambered onto the best-seller list and remained there for more than a year.

The book's success confirmed its central premise: that American men who had renounced the Vietnam War and embraced feminism now fear they have become too soft. Having drifted far from traditional manhood, they need help finding their way back. Such men are drawn to Iron John—a Wildman who led boys from the suffocating confines of childhood into the liberating expanses of manhood. Bly believes the story outlines the initiatory process by which boys become men in most societies. Though deprived of such guidance, American men need not despair, for the requisite rituals are too deeply embedded in the human psyche to be forever lost, or so Bly maintains.

Some of Bly's readers, calling themselves mythopoets, resolved to exhume those rituals and breathe into them new life. They scoured the works of Joseph Campbell and Mary Stewart for mythological or historical examples of men's rituals that could be "adapted" for mod-

As Bly's boys tried to create and perform rituals dating back to the Bronze Age, they overlooked a less remote source.

ern usage. Other Bly enthusiasts published magazines and placed ads in newspapers to attract like-minded men to share the experience. Still others— some one hundred thousand strong— sought to identify with their hoary male forebears by attending weekend "man-camps" in the woods (or in suitably bucolic convention centers). Soon the mythopoetic army overran the tiny outposts of "pro-feminist" academics and men's-rights activists, each of which until then had claimed the men's movement as its own.

But as Bly's boys tried to create and perform initiatory rituals dating back to the Bronze Age, they overlooked a less remote source: the Gilded Age of nineteenth-century America, when literally millions of men—members of the Freemasons, Odd Fellows, Knights of Pythias, and hundreds of similar societies—each week performed elaborate initiatory rituals.

The oldest and most imitated of the fraternal orders was Freemasonry. Founded in late-seventeenth-century England as a stonemasons' guild, the group evolved into a drinking and eating club for tradesmen, merchants, and some noblemen. Its special cachet was secrecy. Members used hand signals and passwords to identify one another; soon they devised a legend about Hiram Abiff, the master mason of Solomon's Temple who was assassinated by rivals and "raised" back to life. Eventually new members underwent a simple initiation, during which they learned the secret signals and heard Abiff's story. Then everyone hastened to the wine steward.

By the mid-1700s Freemasonry had diffused through much of the Western world. In France it was taken up by freethinkers and evolved into a shadowy political force that attached itself to various conspiracies against church and monarchy. In Germany it served as the inspiration among a group of intellectuals for an elevated mysticism that culminated in Mozart's *The Magic Flute*.

But it was chiefly as a drinking society that Freemasonry crossed the Atlantic and took root in the English colonies. In America nearly all the lodges were located in taverns. Often the three "degrees," or ritual ranks, were conferred in a single evening by members who, having lingered too long at the punch bowl, stumbled over the oaths, passwords, and whatever else they happened upon. Their revelries commonly spilled beyond the tavern, and constables learned to exercise special vigilance on nights the "merry Masons" were abroad.

The character of American Freemasonry changed after 1826. That year William Morgan, who had joined a Masonic lodge in Rochester, New York, moved to Batavia, New York, but was denied admission to the lodge there. Disdaining his oath of secrecy, Morgan announced plans to publish the Masonic signs and lectures. Several weeks later some mysterious strangers showed up, told Morgan that he was under arrest for unpaid debts, and took him to Fort Niagara. Then he disappeared, never to be seen again. Rumors abounded that he had been tossed into the rapids by Freemasons; members of the order suggested that Morgan had fled town and changed his name to avoid creditors.

What happened next is beyond dispute: Two dozen Masons were indicted for conspiring to abduct Morgan, conspiracy being the most serious charge that could be lodged in the absence of a body. Though the evidence against the defendants was damning, only a handful were convicted, and their sentences were brief. But a public tumult ensued when it was learned that Gov. De Witt Clinton, as well as some of the prosecutors, judges, and jurors were members of the order. Ministers raged against Freemasonry. Politicians, insisting that both political parties had been tainted by the order, founded the nation's first third party, the Anti-Masonic party.

Tens of thousands of Masons withdrew from the order, many lodges ceased meeting, and some officials closed their doors for what they assumed would be the final time. But the Morgan debacle indirectly reinvigorated the fraternal movement by turning it over to an emerging middle class of businessmen, clerks, lawyers, and doctors. Many ex-Freemasons flocked to the Odd Fellows, formerly a working-class club, and took control of it. They sold the punch bowls and banned alcohol, they investigated the morals of prospective initiates and hauled wayward members before lodge tribunals, and they ceased passing the hat for needy members and established an insurance system based on fixed weekly assessments. These, however, were simply the means to promote the order's chief new purpose: initiation.

The ceremonies were drafted by a special committee on ritual, which included several former Freemasons. They wrote an hour-long pageant based loosely on the story of Genesis, with the initiate playing Adam. Because Adam was naked, the initiate's shirt was removed. "Thou art dust," he was told, and chains were wound around his body to symbolize his "guilty soul." He was led blindfolded around the lodge room four or five times as officers lectured on mortality, God, and the meaning of life. Suddenly the blindfolds were snatched away. A skeleton loomed in the torchlight. "Contemplate that dismal, ghastly emblem of what thou art sure to be, and what thou mayst soon become," an officer intoned.

Odd Fellows found this ritual inspiring and craved more like it. But English officials, who had chartered the first American lodges, were dumbfounded. To them the lodge was a place for workers to unwind, perhaps over a tankard of beer, and to help one another when times were bad. Workers needed tangible assistance and support, not long-winded lectures on morality and religion. Relations between American and English branches smoldered as droves of bibulous English emigrants knocked on the doors of the American lodges, took seats in awe-inspiring "temples," and stared in disbelief as lamps were extinguished, torches lit, and robes, altars, and skeletons prepared. As speakers droned on, with no one stirring to prepare libations, the Englishmen's wonder turned to anger. During the 1840s English officials demanded that the Americans abandon the new rituals on pain of having their charters revoked. The Americans refused, explaining that Odd Fellowship had grown in America only after it had discarded "conviviality" and instituted religious rituals. "Our career affords an example not unworthy of your imitation," American officials noted pointedly.

In 1844 the Americans broke loose and established the "Independent" Order of Odd Fellows. Free to develop on its own terms, American Odd Fellowship created a sequence of nine elaborate rituals, most of them derived from the Old Testament. In one, for example, the initiate became Isaac, the son of Abraham, who journeyed across a desert wilderness to Mount Moriah (several blind-folded circuits of the lodge room). Then he was tied up and placed upon an altar. Firewood was piled beneath it, a torch was lit, and the Twenty-third

Psalm read. After explaining that Isaac was to be sacrificed, Abraham struck a match and leaned toward the wood. Then a gong sounded. God, Abraham announced, had decided to save Isaac and had commanded that he be admitted as a patriarch of Abraham's family. Odd Fellows reported that such a rite "fully satisfied" their "desire" and elevated their order "almost to the dignity of a religion." The Odd Fellows grew from some thirty thousand members in 1843, just prior to the new rituals, to two hundred thousand by 1860 and nearly a million by 1900.

American Freemasonry developed along similar lines, especially the Scottish Rite, the most prestigious branch of the fraternity, which greatly expanded its twenty-nine rituals during the 1850s and 1860s; the new sequence filled eight hundred printed pages. Although a few traditionalists claimed that Freemasonry had been "murderously perverted" by the revisions, most credited the new rituals for the order's growth from forty thousand members in the 1830s to nearly three-quarters of a million by the close of the nineteenth century.

During the 1860s and 1870s hundreds of fraternal organizers imitated the Odd Fellows and Freemasons. The Knights of Pythias, founded in 1864, devised a set of five wildly eclectic rituals: Roman senators sauntered through Hades, and crusaders through medieval castles. Within a decade membership in the order exceeded a quarter of a million, a figure that doubled by the end of the century. An official in 1887 attributed the order's growth to a ritual that had "taken hold of the hearts of men."

The craving was so widespread that entrepreneurs proffered initiatory ritual rather like the way Publishers' Clearinghouse exploits the gambling itch to sell magazines. Victorian insurance promoters, recognizing that men would more likely buy a policy if it came with evenings of initiation, created scores of ritualistic beneficiary societies. One syndicate approached Lew Wallace to transform his best-selling novel into a ritual for the Knights of Ben-Hur. After eliminating the anachronism, Wallace agreed, and within a

decade more than a hundred thousand men—initiates of the Tribe of Ben-Hur—had raced "chariots," done time on "Roman" galleys, and forked over substantial premiums for the Tribe's life insurance. Life insurance companies, lacking such rituals, fought hard to gain control of the market. But as late as 1900 a half-million more Americans were insured by fraternal societies than by insurance companies.

Wherever Victorian men came together, someone, it seemed, would propose formal initiations. The Grand Army of the Republic, a veterans' organization, offered three separate rituals, much to the dismay of politically ambitious men such as Oliver Wilson of Indiana who complained that GAR members cared more about the "bauble of ritualism" than pensions. The Knights of Labor, the largest of the post-Civil War labor organizations, provided its membership with three lengthy ceremonies. When Terence Powderly took charge of the Knights, he fought to eliminate the rituals. "The best part of each meeting was taken up in initiating new members, in instructing them in the use of symbols, in hymns and formula that could not be put in the interest of labor outside the meeting room," he complained in his autobiography. But the Knights refused to give up their ceremonies.

By the turn of the century, up to 40 percent of all adult men belonged to at least one lodge.

At the turn of the century observers estimated that from 20 to 40 percent of all adult men belonged to at least one of the nation's seventy-thousand lodges. Because only the highest-paid manual workers could afford the dues, paraphernalia, and initiation fees, and because Catholic lodge members were threatened with excommunication, the fraternal movement was chiefly an activity of middle-class Protestant men, many of whom belonged to several orders. Initia-

tion was arguably their chief leisure activity.

The money spent on ritual, though incalculable, was by any standard staggering. During the last third of the nineteenth century the Odd Fellows' total revenue was about $150 million; the Freemasons, far more affluent, surely took in several times this amount. The insurance industry estimated the revenue of beneficiary societies at $650 million. All told, fraternal income perhaps approached $2 billion, about what federal government spent on defense during the same period.

Some of this wealth went into costumes, pensions, charity, or the pockets of unscrupulous officials, but much was expended on the temples themselves. In nearly every community the temple of the Masons, Odd Fellows, or Knights of Pythias was a landmark. The spectacular Masonic Temple in Philadelphia, built during the 1870s at a cost of $1.5 million, rivaled Wanamaker's across the street. The Masonic Temple in Chicago, completed in time for the world's fair in 1893, was the tallest building in the world.

We neglect fraternal orders partly because they declined so rapidly in the twentieth century. A new generation of men, when dragged to the lodge by their bosses or fathers-in-law, choked down laughter as the neighborhood grocer, donning the miter of Jewish high priest, fumbled through an Old Testament lesson for the Odd Fellows or as the superintendent of the ironworks, wearing the headdress of an Iroquois sagamore, brandished a tomahawk and challenged the initiate's fitness for the Improved Order of Red Men. Many young men regaled friends with hilarious accounts of what had transpired at the lodge, and they never went back. Hundreds of smaller orders quietly passed out of existence. Most beneficiary societies, financially dependent on an infusion of young members, were in serious trouble by the 1920s. The Depression finished them off and also wiped out thousands of lodges that could no longer make the mortgage payments on their temples. Within a few years most Americans would associate the orders with Ralph Kramden and Ed Norton of the Loyal Order of Raccoons.

The historical profession came of age during these skeptical years, and academics saw no reason to pay much attention to institutions that were intentionally behind the times. Scholars who bothered to look at the rituals dismissed them as hokum; they assumed that businessmen joined to make contacts, workers to acquire insurance, and others because there was not much else to do. With the development of trade associations and businessmen's clubs, private and governmental insurance, and movies and television, most of the orders expired out of sheer inanity.

But historians erred in thinking of the orders as yet another manifestation of the backwardness of small-town America. The orders in fact thrived especially in large cities. And the businessmen, engineers, and lawyers who spent evenings pretending to be medieval knights or Indian chiefs were by day transforming the United States into an urban-industrial nation.

The popularity of *Iron John* in recent years further confirms that male rituals are not incompatible with modernity. At first glance the slouching, dungareed participants at Bly's mancamps little resemble the somber, stiff faces that stare out from nineteenth-century lodge photographs. But the rituals invented by Bly's mythopoets are uncannily similar to those performed in fraternal lodges more than a century ago.

Both sets of rituals attempted to establish a link to primitive or ancient peoples. Bly proposes that the story of Iron John, though based on a tale the Grimm brothers set down in 1820, may have originated twenty thousand years earlier. Men's movement enthusiasts exalt drumming as an "ancient ritual" and carve wooden masks in honor of "old gods" such as Pan, Orpheus, Shiva, and Dionysus.

More than a hundred years ago Albert Pike—poet, lawyer, Confederate general, and Masonic ritualist—similarly called for a return to the primitive truths that "faded out from men's souls before the world grew old." He viewed Freemasonry as a faint echo of rites practiced by druidic shamans, Eleus-

inian mystics, and Zoroastrian priests. The Ancient Order of United Workmen and the Improved Order of Red Men in their very names suggested a link to the distant past. They did so not from any romantic attachment to Noble Savages—Native Americans who sought admission to the Red Men were turned away—but to lay claim to rites of prehistoric origin. For much the same reason the Knights of Pythias identified Pythagoras as the first member of their order.

Once they had settled into their tribal sweat lodge, Solomonic temple, or medieval castle, initiates for both the fraternal orders and modern men's groups underwent an initiatory sequence with comparable motifs. After being depicted as deficient or immature, they embarked on arduous journeys revealing the knowledge necessary for self-transformation. Fraternal initiates, their shirts removed or disarranged, were blindfolded and prodded around the lodge. The ritual climaxed when the blindfolds were snatched away. "God said, 'Let there be light,'" Masons were informed.

Men's movement initiates, also blindfolded and their faces smudged or covered with masks, are carried over the heads of members or obliged to crawl on hands and knees. As the drumming reaches a crescendo, the blindfolds are removed. Newcomers to one men's group, after scrambling through a tunnel, are told, "Go, The light is gold."

All fraternal initiates swore themselves to secrecy on pain of allowing brethren to "thrust my tongue through with a red-hot iron" or words to that effect. Fearsome oaths notwithstanding, the orders were remarkably lax. Some, fearing that another would steal an affecting ritual, copyrighted their "secret" work. Everyone recognized that meaningful secrets could not be kept among a million members. Secrecy was chiefly symbolic, a means of strengthening the bond among men by underscoring the exclusion of women. Indeed, no offense was more serious than to tell one's wife the "concerns of the order." Women, for their part, resented the large sums spent on dues and paraphernalia and chafed at

their husbands' absence on the frequent lodge nights. In the 1850s the Odd Fellows, seeking to "lessen and ultimately destroy the prejudice of the fairer sex," created a women's auxiliary called the Degree of Rebekah. Still, women were to have no part in men's initiations. "The simple truth is this," one official explained in 1867: "Woman is not entitled to and seeks not a place among us."

Bly's mythopoets initially took a more moderate stand. Because some men's groups met in family rooms or booked events in public facilities, women came and went pretty much as they wished. But it soon became apparent that even their fleeting presence somehow interfered with the proceedings. "Don't have a woman near the meeting space," men's organizers warned. The need for secrecy and exclusion was driven home after one exuberant group invited the media to a weekend mancamp. Bly telegrammed a warning: The mythopoetic movement was still in its "infancy," and its rituals would be ridiculed by the public. But by then a small army of freelance journalists had already filled their notebooks with arch accounts of what they had seen. "A luscious hologram of multilayered idiocy," Joe Queenan of *GQ* wrote. Now most men's groups exclude women and outsiders. Many swear participants to secrecy—one reason less has been heard of them in recent months.

If women were conspicuous by their absence, "fathers" were omnipresent—in both fraternal and men's groups. The central drama of fraternal rituals derived from the hostility of "elderly" officers—patriarchs with flowing white beards or sachems leaning upon walking sticks—toward the callow initiates—"squaws," "pages," "children." Tension between surrogate father and son rose to a climax. Suddenly, usually on completion of the initiatory journey, the officer embraced the initiate. Father and son had become brothers.

Bly's goal is similar. Young men today do not know what it means to be a man because their fathers—"enfeebled, dejected, paltry"—failed to teach them. Bly's hairy Wildman serves as a surrogate for the clean-shaven (or absent) male cipher of the modern family. Some men's groups place an empty "Spirit Chair" at the front of the room, a mute reminder (and perhaps indictment) of the missing fathers.

Rituals such as these, abstracted from a "sacred" context and a community of shared sentiment, seem so artificial as to verge on fraud. (Some wags during the nineteenth century said that the orders had been invented by novelty companies; today critics propose that men's group organizers have a stake in drum companies). Many find it hard not to agree with Lance Morrow of *Time*, who called the men's movement a "depthless happening in the goofy circus of America," language reminiscent of the nineteenth-century criticisms of the lodges.

But though contrived, the rituals—then and now—are not without effect. Mancamp participants are commonly convulsed with sobs. A reporter for *Esquire*, while sniggering at what he described as a "Three Stooges skit," was taken aback by the "murderously authentic" moans and weeping around him. In 1877 the *Voice of Masonry* observed that fraternal initiates became "so wrought upon and their feelings so excited that they shed tears." The National Christian Association, founded in 1867 to rid the nation of the orders, acknowledged the mysterious power of the rituals and identified Satan as their source. Members took degree after degree "as a charmed frog goes into a snake's mouth."

To what, indeed, can we attribute the enduring attraction of men's rituals? Bly, whose views matter if only because he predicted the movement his book inspired, responds that all men possess an intuitive attraction to the requisite rituals of manhood, which are "still very much alive in our genetic structure." But until scientists find a peptide chain curled along the Y chromosome that impels men to caper in mudholes or don outlandish headgear, his argument will persuade few who are not already wedded to Jung's notion that some ideas are factory-installed in the brain. Moreover, Bly's belief that men are predisposed to such rituals fails to explain why American men had to invent them in the first place or why so many of their great-grandchildren scorned their vaunted rites.

Some social scientists regard male rites as attempts by men to assert their fading power over women. In this vein, many feminists view the mythopoets as part of a backlash against their movement, a longing for the good old days when men were Wildmen and women chattel; they brush aside the pro-feminist protestations of Bly and his followers as little more than a smoke screen.

The charge that men's rituals are a reaction against the advancement of women is probably not far from wrong.

Many women in the nineteenth century, particularly those active in reform and women's rights, had similar misgivings about what transpired behind the lodge's thick veil of secrecy. If, as defenders of the orders claimed, fraternal rituals were designed to make initiates "gentle, charitable, and tender as a woman," why weren't women permitted to see what went on? If the purpose of the orders were laudable, why were they so elaborately cloaked in secrecy? The charge that men's rituals are a male reaction against the advances of women has surfaced repeatedly; it is probably not far from wrong.

By the first few decades of the nineteenth century, women were assuming a new place within the homes of the emerging middle classes. At a time when lawyers and merchants—not to mention legions of ambitious inventors and clerks—fastened their attention upon the prospects of making money within the rapidly expanding national economy, they all but abandoned patriarchal traditions of men's religious and moral guidance. And women, delivered from many of the crushing burdens of farm life, eagerly filled the void left by men's withdrawal from the "domestic sphere." Their special task, women now proclaimed, was to redeem the nation from a hardhearted materialism by instilling in children the gentle and self-effacing virtues of Christ.

When the men who had been reared in such homes came of age, they found themselves inhabiting a competitive world where the government safety net was but a few filaments in the imaginations of the likes of Edward Bellamy and Henry George. How were these young men to reconcile the demands of bosses and the remorseless workings of the market with the lessons of love learned at a mother's knee? How reconcile the Darwinian world of adult men with the peaceable promises of childhood?

Fraternal rituals offered psychological guidance by leading men from the precepts and enticements of childhood into a closer affinity with bosses and bankers, customers and colleagues. It did so by attenuating adult men's associations with childhood and women and by strengthening the ties amongst themselves. The rituals provided a religious experience antithetical to what they had learned as youths and supplanted the familial bonds of childhood with the brotherhood of the lodge.

Lodge officials insisted that their rites accorded with Christianity. There was seemingly no reason for initiates to view the religion of the lodge with suspicion: lodge meetings usually began with a minister offering a prayer, all initiates were obliged to profess belief in God, most rituals were drawn from the Bible, and the setting itself resembled nothing so much as the church. But the altars, chalices, coffins, and flickering candles, when used as props to enact the destruction of King Solomon's Temple (Royal Arch Masonry), the execution of a spy (Grand Army of the Republic), or a sojourn through the "calcined wastes" of Hades (Knights of Pythias), conveyed lessons far different from what ministers imparted to their flocks on Sunday. The deity of the lodge was distant and impersonal, totally unlike the loving God that then prevailed in Protestant churches.

The rituals, too, provided a family psychodrama that drew initiates from the feminine attachments of childhood and brought them, by means of an initiatory "rebirth," into a new family of brothers. This transference climaxed with the reconciliation of the initiate—the son—with his new father.

The rituals of Bly's mythopoets seem to function much the same way, evoking the "old gods" of patriarchal tradition, imitating the warrior rites of tribal societies, enshrining ancient kings and heroes. From these imaginative realms women are almost entirely absent. Modern men cling tightly to Iron John partly because he carries them into a world where manhood is unencumbered by gender-role ambiguities. The leaders of fraternal orders nowadays take unabashed pride in the "masculine" character of their rites and express misgivings over what they regard as the "feminine" inventions of the men's movement: the "touchy-feely" quality of the steam baths, naked romps in the woods, the self-revelatory discussions that stretch deep into the night. Such experiences may well be therapeutic, states Harry E. Echols, a lawyer and prominent Odd Fellow and Freemason in Washington, D. C., but they lack the ongoing fellowship of the lodge and meaningful rituals that, burnished by the passage of time, reflect the wisdom of the past.

Victorian men retreated on lodge nights into a mystic wonderland inhabited by gods and heroes.

Echol's statement points out that more than gender is involved in the appeal of men's rituals. The orders and the men's groups seize upon the distant past because it offers something of an antidote to the modern world. Victorian men, driven by sales and production quotas, buffeted by the vagaries of distant markets, and trapped in widening webs of corporate bureaucracies, retreated on lodge nights into a mystic wonderland inhabited by gods and heroes, kings and knights, a place where identity was conferred rather than imperiled. The unreality of the lodge was its chief attraction.

The same may be true of mancamps. When one participant complained that its rituals were ridiculous, an organizer explained that the weekend's purpose was to let people "get beyond the logical world." The rational demands of the modern world for system, regularity, and order may spawn an antithetical world of fantasy and emotional expression. Tocqueville put it somewhat differently: The material satisfactions of life notwithstanding, "the soul has needs that must be fulfilled."

The emergence of Bly and of the Wildman he brought back from the primordial depths of the human soul serves as a reminder that the road to the future may take some strange detours. The enduring appeal of compensatory anachronisms—not to mention the resurgence of religious fundamentalism and ethnic nationalism—shows the emotional power of pre-modern values and beliefs. When we finally arrive at the year 2001, it may bear less resemblance to the aseptic and androgynous landscapes of Stanley Kubrick than to terrain through which we passed centuries ago.

Mark Carnes is chair of the history department at Barnard College, Columbia University. His book Secret Ritual and Manhood in Victorian America *was published by Yale University Press.*

Unit Selections

Key Points to Consider

❖ Compare the response to more recent acts of terrorism, such as the 1995 bombing in Oklahoma, with that caused by the Haymarket affair. Why are Americans so quick to accept the idea of conspiracy?

❖ What were the outstanding issues of the presidential election of 1896? Why did the Democrat-Populist, William Jennings Bryan, fail to appeal to urban workers?

❖ Discuss the consequences of the Spanish-American War on world power alignments. Did the Philippine insurrection offer any lessons that we might have learned for the war in Vietnam?

❖ Evaluate Teddy Roosevelt's presidency. What were his failures? His achievements?

 **Links** **www.dushkin.com/online/**

11. **Chicago Historical Society/Northwestern University**
    http://www.chicagohs.org/fire/
12. **Jim Zwick/Syracuse University**
    http://home.ican.net/~fjzwick/ail98-35.html
13. **Ohio State University/Department of History**
    http://www.cohums.ohio-state.edu/history/projects/McKinley/
14. **Small Planet Communications/"The Age of Imperialism"**
    http://www.smplanet.com/imperialism/toc.html

These sites are annotated on pages 4 and 5.

Industrialization and urbanization were the two major developments of post–Civil War America. Corporations came to dominate the marketplace; some of them attained a previously undreamed of size. Individuals who ran these corporations amassed huge fortunes on which they paid no income taxes. Some of them flaunted their wealth by building ornate mansions, collecting art treasures from all over the world, and trying to outspend one another on lavish parties and balls. Ordinary people fared less well. Urban workers, who included men, women, and children, often lived in unhealthy squalor and worked long hours in dreary factories and mills. Farmers had to sell what they produced in markets that fluctuated widely. They also had to contend with the monopolistic practices of railroads, which charged "all the traffic would bear" for shipping and storing farm products.

The article "Terrorism Revisited" focuses on what became known as the "Haymarket affair" of 1886. During a labor rally in Chicago's Haymarket Square, someone threw a bomb that killed or fatally wounded seven policemen. Though no one knew who was responsible, blame was cast upon "anarchists," and the belief grew that these individuals represented a foreign conspiracy that was trying to destroy the nation. The incident and its aftermath tells how fear of the "anarchists" was manipulated to help destroy the burgeoning labor movement.

Farm organizations grew in response to the many grievances harbored by those who tilled the land. Some created cooperatives to get higher prices for the goods they produced and lower prices for the supplies and machinery they purchased. When it appeared that neither the Republican nor Democratic Party was responsive to the needs of farmers, they moved to form the People's Party, better known as the Populists. The Populists favored more government intervention against the corporations that they had to deal with and to provide, among other things, cheaper credit for farmers. The Populists formed a third party in 1892, but the combination of an uninspiring presidential candidate, lack of funds, and the taint of "radicalism" prevented them from doing very well.

The onset of a major depression in 1893 resulted in large scale unemployment, violent labor disputes, and an unprecedented number of farm foreclosures. Populist strength grew in rural areas, but a doubt that they could win a national election even under these conditions caused them to endorse the Democratic candidate, William Jennings Bryan, in 1896. Bryan attached himself to the cause of "free silver," which farmers thought would result in higher prices for agricultural products. In "Electing the President, 1896," Edward Ranson discusses that campaign and concludes that Bryan lost because he championed an older, rural America against those who represented a modernizing, industrial nation.

The return of prosperity and the outbreak of the Spanish-American War ended the Populist crusade.

American foreign policy became more assertive during the 1880s and 1890s. Various theories were put forward to justify American expansion into the Pacific: the need for Asian markets, the acquisition of coaling stations for merchant and naval vessels, and taking up the "white man's burden" among them. The Spanish-American War provided an opportunity to put these ideas into practice. Although events in Cuba provided the immediate cause of the war, by its end the United States had acquired the Philippines and other Pacific islands. Although it lasted only a few months and casualties were relatively low, what a contemporary referred to as a "splendid little war" actually had very significant consequences. In "The Meaning of '98," John Lukacs describes how it brought about a realignment of the major powers and set the stage for a Pacific rivalry between the United States and Japan.

Rebels in the Philippine Islands had been fighting for liberation from Spanish rule for years. They had reason to believe that if they collaborated with the United States in its war against the Spanish they would receive independence. When it became clear that this was not to be, Filipino rebels led by Emilio Aguinald launched a guerrilla war against the United States that lasted until 1902. Casualties on both sides during this conflict far exceeded those of the Spanish-American War. "Our First Southeast Asian War" describes this bloody endeavor, and authors David Kohler and James Wensyel draw parallels with the more recent Vietnam War.

"How We Lived" consists of interviews with centenarians who describe their experiences during the first decades of the twentieth century. This was an age when telephones were a novelty, people used pages from the Sears, Roebuck & Company catalogue for toilet tissue, and collected water in rain barrels to do their laundry. There are also accounts of the primitive methods then used to treat illnesses.

Teddy Roosevelt's public career began during the years covered in this unit and continued into the progressive era. Teddy came into national prominence as head of the "Rough Riders" (he actually was second in command, but his flamboyance overshadowed the other man) during the Spanish-American War. He exploited this adventure in his bid for high offices, first in running for governor of the State of New York then for the vice presidency of the country. The assassination of William McKinley catapulted Roosevelt into the presidency, a position he coveted and clearly enjoyed. "Theodore Roosevelt," by Edmund Morris, acknowledges Teddy's bumptious behavior in office but concludes that he fought for many good causes, including the protection of the environment.

The Emergence of Modern America

Terrorism Revisited

Terrorists armed with high explosives have been busy on our shores lately. America has weathered such attacks before.

By Bernard A. Weisberger

Dynamite! of all the good stuff, this is the stuff. Stuff several pounds ... into an inch pipe ... in the immediate neighborhood of a lot of rich loafers ... and light the fuse. A most cheerful and gratifying result will follow. ... [It] beats a bushel of ballots all hollow, and don't you forget it." This sunny exhortation was part of a letter to the editor that appeared in an anarchist newspaper in Chicago in 1885. A year later, when a bomb that killed one policeman and mortally wounded seven others was thrown at a mass meeting in an open square of the city known as the Haymarket, it was enough to get two of *The Alarm*'s editors (and two other men) hanged, even though no concrete evidence connected them in any way to the actual offense.

I am reminded of this dark event by the news of the arrest of the "Islamic fundamentalists" charged with conspiring to blow up New York's World Trade Center early this year. We are possibly at the start of a new upsurge of panic over terrorists—particularly terrorists armed with high explosives—and a ret-

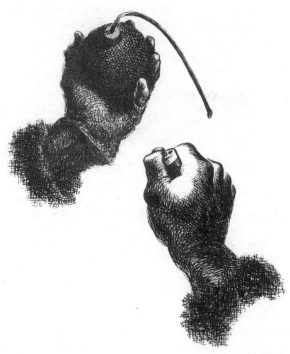

GIL EISNER

rospective look at earlier epidemics of the fever may prove useful.

The first outbreak, around the time of the Haymarket affair, was a response to the perceived popularity, at the end of the 1880s, of the doctrine of anarchism—or rather of one strain of it. Anarchists held that government, any government, was in itself an oppressive

device used by the rich and powerful to help them rob the downtrodden toilers of the earth. All of them hoped for the eventual disappearance of the state, but some—and only some—believed that the process could be hurried along by stirring the wretched of the earth to revolution. One way to do this was through dramatic acts of antiestablishment violence that would show the vulnerability of the ruling classes. A single assassination might be the push needed to bring down the whole rotten structure. Believers in this "propaganda of the deed" were to be found in major industrial cities of the United States, primarily among foreign-born pro-labor activists.

Eight such agitators were rounded up after the Haymarket bombing and charged with being accessories. One, Albert Parsons, was a native-born American—and, moreover, a Confederate war veteran. The trial was conducted by a patently biased judge in a hostile atmosphere, for the overwhelming majority of Americans shared the sentiments of the newspaper editors who referred to the presumed perpetrators as "foreign savages," "desperate fanatics," and "pirates" who deserved to be "repressed, swiftly, sternly and without parley." It was anarchism (generally lumped in the press with "socialism" and "communism") that was in the dock, and a guilty verdict was predictable from the start, though no one knows to this day who actually threw the bomb. Seven men were sentenced to death, and one to jail. On November 10, 1887, one committed suicide in his cell; Gov. Richard Oglesby commuted the sentence of two more to life imprisonment; the other four (Parsons among them) died on the gallows. Six years later a new Illinois governor, John P. Altgeld, after reviewing the record, pardoned the three survivors in a show of courage that turned out to be an act of political suicide as well.

To say that the Haymarket eight were unfairly treated under the law is by no means to deny the reality of danger from violence-prone anarchists. Between 1894 and 1900 four European heads of state—a President of France, the Prime Minister of Spain, the Empress of Austria, and the King of Italy—were assassinated by professed anarchists. Then, on September 6, 1901, President William McKinley, visiting the Pan-American exposition in Buffalo, was fatally wounded by Leon Czolgosz, who declared prior to his execution: "I don't believe we should have any rulers. It is right to kill them." But these assaults, committed with daggers and revolvers, were less unnerving than dynamite attacks on "bourgeois" cultural and institutional centers. In France and Spain during the 1890s, bombs were flung into an opera house, a police station, a church, a mining company's Paris office, and the Chamber of Deputies. Innocent bystanders, women and children, were blown to bits. Such episodes justified the use of the term *terrorism*. Nothing could be more paralyzing—literally more full of terror—to the average citizen, far removed from power, than the fear of death or mutilation at any moment, in any place, at the hands of an unknown fanatic. In the United States the image of the terrorist as a whiskered foreigner, holding a round bomb with a sputtering fuse, became a fixture of cartoonists' repertories and

the public's consciousness. After McKinley's death, President Theodore Roosevelt declared that anarchism was "a crime against the whole human race" and asked that the immigration laws be amended to exclude persons "teaching disbelief in or opposition to organized government." They were.

After 1901 individual acts of terror subsided, and the center of gravity of anarchist activism shifted into syndicalist trade unions, which favored the general strike as the battering ram of choice to pulverize the bourgeois state apparatus. In 1914 the struggle was submerged in the overall slaughter of the Great War. Out of that conflict came the Bolshevik Revolution and in the United States, in 1919, a second great wave of antiradical fear and loathing.

The setting was perfect. Wartime patriotic fervor and suspicion of dissenters still smoldered. Meanwhile, the economic shock of demobilization and reconversion launched a wave of strikes—in the steel mills of Pittsburgh, the coal mines of West Virginia, even among the police of Boston. In Seattle a general strike shut down the city for

---

The Attorney General was targeted, but the assassin blew himself into unidentifiable fragments near the A.G.'s door.

---

five days. At the same time, the American branch of the Communist party was born, as was the Third International, which called for worldwide revolution.

To this combustible mixture, real fire was applied by parties unknown. A bomb was mailed to the former senator Thomas Hardwick of Georgia and blew

off the hands of the maid who opened the package. Then, in the New York post office, sixteen similar parcels were identified, each containing explosives and destined for an honor list that included Justice Oliver Wendell Holmes, Postmaster General Albert S. Burleson, Attorney General A. Mitchell Palmer, John D. Rockefeller, and J. P. Morgan. (There was also a bomb attempt against Morgan's office in Wall Street, but that was not until autumn of 1920.) A month after May Day, marked by riots that disrupted "Red" parades in several cities, more bombs were detonated in the homes of officials in Cleveland, Boston, New York, and Pittsburgh. Palmer's Washington residence was targeted, but the assassin accidentally blew himself into unidentifiable fragments before reaching the Attorney General's front door.

REIGN OF TERROR PLANNED, ran one typical headline; PLANS FOR VIOLENCE AND MURDER, another proclaimed. The nation braced for a Fourth of July uprising that never materialized. But in November police raided the Russian People's House, the New York headquarters of a pro-Soviet organization, and declared that they found "material for 100 bombs" there. RED BOMB LABORATORY FOUND, said the next day's *Times.* Convinced (like the Bolsheviks themselves) that revolution was imminent, Palmer's Department of Justice struck back. On December 21 it deported 249 foreign-born alleged anarchists to Russia (including Emma Goldman and Alexander Berkman, who had in fact tried to kill the industrialist Henry Clay Frick in 1892). Then, in a sweeping nationwide series of raids on January 2, 1920, more than 4,000 suspected radicals were rounded up, detained under appalling conditions, questioned, and sometimes beaten up. A relative handful suffered deportation; the rest were released without apology or redress. Most newspapers reacted with satisfaction. The Washington *Evening Star* said that the raids were justified by a threat that was "no mere scare, no phantom of heated imagination." The *Post* agreed: "There is no time to waste on hairsplitting over infringement of liberty."

The Red scare of 1919–20 eventually faded away. That of 1948–53, the first of the Cold War, was primarily sparked by fear of espionage—treason by stealth, rather than by violence. Beginning in the 1970s, however, the old anxieties were rekindled by such bloody events as the kidnappings and murders organized by Italy's Red Brigades, the hijackings of planes on international air routes, indiscriminate shoot-outs in airports serving Tel Aviv and Rome, the massacre of Israeli athletes at the 1972 Olympic Games, and the attempted assassination of the pope. The Soviet Union was seen as the instigator of a good deal of this mayhem, but now, with the Cold War ended, it is the "Islamic fundamentalist" who holds that ever-ready, lethally hissing, globe-shaped bomb of folk memory.

I don't want to be misunderstood. Terrorist attacks are genuine and often despicable crimes, no less so for being described by their authors as political acts. The criminals deserve maximum punishment if convicted after fair trials under American standards of justice. And reasonable police vigilance to prevent the recurrence of such horrors as the World Trade Center bombing is justified.

Yet I can't forgo a certain wariness. I note the way in which our own government condemns regimes that sponsor terrorism but looks the other way when diplomatic convenience so dictates, not to mention how conveniently certain nations can dismiss an entire nationalist movement because some of its adherents advocate terror.

Closer to home, I would hope that Americans do not need reminding that not all Muslims are fundamentalists, and not all fundamentalists are fanatics and killers. The loose and lordly journalistic use of these terms gives me some concern. So far, happily, there have been no witch hunts. But history, properly studied, provides the raw material of both idealism and skepticism, and it will not harm the legitimate condemnation of terrorism to remember that the term itself is potentially dangerous when tossed around lightly. Sort of like a loaded bomb, you might say.

Electing The President, 1896

Edward Ranson *on the White House race that split and defined a fin-de-siècle US.*

On the eve of the American presidential and congressional elections in November 1896 the mood of the country was tense. In some quarters, especially in the ranks of nervous bankers, financiers, businessmen and property owners it approached hysteria. Both major parties warned of the dire consequences of a victory for the other side, of the cataclysmic economic results that would follow, of the resultant sectional hostility and of class conflict. Politicians, editors and clergymen all used military metaphors in their appeals to the electorate. Although feelings ran high and voting was heavy (nearly 14 million ballots were cast—a figure that would not be exceeded until 1908), polling day, November 3rd, passed without serious incident.

William McKinley, the Republican candidate, achieved a clear victory, though not a landslide, receiving 7,102,246 votes (51 per cent) to the 6,492,559 (46 per cent) cast for William Jennings Bryan, the Democratic standard-bearer, minor candidates sharing the remaining 3 per cent. Although McKinley carried only twenty-three states to Bryan's twenty-two he won in the electoral college 271–176 because his appeal was greatest in the most populous areas of the country; the demographic and economic trends of the 1890s were in the Republicans' favour. Urban and industrial America, the backbone of McKinley's support, was growing, and Bryan failed to attract the working classes in these areas. On the other hand, rural and agrarian America, the natural constitu-ency of Bryan and the Democrats, was losing its economic and political influence.

True, presidential elections between the end of the American Civil War in 1865 and 1896 had often stimulated high levels of voter interest and participation and provoked intense partisan passions. Bitter recollections of the Civil War and Reconstruction on both sides, and the rough political equilibrium which existed at the national level between the Democrats and the Republicans, ensured that political managers would stoop to any expedient to win over particular groups in the electorate or to carry key states. As Republican Senator Ingalls of Kansas wrote in 1890, 'The Decalogue and the Golden Rule have no place in a political campaign. The object is success.'

Yet for most of this period, party and presidential politics were not concerned with philosophies, programmes or policies, but focused rather upon personalities and patronage. Party loyalty was fierce, political apostasy despised, and breakaway movements and third parties rarely exercised more than temporary influence. Success could rest on wafer

Corbis/Bettmann

On the stump: (far left) the charismatic orator and Democratic candidate for the Presidency, William Jennings Bryan, on the campaign trail leaving Galion, Ohio, by train with his wife and supporters.

thin margins in pivotal states like Indiana, Illinois or New York, and candidates were chosen, in part at least, because of their local associations and their perceived ability to win in these vital areas. Hence it came to be said that while some men were born great, and some had greatness thrust upon them, others came from Ohio.

The political battles of the late nineteenth century were fought against a background of social, economic and cultural change. The population grew from 39.8 million in 1870 to 75.9 million in 1900, an increase of 25 per cent in each decade. At the same time the nation experienced rapid urbanisation and industrialisation. The costs of these changes included heightened urban-rural tensions, growing hostility between capital and labour, increasing poverty and rising resentment against social inequalities. Although the Republican Party usually supported a high protective tariff, as a means of aiding American industry and securing full employment, while the Democrats favoured a tariff for revenue purposes only as a way of helping American farmers, politicians of the 1870s and 1880s, imbued with *laissez-faire* ideas, generally chose to ignore domestic social and economic problems.

By the 1890s social, economic and political discord had created a climate close to national crisis. Men of power and property even pondered the likelihood of revolution. It was in such an atmosphere that the presidential campaign of 1896 was conducted, a campaign that for the first time in decades saw serious debate on economic and social issues which deeply divided America along unfamiliar socio-economic fissures, rather than according to traditional party lines.

The Democrats, led by Grover Cleveland, had won control of Congress and the White House in 1892, and the prospects seemed set for Cleveland to redeem his campaign promise to reduce the tariff. Within weeks of his taking office in March 1893, however, economic confidence evaporated, stock prices fell, production slowed and unemployment rose alarmingly to 2,500,000 by January 1894. By that time 642 banks had closed, and by mid-1894 156 railroads

Corbis/Bettmann

Republican contender (and victor in the 1896 White House race) William McKinley pictured here with his wife; a stiff pose that reflected his rather 'stuffed shirt' persona.

with 30,000 miles of track were in the hands of receivers. Agricultural prices dropped precipitously, tens of thousands of farmers faced bankruptcy and foreclosure of their mortgages, and agrarian distress was widespread.

The nation blamed the Democratic Party in general, and the Cleveland administration in particular, for their tribulations, with public soup kitchens being christened 'Cleveland Cafés.' The political prospects of the Democrats depended on how the administration responded to this crisis, but, in fact, both the economic and political situations quickly went from bad to worse. In the face of Republican opposition, and Democratic defections by those who believed the circumstances had changed or had special interests to protect, Cleveland was unable to persuade Congress to agree [on] a significantly lower tariff. The resultant act of August 1894 was referred to by the President as falling 'far short of the consummation for which we have long labored', and as the result of 'party perfidy and party dishonor'. The new tariff became law without his signature, an action which amounted to a public acknowledgement of the deep rifts apparent in Democratic ranks.

Other problems also had to be faced in 1893–94. Several 'armies' of unemployed men marched on Washington, including the group led by 'General' Jacob S. Coxey, an Ohio businessman, who sympathised with the victims of the depression. The march, which began on March 25th, 1894, never exceeded a few hundred men, but attracted considerable publicity. Although the episode ended in farce on May 1st, when Coxey and other leaders were arrested for trespassing on the grass outside the Capitol Building, it was a graphic illustration of the plight and desperation of many.

Labour-capital relations were also at a low ebb, sometimes approaching a state of industrial warfare. The best known confrontations of the period included the Homestead strike of 1892, which took place before the panic and Depression of 1893 began. The refusal of the management at the Homestead, Pennsylvania, iron and steel works to negotiate conditions or to grant full union recognition led to a strike in July 1892. Violence flared with a pitched battle between the strikers and Pinkerton agents, but the end result was a victory for the management which left bad feelings on both sides.

Hard times served only to intensify labour problems as shown by the Pullman strike of 1894. George M. Pullman, head of the Pullman Palace Car Company which built and operated railroad diner, parlor and sleeping cars, saw himself as a philanthropist, but his employees resented high rents and service charges for company housing and the stifling paternalism. Despite the Depression Pullman maintained profits and dividends, but he repeatedly cut wages and his workers turned to the new American Railway Union headed by Eugene V. Debs. When his workers went on strike in May 1894, Pullman assumed an intransigent position, and the dispute escalated into a national railroad strike.

The workers were eventually defeated when the conservative Railroad Brotherhoods and the American Federation of Labor declined to help, when the General Managers Association co-ordinated the activities of the railroads and when the Federal Government, on the excuse that the mails were being interfered with, employed court injunctions and deployed troops. Just as the battle over the tariff had opened up divisions in the Democratic Party so too did the administration's actions during the Pullman strike. Conservatives supported the President, while radicals sympathised with the strikers.

The Depression, the tariff fiasco, Coxey's army, the Pullman strike, all undermined the unity of the Democrats and their chances in the 1894 mid-term elections. To compound their troubles the Democrats also divided bitterly over whether to repeal the 1890 Sherman Silver Purchase Act. Under its provisions the Secretary of the Treasury was required to purchase 4.5 million ounces of silver every month—the estimated American production—and to issue in payment treasury notes of full legal-tender value redeemable in gold or silver at the discretion of the government. The act also proclaimed it to be 'the established policy of the United States to maintain the two metals on a parity with each other upon the present legal ratio or such ratio as may be provided by law'.

To understand the importance of the money question during this period one must remember that gold had become a symbol of conservative eastern and northern financial and business corporations. These institutions were perceived to be ruthlessly exploiting western and southern debtors, mainly farmers, who favoured inflationist policies, including the monetarisation of silver, as a means of raising prices, restoring prosperity and escape from their burdens of debts. While the debate was sometimes conducted with the intellectual dexterity and complexity of a medieval theological dispute, there was often a tendency on both sides to simplify the arguments, to take extreme positions, and to appeal to emotions and morality as much as to economic theory.

In the straightened financial circumstances of 1893 the obligations to purchase large quantities of silver and to redeem treasury notes were considered by the administration to be too onerous, and Cleveland called for the repeal of the Silver Purchase Act. The ensuing debate in Congress divided both parties on sectional lines, with members from the north and east favouring repeal and those from the south and west making impassioned appeals to retain the legislation. Young William Jennings Bryan, a Democratic representative from Nebraska, made a brilliant three-hour speech that presaged the 1896 campaign, claiming the debate was between over-privileged corporate interests and the frequently ignored down-trodden masses. The repeal of the Act in October 1893 was achieved by a ruthless use of patronage, but it led to a further serious breach in the ranks of the Democrats.

The Republicans skillfully placed the blame for the Depression, unemployment and the farmers' woes on the shoulders of the Democrats, but they said nothing as severe as the Democrats were saying about each other. Republican representative Thomas Reed predicted, 'The Democratic mortality will be so great next fall that their dead will be buried in trenches and marked "Unknown",' and events bore him out. The great Democratic majorities of 1892 were overturned and one Democrat, Champ Clark of Missouri, referred to 1894 as the greatest 'slaughter of the innocents' since the days of Herod.

Rising partisan, sectional and class antagonisms were soon exacerbated by three ultra-conservative Supreme Court decisions in 1895. In January the Court held in the E. C. Knight case that the American Sugar Refining Company, which processed 94 percent of the nation's sugar, had not violated the Sherman Anti-trust Act. In May, in Pollock v. Farmers' Loan and Trust Company, the Court outlawed the income tax provisions of the 1894 Tariff Act, provisions that men of poverty had seen as a dangerous assault on wealth. The same month the Court upheld the use of an injunction issued in 1894 against Eugene V. Debs during the Pullman strike.

By 1895 the money question, and the belief in the merits of deliberately inflating the currency, so-called 'free silver', had become the dominant political and economic issue. President Cleveland, whose belief in conservative fiscal policies and 'sound' money was unshakeable, tried in vain to prevent the spread of the silver infection through his party. His efforts only intensified the strong, indeed bitter, feelings against him, without preventing the silverites gaining additional converts in both country and party.

The growth of pro-silver sentiment among the Democrats posed a dilemma for the Populist or People's Party which had supported free silver since 1892. Their candidate for President in 1892, General James B. Weaver of Iowa, had polled over one million votes and won 22 electoral votes, a good result for a third party. The Populist problem was whether to continue to fight for a broad spectrum of political and economic reforms or to concentrate on silver. They had also to decide whether to co-operate with their political rivals, the Democrats, or to remain independent.

Even the Republicans were not immune from the growing silver sentiment. Republicans from the western farming states had at least to express sympathy with free silver ideas in order to win re-election. For Senator Henry Moore Teller of Colorado, a silver mining state, free silver was not just a tactical necessity, but a matter of conscience, and he threatened to leave the Republican Party in 1896. However, the disaffection in Republican ranks was limited, and in any case they hoped to fight the election on the issue of the protective tariff which had added electoral attractions in a depression.

Democratic disarray foretold Republican success in 1896, and there was no shortage of aspirants for the Grand Old Party's nomination. The anticipated prominence of the tariff issue gave the advantage to fifty-three year-old William McKinley from the key state of Ohio. 'Major' McKinley had a respectable Civil War record, and had served in Congress between 1877–91 followed by two successive terms as Governor of Ohio. He was best-known as an expert on the tariff, was sometimes called the High Priest of Protection—the 1890 Tariff Act carried his name. In the 1894 elections, though not a candidate himself, he was much in demand as a speaker and he enhanced his personal reputation by making 371 appearances in sixteen states, including twenty-three speeches in a single day.

The genial McKinley was a moderate in politics, had led a blameless personal life, and inspired trust and loyalty. Even those who disagreed with him found it difficult to dislike him. McKinley also had the advantage of a talented political manager and personal friend in the energetic Cleveland industrialist, Marcus Monzo Hanna. By the time the Republican national convention opened in St Louis in June 1896 Hanna had corralled enough delegates virtually to ensure McKinley's nomination.

The Republican platform damned the Democrats and all their works, blaming them for the Depression and all its consequences. The Republicans declared 'unreservedly for sound money', but devoted their greatest attention to the tariff issue. Unable to support the platform Senator Teller and twenty-one other delegates walked out to cries of 'Go to Chicago', where the Democrats were due to meet. Thereafter McKinley was easily nominated on the first ballot.

Whereas the silver rebellion in the Republican ranks was minor, the advocates of free silver in the Democratic Party experienced sweeping successes in 1895 and 1896, winning control over one state delegation to Chicago after another. When the Democratic national convention opened on July 8th it was soon clear that silver men were in the saddle and they wrote into the platform the statement: 'We demand the free and unlimited coinage of both silver and gold at the present legal ratio of 16 to 1'. The platform also preferred a lowering of the tariff, but not 'until the money question is settled.'

While the silver forces had indeed captured the Democratic Party, repudiated President Cleveland and written the platform, no outstanding spokesman and potential presidential nominee had emerged. To some extent this was deliberate as silver supporters believed the cause was greater than the ambitions of any individual. Leading possibilities included former congressman Richard Parks 'Silver Dick' Bland of Missouri who had a long and distinguished history of supporting free silver. 'Bland's major political liabilities were the facts that he came from a relatively unimportant state and was *persona non grata* with the Populists whose support was necessary for any silver Democrat to avoid splitting the anti-gold vote. Former governor Horace Boies of Iowa was another hopeful, and there was even a suggestion that Senator Teller, the silver Republican, might be selected to unite the silver vote.

One of the myths of the 1896 campaign is that William Jennings Bryan, the eventual Democratic nominee, was virtually unknown before the Chicago convention. Bryan, who was born in Illinois in 1860, had moved to Lincoln, Nebraska, in 1887 and made a name for himself as a politician, a supporter of free silver and a noted public speaker. Known as 'the boy orator from the Platte', or as 'the silver tongued orator', he had served four years in Congress, but failed to get elected to the Senate in 1894. Only thirty-six in 1896 Bryan was a man with a deep religious commitment, impeccable moral standards, a social conscience and a magnetic personality. He inspired supporters with his sincerity and could captivate audiences with his wonderful voice and dramatic abilities. Bryan's weaknesses were his inexperience and his tendency to suggest simple answers to complicated problems. He conducted a skillful campaign for two years before the Chicago convention to advance the cause of free silver and to win personal recognition within the ranks of the silverites.

At Chicago good fortune and deft manipulation gave Bryan the opportunity to speak last in the debate on the party platform. He delivered a carefully rehearsed address that came to be known as 'The Cross of Gold speech', but made it appear to be spontaneous. He began by telling his listeners that he came to speak to them in defence of a cause as holy as that of liberty, namely the cause of humanity. He reviewed the history of the struggle over money, paraded the arguments in favour of free silver, then reached a thrilling climax with the words:

> . . . Having behind us the producing masses of this nation and the world, supported by the commercial interests, the laboring interests, and the toilers everywhere, we will answer their demand for a gold standard by saying to them: You shall not press down upon the brow of labor this crown of thorns, you shall not crucify mankind upon a cross of gold.

Bryan was nominated the next day with Arthur Sewall of Maine as his running mate. Subsequently the silver Republicans and the small National Silver Party endorsed these selections.

The Populist Party problems now came to a head. Should they accept Bryan and Sewall and the Chicago platform, and effectively fuse with the Democrats, thus sacrificing their independence and broad programme of reforms? If they stubbornly maintained their independence they would probably suffer major desertions to the stronger Democrats and bear the responsibility of handing the election to McKinley and the Republicans. With much heart-searching and many cries of betrayal the Populists, in a turbulent convention, solved their dilemma by adopting their own platform while nominating Bryan, but rejecting Sewall in favour of their own candidate for Vice-President, Tom Watson of Georgia. Thus Bryan actually had the nomination of four political groups, while McKinley was the standard bearer only for the Republican. The gold Democrats, who did not walk out at Chicago, could not bring themselves to vote for either of the major candidates and later made the gesture of selecting Senator John M. Palmer of Illinois for President and former Confederate General Simon Bolivar Buckner of Kentucky for Vice-President.

The two major candidates conducted quite different campaigns. The Democrats had a cause and a leader, but they lacked organisation, money and press support—in the past these had been supplied by the conservatives in the party who now stood aside. Bryan compensated in part by undertaking strenuous speaking tours. He travelled 18,000 miles in twenty-seven states making hundreds of appearances, often before very large crowds, including twenty-seven speeches on the final day. For Bryan silver became the symbol of the aspirations of the exploited masses, but his speeches were stronger on rhetoric than in dealing with economic realities; the beneficial effects of free silver were taken as articles of faith.

Bryan's effort was heroic, especially as he was often left to arrange details of his tours that should have been handled by others. Yet, despite the Democrats' promises of social and economic reform, Bryan converted few eastern working men to his cause. His platform rhetoric appealed to southern and western farmers.

Meanwhile McKinley, billed as the advance agent of prosperity, conducted a front porch campaign. He knew he could not compete with Bryan as an orator, and moreover, believed that to tour the country in pursuit of the presidency demeaned the office. Instead hundreds of delegations of faithful Republicans made a pilgrimage to McKinley's home in Canton, Ohio. Perhaps 750,000 people came to listen to his well-rehearsed responses to their prearranged addresses and questions. Thus it was said that while Bryan went to the people, the people came to McKinley.

The Republicans enjoyed many advantages thanks to Mark Hanna who ran the election campaign as Chairman of the National Republican Committee. He created the finest political organisation yet seen, with headquarters in New York and Chicago, and raised a campaign chest of between $3\frac{1}{2}$ and 4 million dollars via contributions from businesses with an interest in a Republican victory. The electorate was educated as to the advantages of the gold standard and to the threat of free silver through millions of pamphlets published in several languages relating to the currency and tariff issues. Appeals were often aimed at particular economic, ethnic or special interests groups, even to cyclists! Newspapers and magazines were supplied with articles, posters, cartoons and campaign badges. Hundreds of speakers were employed and the party strategists even appropriated the national flag as a partisan symbol. It was also to their advantage that the Republican message— that a high tariff protected American living standards against cheap foreign competition and that free silver would unsettle business conditions—was far easier to understand than the Democratic theories which sometimes approached the metaphysical. As Hanna said of Bryan 'He's talking silver all the time, and that's where we've got him.' Republicans portrayed Bryan as a wild-eyed radical, even a revolutionary and as a dangerous free trader.

Businessmen indoctrinated their employees with placards in the work place, pamphlets and lunchtime speeches. Printed slips in pay packets warned that the election of Bryan and the adoption of radical financial policies might mean job losses and a fall in the purchasing power of wages. Some business contracts were signed with let-out clauses in case of a Democratic victory, insurance companies put pressure on their policy holders, and mortgage companies threatened to curtail credit, though it is difficult to know how effective this was. Some clergymen, both Protestant and Catholic, broke with the practice of political neutrality by endorsing McKinley, as they saw Bryan as a dangerous socialist, and because they objected to his use of phrases like 'crown of thorns' and 'cross of gold' as blasphemous.

Unable to find a chink in McKinley's political or personal armour the Democrats concentrated much of their fire upon Hanna, an acknowledgement of his importance in the campaign and the later source of the popular, though erroneous, belief that he possessed a dominating influence over McKinley.

The election had its lighter side, of course. The Democrats sang to the tune 'Marching Through Georgia':

> Sound the good old bugle with a bi-metallic ring,
> Silver free from sea to sea with lusty voice-sing,
> Our banner with its silver stars to waiting breezes fling,
> While we go marching to victory.

Republicans replied to the tune 'Battle Cry of Freedom' with:

> We will welcome to our numbers all honest men and true,
> Shouting sound money and protection,
> And the rich and poor shall share in the wages when they're due,
> Shouting sound money and protection.
> Protection forever, hurrah! boys, hurrah!
> Down with 'free silver,' and stop Bryan's 'jaw,'
> Then we'll rally 'round McKinley, we'll rally once again,
> Shouting sound money and protection.

The 1896 election allowed the demands for reform to be channelled via the established political processes rather than be disputed on the streets. Both the Republican and Democratic parties were affected by the campaign as they had to face up to new policies, new methods and a changing electorate. The presentation of candidates and issues, the refinement of campaign techniques, the use of slogans and images were all advanced at this time.

In reality both sides were offering the electorate panaceas, the Democrats free silver and the Republicans protection. The Democrats lost because of inferior organisation, pitifully inadequate funds, and because their remedy for the nation's ills was both too radical and untried compared to the Republican programme. Not that the election was a simple fight between the two major parties. The presence of the Populists helped to bring the silver question into the limelight, though Bryan found their endorsement a mixed blessing. Both the Populists and the Democrats concentrated in 1896 on the currency issue at the expense of the rest of their programme and there is some truth, at least, in the comment of the noted reformer Henry Demarest Lloyd that free silver 'was the cowbird of the Reform movement', which 'waited until the nest had been built by the sacrifices and labour of others, and then laid its egg in it, pushing out the others which lie smashed on the ground'.

While the Democrats did eventually win the White House in 1912, the Populists would never recover from their defeat in 1896. Yet many of the reforms they advocated in the 1890s, like the direct election of United States senators, a federal income tax, and stricter regulation of banks and corporations, measures considered dangerous innovations at the time, were actually achieved in the early twentieth century during the calmer Progressive Era.

Bryan fought a courageous campaign in 1896, which he referred to as 'The First Battle', intending to continue the fight. Indeed, 1900 was a rematch between McKinley and Bryan, but by then prosperity had returned and the emergence of imperialism as an issue after the 1898 Spanish-American War made free silver redundant. Bryan and the Democrats, the intellectual heirs of Thomas Jefferson and his belief in the virtues of rural life and the vices of urban living, were unable to adapt to the fact that political power had shifted to the burgeoning industrial towns. Whether he realised it or not Bryan was the champion of old America in a vain struggle against an emerging twentieth-century new America.

FOR FURTHER READING:

William M. Bryan, *The First Battle, A Story of the Campaign of 1896* (Chicago, 1896); Robert F. Durden, *The Climax of Populism: The Election of 1896* (University of Kentucky Press, 1965); Paul W. Glad, *McKinley, Bryan and the People* (Philadelphia, Lippincott, 1964); Stanley L. Jones, *The Presidential Election of 1896* (University of Wisconsin Press, 1964); Lewis L. Gould, *The Presidency of William McKinley* (University of Kansas Press, 1980); H. Wayne Morgan, *From Hayes to McKinley, National Party Politics, 1877–1896* (Syracuse University Press, 1969); Arthur M. Schlesinger, Jr., (ed), *History of American Presidential Elections 1789–1968, Vol II* (Chelsea, New York, 1971).

Edward Ranson is Lecturer in American History at the University of Aberdeen and author of British Defence Policy and Appeasement Between the Wars 1919–1939 *(The Historical Association, 1993)*

The Meaning of '98

Our War with Spain Marked the First Year of the American Century

By John Lukacs

One hundred years ago, in April 1898, the American Century suddenly began. "Suddenly" because what happened then—the declaration of war against Spain—led to a rapid crystallization of a passionate nationalism. The American longing for national aggrandizement existed before 1898—indeed it was gathering momentum—but as the great French writer Stendhal wrote in his essay "On Love," passion has a way of "crystallizing" suddenly, as a reaction to external stimuli. Such a stimulus, in the history of the United States, was the Spanish-American War in 1898. When it was over, in a famous (or infamous) phrase John Hay would call it "a splendid little war." Well, as far as wars go (and many of them tend to go unexpectedly far), it *was* "a splendid little war." But its consequences were not little at all. They were enormous, and one hundred years later we live with them still. So allow me to begin this essay with a brief summary of the Spanish-American War.

The island of Cuba was one of the last (and the largest remaining) Spanish colonies in the Western Hemisphere. Its political class wanted independence from Spain. It could not achieve this by itself. There was nothing very new about that. Trouble in Cuba had flared up often during the nineteenth century. But in 1895 there arose conditions resembling a civil war (or, more precisely, a guerrilla war). At first the Spanish military reacted energetically. Soon it became evident that the problem was triangular, involving not only Spain and the Cuban rebels but also the United States. For one thing, the rebels depended more and more on American

support, and particularly on their abettors in Florida. (What else is new?) Perhaps more important was a surge of American public and popular opinion, which was dishonestly inflated by the novel element of the "yellow press," the national chains of Hearst and Pultizer newspapers, proclaiming the Cuban situation to be intolerable. "Intolerable" is, of course, what people think must not be tolerated, and that was the continued presence of Spain in Cuba. In the late 1897 the Spanish government showed a very considerable willingness to compromise, whereby all sensible reasons for an American intervention in Cuba could be eliminated. But passion is not governed by reason, and there were many groups of people with reasons of their own. On February 15, 1898, the U.S. battleship *Maine* blew up in Havana Harbor. There was a large loss of American lives and an immediate clamor for war. "Remember the *Maine*!" One hundred years later we do not know what caused the explosion. Possibly it was the work of Cubans, hoping to incite Americans thereby for the sake of their "liberation" from Spain. (Sixty years later a Cuban leader arose whose main purpose was to declare Cuba's "liberation" not from Spain but from the United States. Fidel Castro was not anti-Spanish but anti-American. His ancestors were Spanish-Cubans in 1898; he maintained cordial relations with Generalissimo Franco, the anti-Communist dictator of Spain, upon whose death Castro declared three days of national mourning in Cuba. Such is the irony of history—or, rather, of human nature.)

After the catastrophe, the Spanish government was willing to settle almost

everything to the satisfaction of the United States, but it was too late—too late because of the inflamed state of American public opinion. President McKinley did not have the will to oppose anything like that. On April 11, 1898, he sent a message to Congress; the formal declaration of war came two weeks afterward.

One week later Commodore (soon to become Admiral) George Dewey destroyed a Spanish squadron on the other side of the world, in Manila Bay. Some of his warships now raced across the southern Pacific and around the Horn to help blast another Spanish squadron out of the warm waters of Santiago Bay. Meanwhile, American troops had landed, unopposed, in Cuba and then won battles (in reality, successful skirmishes) at El Caney and San Juan Hill. Later in July Americans, again unopposed, invaded Puerto Rico. The war was over. Spain asked for peace. An armistice was signed on August 12, and the final terms were nailed down in Paris in December. American losses were minimal: a few hundred men. The United States insisted on, and got, Cuba, Puerto Rico, the Philippines, and Guam.

And also Hawaii, whose annexation had been—unsuccessfully—urged on two Presidents by American intriguers and filibusters. President Cleveland, and for a while McKinley, refused the annexation. But by July 1898 the nationalist tide was too much for this President and for much of the Congress: The United States annexed Hawaii.

It was thus that one hundred years ago the United States—which, during the first century of its existence, thought of itself as the prime power in the

From *American Heritage*, May/June 1998, pp. 72-80. © 1998 by Forbes, Inc. Reprinted by permission of *American Heritage* magazine, a division of Forbes, Inc.

Americas, a hemispheric power—became a world power imperiously, geographically, a world power of the first rank, with incalculable consequences.

In 1898 there were no Gallup Polls; there was no such thing as public-opinion research. Still, it is possible to reconstruct the main elements of what the people of the United States thought (and perhaps felt) about these events.

That tremendous surge of national self-confidence, debouching into super-nationalism (in reality, imperialism, though most Americans would shy away from such a word), must not obscure the fact that as in every war in the history of this country, Americans were divided. On one side, which turned out to be the dominant one, were the expansionists of 1898. Of their many and increasingly vocal declarations let me cite but one or two. There was Sen. H. M. Teller of Colorado, who as early as 1893 proclaimed: "I am in favor of the annexation of Hawaii. I am in favor of the annexation of Cuba. I am in favor of the annexation of the great country lying north of us." (He meant Canada.) The language of Sen. E. O. Wolcott of Colorado was more florid: "Who is to say that in the evolution of such a Republic as this the time has not come when the immense development of our internal resources and the marvelous growth of our domestic and foreign commerce and a realization of our virile strength have not stimulated that Anglo-Saxon restlessness which beats with the blood of the race into an activity which will not be quenched until we have finally planted our standard in that far-off archipelago which inevitable destiny has intrusted to our hands?" (He meant the Philippines.) And when the war was over, Sen. Orville H. Platt of Connecticut said: "The same force that had once guided Pilgrim sails to Plymouth Rock had impressed our ships at Manila and our army at Santiago. Upon us rested the duty of extending Christian civilization, of crushing despotism, of uplifting humanity and making the rights of man prevail. Providence has put it upon us." On the other side of Congress were the opponents of the expansionists. There was Sen. George F. Hoar: "The Monroe

Doctrine is gone." Or Sen. Donelson Caffery: "Sir, Christianity can not be advanced by force." What drove the expansionists was "lust of power and greed for land, veneered with the tawdriness of false humanity."

It is at this point instructive to look at the character and the development of these divisions of American opinion. The twentieth-century terminology of "internationalists versus isolationists" does not apply. Besides the fact that "isolationism" as a category came into usage only after World War I, the expansionists of 1898 were American unilateralists, not internationalists, while their opponents were not isolationists either. What clashed were two different visions of American destiny. These were already visible well before 1898, to which I shall soon turn. More germane to the national debate of 1898 were the differing tendencies of political parties, national regions, and portions of society. With few exceptions Republicans were expansionists; Democrats were not. That was already evident earlier in the 1890s, when the Republican President Benjamin Harrison and his Secretary of State, John W. Foster (grandfather of John Foster Dulles), were in favor of the forced annexation of Hawaii, whereas the Democratic President Grover Cleveland and his Secretary of State, Walter Q. Gresham, were not. These divisions were not absolute; there were a few anti-imperialist Republicans. Yet it ought to be observed that the Republicans were the more *nationalist* party of the two, something that, by and large, remained true for most of the following century and is discernible even now. (In 1892 the Republican party platform called for "the achievement of the manifest destiny of the Republic in the broadest sense." In 1956 the Republican party platform called for "the establishment of American air and naval bases all around the world." The man who coined the term manifest destiny in the 1840s, John L. O'Sullivan, was a Democrat, who later condemned "wicked and crazy Republicanism." He died in 1895.) It is significant to note that many of the opponents of the expansionists were Southern Democrats, including such unreconstructed populists as "Pitchfork Ben" Tillman—which is interesting, since forty

years earlier it was the South that had proposed the acquisition of Cuba. Many, certainly the most vocal, expansionists were Protestant churchmen; the hierarchy of American Catholics was, for the most part, not. The leaders of American finance and business (Andrew Carnegie, James J. Hill, J. P. Morgan, and most of Wall Street) opposed the war—at least for some time.

But much of this was soon swept away. Immediately after the declaration of war the businessmen's and financiers' opposition crumbled (another instance of the limitations of the economic interpretation of history, or of the flag following trade; the reverse is rather true). In the hot skillet of nationalist emotions, the opposition of most Catholics melted away fast. Two former Confederate generals, Joe Wheeler and Fitzhugh Lee, were now major-generals of the United States Army. Fifteen Democrats and Populists voted for the ratification of the peace treaty with Spain; only two Republicans voted against it. The vote was 57 to 27 in the Senate, one above the needed two-thirds majority. William Jennings Bryan, once an anti-expansionist, urged a speedy ratification. It did not do much for him; in 1900 McKinley beat him by a landslide. Less than a year later McKinley was dead, the President was now Theodore Roosevelt, and the American Century was on.

In 1898 the Spanish-American War was the culmination of a great wave of national sentiment that had begun to rise many years before. There was a change, less in the temperature of patriotism than in the national vision of the destiny of the United States, after the end of the first century of its existence. In sum, the time had come for the United States to expand not only its light and its example but its power and its institutions all around the globe. When the Chicago world's fair opened in 1893, Chauncey M. Depew gave the speech of dedication. "This day," he said, "belongs not to America but the world. . . . We celebrate the emancipation of man." No one had spoken in such tones at the Centennial in 1876 in Philadelphia. But now in March 1893 the Philadelphia *Press* proclaimed, "Our nation stands on the threshold of a new policy as surely as it did in 1803, when Jefferson annexed Louisiana and the United States realized it must govern it."

It is wrong to think that this rise of a national sentiment was nothing but emotional, fueled by war fever and declamatory rhetoric. What had begun to change the course of the mighty American ship of state was a change of mentality, including a powerful intellectual impulse. Its proponents included some of the most intelligent, and learned, Americans of a generation. The usage of the noun *intellectual* (adopted from the Russian, designating a certain kind of person) had hardly begun to appear in the American language in the 1890s, but the adjective was properly applicable to the capacities of such men as Theodore Roosevelt, Henry Cabot Lodge, Alfred Thayer Mahan, John Hay, Whitelaw Reid, and Albert J. Beveridge. Far from being provincial, they looked around the world and saw how the European powers had embarked on their imperialist expansion. For the United States to opt out from a course of spreading its influence beyond its continental boundaries would be a sickening symptom of a materialist small-mindedness.

And what were the ingredients of this philosophy—for a kind of philosophy it was. It amounted to more than a mere emulation of the other Great Powers of the present. One principal ingredient was the belief in sea power. That was the key to modern history, as Alfred Mahan wrote in his famous book *The Influence of Sea Power Upon History* in 1890, and it was more than coincidental that a Republican President and Congress embarked on a Big Navy program in the same year, the first substantial American military expenditure since the Civil War. There was a racial ingredient: the belief that the most advanced, indeed the ruling, people of the globe were of Anglo-Saxon and Teutonic stock. Besides the Roosevelt-Lodge-Mahan-Hay-Reid coterie of progressive imperialists, there were prestigious professors in the leading American universities whose eulogies of the Teutonic-Germanic races were influential as well as popular: John W. Burgess, for example, whose *Political Science* later acquired a foreword by Nicholas Murray Butler, the much-respected president of Columbia University. Very similar were the advocacies of John Fiske of Harvard. The Congregationalist minister Josiah Strong wrote as early as 1885 about the American Anglo-Saxon destined to be his brother's keeper: "If I read not amiss, this powerful race will move . . . down upon Central and South America, or upon the islands of the sea . . . and beyond. And can any one doubt that the result of this competition of races will be 'the survival of the fittest'?" Not many people know that Rudyard Kipling's "Take Up the White Man's Burden" was written for Americans; even fewer are aware that in *The Descent of Man* Charles Darwin wrote about America: "the heir of all ages, in the foremost files of time." Such a concordance of Darwinism and of racism and of Protestant Christianity sounds strange now. In the 1890s it was not. In 1894 Mahan wrote: "Comparative religion teaches that creeds which reject missionary enterprise are foredoomed to decay. May it not be so with nations?" Many of the shrill proposals for American imperialism in the name of Protestant Christianity were reconstructed later by historians, foremost among them Julius W. Pratt. Thus the editorial of the *Christian and Missionary Alliance* in April 1898: "God is stronger than either the Romish Church or the Catholic powers of Europe. We should pray not only that Cuba be free, but that these fair Eastern isles shall become scenes of gospel triumphs and the salvation of countless souls. . . ." And *The Christian Standard:* The time has arrived "to crack the Monroe Doctrine like a shell, and to introduce the nation to an enlarged mission. . . . The Lord has not raised up this mighty people to dwell in selfish contentment, indifferent to the wrongs and oppressions of other lands. . . . The magnificent fleets of Spain have gone down as marvellously, as miraculously, as the walls of Jericho went down."

Such were many of the voices current in 1898. They were not necessarily what the majority of Americans thought. But such influences cannot be precisely defined. Hard and determined minorities may acquire an impact on a majority beyond numerical calculations. Still, in any event, they cannot be very influential when they represent something quite different from broader popular inclinations. The politicians knew that. So did the progressive intellects. When Captain (later Admiral) Mahan wrote that the Navy must have bases abroad, he added: "At present the positions of the Caribbean are occupied by foreign powers, nor may we, however disposed to acquisition, obtain them by means other than righteous; *but a distinct advance will have been made when public opinion is convinced."* (The italics are mine.) In 1890 a Republican Congress voted on seven battleships and eventually authorized the building of three first-class battleships, even though the Secretary of the Navy had asked only for two. The former Republican presidential candidate James G. Blaine wrote to President Harrison in 1891 that the United States should annex Cuba and Puerto Rico and perhaps all of the West Indian islands. In June 1896 the *Washington Post* editorialized: "A new consciousness seems to have come upon us—the consciousness of strength—and with it a new appetite, the yearning to show our strength. . . . Ambition, interest, land hunger, pride, the mere joy of fighting, whatever it may be, we are animated by a new sensation. We are face to face with a strange destiny. The taste of Empire is in the mouth of the people even as the taste of blood in the jungle. It means an Imperial policy, the Republic, renascent, taking her place with the armed nations."

It was thus that in 1898 the majority of the American people took satisfaction from the pictures of the Stars and Stripes solidly planted on faraway islands and floating over the oceans, just as their ears took satisfaction from the originally somewhat odd, but soon intensely familiar, martial band music of John Philip Sousa, music with a Central European flavor, but no matter, for it was at that time that American popular music—indeed, the tuning of American ears—was changing too, from the simpler Anglo-Celtic strains to newer rhythms and melodies. It was thus that the American Dominion Over Palm and Pine came into being at the very time when Kipling in his *Recessional* warned

Save the Olympia!

The flagship Dewey took into Manila Bay still survives, but it needs help

By John Steele Gordon

As April 30, 1898, turned into May 1, the USS *Olympia* steamed down the west coast of Luzon Island in the Philippines and entered Manila Bay through the Boca Grande, the wider of the two channels created by the island of Corregidor. The cruiser, flagship of the United States Asiatic Squadron, was blacked out except for a single stern light to guide the three other cruisers, two gunboats, two colliers, and cutter that steamed in two lines behind her.

The squadron's commander, Commodore George Dewey, could see the pearly glow of Manila, far across the wide bay, lighting the sky to the northeast. Just south lay the Spanish naval station of Cavite, where he knew the Spanish fleet awaited his arrival. He approached Manila to within a mile, and then, at dawn, he steamed toward his objective. At 5:15 A.M. the Spanish opened fire, but Dewey, nervous about his supply of ammunition, held off until he thought his ships were at optimum range. Finally, at 5:40, standing on the starboard side of the flying bridge of the *Olympia*, he gave the now-famous order to his flag captain: "You may fire when you are ready, Gridley."

The American fleet, modern, mobile, well maintained, and massively gunned, far outclassed the ancient, decrepit, and an-

INDEPENDENCE SEAPORT MUSEUM, PHILADELPHIA

The *Olympia* spends her days alongside a World War II submarine.

chored Spanish ships. In a few hours the latter were little more than twisted heaps at the bottom of the anchorage, 381 of their sailors dead or wounded. The American fleet, virtually unscarred, had suffered only 7 casualties and no combat deaths.

In future years historians would note that this was a moment of profound transition for the world. The country that had built and dispatched Dewey's fleet had spent the previous century growing, in splendid isolation, from a fledgling republic into a colossus. Now for the first time it was projecting its immense power far abroad, and it would spend the next century, ever increasingly, as the world's dominant military, economic, technological, political, and cultural power. For Spain, on the other hand, the Battle of Manila Bay was a pathetic end of nearly four hundred years of empire.

Today the *Olympia,* moored on the Philadelphia waterfront, is the very embodiment of the era of technological and geopolitical transition in which she lived. The full-rigged sailing ship had dominated sea warfare for three centuries after its development in the late 1400s, and the last battle fought entirely under sail, Navarino, had taken place as recently as 1827, during the Greek War for Independence. But the Industrial Revolution affected na-

America's British cousins that *their* dominion over palm and pine might be short-lived: "Lest we forget!"

In an article entitled "Our Blundering Foreign Policy," Henry Cabot Lodge wrote in March 1895: "Small states are of the past and have no future. . . . The great nations are rapidly absorbing for their future expansion and their present defense all the waste places of the earth. It is a movement which makes for civilization and the advancement of the race. As one of the great nations of the world, the United States must not fall out of the line of march." During the war Theodore Roosevelt wrote him: "You must get Manila and Hawaii; you must prevent any talk of peace until we get Porto Rico and the Philippines as well as secure the independence of Cuba."

Would the United States have become a world power in the early twentieth century even without the Spanish-American War and the events of 1898? Probably. But the consequences of 1898 are still with us.

Was it worth it? That was the question that American opponents of the War of 1898 were asking, among them Mark Twain. Their vision of American destiny was different, but then they were overwhelmed by the great national success of the war. However—sooner rather than later—events themselves accumulated to reveal that all was not well with this acquisition of peoples in distant parts of the world. Only a few months after the "liberation" of Manila, a rebellion in the

Philpines broke out against the American occupiers. Its suppression took two years and hundreds of lives. The "liberation" of Cuba from the "tyranny" of Spain led to the rule of that island by a series of native tyrants of whom the last (and still present) one has been obsessively anti-American, in one instance not unwilling to inveigle the United States into a potential nuclear war with the distant Soviet Union. Whether the acquisition of Puerto Rico and of its people by the American Republic was a definite gain is still an open question, as is the future status of that island. One may even speculate that had Hawaii remained a Pacific kingdom the tragedy at Pearl Harbor or perhaps even a Japanese-American war might not have occurred—but that carries speculation too far.

val warfare no less profoundly than it affected everything else. At first, steam merely supplemented sails for power, and wood remained the primary construction material. Then, in 1860, the Royal Navy built its first iron-hulled and armored ship, HMS *Warrior*. But the *Warrior* remained, essentially, an updated version of the old ships of the line, with a full suit of sails and many relatively small guns arrayed along her sides.

The USS *Monitor*, built two years later, was the first truly modern warship, for her two massive guns were mounted in a turret that could turn to fire in any direction. The *Iowa*-class battleships of World War II were really nothing more than vastly enlarged and elaborated *Monitors*.

The *Olympia* is roughly halfway between the *Monitor* and the *Iowa* in terms of development. She carries four 8-inch guns in two turrets along with ten 5-inch guns and numerous smaller ones. But the "officers' country" is still located over the stern, where it was in sailing days, rather than forward, as in twentieth-century warships. And the officers' quarters more closely resemble those on a yacht than on a modern warship. The admiral's cabin even has a fireplace. Meanwhile, the enlisted men still slept in hammocks, slung wherever there was room, just as Nelson's sailors had a hundred years earlier. The *Olympia*'s engines, powered by coal that was shoveled by hand, could drive her at twenty-two knots, but they were of a piston-driven, reciprocating design that, basically, dated back to Robert Fulton. The stokers and others who labored in the engine space had to endure nearly inhuman conditions.

In 1906, fourteen years after the *Olympia*'s launch, HMS *Dreadnought* introduced the all-big-gun design and turbine engines that quickly rendered ships like the *Olympia* obsolete. Still, the *Olympia* had a long career after her day of glory in Manila Bay. For more than a decade she served as the flagship of the North Atlantic Squadron, and she remained in commission until 1922. The year before, she was chosen to convey the body

LIBRARY OF CONGRESS

A chromolithograph shows the *Olympia* firing in Manila Bay.

of America's unknown soldier back from France to rest in honor at Arlington National Cemetery.

She was laid up at the Philadelphia Naval Yard and was very nearly broken up at the outbreak of World War II, when the Navy was desperate for scrap steel. Only President Franklin Roosevelt's deep interest in naval history saved her. But the Navy was uninterested in its own history, and the *Olympia* languished in decay, as did such other historic vessels as Farragut's flagship, the USS *Hartford*. In the 1950s most (including, inexcusably, the *Hartford*) were broken up, and the *Olympia* was systematically vandalized of many bronze fittings, which were illegally sold for scrap. Nevertheless, she survived, and a local group, the Cruiser Olympia Association, opened her as a historical exhibit.

Today she remains a singularly important relic of the past, not only a central player in a very important moment in American History but also one of only half a dozen ships—dispersed all over the globe in Russia, Britain, the United States, Chile, and Japan—that survive from the long period between the end of the age of sail and the beginning of World War II.

The *Olympia* was recently turned over to Philadelphia's Independence Seaport Museum, which has impressive expertise in historic preservation, and she remains open to the public. She was long in shocking disrepair, but today her situation is beginning to change. She was totally repainted in the fall of 1997, at a cost of no less than $250,000, and her decking and electrical wiring was replaced. But another $5 million, at a minimum, must be found to put the *Olympia* in the tiptop shape so important a relic deserves. If you would like to contribute to this worthy project (fully tax-deductible), write to the Independence Seaport Museum at the Olympia Fund, 211 South Columbus Blvd., Philadelphia, PA 19106-3199.

John Steele Gordon writes "The Business of America" in each issue of American Heritage.

There may be another consideration, on a different level. For Spain the loss of its colonies in 1898 marked the lowest point of a decline that may have begun three hundred years earlier, with the defeat of its armada by Drake. Yet that amputation in 1898 proved to be a blessing in disguise for the Spanish spirit. Reacting against antiquated institutions and mental habits of their country, a Generation of '98 arose, an intellectual revival that produced some of the leading minds not only of Spain but of the twentieth century: Miguel de Unamuno y Jugo, José Ortega y Gasset, and other great names in the arts. On the other side of the ocean, the rise of American arts and letters had nothing to do with the Spirit of '98. Years later great American writers such as Henry James and

Thomas Stearns Eliot chose to abandon their American citizenship and live in England. Twenty years had to pass until American arts and letters—and popular music—began to impress the world.

And yet . . . and yet . . . all in all, and for all its strident excrescences, the rising spirit of American imperialism in 1898 was not ungenerous. Not even in the short run; if there was any popular hatred for Spain in 1898, it burned out instantly (as manifest in the words of the captain of the USS *Texas* when his men roared their approval while an ungainly Spanish war vessel sank rapidly at Santiago: "Don't cheer, boys, the poor devils are dying!"). American rule in the Philippines, in Puerto Rico, in Cuba led to a rapid and impressive improvement of living conditions, education, institu-

tions of self-government, sanitation; under the command of the very able Brig. Gen. Leonard Wood, American Army doctors, foremost among them William Gorgas, extinguished yellow fever in Cuba within a year or two. Every foreign government expected the United States to annex Cuba. It did not do so, though an amendment proposed by Senator Platt allowed the United States to intervene there militarily, but then President Franklin D. Roosevelt abolished the Platt Amendment too. In 1946 the Philippines, one year after their American liberation from the Japanese, became fully independent. In 1959 Hawaii became the fiftieth state of the Union. Surely in the long run the record of American imperialism compares favorably with that of many other powers.

History—indeed all human thinking—depends on retrospect. And retrospect too—again, as all human thinking—has its own limitations. We may judge the past according to our standards of the present, but we ought to know that such standards are not perennial and not categorically applicable to people and events of the past. A man such as Theodore Roosevelt had his faults (who hasn't?), but his American imperialism may still have been preferable to that of the small-minded trumpeteers of Manifest Destiny, or to the cloudy evangelical populism of William Jennings Bryan, or to the imperialism of some of Roosevelt's foreign contemporaries-William II, for instance, the German kaiser. In *The Oxford History of the American People,* Samuel Eliot Morison describes William McKinley as "a kindly soul in a spineless body"—and who was our last American President with a "kindly soul"? The origins of the War of 1898—and the intentions of many of its proponents—were not simple.

And now we have to turn to its consequences to the world at large.

In the sixteenth century Spain became the greatest power in the world. In the seventeenth century it was France. In the eighteenth century France and Britain fought a series of world wars—of which the American War of Independence was but one—mainly over the inheritance of the then decaying Spanish Empire. During the nineteenth century the greatest world power was Britain. In 1823 Thomas Jefferson wrote to President James Monroe: "Great Britain is the nation which can do us [the] most harm of any one . . . and, with her on our side, we need not fear the whole world." In 1898, seventy-five years later, this relationship was reversed.

Between 1895 and 1898 there occurred a revolution in the relationship of Great Britain and the United States, a subtle and undramatic adjustment but one that had momentous consequences. In 1895 there arose a controversy between Washington and London over a boundary question in Venezuela. After a few exchanges of notes, both sides climbed down. When, less than three years later, the United States provoked a war with Spain over Cuba, the British government sided with the United States without reservation. And not only the government; in 1898 the vast majority of British public opinion and the press took our side. The global implications of this change were immense. Since 1898 there has not been a single instance when a British government opposed the United States—indeed, when a principal consideration of a British government was not the securing of American goodwill. And there was more to that. Soon after 1898 the British, for the first time in their history, were beginning to be anxious about Germany. In order to be able to respond to a German challenge, they had to secure the friendship of the United States, at almost any price. This American factor was one of the elements behind the British decision to arrive at an entente with France in 1904. Eventually this policy bore fruit: In both world wars of the twentieth century, the United States stood by Britain. This alliance brought them victory—as well as the gradual abdication of the British Empire and the continuing rise of an American one. And this went beyond and beneath governmental calculations. As early as 1898 the young Winston Churchill (he was twenty-three years old then) began to think (and write) about an ever-closer British-American alliance, perhaps even leading to an eventual confederation of the English-speaking peoples of the world. To replace the Pax Britannica with a Pax Anglo-Americana: This was the vision he pursued throughout his long life. It was not to be; but that is another story, though not unrelated to the above.

But the Spanish-American War had an immediate effect on the other European powers too. At first many of them were shocked at the sight of the aggressive newcomer bullying Spain. In December 1897 Count Goluchowski, the foreign minister of the creaking old Austrian Empire, wrote that the United States now represented "a common danger to Europe . . . the European nations must close their ranks in order successfully to defend their existence." They did nothing of the sort. None of them did anything to help Spain. As a matter of fact the Russians kept urging the United States to take Hawaii, in order to cause trouble between the United States and Britain (as they had done during the Civil War and even after). It did not work out that way. Less than ten years after 1898, the Russians composed their differences with Britain because of Germany. A few years later Britain, France, Russia, and the United States became allies in World War I, against Germany. Had Germany won the First or the Second World War—and those were the last attempts of a European power to become the main power in the world—the twentieth century would have been a German one. It became the American Century instead.

In 1898, for the first time, the world became round-politically and not merely geographically. Until 1898 all the Great Powers were European ones. Now two other world powers arose: the United States and Japan. What was now happening in the Far East had a direct impact on the relationship of the powers in Europe and also the reverse. Thus there were seven Great Powers now, but less than fifty years later there were only two, the United States and Soviet Russia, and less than another fifty years later the United States stood alone at the end of a century that may properly be designated the American one.

Will the twenty-first century—the third century in the history of the United States—still be the American one? We may speculate on that. Yet it behooves us to recognize that the American Century began not in 1917 or in 1945 but in 1898.

John Lukacs is the author of the recently published A Thread of Years *(Yale University Press).*

BATTLES WON AND LOST

Our First Southeast Asian War

America's turn-of-the-century military campaign against Philippine insurgents consumed three years, involved 126,000 troops, and cost 4,000 lives. The lessons we learned could have been used in Vietnam sixty years later.

David R. Kohler and James W. Wensyel

David R. Kohler, Commander, U.S. Navy, is a Naval Special Warfare officer who has served multiple tours in UDT (underwater demolition) and SEAL (sea, air, land) teams. He has a master's degree in national security affairs from the Naval Postgraduate School in Monterey, California.

James W. Wensyel, a retired Army officer, is the author of three published books and numerous articles. His article on the crash of the dirigible Shenandoah *appeared in the February 1989 issue of* American History Illustrated. *He resides with his wife Jean in Newville, Pennsylvania.*

Guerrilla warfare ... jungle terrain ... search and destroy missions ... benevolent pacification ... strategic hamlets ... terrorism ... ambushes ... free-fire zones ... booby traps ... waning support from civilians at home. These words call forth from the national consciousness uncomfortable images of a war Americans fought and died in not long ago in Southeast Asia. But while the phrases may first bring to mind America's painful experience in Viet-

nam during the 1960s and '70s, they also aptly describe a much earlier conflict—the Philippine Insurrection—that foreshadowed this and other insurgent wars in Asia.

The Philippine-American War of 1898–1902 is one of our nation's most obscure and least-understood campaigns. Sometimes called the "Bolo War" because of the Filipino insurgents' lethally effective use of razor-sharp bolo knives or machetes against the American expeditionary force occupying the islands, it is often viewed as a mere appendage of the one-hundred-day Spanish-American War. But suppressing the guerrilla warfare waged by Philippine nationalists seeking self-rule proved far more difficult, protracted, and costly for American forces than the conventional war with Spain that had preceded it.

America's campaign to smash the Philippine Insurrection was, ironically, a direct consequence of U.S. efforts to secure independence for other *insurrectos* halfway around the world in Cuba. On May 1, 1898, less than a week after Congress

declared war against Spain, a naval squadron commanded by Commodore George Dewey steamed into Manila Bay to engage the Spanish warships defending that nation's Pacific possession. In a brief action Dewey achieved a stunning victory, sinking all of the enemy vessels with no significant American losses. Destroying the Spanish fleet, however, did not ensure U.S. possession of the Philippines. An estimated 15,000 Spanish soldiers still occupied Manila and the surrounding region. Those forces would have to be rooted out by infantry.

President William McKinley had already ordered a Philippine Expeditionary Force of volunteer and regular army infantry, artillery and cavalry units (nearly seven thousand men), under the command of Major General Wesley Merritt, to "reduce Spanish power in that quarter [Philippine Islands] and give order and security to the islands while in the possession of the United States."

Sent to the Philippines in the summer of 1898, this limited force was committed without fully considering the operation's potential length and cost. American military and government leaders also failed to anticipate the conse-

From *American History Illustrated*, January/February 1990, pp. 19-30. Reprinted through the courtesy of Cowles Magazines, publishers of *American History Illustrated*.

quences of ignoring the Filipino rebels who, under Generalissimo Don Emilio Aguinaldo y Famy, had been waging a war for independence against Spain for the past two years. And when American insensitivity toward Aguinaldo eventually led to open warfare with the rebels, the American leaders grossly underestimated the determination of the seemingly ill-trained and poorly armed insurgents. They additionally failed to perceive the difficulties involved in conducting military operations in a tropical environment and among a hostile native population, and they did not recognize the burden of fighting at the end of a seven-thousand-mile-long logistics trail.

Asian engagements, the Americans learned for the first time, are costly. The enterprise, so modestly begun, eventually saw more than 126,000 American officers and men deployed to the Philippines. Four times as many soldiers served in this undeclared war in the Pacific as had been sent to the Caribbean during the Spanish-American War. During the three-year conflict, American troops and Filipino insurgents fought in more than 2,800 engagements. American casualties ultimately totaled 4,234 killed and 2,818 wounded, and the insurgents lost about 16,000 men. The civilian population suffered even more; as many as 200,000 Filipinos died from famine, pestilence, or the unfortunate happenstance of being too close to the fighting. The Philippine war cost the United States $600 million before the insurgents were subdued.

The costly experience offered valuable and timeless lessons about guerrilla warfare in Asia; unfortunately, those lessons had to be relearned sixty years later in another war that, despite the modern technology involved, bore surprising parallels to America's first Southeast Asian campaign.

ORIGINS

America's war with Spain, formally declared by the United States on April 25, 1898, had been several years in the making. During that time the American "yellow press," led by Joseph Pulitzer's *New York World* and William Randolph

Hearst's *New York Journal,* trumpeted reports of heroic Cuban *insurrectos* revolting against their cruel Spanish rulers. Journalists vividly described harsh measures taken by Spanish officials to quell the Cuban revolution. The sensational accounts, often exaggerated, reminded Americans of their own uphill fight for independence and nourished the feeling that America was destined to intervene so that the Cuban people might also taste freedom.

Furthermore, expansionists suggested that the revolt against a European power, taking place less than one hundred miles from American shores, offered a splendid opportunity to turn the Caribbean into an American sea. Businessmen pointed out that $50 million in American capital was invested in the Cuban

sugar and mining industries. Revolutions resulting in burned cane fields jeopardized that investment. As 1898 opened, American relations with Spain quickly declined.

In January 1898 the U.S. battleship *Maine* was sent to Cuba, ostensibly on a courtesy visit. On February 15 the warship was destroyed by a mysterious explosion while at anchor in Havana harbor, killing 262 of her 350-man crew. The navy's formal inquiry, completed on March 28, suggested that the explosion was due to an external force—a mine.

On March 29, the Spanish government received an ultimatum from Washington, D.C.: Spain's army in Cuba was to lay down its arms while the United States negotiated between the rebels and the Spaniards. The Spanish forces were

KEYSTONE-MAST COLLECTION. CALIFORNIA MUSEUM OF PHOTOGRAPY, UNIVERSITY OF CALIFORNIA, RIVERSIDE

Manila-bound soldiers on a troopship pulling away from a San Francisco pier watch as the last man climbs aboard (right). At the height of the Spanish-American War, President William McKinley sent a seven-thousand-man expeditionary force to occupy the Philippines; during the next three years nearly twenty times that number of Americans would become involved in operations against Filipino insurgents.

also told to abolish all *reconcentrado* camps (tightly controlled areas, similar to the strategic hamlets later tried in Vietnam, where peasants were regrouped to deny food and intelligence to insurgents and to promote tighter security). Spain initially rejected the humiliation of surrendering its arms in the field but they capitulated on all points. The Americans were not satisfied.

On April 11, declaring that Spanish responses were inadequate, President McKinley told a joint session of Congress that "I have exhausted every effort to relieve the intolerable condition at our doors. I now ask the Congress to empower the president to take measures to secure a full and final termination of hostilities in Cuba, to secure . . . the establishment of a stable government, and to use the military and naval forces of the United States . . . for these purposes . . ."

Congress adopted the proposed resolution on April 19. Learning this, Spain declared war on the 24th. The following day, the United States responded with its own declaration of war.

The bulk of the American navy quickly gathered on the Atlantic coast. McKinley called for 125,000 volunteers to bolster the less than eighty-thousand-man regular army. His call was quickly oversubscribed; volunteers fought to be the first to land on Cuba's beaches.

The first major battle of the war, however, was fought not in Cuba but seven thousand miles to the west—in Manila Bay. Dewey's victory over Spanish Admiral Patricio Montojo y Pasarón (a rather hollow victory as Montojo's fleet consisted of seven unarmored ships, three of which had wooden hulls and one that had to be towed to the battle area) was wildly acclaimed in America.

American leaders, believing that the Philippines would now fall into America's grasp like a ripe plum, had to decide what to do with their prize. They could not return the islands to Spain, nor could they allow them to pass to France or Germany, America's commercial rivals in the Orient. The American press rejected the idea of a British protectorate. And, after four hundred years of despotic Spanish rule in which Filipinos had little or no chance to practice self-government, native leaders seemed unlikely candidates for managing their own affairs. McKinley faced a grand opportunity for imperialistic expansion that could not be ignored.

The debate sharply divided his cabinet—and the country. American public opinion over acquisition of the Philippines divided into two basic factions: imperialists versus anti-imperialists.

The imperialists, mostly Republicans, included such figures as Theodore Roosevelt (then assistant secretary of the navy), Henry Cabot Lodge (Massachusetts senator), and Albert Beveridge (Indiana senator). These individuals were, for the most part, disciples of Alfred Thayer Mahan, a naval strategist who touted theories of national power and prestige through sea power and acquisition of overseas colonies for trade purposes and naval coaling stations.

The anti-imperalists, staunchly against American annexation of the Philippines, were mainly Democrats. Such men as former presidents Grover Cleveland and Rutherford B. Hayes, steel magnate Andrew Carnegie, William Jennings Bryan, union leader Samuel Gompers, and Mark Twain warned that by taking the Philippines the United States would march the road to ruin earlier traveled by the Roman Empire. Furthermore, they argued, America would be denying Filipinos the right of self-determination guaranteed by our own Constitution. The more practical-minded also pointed out that imperialistic policy would require maintaining an expensive army and navy there.

Racism, though demonstrated in different ways, pervaded the arguments of both sides. Imperialists spoke of the "white man's burden" and moral responsibility to "uplift the child races everywhere" and to provide "orderly development for the unfortunate and less able races." They spoke of America's "civilizing mission" of pacifying Filipinos by "benevolent assimilation" and saw the opening of the overseas frontier much as their forefathers had viewed the western frontier. The "subjugation of the Injun" (wherever he might be found) was a concept grasped by American youth— the war's most enthusiastic supporters (in contrast to young America's opposition to the war in Vietnam many years later).

The anti-imperialists extolled the sacredness of independence and self-determination for the Filipinos. Racism, however, also crept into their argument, for they believed that "protection against race mingling" was a historic American policy that would be reversed by imperialism. To them, annexation of the Philippines would admit "alien, inferior, and mongrel races to our nationality."

As the debate raged, Dewey continued to hold Manila Bay, and the Philippines seemed to await America's pleasure. President McKinley would ultimately cast the deciding vote in determining America's role in that country. McKinley, a genial, rather laid-back, former congressman from Ohio and one-time major in the Union army, remains a rather ambiguous figure during this period. In his Inaugural Address he had affirmed that "We want no wars of conquest; we must avoid the temptation of territorial aggression." Thereafter, however, he made few comments on pacifism, and, fourteen weeks after becoming president, signed the bill annexing Hawaii.

Speaking of Cuba in December 1897, McKinley said, "I speak not of forcible annexation, for that cannot be thought of. That, by our code of morality, would be criminal aggression." Nevertheless, he constantly pressured Madrid to end Spanish rule in Cuba, leading four months later to America's war with Spain.

McKinley described experiencing extreme turmoil, soul-searching, and prayer over the Philippine annexation issue until, he declared, one night in a dream the Lord revealed to him that "there was nothing left for us to do but to take them all [the Philippine Islands] and to educate the Filipinos, and uplift, and civilize, and Christianize them." He apparently didn't realize that the Philippines had been staunchly Roman Catholic for more than 350 years under Spanish colonialism. Nor could he anticipate the difficulties that, having cast its fortune with the expansionists, America would now face in the Philippines.

PROSECUTING THE WAR

Meanwhile, in the Philippine Islands, Major General Wesley Merritt's Philippine Expeditionary Force went about its job. In late June, General Thomas Anderson led an advance party ashore at Cavite. He then established Camp Merritt, visited General Aguinaldo's rebel forces entrenched around Manila, and made plans for seizing that city once Merritt arrived with the main body of armed forces.

Anderson quickly learned that military operations in the Philippines could be difficult. His soldiers, hastily assembled and dispatched with limited prior training, were poorly disciplined and inadequately equipped. Many still wore woolen uniforms despite the tropical climate. A staff officer described the army's baptism at Manila: " . . . the heat was oppressive and the rain kept falling. At times the trenches were filled with two feet of water, and soon the men's shoes were ruined. Their heavy khaki uniforms were a nuisance; they perspired constantly, the loss of body salts inducing chronic fatigue. Prickly heat broke out, inflamed by scratching and rubbing. Within a week the first cases of dysentery, malaria, cholera, and dengue fever showed up at sick call."

During his first meeting with Dewey, Anderson remarked that some American leaders were considering annexation of the Philippines. "If the United States intends to hold the Philippine Islands," Dewey responded, "it will make things awkward, because just a week ago Aguinaldo proclaimed the independence of the Philippine Islands from Spain and seems intent on establishing his own government."

A Filipino independence movement led by Aguinaldo had been active in the islands since 1896 and, within weeks of Dewey's victory, Aguinaldo's revolutionaries controlled most of the archipelago.

Aguinaldo, twenty-nine years old in 1898, had taken over his father's position as mayor of his hometown of Kawit before becoming a revolutionary. In a minor skirmish with Spanish soldiers, he had rallied the Filipinos to victory. Thereafter, his popularity grew as did his ragtag but determined army. Aguinaldo was slight of build, shy, and soft-spoken, but a strict disciplinarian.

As his rebel force besieged Manila, Aguinaldo declared a formal government for the Philippines with himself as president and generalissimo. He proclaimed his "nation's" independence and called for Filipinos to rally to his army and to the Americans, declaring that "the Americans . . . extend their protecting mantle to our beloved country. When you see the American flag flying, assemble in numbers: they are our redeemers!" But his enthusiasm for the United States later waned.

Stymied by the Filipinos' use of guerrilla warfare, the Americans were forced to change their strategy.

Merritt put off Aguinaldo's increasingly strident demands that America recognize his government and guarantee the Filipinos' independence. Aguinaldo perceived the American general's attitude as condescending and demeaning.

On August 13, Merritt's forces occupied Manila almost without firing a shot; in a face-saving maneuver the Spanish defenders had agreed to surrender to the Americans to avoid being captured—and perhaps massacred—by the Filipino insurgents. Merritt's troops physically blocked Aguinaldo's rebels, who had spent weeks in the trenches around the city, from participating in the assault. The Filipino general and his followers felt betrayed at being denied a share in the victory.

Further disenchanted, Aguinaldo would later find his revolutionary government unrepresented at the Paris peace talks determining his country's fate. He would learn that Spain had ceded the Philippines to the United States for $20 million.

Officers at Merritt's headquarters had little faith in the Filipinos' ability to govern themselves. "Should our power . . . be withdrawn," an early report declared, "the Philippines would speedily lapse into anarchy, which would excuse . . . the intervention of other powers and the division of the islands among them."

Meanwhile, friction between American soldiers and the Filipinos increased. Much of the Americans' conduct betrayed their racial bias. Soldiers referred to the natives as "niggers" and "gugus,' epithets whose meanings were clear to the Filipinos. In retaliation, the island inhabitants refused to give way on sidewalks and muscled American officers into the streets. Men of the expeditionary force in turn escalated tensions by stopping Filipinos at gunpoint, searching them without cause, "confiscating" shopkeepers' goods, and beating those who resisted.

On the night of February 4, 1899, the simmering pot finally boiled over. Private William "Willie" Walter Grayson and several other soldiers of Company D, 1st Nebraska Volunteer Infantry, apprehended a group of armed insurgents within their regimental picket line. Shots were exchanged, and three Filipino *insurrectos* fell dead. Heavy firing erupted between the two camps.

In the bloody battle that followed, the Filipinos suffered tremendous casualties (an estimated two thousand to five thousand dead, contrasted with fifty-nine Americans killed) and were forced to withdraw. The Philippine Insurrection had begun.

GUERRILLA WARFARE

The Americans, hampered by a shortage of troops and the oncoming rainy season, could initially do little more than extend their defensive perimeter beyond Manila and establish a toehold on several islands to the south. By the end of March, however, American forces seized Malolos, the seat of Aguinaldo's revolutionary government. But Aguinaldo escaped, simply melting into the jungle. In the fall, using conventional methods of warfare, the Americans first struck south, then north of Manila across the central Luzon plain. After hard marching and tough fighting, the expeditionary force occupied northern Luzon, dispersed the rebel army, and barely missed capturing Aguinaldo.

Believing that occupying the remainder of the Philippines would be easy, the Americans wrongly concluded that the war was virtually ended. But when the troops attempted to control the territory they had seized, they found that the Filipino revolutionaries were not defeated but had merely changed strategies. Abandoning western-style conventional warfare, Aguinaldo had decided to adopt guerrilla tactics.

Aguinaldo moved to a secret mountain headquarters at Palanan in northern Luzon, ordering his troops to disperse and avoid pitched battles in favor of hit-and-run operations by small bands. Ambushing parties of Americans and applying terror to coerce support from other Filipinos, the insurrectionists now blended into the countryside, where they enjoyed superior intelligence information, ample supplies, and tight security. The guerrillas moved freely between the scattered American units, cutting telegraph lines, attacking supply trains, and assaulting straggling infantrymen. When the Americans pursued their tormentors, they fell into well-planned ambushes. The insurgents' barbarity and ruthlessness during these attacks were notorious.

The guerrilla tactics helped to offset the inequities that existed between the two armies. The American troops were far better armed, for example, carrying .45-caliber Springfield single-shot rifles, Mausers, and then-modern .30-caliber repeating Krag-Jorgensen rifles. They also had field artillery and machine guns. The revolutionaries, on the other hand, were limited to a miscellaneous assortment of handguns, a few Mauser repeating rifles taken from the Spanish, and antique muzzle-loaders. The sharp-edged bolo knife was the revolutionary's primary weapon, and he used it well. Probably more American soldiers were hacked to death by bolos than were killed by Mauser bullets.

KEYSTONE-MAST COLLECTION, CALIFORNIA MUSEUM OF PHOTOGRAPHY, UNIVERSITY OF CALIFORNIA, RIVERSIDE

U.S. troops found the tropical climate and Southeast Asian terrain almost as deadly as combat. Thousands of soldiers were incapacitated by dysentery, malaria, and other tropical maladies. The first troops sent to the archipelago wore unsuitable woolen uniforms; these men, photographed in 1900, had at least been issued ponchos for use during the rainy season.

As would later be the case in Vietnam, the guerrillas had some clear advantages. They knew the terrain, were inured to the climate, and could generally count on a friendly population. As in Vietnam, villages controlled by the insurgents provided havens from which the guerrillas could attack, then fade back into hiding.

Americans soon began to feel that they were under siege in a land of enemies, and their fears were heightened because they never could be sure who among the population was hostile. A seemingly friendly peasant might actually be a murderer. Lieutenant Colonel J. T. Wickham, commanding the 26th Infantry Regiment, recorded that "a large flag of truce enticed officers into

ambushes... Privates Dugan, Hayes, and Tracy were murdered by town authorities... Private Nolan [was] tied up by ladies while in a stupor; the insurgents cut his throat... The body of Corporal Doneley was dug up, burned, and mutilated... Private O'Hearn, captured by apparently friendly people, was tied to a tree, burned over a slow fire, and slashed up... Lieutenant Max Wagner was assassinated by insurgents disguised in American uniforms."

As in later guerrilla movements, such terrorism became a standard tactic for the insurgents. Both Filipinos and Americans were their victims. In preying on their countrymen, the guerrillas had a dual purpose: to discourage any Filipinos disposed to cooperate with the

Americans, and to demonstrate to people in a particular region that they ruled that area and could destroy inhabitants and villages not supporting the revolution. The most favored terroristic weapon was assassination of local leaders, who were usually executed in a manner (such as beheading or burying alive) calculated to horrify everyone.

By the spring of 1900 the war was going badly for the Americans. Their task forces, sent out to search and destroy, found little and destroyed less.

The monsoon rains, jungle terrain, hostile native population, and a determined guerrilla force made the American soldiers' marches long and miserable. One described a five-week-long infantry operation: " . . . our troops had been on half rations for two weeks. Wallowing through hipdeep muck, lugging a ten-pound rifle and a belt . . . with 200 rounds of ammunition, drenched to the skin and with their feet becoming heavier with mud at every step, the infantry became discouraged. Some men simply cried, others slipped down in the mud and refused to rise. Threats and appeals by the officers were of no avail. Only a promise of food in the next town and the threat that if they remained behind they would be butchered by marauding bands of insurgents forced some to their feet to struggle on."

News reports of the army's difficulties began to erode the American public's support for the war. "To chase barefooted insurgents with water buffalo carts as a wagon train may be simply ridiculous," charged one correspondent, "but to load volunteers down with 200 rounds of ammunition and one day's rations, and to put on their heads felt hats used by no other army in the tropics. . . . to trot these same soldiers in the boiling sun over a country without roads, is positively criminal. . . . There are over five thousand men in the general hospital."

Another reported that the American outlook "is blacker now than it has been since the beginning of the war . . . the whole population . . . sympathizes with the insurgents. The insurgents came to Pasig [a local area whose government cooperated with the Americans] and their first act was to hang the 'Presidente' for treason in surrendering to Americans. 'Presidentes' do not surrender to us anymore."

NEW STRATEGIES

Early in the war U.S. military commanders had realized that, unlike the American Indians who had been herded onto reservations, eight million Filipinos (many of them hostile) would have to be governed in place. The Americans chose to emphasize pacification through good works rather than by harsh measures, hoping to convince Filipinos that the American colonial government had a sincere interest in their welfare and could be trusted.

As the army expanded its control across the islands, it reorganized local municipal governments and trained Filipinos to take over civil functions in the democratic political structure the Americans planned to establish. American soldiers performed. police duties, distributed food, established and taught at schools, and built roads and telegraph lines.

As the war progressed, however, the U.S. commanders saw that the terrorism practiced by Aguinaldo's guerrillas was far more effective in controlling the populace than was their own benevolent approach. Although the Americans did not abandon pacification through good works, it was thereafter subordinated to the "civilize 'em with a Krag" (Krag Jorgensen rifle) philosophy. From December 1900 onward, captured revolutionaries faced deportation, imprisonment, or execution.

The American army also changed its combat strategy to counter that of its enemy. As in the insurgents' army, the new tactics emphasized mobility and surprise. Breaking into small units—the battalion became the largest maneuver force—the Americans gradually spread over the islands until each of the larger towns was occupied by one or two rifle companies. From these bases American troops began platoon- and company-size operations to pressure local guerrilla bands.

Because of the difficult terrain, limited visibility, and requirement for mobility, artillery now saw limited use except as a defensive weapon. The infantry became the main offensive arm, with mounted riflemen used to pursue the fleeing enemy. Cavalry patrols were so valued for their mobility that American military leaders hired trusted Filipinos as mounted scouts and cavalrymen.

The Americans made other efforts to "Filipizize" the war—letting Asians fight Asians. (A similar tactic had been used in the American Indian campaigns twenty years before; it would resurface in Vietnam sixty years later as "Vietnamization.") In the Philippines the Americans recruited five thousand Macabebes, mercenaries from the central Luzon province of Pampanga, to form the American officered Philippine Scouts. The Macabebes had for centuries fought in native battalions under the Spanish flag—even against their own countrymen when the revolution began in 1896.

Just as a later generation of American soldiers would react to the guerrilla war in Vietnam, American soldiers in the Philippines responded to insurgent terrorism in kind, matching cruelty with cruelty. Such actions vented their frustration at being unable to find and destroy the enemy. An increasing number of Americans viewed all Filipinos as enemies.

"We make everyone get into his house by 7 P.M. and we only tell a man once," Corporal Sam Gillis of the 1st California Volunteer Regiment wrote to his family. "If he refuses, we shoot him. We killed over 300 natives the first night. . . . If they fire a shot from a house, we burn the house and every house near it."

Another infantryman frankly admitted that "with an enemy like this to fight, it is not surprising that the boys should soon adopt 'no quarter' as a motto and fill the blacks full of lead before finding out whether they are friends or enemies."

That attitude should not have been too surprising. The army's campaigns against the Plains Indians were reference points for the generation of Americans that took the Philippines. Many of the senior officers and noncommissioned officers—often veterans of the Indian wars—considered Filipinos to be "as full of treachery as our Arizona Apache." "The country won't be pacified," one soldier told a reporter, "until the niggers are killed off like the Indians." A popular soldiers' refrain, sung to the tune of "Tramp, tramp, tramp, the boys are marching," began, "Damn, damn, damn the Filipinos," and again spoke of "civilizing 'em with a Krag."

Reprisals against civilians by Americans as well as insurgents became common. General Lloyd Wheaton, leading a U.S. offensive southeast of Manila, found his men impaled on the bamboo prongs of booby traps and with throats slit while they slept. After two of his companies were ambushed, Wheaton ordered that every town and village within twelve miles be burned.

The Americans developed their own terrorist methods, many of which would be used in later Southeast Asian wars. One was torturing suspected guerrillas or insurgent sympathizers to force them to reveal locations of other guerrillas and their supplies. An often-utilized form of persuasion was the "water cure," placing a bamboo reed in the victim's mouth and pouring water (some used salt water or dirty water) down his throat, thus painfully distending the victim's stomach. The subject, allowed to void this, would, under threat of repetition, usually talk freely. Another method of torture, the "rope cure," consisted of wrapping a rope around the victim's neck and torso until it formed a sort of girdle. A stick (or Krag rifle), placed between the ropes and twisted, then effectively created a combination of smothering and garroting.

The anti-imperialist press reported such American brutality in lurid detail. As a result, a number of officers and soldiers were court-martialed for torturing and other cruelties. Their punishments, however, seemed remarkably lenient. Of ten officers tried for "looting, torture, and murder," three were acquitted; of the seven convicted, five were reprimanded, one was reprimanded and fined $300, and one lost thirty-five places in the army's seniority list and forfeited half his pay for nine months.

Officers and soldiers, fighting a cruel, determined, and dangerous enemy, could not understand public condemnation of the brutality they felt was necessary to win. They had not experienced such criticism during the Indian wars, where total extermination of the enemy was condoned by the press and the American public, and they failed to grasp the difference now. Press reports, loss of public support, and the soldiers' feeling of betrayal—features of an insurgent war—would resurface decades later during the Vietnam conflict.

SUCCESS

Although U.S. military leaders were frustrated by the guerrillas' determination on one hand and by eroding American support for the war on the other, most believed that the insurgents could be subdued. Especially optimistic was General Arthur MacArthur, who in 1900 assumed command of the seventy thousand American troops in the Philippines. MacArthur adopted a strategy like that successfully used by General Zachary Taylor in the Second Seminole War in 1835; he believed that success depended upon the Americans' ability to isolate the guerrillas from their support in the villages. Thus were born "strategic hamlets," "free-fire zones," and "search and destroy" missions, concepts the American army would revive decades later in Vietnam.

MacArthur strengthened the more than five hundred small strong points held by Americans throughout the Philippine Islands. Each post was garrisoned by at least one company of American infantrymen. The natives around each base were driven from their homes, which were then destroyed. Soldiers herded the displaced natives into *reconcentrado* camps, where they could be "protected" by the nearby garrisons. Crops, food stores, and houses outside the camps were destroyed to deny them to the guerrillas. Surrounding each camp was a "dead line," within which anyone appearing would be shot on sight.

Operating from these small garrisons, the Americans pressured the guerrillas, allowing them no rest. Kept off balance,

short of supplies, and constantly pursued by the American army, the Filipino guerrillas, suffering from sickness, hunger, and dwindling popular support, began to lose their will to fight. Many insurgent leaders surrendered, signaling that the tide at last had turned in the Americans' favor

In March 1901, a group of Macabebe Scouts, commanded by American Colonel Frederick "Fighting Fred" Funston, captured Aguinaldo. Aguinaldo's subsequent proclamation that he would fight no more, and his pledge of loyalty to the United States, sped the collapse of the insurrection.

As in the past, and as would happen again during the Vietnam conflict of the 1960s and '70s, American optimism was premature. Although a civilian commission headed by William H. Taft took control of the colonial government from the American army in July 1901, the army faced more bitter fighting in its "pacification" of the islands.

As the war sputtered, the insurgents' massacre of fifty-nine American soldiers at Balangiga on the island of Samar caused Brigadier General Jacob W. "Hell-Roaring Jake" Smith, veteran of the Wounded Knee massacre of the Sioux in 1890, to order his officers to turn Samar into a "howling wilderness." His orders to a battalion of three hundred Marines headed for Samar were precise: "I want no prisoners. I wish you to kill and burn, the more you kill and burn the better it will please me. I want all persons killed who are capable of bearing arms against the United States." Fortunately, the Marines did not take Smith's orders literally and, later, Smith would be court-martialed.

On July 4, 1902, the Philippine Insurrection officially ended. Although it took the American army another eleven years to crush the fierce Moros of the southern Philippines, the civil government's security force (the Philippine Constabulary), aided by the army's Philippine Scouts, maintained a fitful peace throughout the islands. The army's campaign to secure the Philippines as an American colony had succeeded.

American commanders would have experienced vastly greater difficulties except for two distinct advantages: 1) the enemy had to operate in a restricted area, in isolated islands, and was prevented by the U.S. Navy from importing weapons and other needed supplies; and 2) though the insurgents attempted to enlist help from Japan, no outside power intervened. These conditions would not prevail in some subsequent guerrilla conflicts in Asia.

In addition to the many tactical lessons the army learned from fighting a guerrilla war in a tropical climate, other problems experienced during this campaign validated the need for several military reforms that were subsequently carried out, including improved logistics, tropical medicine, and communications.

The combination of harsh and unrelenting military force against the guerrillas, complemented by the exercise of fair and equitable civil government and civic action toward those who cooperated, proved to be the Americans' most effective tactic for dealing with the insurgency. This probably was the most significant lesson to be learned from the Philippine Insurrection.

LESSONS FOR THE FUTURE

Vietnam veterans reading this account might nod in recollection of a personal, perhaps painful experience from their own war.

Many similarities exist between America's three-year struggle with the Filipino *insurrectos* and the decade-long campaign against the Communists in Vietnam. Both wars, modestly begun, went far beyond what anyone had foreseen in time, money, equipment, manpower, casualties, and suffering.

Both wars featured small-unit infantry actions. Young infantrymen, if they had any initial enthusiasm, usually lost it once they saw the war's true nature; they nevertheless learned to endure their allotted time while adopting personal self-survival measures as months "in-country" lengthened and casualty lists grew.

Both wars were harsh, brutal, cruel. Both had their Samar Islands and their My Lais. Human nature being what it is, both conflicts also included acts of great heroism, kindness, compassion, and self-sacrifice.

Both wars saw an increasingly disenchanted American public withdrawing its support (and even disavowing its servicemen) as the campaigns dragged on, casualties mounted, and news accounts vividly described the horror of the battlefields.

Some useful lessons might be gleaned from a comparison of the two conflicts. Human nature really does not change—war will bring out the best and the worst in the tired, wet, hungry, and fearful men who are doing the fighting. Guerrilla campaigns—particularly where local military and civic reforms cannot be effected to separate the guerrilla from his base of popular support—will be long and difficult, and will demand tremendous commitments in resources and national will. Finally, before America commits its armed forces to similar ventures in the future, it would do well to recall the lessons learned from previous campaigns. For, as the Spanish-born American educator, poet, and philosopher George Santayana reminded us, those who do not learn from the past are doomed to repeat it.

Recommended additional reading: Benevolent Assimilation: The American Conquest of the Philippines, 1899–1902 by *Stuart C. Miller (Yale University Press, 1982)*; In Our Image: America's Empire in the Philippines by *Stanley Karnow (Random House, 1989);* Little Brown Brother *by Leon Wolff (Doubleday and Co., Inc., 1961)*; Muddy Glory *by Russell Roth (Christopher Publishing house, 1981); and* Soldiers in the Sun *by William T. Sexton (Books for Libraries Press, 1971).*

How We Lived

They were so mundane, then, the habits that now seem worthy of Ripley's Believe It or Not: *Housewives collected rainwater in barrels to wash their clothes. In the days before toilet paper, people used pages from the Sears, Roebuck and Co. catalog. The job of running a home at the turn of the century, especially a prairie home like the one in west Texas run by* **Mary McQuerry,** *104, required enormous endurance. Some 1.6 million families received land under the program between 1863 and 1967 and like many of them, McQuerry's family arrived on its land by covered wagon:*

. . . My day began at 4 a.m. My husband, James, and I milked about 130 dairy cows by hand. He'd load the wagon to head for the creamery while I gathered wood for the stove and began the first of my many trips to the water well. It took maybe an hour for the oven to heat up right and then I made breakfast from scratch—eggs, biscuits, homemade jellies and jams, bacon from our hogs. The stove was great in the winter, but when it was canning season in the summer, it was brutal. Canning peaches took me two or three days of constant work at the stove in the Texas heat in July. But if I didn't make them, we didn't eat in the winter.

Mondays were wash days. You scrubbed on a board, then stirred them in boiling water and then through two rinse tubs and some bluing. It took till early afternoon. Tuesday was ironing day. The irons were 6 or 7 pounds. You heated them in the fireplace and the process took all day. I did gardening a lot during the rest of the week. And Sun-

day I rested. Before church, I'd catch a chicken and pin it to the ground under my foot. Then I'd pull its head off with my hands. I never got the hang of wringing their necks.

Beyond daily hardships, life on the frontier contained other perils, according to **Pauline McCleve,** *100, who recounts her memories of desolate Arizona:*

. . . There were Indians and outlaws all around. They would steal our cattle, and there would be killings. My father always rode with six-shooters at each

---

PAULINE McCLEVE, 100

Her parents were Mormon pioneers in Arizona. She now lives in Tempe and for 50 years ran a beauty salon. *Family Profile:* **married for 65 years; husband is deceased; five children.** *Family lore:* **Before she married, her mother accidentally shot a hole in her father's hat at a picnic. "Mother never did shoot well," the father opined.** *Beauty secret:* **As a child, she made shampoo from yucca root.** *Midwife's bill for delivery of her first baby:* **$10.**

---

side. It was just part of the attire. Sometimes he'd wear two gun belts—four guns, in all. Billy the Kid came by the house one day before I was born and wanted to kill my mother's dog for barking at him. But the Indian that was with

him said, "No! No!" So they went away. When people in the town found out, they formed a posse to try to catch Billy. They didn't. But two men who were separated from the posse were found shot and killed by the outlaws.

In cities, a small army of tradesmen and merchants moved through neighborhoods. **Sidney Amber,** *109, describes early San Francisco:*

. . . My mother left the milk jug in front of the door. In the morning the milkman came and filled it up. The tea man delivered tea for 25 cents per pound. And the vegetable man or fruit man came in a wagon on the street, hollering: "Fresh fruit! Fresh vegetables!" You went out to look it over. They'd usually come every other day. Wood and coal were delivered. And so was ice—they cut it to the size you wanted.

Buying meat meant a trip to the butcher, recalls **Annie Cecelia Maddigan Healey,** *101:*

. . . There was no refrigeration. They had a big room out in back, and they used to put great big blocks of ice, and they'd hang the critters up, like a lamb or a pig. And you'd say you want some pork chops, and he'd go in this room with a cleaver—crack, crack—and get the chops and throw the fat away in a barrel.

Indoor plumbing was an urban luxury 100 years ago. The first major sewer system was designed in 1885 in Chicago. Utility companies were providing about 3 billion gallons of water a day in 1900, compared with 41 billion gal-

---

lons' in 1990. The first large-scale purification was launched by a Jersey City company in 1908, and chlorination quickly spread. Before all that, most kept chamberpots by their beds for middle-of-the-night emergencies or relied on outhouses. **Miriam Eliason,** *104, recalls living in her later home of Zion, Ill:*

. . . Everybody had a privy on the end of the lot at the alley, and away from the well so [sewage] wouldn't seep into the water supply. A man would come along once a week with a big covered wagon that had a galvanized can. He'd clean out the privy and dump [the waste] in his wagon. In the wintertime, he had a charcoal affair on the side of his wagon to set the can on to thaw the waste out. It would be frozen.

If you didn't have running water says **Bernice Isaacson,** *100, you just made do:*

. . . When we first moved to the Minnesota north woods, we had to borrow drinking water from neighbors who lived more than a mile away. There was a pond on our ground, and my uncle said that we would have to use that water. I said, "Oh, there's worms in there." He said, "If they can live in there, it's pure." We got a pailful and Grandma took a tea towel and strained it and put it on the stove and sterilized it. I remember all those black wiggler worms and polliwogs in that cloth.

Homes were mostly outfitted with handmade goods or things bought from catalogs. Though Benjamin Franklin introduced the first mail-order catalog to America in 1744, it didn't become a truly national market force until a decade after 1886 when Richard Sears and Alvah Roebuck published a 196-page catalog. Circulation of the catalog grew from 318 in 1897 to more than 1 million in 1904 as it became a staple in homes like **Bernice Isaacson's:**

. . . We ordered most everything from Sears, Roebuck catalogs. When my aunt and uncle's house in Iowa burned down some time around 1910, they ordered everything from Montgomery Ward. We laughed about it because they ordered

everything down to an eggbeater. But the first thing I bought after I began to work is a lady's desk from Sears. It's still in the other room.

CONVENIENCES

"Everything changed with electricity," says **Pauline McCleve.** *Just weeks after Thomas Edison lit a filament in October 1879, Charles Brush thrilled Cleveland residents by illuminating the town square. By 1888, 53 municipalities had light and power systems; that number rose to 800 municipal systems by 1900. Government regulation began in states in 1907 and the federal government*

SIDNEY AMBER, 109

He owned two restaurants in Los Angeles and still works as maître d' today; also ran two retail stores and did graphic arts. *Family profile:* **two marriages; both wives deceased; no children.** *Celebrities he has known:* **singer Al Jolson, magician Harry Houdini, heavyweight champion Jack Johnson.** *Price of his first Cadillac:* **$800.** *Vivid memories:* **his mother being thrown from bed in the 1906 San Francisco earthquake; Lindbergh baby kidnapping.**

---

broke up the monopoly power of big utility holding companies in 1935. Families greeted the arrival of electrical household devices like magical talismans. McCleve still speaks with rapture about "my beautiful Blue Bird washing machine" and other advances:

. . . A man down the street had a vacuum cleaner and would rent it to people. My mother used to take the rugs up twice a year and take them out on the line and beat them to get the dirt out. But once she used that vacuum cleaner, she never had to take them up again.

Two years after Alexander Graham Bell patented the telephone in 1876, the first

commercial phone exchange opened in New Haven. The phone's use exploded after that: There were 150,000 phones in the country in 1887 and 2,371,000 by 1902. That's 1 for every 33 Americans. They opened vast new worlds, though at first the newfangled contraption mystified some like **Pauline McCleve**'s father:

. . . I followed Papa down to the post office, where he was going to make his first phone call. A little local girl was missing, and he wanted to know if they had found her. He picked up the phone and was screaming into it, thinking that the person he was talking to was so far away that he had to yell. The postmaster, John Dilavitz, finally said, "Dick, you don't have to yell. Just use your ordinary voice."

Everybody was on a party line, says **Jennie Brown,** *101, so "you didn't tell any secrets."* **Bernice Isaacson** *says making calls was a pretty elaborate event:*

. . . A neighbor helped me get a summer job with the phone company when I was a freshman in high school about 1910. I learned to "throw the plugs." Callers had to pick up the phone, put it to their ear and then ring by winding it. Then, I'd help with their connections. They put me on long distance when I was 15. People would tell me where they wanted to call, then hang up and wait a half-hour till I could call back.

HEALTH

Killer diseases and the complications of giving birth and getting sick were omnipresent in homes at the turn of the century. The scourges included polio, measles and mumps (for which vaccines were invented in 1954, 1963 and 1967, respectively) and influenza. **Leola Peoples,** *101, had medical training and volunteered in Washington, D.C., to fight the 1918 flu epidemic that killed 675,000 Americans overall between September 1918 and June 1919:*

. . . We worked in a makeshift hospital. People would bring bodies in and just drop them in a bed anywhere. I went to work one night, passed 25 beds, and all of them had dead bodies. They couldn't even get enough caskets to bury them. The government gave us whiskey and quinine to give to the sick. That's all they knew as treatments.

There were just two of us black volunteers. A lot of the others were Catholic sisters, and many died. For 700 patients, they had two doctors and 12 nurses. They couldn't get anybody to work, because they were scared. But even with that, the old head nurse didn't want us to eat with the other volunteers because we were black. Can you imagine? We were putting our lives in danger, but she didn't want us to be eating in there with the white people! I never went back in that cafeteria anymore.

When you got sick yourself, says **Miriam Eliason,** *even common complaints could be frightful:*

. . . I wasn't a very healthy child. My father tried to cure my problem with my tonsils by painting them with iodine. When that didn't work, he took me one day on a big old-fashioned bicycle to the doctor's office. They laid me on a table, my father held my head and another man held my feet on the table. The doctor stood over me with that long, shiny instrument, and my mouth was propped open. My screams and struggles were in vain, and the blood was wiped up with towels. And I rode home on the bicycle. They didn't have any such thing as painkillers in those days.

Quarantine signs were a commonplace sight. The family of **Joseph Hankinson,** *100, paid dearly when scarlet fever struck:*

. . . My sister died of it in three days. My mother was at her sister's funeral—my aunt—and Mother came home to find her daughter was dead. When my other sister got sick, we were quarantined—a sign with big red letters right on our front door: "NOTICE: KEEP OUT!" After she got better, they [health authorities] fumigated the house, stuck a pipe through the front door after cork-

ing up all the windows and pumped something in.

Childbirth was hardly routine. **Ora Glass,** *103:*

. . . I gave birth in a regular hospital in Omaha. I don't remember having any painkillers. After the birth, I stayed in the hospital to be a wet nurse, because I had so much milk and my boy only took one breast because one breast has an inverted nipple. He didn't like that one. Sometimes, they'd pump the milk out of my breast to feed other babies, and sometimes they'd bring the white

---

LEOLA PEOPLES, 101

She attended Meharry Medical School in Nashville and got a medical license in 1915. But her training was not equal to that of whites and her poor clientele often couldn't pay, so she moved to the North and became a porter, waitress and nurse's aide. *Family profile:* **married briefly; now lives in Manhattan.** *Favorite memory:* **In 1918, to keep her brother in school, she gambled $5 on a horse race and won $350. He ultimately graduated from Harvard Law School.**

---

babies in. About three or four needed nourishment every day—something was wrong with their mothers. I stayed in the hospital for a few months just to help these babies out.

The hospital was segregated. A lot of Negro mothers in there said, "I don't see how you can do that." I said, "They need nourishment. Why be so cruel when you can help somebody? If my baby needed it, I'd be happy for somebody to help him."

WOMEN AT WORK

Women entered the work force in increasing numbers after the turn of the century: Five million worked outside the home in 1900. That figure grew to 10.4

million in 1930 and, spurred by the women's movement, hit 30 million by 1970. Many of the things women did by hand are now done by technology or cheaper labor abroad. **Annie Healey** *worked in mills in Middleboro, Mass., as a teenager in the 1910s:*

. . . When I was 14 years old my father went to town hall and got permission for me to work at the Star Mill that made beautiful, woolen men's suits. I worked from 6:30 in the morning when the bell rang until 6 at night. At noon, I had three quarters of an hour off for lunch and I'd go home for it. When we moved farther away, I got a job when I was around 15 in a factory where they made candy boxes and shoe boxes. We worked six days a week from 7 until 5, for 50 cents a day. I used to give my mother all the money because my family was buying a house. At first, unions helped get rid of things like child labor, but then they caused some trouble. In Middleboro, we lost three factories after unions got higher wages for workers. The factories were moved to Mexico.

The medical training **Leola Peoples** *got made her one of the first black women to get a physician's license in Georgia. But schools for blacks were so poor that she never learned the more advanced techniques of her white counterparts. She found she could earn more money in the North by being a waitress and working for the railroad:*

. . . I worked in a little hospital in Forsyth, Ga., after I got my doctor's license. I delivered a lot of babies, but all you did then was wash your hands and try to help them pull the baby out. They hadn't heard of C-sections, so women with breech babies often just died.

Few people could pay, so I didn't make money there or in the hospital where I worked in Baldwin, Ala., so I moved to Atlantic City and learned how to be a waitress. There was an old Irish fisherman who saw me on the boardwalk and said, "You got a sad face today." I told him I'd like to be a waitress. I helped him carry fish into the restaurant and was hired.

The most money I ever made in my life was during World War II, working for the Pennsylvania Railroad. The tips were great on the run from Boston to Washington. You'd give [the great actor] Paul Robeson orange juice and coffee and he'd leave a $2.50 tip. When the men came back from the war, they laid the women off.

I became a nurse's aide at Columbia Presbyterian Medical Center in New York and helped some beautiful people. Elizabeth Taylor always suffered from back pain—a slipped disk. She was a nice patient, a good tipper. She'd leave all her jewels right on the table. We'd say, "Miss Taylor, put your stuff away. Anybody can pick that up." She'd laugh. "I don't care, I can get some more."

One of the toughest businesses for women to break into was journalism. **Marjory Stoneman Douglas,** *105, didn't have that much trouble, though, because her father founded and edited the* Miami Herald:

. . . I'd been in Miami a short while when my father asked me to fill in for the society editor, who was off because her mother was sick. I worked from the house. I'd call up two or three women from the women's club to get the news, and the *Herald* would send a boy on a motorcycle to get my copy. After a short period of filling in, I took over the society editor's job full time.

Once in a while my column would make a difference to somebody. In the early 1920s, a story came out that a North Dakota boy named Martin Tabert was arrested here and put in a labor camp as a vagrant. He was beaten to death in the labor camp. The news of his death shocked me so much I wrote a simple ballad [about it]. It received enormous attention. It was read in Tallahassee in the Legislature and as a result they abolished beating in the labor camps forever.

PROHIBITION

Everyone has stories about how his family or friends got around the law ban-

ning alcohol that was enacted in 1919. **Dominic Cali,** *102, says everybody made his own beer without fear of reprisal from the 1,550 federal prohibition agents. Still, 500,000 were convicted of alcohol-related activities and paid $75 million in fines during Prohibition. Some companies found enterprising ways to skirt the law, says* **Tom Lane,** *101:*

. . . You could get a cask of [prefermented juice] from California, and it came with a little leaflet that said something like, "Do not put a hose into the cask, and let it stand for one month or it will turn into wine and that is against the law." They told you just how to make it!

SADIE NICKELSON, 100

She was a homesteader in Thermopolis, Wyo.; worked as a cowgirl doing ranch work. Still lives there. *Family profile:* **married twice (she and her first husband walked to a preacher's house and got him to perform the service on the spot); two children; one grandchild; three great-grandchildren.** *Childhood lore:* **She discovered an Indian grave site at the top of a tree. Later, she lived in a boxcar turned into a home for railroad workers like her father.**

There were as many as 219,000 illegal saloons at the height of Prohibition. And violence became part of the liquor business. The national murder rate rose from 6 per 100,000 of population to 10 per 100,000 in 1933. **Sadie Nickelson,** *100, describes how violence seeped into her hometown, Thermopolis, Wyo.:*

. . . Prohibition was the worst thing the government ever did. It made more trouble—shootings and killings. Once, there was a man who had a load of whiskey who had to cross a bridge at Gooseberry Creek. The local game war-

den, the only one who had the authority to stop the car and search it, approached the car. But when he looked in, the driver shot him dead.

That wasn't the only fatality. A local farmer, just as a curiosity, decided to watch from behind some trees as a shipment of whiskey came through. The fellow [who] was driving the car just shot him, even though he was innocent—wasn't a threat at all.

CLOTHING

Function prevailed over fashion in clothes for most at the dawn of the century. Onetime seamstress **Lucille Mosditchian,** *100, knew how important it was to make clothes well:*

. . . Clothing had to be perfect or you couldn't sell it. In those days, I mostly made dresses for women. Like most women, I wore dresses all the time around the house. I never thought that women would wear pants like they do now. The first pair of pants I wore, my husband nearly killed me. They didn't believe in that those days. But I felt good in them.

But when folks got interested in fashion, **Sidney Amber** *remembers, they went all out:*

. . . Women always wore gloves, a hat, a bustle, long skirts. They always looked very beautiful in their garments. A hat would cost around $2.50, $2.75, and that's for a very gorgeous hat with a beautiful plume on it. But now, hats are of the past.

In upscale families, clothes were changed at different parts of the day. **Miriam Eliason:**

. . . My mother always dressed up in the afternoon. After she'd get the dinner dishes washed, she'd wear a skirt and a dressing sack. Women also wore cotton pants with legs that would overlap in the back. There wasn't any underwear. They wore two or three long petticoats, too. My mother would sweat; her dress would be wet.

MANNERS

Many centenarians are unhappy about the coarsening of everyday life. The views of 102-year-old **Mary Corinne Rosebrook,** *a onetime Latin teacher are typical:*

. . . I think that generally speaking there's more informality and relaxation these days. But I think manners mattered more some years ago. There have to be some standards. There's nothing unjust about that. In my schools we always had high standards, and the children had reason to respect the authorities. Schools used to be a safe place, but it doesn't seem that way today.

Ora Glass *recalls that formal schooling in manners was common:*

. . . When I was young we took a course at the YMCA on table manners and how to act at different receptions and the like, on how you're supposed to address people. Today, some places you go to even the clerks in the stores aren't very mannerly. Some are so rude.

A becoming modesty is what **Pauline McCleve** *remembers about the way her parents related to each other.*

. . . We bathed in a tin tub when we were growing up. Once, I went in the bathroom and found that even though Mother was all alone, she had put chairs up and quilts around to protect the view of her bathing. I said, "Mother, you put those barriers up and you're all alone here except for Father." She said she was afraid he might come in while she was bathing, and she didn't want him to see her bathing.

DEALING WITH OTHERS

Many of these centenarians say they experienced profound love, enjoyed their families and communities and regret that today's families and relationships don't seem as satisfying as theirs. But that was not a universal circumstance.

Relations between men and women were often shrouded in mystery, according to **Marjory Stoneman Douglas:**

. . . In the early 1900s, girls weren't brought up to be competitive, unless you consider their attractiveness to males. We were more or less sheltered from everything and especially from sex. In junior and senior year [at Wellesley College], we had lectures behind locked doors. One girl fainted when the lecturer showed a picture of a pregnant woman. In zoology class, we saw pictures of

---

BERNICE ISAACSON, 100

Her mother died when she was 6; her father was an alcoholic. She was raised by relatives. Now lives in Omaha. *Family profile:* **married at 20; husband deceased; two sons; four grandchildren; seven great-grandchildren.** *First job:* **telephone operator as a young teenager, earning $5 a week; specialized in long-distance calls at age 15.** *Earliest memory:* **at age 2½, singing "McKinley's elected, Bryan's a fool, sitting on a haystack, looking like a mule!"**

---

copulating earthworms, and a good deal was said about frogs. But outside of the general idea that something had to happen between the male and female, we were completely vague. I had some dim idea it had something to do with the navel.

Racial segregation was a deeply wounding and debilitating reality, recalls **Leola Peoples:**

If you were black, you had to go to the black section of everything. If you rode a train, you had to ride right up in front by the engine where you'd get all that smoke. When I got to Atlantic City from the South, black people could not bathe

in the ocean with the whites. I guess white people didn't want to go in the water with the black folks.

After I moved to New York, I went to Brooklyn a lot to see Jackie Robinson play. They used to throw bottles at him from the seats. But he stuck with it. He sure helped his people.

Black people fought like heck for civil rights. But then we had our own troubles. Mayor John Lindsay [of New York] was a good leader. They had a riot up here in the late 1960s that started at a five-and-dime store. He came up here on a big truck with a big bullhorn. He rode through 125th Street and said, "This isn't getting you anywhere. Put down those bottles and rocks you're throwing. I know what you're going through. I just want you to remember that the man underneath today could be on top tomorrow."

Mary Okinaga, *100, was one of the 110,000 Japanese-Americans sent to internment camps in 1942 during World War II—even though she had been in the United States for 25 years, considered herself "a full American" and blamed Japan for starting the war:*

. . . I was in San Francisco when Pearl Harbor happened. When the executive order [establishing the internment camps] came out, I personally didn't fight against it. The government took us by train. We could bring only what we could carry in our hands.

I went to Heart Mountain, Wyo. It was snowing when I got there, and I didn't like the cold. But I got used to it. I was a janitor in the hospital inside the camp. I got $6 a month for the work, and there was no other place to spend that money, so I saved some up.

At the end of the war, we went back to San Francisco. Everything in our home had been looted. All gone. I had stored some of my personal belongings at the Buddhist temple's storage place. And when I came back, it was gone, too.

Theodore Roosevelt

*With limitless energy and a passionate sense of the nation, he
set the stage for the American century*

By Edmund Morris

They don't hold White House lunches the way they used to at the beginning of the century. On Jan. 1, 1907, for example, the guest list was as follows: a Nobel prizewinner, a physical culturalist, a naval historian, a biographer, an essayist, a paleontologist, a taxidermist, an ornithologist, a field naturalist, a conservationist, a big-game hunter, an editor, a critic, a ranchman, an orator, a country squire, a civil service reformer, a socialite, a patron of the arts, a colonel of the cavalry, a former Governor of New York, the ranking expert on big-game mammals in North America and the President of the U.S.

All these men were named Theodore Roosevelt.

In his protean variety, his febrile energy (which could have come from his lifelong habit of popping nitroglycerin pills for a dicey heart), his incessant self-celebration and his absolute refusal to believe there was anything finer than to be born an American, unless to die as one in some glorious battle for the flag, the great "Teddy" was as representative of 20th century dynamism as Abraham Lincoln had been of 19th century union and George Washington of 18th century independence.

Peevish Henry Adams, who lived across the square from the White House and was always dreading that the President might stomp over for breakfast (T.R. thought nothing of guzzling 12 eggs at a sitting), tried to formulate the dynamic theory of history that would explain, at least to Adams' comfort, why America was accelerating into the future at such a frightening rate. His theory was eventually published in *The Education of Henry Adams* but makes less sense today than his brilliant description of the President as perhaps the fundamental motive force of our age: "Power when wielded by abnormal energy is the most serious of facts... Roosevelt, more than any other man living within the range of notoriety, showed the singular primitive quality that belongs to ultimate matter—he was pure Act."

In his youth, as indeed during his infamous "White House walks," which usually culminated in a nude swim across the Potomac, Theodore Roosevelt's cross-country motto was "Over, Under or Through—But Never Around." That overmastering directness and focus upon his objective, be it geological or political or personal, was the force that Adams identified. But T.R., unlike so many other active (as opposed to reactive) Presidents, also had a highly sophisticated, tactical mind. William Allen White said that Roosevelt "thought with his hips"—an aperçu that might better be applied to Ronald Reagan, whose intelligence was intuitive, and even to Franklin Roosevelt, who never approached "Cousin Theodore" in smarts. White probably meant that T.R.'s mental processor moved so fast as to fuse thought and action.

He was, after all, capable of reading one to three books daily while pouring out an estimated 150,000 letters and conducting the business of the presidency with such dispatch that he could usually spend the entire afternoon goofing off, if his kind of mad exercise can

Harvard University

ATHLETIC AT HARVARD

> **BORN** Oct. 27, 1858, in New York City
> **1897** Named Assistant Secretary of the Navy
> **1898** Leads Rough Riders in Spanish-American War. Elected Governor of New York
> **1900–1901** Elected Vice President. McKinley shot; T.R. becomes President; begins Panama Canal
> **1906** Wins Nobel Peace Prize
> **1912** Loses bid for the presidency
> **1919** Dies in his sleep

be euphemized as goofing off. "Theodore!" Senator Henry Cabot Lodge was once heard shouting, "if you knew how ridiculous you look up that tree, you'd come down at once!"

The obvious example of T.R.'s "Never Around" approach to statesmanship was the Panama Canal, which he ordered built in 1903, after what he called "three centuries of conversation." If a convenient revolution had to be fomented in Colombia (in order to facilitate the independence of Panama province and allow construction to proceed p.d.q.), well, that was Bogotá's bad luck for being obstructionist and good fortune for the rest of world commerce. Being a historian, T.R. never tired of pointing out that *his* Panamanian revolution had been merely the 53rd anti-Colombian insurrection in as many years, but he was less successful in arguing that it was accomplished within the bounds of international law. "Oh, Mr. President," his Attorney General Philander Knox sighed, "do not let so great an achievement suffer from any taint of legality."

Dubious or not as a triumph of foreign policy, the canal has functioned perfectly for most of the century, and still does so to the honor of our technological reputation, although its control has reverted to the country T.R. allowed to sprout alongside, like a glorified right of way.

But T.R. deserves to be remembered, I think, for some acts more visionary than land grabbing south of the border. He fathered the modern American Navy, for example, while his peacemaking between Russia and Japan in 1905 elevated him to the front rank of presidential diplomats. He pushed through the Pure Food and Meat Inspection laws of 1906, forcing Congress to acknowledge its responsibility as consumer protector.

Many other Rooseveltian acts loom larger in historical retrospect than they did at the time, when they passed unnoticed or unappreciated. For example, T.R. was the first President to perceive, through his own pince-nez, that this nation's future trade posture must be toward Asia and away from the Old World entanglements of its past. Crossing the Sierra Nevada on May 7, 1903, he boggled at the beauty and other worldliness of California. New York—his birthplace—seemed impossibly far away,

Europe antipodean. "I felt as if I was seeing Provence in the making."

There was no doubt at all in T.R.'s leaping mind which would be the world's next superpower. Less than five years before, he had stormed San Juan Heights in Cuba and felt what he described as the "wolf rising in the heart"—that primal lust for victory and power that drives all conquerors. "Our place . . . is and must be with the nations that have left indelibly their impress on the centuries!" he shouted in San Francisco.

> *"He was so alive at all points, and so gifted with a rare faculty of living intensely . . . in every moment . . . "*
>
> **EDITH WHARTON,** at Roosevelt's burial, January 1919

It's tempting to speculate how T.R. might behave as President if he were alive today. The honest answer, of course, is that he would be bewildered by the strangeness of everything, as people blind from birth are said to be when shocked by the "gift" of sight. But he certainly would be appalled by contemporary Americans' vulgarity and sentimentality, particularly the way we celebrate nonentities. Also by our lack of respect for officeholders and teachers, lack of concern for unborn children, excessive wealth and deteriorating standards of physical fitness.

Abroad he would admire our willingness to challenge foreign despots and praise the generosity with which we finance the development of less-fortunate economies. At home he would want to do something about Microsoft, since he had been passionate about monopoly from the moment he entered politics. Although no single trust a hundred years ago approached the monolithic immensity of Mr. Gates' empire, the Northern Securities merger of 1901 created the greatest transport combine in the world,

controlling commerce from Chicago to China.

T.R. busted it. In doing so he burnished himself with instant glory as the champion of American individual enterprise against corporate "malefactors of great wealth." That reputation suited him just fine, although he privately believed in Big Business and was just as wary of unrestrained, amateurish competition. All he wanted to establish, early in his first term, was government's right to regulate rampant entrepreneurship.

Most of all, I think, Theodore Roosevelt would use the power of the White House in 1998 to protect our environment. His earliest surviving letter, written at age 10, mourns the cutting down of a tree, and he went on to become America's first conservationist President, responsible for five new national parks, 18 national monuments and untold millions of acres of national forest. Without a doubt, he would react toward the great swaths of farmland that are now being carbuncled over with "development" as he did when told that no law allowed him to set aside a Florida nature preserve at will.

"Is there any law that *prevents* me declaring Pelican Island a National Bird Sanctuary?" T.R. asked, not waiting long for an answer. "Very well, then," reaching for his pen, "I do declare it."

Edmund Morris, whose biography of Ronald Reagan will be published this fall, won a Pulitzer for his 1980 biography of Theodore Roosevelt

Unit Selections

Key Points to Consider

❖ The Populist reform movement developed in response to economic hardship that was made worse by the onset of depression. How do you account for the rise of progressivism in times of relative prosperity? Discuss the legislation passed during Woodrow Wilson's presidency. Did it succeed in achieving its goals? Why or why not?

❖ Why was Margaret Sanger's campaign to disseminate information about birth control so controversial? Which groups opposed her and why?

❖ Discuss the article on Leo Frank and the one on the Ku Klux Klan. Why do you think people are so willing to discriminate against others of different ethnic, racial, or religious backgrounds?

❖ Why did Prohibition fail in the end? What effects did it have while it lasted? Can the "Great Experiment" tell us anything about modern campaigns against alcohol and drugs? Defend your answer.

 **Links** | **www.dushkin.com/online/**

15. **International Channel**
http://www.i-channel.com/features/
16. **Mike Iavarone,**
http://www.worldwar1.com/
17. **World Wide Web Virtual Library**
http://www.iisg.nl/~w3vl/

These sites are annotated on pages 4 and 5.

The first decade of the twentieth century was one of relative prosperity, although all groups did not share equally. Yet the feeling grew that something was amiss, that the society was being derailed. One conspicuous development was the growing disparity between the extremes of wealth and poverty. In short, the rich were growing richer and the poor, if not growing poorer, still seemed an aberration in such an affluent society. There was growing dissatisfaction over the enormous power wielded by corporations, the corruption that existed in various levels of government, and the lack of minimal standards for men, women, and children, either in the workplace or where they lived. Those whom Teddy Roosevelt would refer to as "muckrakers" (today we would call them investigative reporters), published widely read "exposés" on a number of such conditions.

The Progressive movement generally was led by white, educated, middle- or upper-middle-class men and women. They were not radicals, although their opponents often called them that, and they had no wish to destroy the capitalist system. Instead they wanted to reform it in order to eliminate corruption, to make it function more efficiently, and to provide what we would call a "safety net" for the less fortunate. The reforms they proposed were modest ones, such as replacing political appointees with trained experts, having senators elected directly by the people, and conducting referenda on important issues. The movement arose on local levels, then percolated upward to state governments, then into the national arena.

As president, Teddy Roosevelt had responded to progressive sentiment through actions such as his "trust busting." He did not seek a third term in 1908, and he endorsed William Howard Taft as the Republican candidate for the presidency. Taft won the election but managed to alienate both progressives and conservatives during his tenure of office. By 1912 progressivism was so strong that the Democratic party nominated Woodrow Wilson, who had compiled an impressive record as a reform governor in the state of New Jersey. Roosevelt, now counting himself a full-blown Progressive, bolted the Republican party when Taft won renomination and formed the Progressive, or "Bull Moose," Party. Roosevelt was still popular, but all he managed was to split Republican support with the result that Woodrow Wilson won the election with only 42 percent of the popular vote.

"Woodrow Wilson, Politician" is aptly named, for Wilson is too often remembered only for his foreign policies—his leadership during World War I and his failure to bring the United States into the League of Nations. Author Robert Dallek evaluates Wilson's presidency in the domestic sphere and concludes that his achievements should be ranked along with those of Franklin D. Roosevelt and Lyndon B. Johnson. In "The Burden of Taxation," Edward Oxford describes the origins and passage of the Sixteenth Amendment, a progressive measure providing for the federal taxation of incomes.

Anti-Semitism has a long and dishonorable history in the United States. During the early part of

the century, Jews encountered discrimination in every field. They were excluded from social organizations, the upper echelons of the corporate world (except those they created themselves), and, to a large extent, from academic life. The stereotypical male Jew was a ruthless money-grubber who lusted after Gentile women. "The Fate of Leo Frank," by Leonard Dinnerstein, describes a notorious case in which a Jewish factory manager in Georgia was convicted on the flimsiest evidence of murdering a young employee. When the governor, after reviewing the case, commuted Frank's sentence, an angry mob invaded the jail where he was kept and lynched him.

Like a machine, Margaret Sanger's mother simply wore out after 18 pregnancies and 11 live births. Margaret, while working as a practical nurse and midwife, saw many other women whose health suffered from frequent, unintended, and unwanted pregnancies. She defied existing morality by preaching in favor of, and providing instructions for, birth control. To avoid prosecution for violating postal obscenity laws, she fled to Europe for a year. Later, when the case was dismissed, she continued her crusade for sex education and family planning. Gloria Steinem's "Margaret Sanger" highlights the career of this important forerunner of modern feminism.

Movements favoring the temperate use of alcohol, or its total prohibition, have long flourished in the United States. "Alcohol in American History" traces the course of these campaigns, which fluctuated from moral exhortation directed at individual conduct to seeking legislation to restrict or abolish the use of alcohol. The forces of prohibition triumphed in 1917, when what would become the Eighteenth Amendment passed both houses of Congress. It went into effect in 1920. Author David Musto discusses the positive aspects of "The Great Experiment," such as the lowered incidence of alcohol-related diseases. He also points out, however, that it helped spawn organized crime as bootlegging became a growth industry.

Following a sharp post-war recession, the economy flourished during the 1920s. Although farmers and other groups failed to keep pace, many people had more disposable income than ever before. They purchased automobiles, telephones, radios, and a host of newly available products. More people than ever before began "playing" the stock market. That is, they purchased stocks not for long-term investment but because they hoped to sell them months or even weeks later at higher prices. Stories abounded of individuals who earned fortunes virtually overnight. One Republican president succeeded another during these prosperous times, and party leaders boasted of a "new era" that would last indefinitely.

Terms such as "The Roaring Twenties" or "The Jazz Age" have been used to describe this decade. Motion pictures and popular fiction depicted young, good-looking men and women endlessly dancing the Charleston, drinking from hip flasks, or visiting illegal speakeasies to listen to "hot" jazz. Most people's lives were nothing like this, of course, but these were exciting times for those who could afford it. In "F. Scott Fitzgerald," Edward Oxford discusses the career of an author whose novels and short stories best caught the tenor of the age. Fitzgerald and his wife Zelda lived as if they were characters from Fitzgerald's fiction.

There was a darker side to the decade. Hatred directed against Germans during the Great War and against "Bolsheviks" during the Red Scare contributed to a general suspicion of foreigners. Ethnic and racial discrimination became more virulent than ever before. Bernard Weisberger's essay, "When White Hoods Were in Flower," discusses the revival of the Ku Klux Klan. The first Klan, it will be remembered, was an organization formed in the South in opposition to Radical Reconstruction. The new Klan flourished in the North as well, and targeted Jews, Catholics, and foreigners, as well as blacks.

Woodrow Wilson, Politician

The idealistic architect of a postwar world order that never came into being: such is the popular image of President Woodrow Wilson. What it omits is the savvy, sometimes ruthless politician whose achievements in the domestic sphere were equalled by only two other 20th-century presidents, Franklin Delano Roosevelt and Lyndon Baines Johnson. Robert Dallek here restores the whole man.

Robert Dallek

Robert Dallek is professor of history at the University of California, Los Angeles. He is the author of several books on political and diplomatic history, including Franklin D. Roosevelt and American Foreign Policy, 1932–1945 *(1979), which won a Bancroft Prize, and, most recently,* Lone Star Rising: Lyndon Johnson and His Times, 1908–1960 *(1991).*

Few presidents in American history elicit more mixed feelings than Woodrow Wilson. And why not? His life and career were full of contradictions that have puzzled historians for 70 years. A victim of childhood dyslexia, he became an avid reader, a skilled academic, and a popular writer and lecturer. A deeply religious man, who some described as "a Presbyterian priest" with a dour view of man's imperfectability, he devoted himself to secular designs promising the triumph of reason and harmony in domestic and world affairs. A rigid, self-exacting personality, whose uncompromising adherence to principles barred agreement on some of his most important political goals, he was a brilliant opportunist who won stunning electoral victories and led controversial laws through the New Jer-

sey state legislature and the U.S. Congress. A southern conservative and elitist with a profound distrust of radical ideas and such populists as William Jennings Bryan, he became the Democratic Party's most effective advocate of advanced progressivism. A leading proponent of congressional influence, or what he called "Congressional Government," he ranks with Theodore Roosevelt, Franklin D. Roosevelt, Harry S. Truman, and Lyndon B. Johnson as the century's most aggressive chief executives. An avowed pacifist who declared himself "too proud to fight" and gained reelection in 1916 partly by reminding voters that he had "kept us out of war," he made military interventions in Latin America and Europe hallmarks of his two presidential terms.

There is no greater paradox in Wilson's life and career, however, than the fact that his worst failure has become the principal source of his historical reputation as a great American president. Administrative and legislative triumphs marked Wilson's service as president of Princeton, governor of New Jersey, and president of the United States. But most Americans who would concede Wilson a place in the front

ranks of U.S. chief executives would be hard pressed to name many, if any, of these achievements. To them, he is best remembered as the president who preached self-determination and a new world order. (And not only to Americans: An upcoming Wilson biography by Dutch historian J. W. Schulte Nordholt is subtitled *A Life for World Peace.*) In the 1920s and '30s, when America rejected participation in the League of Nations and a political or military role in a world hellbent on another total war, Wilson's reputation reached a low point. He was a good man whom bankers and munitions makers had duped into entering World War I. He had also led America into the fighting out of the hopelessly naive belief that he could make the world safe for democracy and end all wars.

American involvement in World War II reversed Wilson's historical standing. Now feeling guilty about their isolationism and their rejection of his vision of a world at peace, Americans celebrated him as a spurned prophet whose wisdom and idealism deserved renewed acceptance in the 1940s. A new world league of self-governing nations practicing collective security for the sake of global stability and peace became the great

From *The Wilson Quarterly,* Autumn 1991, pp. 106-114. © 1991 by the Woodrow Wilson International Center for Scholars. Reprinted by permission.

American hope during World War II. When the fighting's outcome proved to be the Soviet-American Cold War, Americans saw it as another setback for Wilson's grand design. Nevertheless, they did not lose faith in his ultimate wisdom, believing that democracy and the international rule of law would eventually have to replace tyranny and lawless aggression if the world were ever to achieve lasting peace.

Now, with America's triumph in the Cold War and the Soviet-American confrontation all but over, the country has renewed faith in a world order akin to what Woodrow Wilson proposed in 1918. The idea took on fresh meaning when President Bush led a coalition of U.N.-backed forces against Iraq's attack upon and absorption of Kuwait. The triumph of coalition arms seemed to vindicate Wilson's belief that collective action through a world body could reduce the likelihood and effectiveness of attacks by strong states against weaker ones and thus make international acts of aggression obsolete.

Yet present hopes for a new world order can plummet overnight—and with them Wilson's standing. If Wilson's reputation as a great president rests upon his vision of a new era in world affairs and the fulfillment of some part of that design in our lifetimes, his place in the forefront of U.S. presidents seems less than secure.

Will the ghost of Wilson be plagued forever by the vagaries of world politics? Only if we fail to give scrutiny to his full record. A careful reassessment of Wilson's political career, especially in domestic affairs, would go far to secure his place as a great American president who has much to tell us about the effective workings of democratic political systems everywhere.

For all his idealism and elitism, Wilson's greatest triumphs throughout his career rested on his brilliance as a democratic politician. He was the "great communicator" of his day—a professor who abandoned academic language and spoke in catch phrases that inspired mass support. He was also a master practitioner of the art of the possible, a leader with an impressive talent for reading the public mood and adjusting to it in order to advance his personal ambition and larger public goals. This is not to suggest that his career was an uninterpreted success. He had his share of spectacular failures. But some of these he converted into opportunities for further advance. And even his unmitigated failures had more to do with circumstances beyond his control than with flaws in his political judgment.

Wilson's early life gave little indication of a master politician in the making. Born in 1856 in Staunton, Virginia, the third of four children, he was the offspring of devout Scotch Presbyterian divines. Thomas Woodrow, his maternal grandfather, came from Scotland to the United States, where he ministered to congregations in small Ohio towns. Jesse Woodrow Wilson, Wilson's mother, was an intensely religious, austere Victorian lady with no sense of humor and a long history of psychosomatic ailments. Joseph Ruggles Wilson, Woodrow's father, was a brilliant theologian and leading light in the southern Presbyterian church, holding pulpits in Staunton, Virginia; Augusta, Georgia; Columbia, South Carolina; and Wilmington, North Carolina. Joseph Wilson enjoyed a reputation as an eloquent and powerful speaker whose "arresting rhetoric and cogent thought" made him one of the leading southern preachers and religious teachers of his time. Woodrow Wilson described his father as the "greatest teacher" he ever knew. Yet theological disputes and clashes with other strong-willed church leaders drove Joseph, who advocated various reforms, from one pulpit to another and left him with a sense of failure that clouded his life. One Wilson biographer notes that "by mid-career, Joseph Wilson was in some ways a broken man, struggling to overcome feelings of inferiority, trying to reconcile a God of love with the frustration of his ambition for success and prominence within the church." To compensate for his sense of defeat, Joseph invested his vaunting ambition in his son Woodrow, whom he hoped would become the "very great man" Joseph himself had wished to be.

Although Joseph imparted a love of literature and politics to his son, Bible readings, daily prayers, and Sunday worship services were centerpieces of Woodrow's early years. His father also taught him the transient character of human affairs and the superiority of religious to secular concerns. Joseph left little doubt in the boy's mind that he foresaw for him a career in the ministry as "one of the Church's rarest scholars ∴ one of her most illustrious reformers … or one of her grandest orators." But Joseph's defeats in church politics in Woodrow's formative adolescent years soured father and son on Woodrow's entrance into the ministry.

Instead, Woodrow, with his father's blessing, invested his ambitions in a political career. As Richard Hofstadter wrote, "When young Tommy Wilson sat in the pew and heard his father bring the Word to the people, he was watching the model upon which his career was to be fashioned." Before college, he hung a portrait of British Prime Minister William Gladstone above his desk and declared: "That is Gladstone, the greatest statesman that ever lived. I intend to be a statesman, too." During his years as a Princeton undergraduate (1875–79), he rationalized his determination to enter politics by describing it as a divine vocation. A career as a statesman was an expression of Christian service, he believed, a use of power for the sake of principles or moral goals. Wilson saw the "key to success in politics" as "the pursuit of perfection through hard work and the fulfillment of ideals." Politics would allow him to spread spiritual enlightenment to the yearning masses.

Yet Wilson, as one of his later political associates said, was a man of high ideals and no principles, which was another way of saying that Wilson's ambition for self-serving political ends outran his commitment to any particular philosophy or set of goals. Like every great American politician since the rise of mass democracy in the 19th century, Wilson allowed the ends to justify the means. But Wilson never thought of himself as an opportunist. Rather, he considered himself a democrat responsive to the national mood and the country's most compelling needs. It is possible to scoff at Wilson's rationalization of his willingness to bend to current demands, but we do well to remember that the country's greatest presidents have all been men of high ideals and no principles, self-serving altruists or selfish pragmatists with a talent for evoking the vision of America as the world's last best hope.

Wilson's path to high political office, like so much else in his life, ran an erratic course. Legal studies at the University of Virginia, self-instruction, and a brief law practice in Atlanta were meant to be a prelude to a political career. But being an attorney had little appeal to Wilson, and he decided to become a professor of politics instead. Consequently, in 1883, at the age of 27, he entered the Johns Hopkins University Graduate School, where he earned a Ph.D. for *Congressional Government* (1885). His book was an argument for a Congress more like the British Parliament, a deliberative body in which debate rather than contending interests shaped legislation. For 17 years, from 1885 to 1902, he taught at Bryn Mawr, Wesleyan, and Princeton, beginning at the last in 1890. By 1898 he had grown weary of what he derisively called his "talking profession," and during the next four years he shrewdly positioned himself to become the unanimous, first-ballot choice of Princeton's trustees as the university's president.

Wilson's eight years as president of Princeton (1902–1910) were a prelude to his later political triumphs and defeats. During the first three years of his Princeton term, Wilson carried off a series of dazzling reforms. Offended by the shallowness of much instruction at Princeton and animated by a desire to make it a special university like Oxford and Cambridge, where undergraduate education emphasized critical thinking rather than "the ideal of making a living," Wilson introduced a preceptorial system. It aimed at transforming Princeton "from a place where there are youngsters doing tasks to a place where there are men doing thinking, men who are conversing about the things of thought. . . ." As a prerequisite to the preceptorial system, Wilson persuaded the faculty to reorganize the University's curriculum and its

structure, creating 11 departments corresponding to subjects and requiring upperclassmen to concentrate their studies in one of them. Wilson's reforms, biographer Arthur S. Unk asserts, "mark him as an educational statesman of originality and breadth and strength." His achievement was also a demonstration of Wilson's political mastery—a case study in how to lead strong-minded, independent academics to accept a sea change in the life of a conservative university.

The fierce struggles and bitter defeats of Wilson's next five years are a measure of how difficult fundamental changes in higher education can be without the sort of astute political management Wilson initially used. Between 1906 and 1910 Wilson fought unsuccessfully to reorganize the social life of undergraduates and to determine the location and nature of a graduate college. In the first instance, Wilson tried to deemphasize the importance of campus eating clubs, which had become the focus of undergraduate life, and replace them with residential colleges, or quadrangles, where students would live under the supervision of unmarried faculty members residing in the colleges. Wilson viewed the clubs as undemocratic, anti-intellectual, and divisive, and the quadrangle plan as a sensible alternative that would advance the university's educational goals and national standing. Wilson assumed that he could put across his plan without the sort of consultation and preparation he had relied on to win approval for the preceptorial system. But his failure to consult alumni, faculty, and trustees was a major political error that led to his defeat. Likewise, he did not effectively marshal the support he needed to win backing for his graduate-school plan, and again it made his proposal vulnerable to criticism from opponents.

Physical and emotional problems caused by strokes in 1906 and 1907 may partly account for Wilson's defeats in the quadrangle and graduate-school fights. But whatever the explanation for his poor performance in these academic struggles, they were by no means without political benefit to Wilson. In fact, what seems most striking about these conflicts is the way Wilson converted them to his larger purposes of running

Reproduction from the Library of Congress

Among Wilson's progressive measures was the Underwood Tariff of 1914, the first downward revision of the tariff since the Civil War.

first for governor of New Jersey and then for president of the United States.

Colonel George Harvey, a conservative Democrat who owned a publishing empire that included the *New York World* and *Harper's Weekly,* proposed Wilson for the presidency as early as 1906. Although Wilson made appropriate disclaimers of any interest in seeking the White House, the suggestion aroused in him the longing for high political station that he had held for some 30 years. In response to Harvey's efforts, Wilson, who was already known nationally as a speaker on issues of higher education, began speaking out on economic and political questions before non-university audiences. His initial pronouncements were essentially conservative verities calculated to identify him with the anti-Bryan, anti-Populist wing of the Democratic Party. "The nomination of Mr. Wilson," one conservative editor wrote in 1906, "would be a good thing for the country as betokening a return of his party to historic party ideals and first principles, and a sobering up after the radical 'crazes.' " In 1907 Wilson prepared a "Credo" of his views, which, Arthur Unk says, could hardly have failed to please reactionaries, "for it was conservative to the core." It justified the necessity of great trusts and combinations as efficient instruments of modern business and celebrated individualism. In

1908 Wilson refused to support Bryan for president and rejected suggestions that he become his vice-presidential running mate.

During the next two years, however, Wilson shifted decidedly to the left. Mindful of the mounting progressive temper in the country—of the growing affinity of middle-class Americans for reforms that would limit the power of corporations and political machines—Wilson identified himself with what he called the "new morality," the need to eliminate fraud and corruption from, and to restore democracy and equality of opportunity to, the nation's economic and political life. His academic fights over the quadrangles and graduate school became struggles between special privilege and democracy. In a speech to Princeton's Pittsburgh alumni in the spring of 1910, Wilson attacked the nation's universities, churches, and political parties as serving the "classes" and neglecting the "masses." He declared his determination to democratize the colleges of the country and called for moral and spiritual regeneration. Incensed at his conservative Princeton opponents, who seemed the embodiment of the privileged interests, and eager to make himself a gubernatorial and then national candidate, Wilson invested idealism in the progressive crusade, leaving no doubt that he was ready to lead a movement that might redeem America.

New Jersey Democratic boss James Smith, Jr., seeing Wilson as a conservative opportunist whose rhetoric would appease progressives and whose actions would favor the corporations and the bosses, arranged Wilson's nomination for governor. Wilson seemed to play his part perfectly during the campaign, quietly accepting Smith's help even as he declared his independence from the party machine and espoused the progressive agenda—the direct primary, a corrupt-practices law, workmen's compensation, and a regulatory commission policing the railroads and public utilities. On election day Wilson swept to victory by a 50,000-vote margin, 233,933 to 184,573, and the Democrats gained control of the normally Republican Assembly. Once in the governor's chair, Wilson made clear that he would

be his own man. He defeated Smith's bid for election to the U.S. Senate by the state legislature and skillfully assured the enactment of the four principal progressive measures. As he told a friend, "I kept the pressure of opinion constantly on the legislature, and the programme was carried out to its last detail. This with the senatorial business seems, in the minds of the people looking on, little less than a miracle in the light of what has been the history of reform hitherto in the State." As Wilson himself recognized, it was less a miracle than the product of constant pressure on the legislature at a time when "opinion was ripe on all these matters." Wilson's break with the machine and drive for reform reflected a genuine commitment to improving the lot of New Jersey's citizens. Most of all, they were a demonstration of how an ambitious politician in a democracy bends to the popular will for the sake of personal gain and simultaneously serves legitimate public needs.

Wilson's nomination for president by a deeply divided Democratic convention in the summer of 1912 was an extraordinary event in the history of the party and the nation. Wilson himself called it "a sort of political miracle." Although Wilson was the frontrunner in 1911 after speaking trips to every part of the nation, by May 1912 aggressive campaigns by Missouri's Champ Clark, speaker of the House of Representatives, and Alabama Representative Oscar W. Underwood made Wilson a decided underdog. When Clark won a majority of the delegates on the 10th ballot, it seemed certain that he would eventually get the two-thirds vote needed for the nomination. In every Democratic convention since 1844, a majority vote for a candidate had translated into the required two-thirds. But 1912 was different. Wilson won the nomination on the 46th ballot after his managers struck a bargain, which kept Underwood's 100-plus delegates from going to Clark. William Jennings Bryan gave Wilson essential progressive support, and the party's most powerful political bosses—the men who, in the words of one historian, had been Wilson's "bitterest

antagonists and who represented the forces against which he had been struggling"—decided to back him.

Wilson's campaign for the presidency was another milestone in his evolution as a brilliant democratic politician. He entered the election without a clear-cut campaign theme. The tariff, which he initially focused on, inspired little popular response. In late August, however, after conferring with Louis D. Brandeis, Wilson found a constructive and highly popular campaign theme. Persuading Wilson that political democracy could only follow from economic democracy or diminished control by the country's giant business trusts, Brandeis sold him on the New Freedom—the idea that regulated competition would lead to the liberation of economic enterprise in the United States. This in turn would restore grassroots political power and control. Wilson accurately sensed that the country's mood was overwhelmingly favorable to progressive reform, especially the reduction of the economic power of the trusts. He also saw correctly that Theodore Roosevelt's plea for a New Nationalism—regulated monopoly and an expanded role for federal authority in the economic and social life of the nation—impressed most voters as too paternalistic and more a threat to than an expansion of freedom. As a result, Wilson won a plurality of the popular vote in the four-way contest of 1912, 42 percent to a combined 58 percent for William Howard Taft, TR, and socialist Eugene V. Debs. Wilson's victory in the electoral column was far more one-sided, 435 to 99 for TR and Taft. His victory was also a demonstration of his talents as a speaker who could satisfy the mass yearning for a new era in national affairs.

Wilson's election represented a triumph of democratic hopes. After nearly five decades of conservative rule by the country's business interests, the nation gave its backing to a reform leader promising an end to special privilege and the economic and political democratization of American life. "Nobody owns me," Wilson declared at the end of his campaign, signaling his readiness to act in behalf of the country's working and middle classes. Despite his own largely conservative background, his political agility and sensitivity to popular demands made it likely that he would not disappoint progressive goals.

His first presidential term represents one of the three notable periods of domestic reform in 20th-century America. What makes it particularly remarkable, notes historian John Milton Cooper, is that Wilson won his reforms without the national emergencies over the economy and civil rights that respectively confronted the country during the 1930s and the 1960s. Wilson, in other words, lacked "the peculiarly favorable political conditions" aiding Franklin Roosevelt and Lyndon Johnson.

Wilson's successful leadership rested on his effective management of his party and Congress. Following the advice of Texas Representative Albert S. Burleson, a superb politician who became postmaster general, Wilson filled his cabinet with "deserving" Democrats and allowed Burleson to use patronage "ruthlessly to compel adoption of administration measures." Despite Bryan's ignorance of foreign affairs, for example, his prominence persuaded Wilson to make him secretary of state. Wilson's readiness to set a bold legislative agenda found support from both a 73-member Democratic majority in the House and a decisive majority of Democratic and Republican progressives in the Senate. The 28th president quickly proved himself to be an able manipulator of Congress. Eager to create a sense of urgency about his legislative program and to establish a mood of cooperation between the two branches of government, Wilson called a special congressional session at the start of his term and then spoke to a joint meeting of both houses. Indeed, he was the first president to appear in person before Congress since John Adams. Presenting himself as a colleague rather than "a mere department of the Government hailing Congress from some isolated island of jealous power," Wilson returned repeatedly to Capitol Hill for conferences to advance his reform program.

In the 18 months between the spring of 1913 and the fall of 1914, Wilson pushed four key laws through the Congress. The Underwood Tariff of October 1914 was the first downward revision of the tariff since the Civil War; it was inspired more by a desire to reduce the cost of living for lower- and middle-class Americans than by any obligation to serve the interests of industrial giants. Wilson drove the bill through the upper house by exposing the lobbyists representing businesses that sought "to overcome the interests of the public for their private profit." Making the tariff law all the more remarkable was the inclusion of the first graduated income tax in U.S. history. Shortly thereafter, Wilson won passage of the most enduring domestic measure of his presidency, the reform of the country's banking and money system. Insisting on pubic, centralized control of banks and the money supply rather than a private, decentralized system, Wilson once again came before Congress to influence the outcome of this debate. The Federal Reserve Act of December 1913 combined elements of both plans, providing for a mix of private and public control. Although further reforms would occur later to make the Federal Reserve system a more effective instrument for dealing with national economic problems, the Wilson law of 1913 created the basic elements of the banking system that has existed for almost 80 years. During the next nine months, by keeping Congress in continuous session for an unprecedented year and a half, Wilson won passage of the Clayton Antitrust and Federal Trade Commission acts, contributing to the more effective regulation of big business and greater power for organized labor.

In November 1914, Wilson announced that his New Freedom program had been achieved and that the progressive movement was at an end. A man of fundamentally conservative impulses (which he believed reflected those of the nation at large), Wilson did not wish to overreach himself. His announcement bewildered advanced progressives, who had been unsuccessfully advocating a variety of social-justice measures Wilson considered too radical to support. Herbert Croly, the editor of the *New Republic,* charged that "any man of President Wilson's intellectual equipment who seriously asserts that the fundamental wrongs of a modern society can be easily and quickly righted as a consequence of a few laws . . . casts suspicion either upon his own sincerity or upon his grasp of the realities of modern social and industrial life." Similarly, Wilson's refusal to establish a National Race Commission and his active commitment to racial segregation in the federal government incensed African-American leaders who had viewed him as a likely supporter of progressive measures for blacks.

Though he did little to reverse course on helping blacks, Wilson stood ready to return to the progressive position for the sake of reelection in 1916. "I am sorry for any President of the United States who does not recognize every great movement in the Nation," Wilson declared in July 1916. "The minute he stops recognizing it, he has become a back number." The results of the congressional elections in 1914 convinced Wilson that the key to success in two years was a campaign attracting TR's Progressive backers to his standard. Consequently, in 1916, he elevated Louis D. Brandeis to the Supreme Court and signed seven additional reform bills into law. Among other things, these laws brought relief to farmers and workers and raised income and inheritance taxes on wealthy Americans. The election results in November vindicated his strategy. Wilson gained almost three million popular votes over his 1912 total and bested Charles Evans Hughes, who headed a reunited Republican party, by 23 electoral votes. On this count alone, Wilson's two consecutive victories as the head of a minority party mark him as one of the century's exceptional American politicians.

Why did Wilson's political astuteness desert him during his second term in his handling of the Versailles Treaty and the League of Nations? The answer is not naiveté about world politics, though Wilson himself believed "it would be the irony of fate if my administration had to deal chiefly with foreign affairs." In fact, the same mastery of Congress he displayed in converting so many significant reform bills into law between 1913 and 1916 was reflected in his creation of a national consensus in 1917 for American participation in the Great War.

At the start of the fighting in 1914, Wilson declared America neutral in thought and deed. And though Wilson himself had a decidedly pro-British bias, he understood that the country then was only mildly pro-Allied and wanted no part in the war. His policies initially reflected these feelings. Only as national sentiment changed in response to events in Europe and on the high seas, where German submarine violations of U.S. neutral rights drove Americans more decisively into the Allied camp, did Wilson see fit to prepare the country for and then lead it into the war. His prewar leadership became something of a model for Franklin Roosevelt in 1939–41 as he maneuvered to maintain a national majority behind his responses to World War II.

Wilson's failure in 1919–20, or, more precisely, the collapse of his political influence in dealing with the peacemaking at the end of the war, consisted of a number of things—most of them beyond his control. His Fourteen Points, his formula for making the world safe for democracy and ending all wars, was beyond the capacity of any political leader to achieve, then and now. Yet there is every reason to believe that Wilson enunciated his peace aims assuming that he would have to accept compromise agreements on many of his goals, as indeed he did in the Versailles negotiations. A number of these compromises on the Fourteen Points went beyond what he hoped to concede, but he recognized that the conclusion of the fighting had stripped him of much of his hold over America's allies and limited his capacity to bend the strong-minded French, British, and Italian leaders to his will or to influence the radical revolutionary regime in Russia. Events were moving too fast in Europe and all over the globe for him to make the world approximate the postwar peace arrangements he had enunciated in 1918.

Faced by such circumstances, Wilson accepted the proposition that a League of Nations, including the United States, would be the world's best hope for a stable peace. Wilson's prime objective after the Versailles conference was to assure American participation in the new world body. But the political cards were stacked against him. After six years of Democratic rule and a growing conviction in Republican Party circles that the Democrats would be vulnerable in 1920, Senate Republicans made approval of the Versailles Treaty and American participation in the League partisan issues which could redound to their benefit. Moreover, between 1918 and 1920, Wilson's deteriorating health, particularly a major stroke in the fall of 1919, intensified a propensity for self-righteousness and made him uncharacteristically rigid in dealing with a political issue that cried out for flexibility and accommodation. As Edwin A. Weinstein has persuasively argued in his medical and psychological biography of Wilson, "the cerebral dysfunction which resulted from Wilson's devastating strokes prevented the ratification of the Treaty. It is almost certain that had Wilson not been so afflicted, his political skills and facility with language would have bridged the gap between [opposing Senate] resolutions, much as he had reconciled opposing views of the Federal Reserve bill . . . or had accepted the modifications of the Treaty suggested in February, 1919."

Wilson's political failure in 1919–20 was a striking exception in a career marked by a substantial number of political victories. His defeat and its consequences were so stunning that they have eclipsed the record of prior achievements and partly obscured Wilson's contributions to American history.

But it is not only the disaster of 1919–20 that is responsible. Mainstream academia today dismisses political history and particularly the study of powerful leaders as distinctly secondary in importance to impersonal social forces in explaining historical change. What seems lost from view nowadays is just how essential strong and skillful political leadership remains in bringing a democracy to accept major reforms. Wilson is an excellent case in point. For all the public's receptivity to progressivism in the first two decades of the century, it took a leader of exceptional political skill to bring warring reform factions together in a coalition that could enact a liberal agenda. By contrast. Wilson's physical incapacity in 1919 assured the defeat of American participation in a world league for 25 years. This is not to say that an American presence in an international body would have dramatically altered the course of world affairs after 1920, but it might have made a difference, and the collapse of Wilson's leadership was the single most important factor in keeping the United States on the sidelines.

Did social and economic and a host of other factors influence the course of U.S. history during Wilson's time? Without a doubt. But a leader of vision and varied abilities—not all of them purely admirable—was needed to seize the opportunities provided by history and make them realities. To forget the boldness of Wilson's leadership, and the importance of political leaders generally, is to embrace a narrow vision of this nation's past—and of its future.

The Burden of Taxation

*The April 15 ritual of last-minute tax filing has its origins in the
Sixteenth Amendment to the U.S. Constitution, whose ratification
in 1913 authorized Congress to institute a graduated income tax
on the earnings of American workers.*

By Edward Oxford

Each year on April 15, as the hands of clocks across America move inexorably toward midnight, time zone by time zone, an unnerving, annual ritual grinds to its conclusion. About one-sixth or so of America's 120-million tax filers—those who have procrastinated or deliberately postponed the inevitable—head to the nation's post offices to thrust their income-tax returns into the waiting hands of clerks called in just to handle the last-minute rush.

In recent years, scattered attempts have been made to ease the anguish of these desperate or defiant taxpayers. In Abilene, Texas, townsfolk put together a street party for late filers. In Santa Rosa, California, a taxpayer could benefit a community fund by paying a dollar to hit an Internal Revenue Service (IRS) agent in the face with a pie. And mirthful postal workers in Cherry Hill, New Jersey, dressed up in convict outfits to discourage tax-scoffing.

Not that such well-intentioned gestures ease much of the pain. Many taxpayers, less than happy with having to hand over their hard-earned dollars to an expectant Uncle Sam, come away from each yearly deadline muttering to themselves.

And their discontent is not without cause. The Tax Foundation calculates that it takes the average U.S. taxpayer about 130 days of working to pay the year's tax bill—a major part of which is federal income tax. By that reckoning, the typical wage-earner does not reach "Tax Freedom Day" until mid-May. The Foundation also points out that all the various taxes added together cost American families more than their food, clothing, and shelter combined.

Dutiful filers can become even more disheartened when they consider that millions of Americans who are legally obliged to file simply do not do so. Something in the magnitude of $1 billion a day, in fact—earned in the nation's "underground economy"—goes almost totally untouched by the IRS.

The idea of paying taxes isn't strange," an IRS spokesperson once said, "We've been doing it all our lives." By that line of reasoning, taxes would seem as American as, say, apple pie, if not nearly so satisfying.

Indeed, taxes have become part of Americana. "The power to tax involves the power to destroy," Chief Justice John Marshall warned in 1819 in rendering his opinion in the precedent-setting case of *McCulloch v. Maryland.* America's great humorist, Mark Twain, asked in 1902: "What is the difference between a taxidermist and a tax collector? The taxidermist takes only your skin." And Albert Einstein, a bona fide genius, allowed that "The hardest thing in the world to understand is the income tax."

Taxes, of course, were not invented by Americans. The word "tax" itself originated with Medieval Latin's *Taxâre,* meaning to touch, reproach, or to reckon. But the concept of taxing can be traced back to the beginnings of recorded history. The ancient Sumerians knelt to pay their cattle-taxes, and a bas-relief from an Egyptian pharaoh's tomb shows the tax collector beating a taxpayer. Centuries later, the first modern income tax financed Great Britain's wars against the French under Napoleon.

With all of these taxes, it was the unhappy lot of the less-privileged—vassals, peasants, and conquered peoples—to support the ruling classes, whether they be the free citizens of Athens, the lords and nobles of feudal baronies, or the courtiers of France's King Louis XIV. "The art of taxation," explained Jean Baptiste Colbert, that king's finance minister, "consists in so plucking the goose as to obtain the largest possible amount of feathers with the smallest possible amount of hissing."

Modern times—against a backdrop of representative government, the Industrial Revolution, and growing social concern—set the stage for taxation that, if not painless, would be less rending than in eras past. "We often forget that this nation was not founded for religious freedom, or freedom of the press or speech," writes columnist Lynn Ashby. "No, what chipped off our ancestors to the point of going to war was taxes. The Stamp Act. The Boston Tea Party. Taxation without representation."

The colonists waged and won the Revolutionary War, but when the new nation began, its coffers were empty. Some means had to be found to sustain the hard-won freedom, but the government operating under the Articles of Confederation had no power to tax. Revenue was to be contributed by the individual states. If they chose not to comply, the central government had no way to force them.

As ratified in 1788, the Constitution accorded the federal government a general taxing power. "The Congress," according to Article 1, Section 8, "shall have Power To lay and collect Taxes, Duties, Imposts and Excises, to pay the Debts and provide for the common Defence and general Welfare of the United States. . . ." But the Constitution required that all taxes be apportioned among the several states by population, a provision that made it unfeasible to collect taxes on individual levels of income. The Founding Fathers, with the taste of British tyranny still fresh in their collective memory, were disinclined to put the citizens' pockets in ready reach of the new central government.

At first, the young nation raised most of its needed moneys through customs duties and tariffs on foreign imports. But before long, Congress imposed taxes on domestically produced goods of an ever-widening variety. An excise tax—sixty cents on each gallon of a whiskey still's capacity or nine cents on each gallon of whiskey actually distilled—set citizen against government, as enraged grain farmers of western Pennsylvania rose in armed revolt. Passed in 1791, the whiskey tax represented an intrusion on the very way of life of that region. For three years, westerners refused to pay, venting their wrath on revenue collectors sent to force their compliance. Several attempts to render the tax more palatable failed, until in 1794 the actions of the rebels forced President George Washington to dispatch armed troops to answer the farmers' blatant defiance of federal authority. The so-called Whiskey Rebellion was put down, ending the nation's first constitutional crisis and making the point that the federal government could and would enforce its laws.

The question of how and what to tax was a continuing dilemma for the government during the first half of the nineteenth century. President Thomas Jefferson, a champion of individual liberty, urged Congress to sweep away just about all of the taxes that had been imposed on the American people. And in 1802, the whiskey tax—as well as other similar, direct taxes (except one on salt)—was repealed. During the next few decades, the federal government got along on tariff revenue. This form of taxation angered the agricultural south, which was heavily reliant on the importation of manufactured goods, and became an important factor in the dissolution of the Union in 1861.

The cataclysmic Civil War forced Congress to look for revenue wherever it could be found. Among the measures adopted was America's first income tax, which Congress passed on August 5, 1861. The Bureau of Internal Revenue, predecessor of the IRS,* was established the next year and dealt with all forms of internal tax, not just the income tax.

The law passed by Congress called for a tax on all income, from "[any] source whatsoever." Incomes of less than $600 per year were exempt, while those falling between that amount and $10,000 were taxed at a rate of three percent. People earning more than $10,000 faced a five percent tax on their incomes. As the war droned on, the federal government required more revenue, leading in 1864 to a rise in the tax rates to five percent for incomes between $600 and $10,000, and to ten percent for those above $10,000.

Despite the urgency of financing the war, some Northerners resented the new taxes. One complained that "Everything is now taxed except coffins." A *New York Tribune* editorial called the income tax "the most inquisitional, vexatious and unjust of all our taxes."

By 1872, the income tax, having been gradually reduced in the immediate postwar years, had been phased out. Once again, the U.S. government turned to tariffs as its primary source of revenue.

*The name of the Bureau of Internal Revenue was changed to the Internal Revenue Service in 1953.

The income tax's disappearance from the scene, however, did not mean that it had been forgotten. The notion of directly taxing those who could afford to pay became more popular, as many realized that indirect taxes such as tariffs and excise duties hit those with lower incomes disproportionately hard. John Sherman, a Republican senator from Ohio, pointed out to his colleagues that "Everything that [the poor man] consumes we tax, and yet we are afraid" to tax the rich. The income tax, he concluded, "is the only one that tends to equalize these burdens between the rich and the poor." Fourteen income tax bills were introduced into the House of Representatives between 1873 and '79, but none became law.

Although a burgeoning populist movement continued to call for an income tax during the 1880s, its members' arguments gained little support, largely due to the healthy state of the national treasury. In 1894, a year after a worldwide financial panic hit the American economy hard, Congress enacted a graduated income tax aimed entirely at the less than one percent of the population with earnings in excess of $4,000 per year. Debate surrounding the tax—dubbed a "punishment for the rich man for being rich" and said to be smacking of "socialism, communism, and devilism"—concentrated on whether a minority of the population could be specifically subjected to a tax by the majority.

In 1895, the Supreme Court ruled the law unconstitutional on the technical grounds that it taxed real estate and as such was a "direct tax" that had to be, according to Article 1 of the Constitution, levied according to population. Justice Stephen Johnson Field, who sided with the majority, stated that "The present assault upon capital is but the beginning. It will be but the stepping stone to others, larger and more sweeping, till our political contests will become a war of the poor against the rich; a war constantly growing in intensity and bitterness." Instead of relying on one segment of society, he argued, "every citizen should contribute his proportion, however small the sum, to the support of government. . . ." One newspaper exclaimed: "Ignorant class hatred has dashed itself in vain against the Constitution."

Despite this setback, support for an income tax remained strong. During his famous acceptance speech at the Democratic National Convention held in Chicago in July 1896, presidential candidate William Jennings Bryan declared: "When I find a man who is not willing to bear his share of the burdens of the government which protects him, I find a man who is unworthy to enjoy the blessings of a government like ours."

In continuing their crusade, advocates of an income tax set their sights on a constitutional amendment. A political wrangle over tariffs during a special session of Congress in 1909 resulted in a resolution calling for such an income-tax amendment being submitted to the states for ratification. But those who had proposed the resolution had done so for political reasons, not because they supported the income tax. They were confident that the amendment would not win approval in the required three-fourths of the states.

However, although it took four years, one state after another did ratify the proposed amendment, which declared that "Congress shall have power to lay and collect taxes on incomes, from whatever source derived, without apportionment among the several States and without regard to any census or enumeration." Finally, in February 1913, Wyoming's legislature cast the thirty-sixth "yes" vote, thus making the Sixteenth Amendment the law of the land.

During the next few months, the details of a new income tax bill were worked out and passed by Congress. In October, President Woodrow Wilson—who had been elected on a platform advocating an income tax—signed the measure into law. Its provisions exempted those with annual incomes below $3,000. Although, given the 1913 dollar value, this tax was not theoretically imposed only on the very rich, allowable deductions once again resulted in only about one percent of the population owing the government money. The top rate, applicable to incomes above $500,000, was seven percent.

At first, few people seemed ruffled by the Wilson tax. One lawmaker announced with a straight face that citizens would fulfill their tax obligation "willingly and cheerfully." Some of the favored few who were obliged to pay income tax even thought the new tax a mark of distinction, since it signified their affluence.

Among those who had grim forebodings about the tax was Dr. Charles Eliot, president of Harvard University, who declared that the tax would ultimately cause Americans to "lose their sturdy, independent, honest and just qualities which alone befit free men." *The Nation* magazine warned: "It is possible for a government to increase repeatedly the rates of such a tax." One lawmaker predicted that " a hand from Washington will stretch out to every man's house. . . ."

No one, not even its sponsors, imagined in 1913 that the personal income tax would in time become a population-wide tax, the basic support of federal spending. "Never since then," *The New York Times* observed years later, "has the taxpayer had it so good."

The income tax had made its debut just in time for World War I. Government spending soared from $1 billion in 1916 to $19 billion three years later. A surtax of 13 percent was assessed on the very highest incomes. And, soon after the U.S. entered the war, Congress voted to lower the exemption from $3,000 to $1,000 for single taxpayers and $2,000 for married couples. The government dispatched a volunteer force of "Four-Minute-Men" to communities across the country to give brief pep-talks urging people to pay their taxes proudly. At moving-picture houses, the words "Give Till It Helps" flashed onto screens.

Out of a population of approximately 105 million, only about 5 million paid income tax. And the tax was nominal—a $10,000-a-year family paid about $500 in income tax. By 1920, the bottom 99 percent of the taxpaying population contributed only 30 percent of all revenue collected through the income tax.

During the "Roaring Twenties," prosperity brought federal budget surpluses, a rarity in the twentieth century. Good times led to tax cuts. But the rise in racketeering during the Prohibition era—1920 to 1933—resulted, in a roundabout way, in an even stronger Internal Revenue presence. While federal agents seized whiskey stills and raided speakeasies, tax collectors reached out for income derived from those enterprises, as well as from extortion, bribery, gambling, and every other illegal pursuit. As one U.S. senator explained: "The law taxes a man on his income. It does not care where he gets it." In its most successful case, the Bureau pointed with pride to the conviction of gangster Al Capone in 1931 on a charge of tax evasion for failing to list all his illicit income.

The growing powers of the tax collectors gave some Americans cause for concern. Critic H. L. Mencken observed in 1926 that "The state has spread out its power until they penetrate to every act of the citizen, however secret; it has begun to throw around its operations with the high dignity and impeccability of a state-religion; its agents become a separate and superior caste, with authority to bind and loose."

With the Great Depression, government revenues plummeted, leading Congress to raise income-tax rates. The election of Franklin D. Roosevelt in 1932 heralded an unprecedented increase in government involvement in the lives of the citizenry. A federal office-building boom in Washington, D.C., symbolized this new activism. The Internal Revenue Building, for example, completed in 1935, covered four entire city blocks. Above its main entrance, carved in stone, were the ennobling, if controversial words of Supreme Court Justice Oliver Wendell Holmes: "Taxes are what we pay for a civilized society."*

Roosevelt's New Deal programs of the 1930s required money. In 1922, the Internal Revenue Bureau had collected $1.6 billion; by 1941, the annual figure had risen to $7.4 billion. Commerce Secretary Harry Hopkins felt that much good could come from taxes. He said,

---

*Justice Holmes, tax historians have duly noted, made his oft-quoted pronouncement in 1904, before the income tax existed. At that time, taxes as a percentage of income averaged only seven percent, as compared with close to forty percent today.

with perhaps partisan verve: "We will tax and tax, spend and spend, elect and elect."

World War II turned the income tax from a "class tax" aimed at the rich into a "mass tax." It was not long before America's more than 130 million people felt the war's seismic fiscal repercussions in their lives. The U.S. government needed vast sums of money to sustain the nation's salient part in the most sweeping conflict in history. As federal spending soared from $9.6 billion in 1940 to $95 billion by war's end, income-tax rates jumped to 19 percent on $2,000 and 88 percent on $200,000. By 1945, 42.7 million Americans were filing income tax returns each year, 38 million more than in 1939 when war broke out in Europe.

Because the United States desperately needed an assured, steady flow of wartime revenue, Congress reintroduced the current "pay-as-you-go" income tax known as "withholding tax," which had been a part of the original 1913 law but was abandoned in 1916.* By this means, the government, in effect, takes a due portion of the taxpayer's income at the source, before he or she ever has possession of it. In a sense, it takes compliance out of the taxpayer's hands. The individual income tax brought the government $150 billion during World War II, surpassing all other sources of federal revenues. That huge amount, however, covered only part of the war's cost. By late 1945, the public debt stood at $280 billion, roughly six times what it had been four years earlier.

During the second half of this century, the income tax has taken a wider,

*The 1913 withholding affected income from all sources, rather than just wages, as is the case today.

deeper hold. Through peace or conflict, prosperity or economic slump, the tax has endured. There have been a mind-boggling number of refinements and alterations, and the debate about which group should bear the brunt of the tax burden continues.

When April 15 comes around, most American taxpayers do their reluctant best to meet their obligations to Uncle Sam. As Scarlett O'Hara fussed in *Gone With the Wind*: "Death and taxes and childbirth! There's never any convenient time for any of them."

Freelance writer Edward Oxford's most recent contribution to American History—"F. Scott Fitzgerald"—*appeared in the November/December 1996 issue.*

The Fate of Leo Frank

He was a Northerner. He was an industrialist. He was a Jew.
And a young girl was murdered in his factory.

By Leonard Dinnerstein

On December 23, 1983, the lead editorial in the Atlanta *Constitution* began, "Leo Frank has been lynched a second time." The first lynching had occurred almost seventy years earlier, when Leo Frank, convicted murderer of a thirteen-year-old girl, had been taken from prison by a band of vigilantes and hanged from a tree in the girl's hometown of Marietta, Georgia. The lynching was perhaps unique, for Frank was not black but a Jew. Frank also is widely considered to have been innocent of his crime. Thus the second "lynching" was the refusal of Georgia's Board of Pardons and Paroles to exonerate him posthumously.

Frank's trial, in July and August 1913, has been called "one of the most shocking frame-ups ever perpetrated by American law-and-order officials." The case became, at the time, a cause célèbre in which the injustices created by industrialism, urban growth in Atlanta, and fervent anti-Semitism all seemed to conspire to wreck one man.

Until the discovery of Mary Phagan's body in the basement of Atlanta's National Pencil Company factory, Leo Frank led a relatively serene life. Born in Cuero, Texas, in 1884, he was soon taken by his parents to Brooklyn, New York. He attended the local public schools, the Pratt Institute, and Cornell University. After graduation he accepted

the offer of an uncle, Moses Frank, to help establish a pencil factory in Atlanta and become both co-owner and manager of the plant. He married Lucille Selig, a native Atlantan, in 1910, and in 1912 he was elected president of the local chapter of the national Jewish fraternity B'nai B'rith. Then, on the afternoon of April 26, 1913, Mary Phagan, an employee, stopped by Frank's factory to collect her week's wages on her way to see the Confederate Memorial Day parade and was murdered.

A night watchman discovered the girl's body in the factory basement early the next morning. Sawdust and grime so covered her that when the police came they could not tell whether she was white or black. Her eyes were bruised, her cheeks cut. An autopsy would reveal

BOTH: COURTESY OF THE ATLANTA HISTORY CENTER

Leo M. Frank, manager and co-owner of National Pencil Company (above), was accused of the murder of Mary Phagan (top right), found dead in the factory's basement.

From *American Heritage*, October 1996, pp. 99-102, 105-109. © 1996 by Forbes, Inc. Reprinted by permission of *American Heritage* magazine, a division of Forbes, Inc.

that her murderer had choked her with a piece of her own underdrawers and broken her skull. The watchman, Newt Lee, summoned the police; they suspected that he might have committed the murder, and they arrested him. After inspecting the scene, the officers went to Frank's home and took him to the morgue to see the body. The sight of the corpse unsettled him, and he appeared nervous. He remembered having paid the girl her wages the previous day but could not confirm that she had then left the factory. The police would find no one who would admit to having seen her alive any later.

A number of unsolved murders had taken place in Atlanta during the previous eighteen months, and the police were under pressure to find the culprit. Early newspaper reports erroneously suggested that Mary Phagan had been raped, and crowds of people were soon milling about the police station, anxious to get their hands on whoever had committed the crime. Frank's uneasy behavior and the public's hunger for justice made him a prime suspect. He was arrested two days later.

Shortly thereafter some factory employees told a coroner's jury, convened to determine the cause of death and suggest possible suspects for investigation, that Frank had "indulged in familiarities with the women in his employ." And the proprietress of a "rooming house" signed an affidavit swearing that on the day of the murder Frank had telephoned her repeatedly, seeking a room for himself and a young girl. Both these charges were later proved false (many witnesses recanted their accusations later), but newspapers headlined them, fueling talk of Jewish men seeking Gentile girls for their pleasure. The solicitor general, Hugh Dorsey, built a case for the prosecution around Frank's alleged perversions. Four weeks after the murder the grand jury granted the indictment Dorsey sought.

Unknown to the members of the grand jury, however, another suspect had also been arrested. He was Jim Conley, a black janitor at the factory who had been seen washing blood off a shirt there. He admitted having written two

Hugh Dorsey built a case around Frank's alleged perversions. Four weeks after the murder the grand jury granted the indictment he sought.

notes found near the body. They read: "Mam that negro hire down here did this i went to make water and he push me down that hole a long tall negro black that hoo it was long sleam tall negro i wright while play with me" and "he said he wood love me land dab n play like the night witch did it but that long tall black negro did buy his slef."

At first almost all investigators assumed that the author of these items had committed the crime. But Conley claimed to have written them as Frank dictated the words, first the day before the murder occurred, then, according to Conley's second affidavit, on the day of the crime.

Conley ultimately signed four affidavits, changing and elaborating his tale each time. Originally he said he had been called to Frank's office the day before the murder and asked to write phrases like "dear mother" and "a long, tall, black negro did this by hisself;" and he claimed to have heard Frank mumble something like "Why should I hang?" But the newspapers found the idea of Frank's having prepared for an apparent crime of passion by asking a black janitor to write notes about it utterly ridiculous. So Harry Scott, the chief detective, said he then "pointed out things in [Conley's] story that were improbable and told him he must do better than that." Another lengthy interrogation led to the second affidavit. It stated that Frank had dictated the notes just after the murder and that Conley had removed the dead body from a room opposite Frank's office, on the second floor, and taken it by elevator to the basement. (Later evidence showed that the elevator had not

been in operation from before the time of the girl's death until after her body was discovered.) A third affidavit spelled out in greater detail the steps Conley had allegedly taken in assisting Frank with the disposal of the dead girl. The Atlanta *Georgian* had already protested after the janitor's second statement that with Conley's "first affidavit repudiated and worthless it will be practically impossible to get any court to accept a second one." But Atlantans had been so conditioned to believe Frank guilty that few protested the inconsistencies in the janitor's tale.

Among those who questioned the prosecution's case against Frank were the members of the grand jury that had originally indicted him. They wanted Dorsey to reconvene them so that they could charge Conley instead. Dorsey refused, so the jury foreman did it on his own. It was the first time an Atlanta grand jury had ever considered a criminal case against the wishes of the solicitor general. Then Dorsey came back before the group and pleaded with them not to indict the black man. Exactly what he told them was not made public, but the next day the Atlanta *Constitution* reported that "the solicitor did not win his point without a difficult fight. He went in with a mass of evidence showing why the indictment of the negro would injure the state's case against Frank and stayed with the grand jurors for nearly an hour and a half."

It is difficult to say why the grand jury ultimately supported Dorsey. Perhaps they accepted the Atlanta *Georgian*'s explanation: "That the authorities have very important evidence that has not yet been disclosed to the public is certain." Or, given Southern values, they may have assumed that no attorney would base his case on the word of a black man "unless the evidence was overwhelming." In any case, the solicitor prevailed and prepared to go to trial.

The trial began on July 28, 1913, and brought forth large and ugly-tempered crowds. The heinous nature of the crime, rumors of sexual misdeeds, newspaper reports of "very important evidence that has not

COURTESY OF THE ATLANTA HISTORY CENTER

Frank's wife, Lucille Selig Frank, sits close by him during the murder trial.

yet been disclosed," the solicitor general's supreme confidence, and anti-Semitism (a Georgia woman had written that "this is the first time a Jew has ever been in any serious trouble in Atlanta, and see how ready every one is to believe the worst of him") combined to create an electric tension in the city. Gossip about Frank had been widespread, and many Georgians wondered if an unbiased jury would be possible. But jury selection was swift, and in an atmosphere punctuated by spontaneous applause for the prosecuting attorney and shouts of "Hang the Jew" from throngs outside the courthouse, the proceedings unfolded.

Solicitor Dorsey opened his presentation by trying to establish where and when the crime had occurred. He elicited testimony from several witnesses about blood spots on the floor and strands of hair on a lathe that Mary Phagan had allegedly fallen against in the room opposite Frank's office. (The state biologist had specifically informed the prosecution that the hair was not Mary Phagan's, and many witnesses testified that the bloodstains could have been merely paint spots; Dorsey ignored them.)

The heart of the state's case, however, revolved around Jim Conley's narrative. Although his story had gone through several revisions during the previous weeks—all of them published in the newspapers—his courtroom account

mesmerized the spectators. Conley told how he had served as a lookout in the past when Frank "entertained" women in the factory (no such women ever appeared at the trial), how after an agreed-upon signal he would lock or unlock the front door or go up to the superintendent's office for further instruction. He claimed that on the fatal day Frank had summoned him to his office, and when he arrived there, he had found his boss "standing up there at the top of the steps and shivering and trembling and rubbing his hands. . . . He had a little rope in his hands. . . . His eyes were large and they looked right funny. . . . His face was red. Yes, he had a cord in his hands. . . . After I got up to the top of the steps, he asked me 'Did you see that little girl who passed here just a while ago?' and I told him I saw one. . . . 'Well . . . I wanted to be with the little girl and she refused me, and I struck her and . . . she fell and hit her head against something, and I don't know how bad she got hurt. Of course you know I ain't built like other men.' The reason he said that was, I had seen him in a position I haven't seen any other man that has got children." Conley did not explain that last sentence; instead he went on to detail how Frank had offered, but never given him, money to dispose of the body. He said Frank had then asked him if he could write and, when he said yes, had dictated the murder notes.

When Dorsey concluded his presentation, *Frost's Magazine* of Atlanta, which had previously made no editorial comment about the case, condemned both the solicitor and Atlanta's chief detective for misleading the public into thinking that the state had sufficient evidence to warrant an accusation against Frank. "We cannot conceive," the commentary read, "that at the close of the prosecution, before the defense has presented one single witness, that it could be possible for any juryman to vote for the conviction of Leo M. Frank."

Frank had retained two of the South's best-known attorneys to defend him: Luther Z. Rosser, an expert at cross-examination, and Reuben R. Arnold, a prominent criminal lawyer. Despite their brilliant reputations, they failed to display their forensic talents when they were most needed. Rosser and Arnold cross-examined Conley for a total of sixteen hours on three consecutive days and could not shake his basic tale. He continually claimed to have forgotten anything that tended to weaken the case against Frank, and some observers thought Conley had been carefully coached by the solicitor general and his subordinates. The murder and disposal of the body would have taken at least fifty minutes to accomplish as the janitor described them, yet witnesses corroborated Frank's recollection of his whereabouts for all but eighteen minutes of that time. Furthermore, much of Conley's narrative depended on his having removed the body to the basement via the elevator, but floor markings, the absence of blood in the elevator, and other incontrovertible evidence proved that he hadn't. Why Frank's attorneys failed to exploit these facts, and why they also failed to request a change of venue before the trial began, has never been explained. But their inability to break Conley undermined their client's case. A reporter who attended every session of the hearings later observed, "I heard Conley's evidence entire, and was impressed powerfully with the idea that the negro was repeating something he had seen. . . . Conley's story was told with a wealth of infinitesimal detail that I firmly believe to be beyond the capacity of his mind, or a far more intelligent one, to construct from his imagination."

Rosser and Arnold's biggest error was probably their attempt to delete from the record Conley's discussion of times he had "watched for" Frank. For a day the two men got the janitor to talk about Frank's alleged relationships with other women, hoping to poke holes in the testimony; then they tried to get the whole discussion stricken. Even one of Dorsey's assistants agreed this information should not have been allowed into the record but added that once Conley had been examined and cross-examined on the subject, it was wrong to try to expunge it. "By asking that the testimony be eliminated," the Atlanta *Constitution* noted, the defense "virtually admit their failure to break down Conley."

It did not matter thereafter that witnesses came in to attest to Frank's good character and his whereabouts before, during, and after the murder. It also made little difference that Frank's explanation of his activities on the day of the murder carried, according to the *Constitution,* "the ring of truth in every sentence." Conley's narrative absolutely dominated the four-week trial.

One juror had allegedly been overheard to say, "I am glad they indicted the God damn Jew. They ought to take him out and lynch him."

In their summations Arnold and Rosser accused the police and solicitor general of having fabricated the evidence. Arnold stated that "if Frank hadn't been a Jew, there would never have been any prosecution against him," and he likened the entire case to the Dreyfus affair in France: "the savagry [*sic*] and venom is . . . the same."

But once again Dorsey emerged the winner. The *Constitution* described his closing argument as "one of the most wonderful efforts ever made at the Georgia bar." The solicitor reviewed the evidence, praised his opponents as "two of the ablest lawyers in the country," and then reemphasized how these men could not break Conley's basic narrative. He went on to state that although he had never mentioned the word *Jew,* once it was introduced he would use it. The Jews "rise to heights sublime," he asserted, "but they also sink to the lowest depths of degradation." He noted that Judas Iscariot, too, had been considered an honorable man before he disgraced himself. The bells of a nearby Catholic church rang just as the solicitor was finishing. Each time Dorsey proclaimed the word *guilty* the

bells chimed, and they "cut like a chill to the hearts of many who shivered involuntarily" in the courtroom.

The jury took less than four hours to find Frank guilty, and the judge, fearing mob violence, asked the defense to keep their client out of court during sentencing. Rosser and Arnold agreed. Solicitor Dorsey requested that they promise not to use Frank's absence as a basis for future appeals—even though barring a defendant from his own sentencing might constitute a denial of his right to due process of law—and the two defense attorneys assented.

Frank's attorneys kept their word and ignored the issue in their appeals for a new trial. According to state law, appeals in a capital case could be based only on errors in law and had to be heard first by the original trial judge. Rosser and Arnold based their appeal on more than 115 points, including the alleged influence of the public on the jury, the admissibility of Conley's testimony about Frank's alleged sexual activities, and affidavits from people who swore that two of the jurors were anti-Semitic. (One had allegedly been overheard to say, "I am glad they indicted the God damn Jew. They ought to take him out and lynch him. And if I get on that jury I'd hang that Jew sure.") Dorsey and his associates countered with affidavits from the jurors swearing that public demonstrations had not affected their deliberations. In his ruling, Leonard Roan, the trial judge, upheld the verdict and commented that although he was "not thoroughly convinced that Frank is guilty or innocent. The jury was convinced."

The next appeal, to the Georgia Supreme Court, centered on Roan's doubt of Frank's guilt, but the justices went along with the earlier decision. This court concluded that only the trial judge could decide whether the behavior of the spectators had prevented a fair trial and whether the jurors had been partial. The judges also ruled Conley's testimony relevant and admissible and dismissed Roan's personal expression of doubt.

At this point Frank replaced his counsel. The new attorneys did not feel

bound by their predecessors' promise to Dorsey, and they pressed the argument that Frank had been denied due process by being absented from his sentencing. But the state supreme court responded that "it would be trifling with the court to . . . now come in and . . . include matters which were or ought to have been included in the motion for a new trial."

The new attorneys went on to try to get the United States Supreme Court to issue a writ of habeas corpus, on the ground that the mob had forced Frank to absent himself from the court at the time of his sentencing, and thus he was being held illegally. The Court agreed to hear arguments on that question and, after two months, rejected the plea by a vote of 7–2.

Justice Mahlon Pitney explained that errors in law, no matter how serious, could not legally be reviewed in a request for a writ of habeas corpus but only in a petition for a writ of error. And Frank's contention of having been denied due process "was waived by his failure to raise the objection in due season. . . ." In a celebrated dissent, Justices Oliver Wendell Holmes and Charles Evans Hughes concluded, "Mob law does not become due process of law by securing the assent of a terrorized jury."

It is difficult for those not well versed in the law to follow the legal reasoning behind such procedural and constitutional questions, especially when judges are not even considering disputes in testimony or blatantly expressed prejudices. Thus many people assumed that the Court was reconfirming the certainty of Frank's guilt. Afterward his attorneys sought commutation to life imprisonment rather than a complete pardon because they concluded that after all the judicial setbacks they would have a better chance with the governor that way.

Once the case came before him, Gov. John M. Slaton moved with dispatch. He listened to oral presentations from both sides, read the records, and then visited the pencil factory to familiarize himself with the scene of the crime. Since the two sides differed in their arguments on where the murder had actually taken place—the metal-lathe room on the second floor versus the factory basement—

and whether the elevator had been used, the governor paid particular attention to those parts of the building. Besides the voluminous public records, Slaton received a personal letter written by the trial judge recommending commutation, a secret communication from one of Hugh Dorsey's law partners stating that Jim Conley's attorney believed his own client was guilty, and a note from a federal prisoner indicating that he had seen Conley struggling with Mary on the day of the murder.

For twelve days Slaton wrestled with the materials. On the last day he worked well into the night, and at 2:00 A.M., on June 21, 1915, he went up to his bedroom to inform his wife. "Have you reached a decision?" she asked.

"Yes," he replied, " . . . it may mean my death or worse, but I have ordered the sentence commuted."

Mrs. Slaton then kissed her husband and confessed, "I would rather be the widow of a brave and honorable man than the wife of a coward."

A ten-thousand-word statement accompanied the governor's announcement. Slaton appeared thoroughly conversant with even the minutiae of the case. He saw inconsistencies in Conley's narrative and zeroed in on them. The first significant discrepancy dealt with the factory elevator. Conley had admitted defecating at the bottom of the shaft on the morning before the murder. When police and others arrived the next day, the feces remained. Not until someone moved the elevator from the second floor was the excrement mashed, causing a foul odor. Therefore, Slaton concluded, the elevator could not have been used to carry Mary Phagan's body to the basement. Furthermore, according to scientific tests, no bloodstains appeared on the lathe or on the second floor—where the prosecution had contended that the murder had taken place—or in the elevator. But Mary's mouth, nostrils, and fingernails had been full of sawdust and grime similar to that in the basement, not on the second floor.

Other details also incriminated Conley. The murder notes found near the body had been written on order pads whose numerical sequence corresponded with those stored in the basement and not at all with those in Frank's office. Another major discrepancy that Slaton noticed concerned the strand of hair found on the metal lathe. Since the state biologist had determined that it could not have come from Mary's head, testimony from Dorsey's witness that "it looked like her hair" had to be dismissed.

Although most of Marietta knew who the killers were, a coroner's jury concluded that Frank had been lynched by persons unknown.

Privately Slaton told friends that he believed Frank was innocent, and he claimed that he would have pardoned him except that he had been asked only for a commutation and he assumed the truth would come out shortly anyway, after which the very people clamoring for Frank's death would be demanding his release. Slaton's announcement of the commutation sent thousands of Atlantans to the streets, where they burned Frank and the governor in effigy; hundreds of others marched toward Slaton's mansion, where state troopers prevented them from lynching him.

A wave of anti-Semitic demonstrations followed. Many Georgians assumed that the governor's "dastardly" actions resulted from Jewish pressures upon him. Atlanta Jews feared for their lives, and many fled the city. Responding to these actions a few days later, Slaton declared: "Two thousand years ago another Governor washed his hands of a case and turned over a Jew to a mob. For two thousand years that Governor's name has been accursed. If today another Jew were lying in his grave because I had failed to do my duty I would all through life find his blood on my hands and would consider myself an assassin through cowardice."

But the mob would not be thwarted. A fellow inmate at the state prison farm cut Frank's throat. While he was recovering in the hospital infirmary, a band of twenty-five men, characterized by their peers as "sober, intelligent, of established good name and character— good American citizens," stormed the prison farm, kidnapped Frank, and drove him 175 miles through the night to Marietta, Mary Phagan's hometown, where, on the morning of August 17, 1915, they hanged him from an oak tree. Although most of the people in Marietta knew who the killers were, a coroner's jury concluded that Frank had been lynched by persons unknown. The Pittsburgh *Gazette* restated that finding: "What the coroner's jury really meant was that Frank 'came to his death by hanging at the hands of persons whom the jury wishes to remain unknown.' "

Many of Frank's friends and later defenders attributed the hanging to unbridled mob passions, but the explanation cannot suffice. "The very best people," a local judge opined at the time, had allowed the Frank case to go through all the courts, letting the judicial process take its course. Then, after every request for a new trial had been turned down, the governor had outrageously stepped in. "I believe in law and order," the judge said. "I would not help lynch anybody. But I believe Frank has had his just deserts."

Obviously, much more than just a wish to carry out the court's decision motivated Frank's killers. The man symbolized all that Georgians resented. He was the Northerner in the South, the urban industrialist who had come to transform an agrarian society, a Jew whose ancestors had killed the Savior and whose co-religionists rejected the truth of Christianity. Thus, despite the fact that the state used a black man as its key witness, something that would have been unthinkable had the accused been a Southern white Christian, Atlantans could easily believe the worst about this particular defendant.

Over the years scores of people have wondered why many Georgians were loath to suspect that a black man might have committed the murder. The answer may have come from the pastor of the Baptist church that Mary Phagan's family attended. In 1942 the Reverend L. O. Bricker wrote: "My own feelings, upon the arrest of the old negro night-watchman, were to the effect that this one old negro would be poor atonement for the life of this little girl. But, when on the next day, the police arrested a Jew, and a Yankee Jew at that, all of the inborn prejudice against the Jews rose up in a feeling of satisfaction, that here would be a victim worthy to pay for the crime."

As time passed, people no longer remembered the specific facts of the case, but they told the story of Mary Phagan and Leo Frank to their children and grandchildren. As with all folktales, some details were embellished, others were dropped; however, as the first three verses of "The Ballad of Mary Phagan" unfold, no listener can have any difficulty knowing what happened:

Little Mary Phagan
She left her home one day;
She went to the pencil-factory
To see the big parade.

She left her home at eleven,
She kissed her mother good-by;
Not one time did the poor child think
That she was a-going to die.

Leo Frank he met her
With a brutish heart, we know;
He smiled and said, "Little Mary,
You won't go home no more."

People have argued the Frank case again and again, but usually without specific knowledge, falling back on hearsay to support their positions. However, in 1982 a dramatic incident put the case back in the public spotlight. Alonzo Mann, who had been a fourteen-year-old office boy in the Atlanta pencil factory in 1913, swore that he had come into the building on the day of the murder and witnessed Jim Conley carrying Mary Phagan's body toward the steps leading to the

basement. The janitor had warned him, "If you ever mention this, I'll kill you." Lonnie Mann ran home and told his mother what he had seen and she advised him to "not get involved." He obeyed her but eventually began telling his tale to friends. Finally, in 1982, two enterprising reporters filed the story in the Nashville *Tennessean.*

Mann's revelations stimulated a renewed effort to achieve a posthumous pardon for Leo Frank. Newspapers editorialized on the need to clear his name, public-opinion polls showed a majority in Georgia willing to support a pardon, and the governor of the state announced in December 1983 that he believed in Frank's innocence. But three days before Christmas the Board of Pardons and Paroles denied the request. It asserted that Mann's affidavit had provided "no new evidence to the case," that it did not matter whether Conley had carried the body to the basement or taken it via the elevator, and that "there are [so] many inconsistencies" in the various accounts of what had happened that "it is impossible to decide conclusively the guilt or innocence of Leo M. Frank."

Once again a storm broke as editorials and individuals excoriated the Board of Pardons and Paroles. The *Tennessean* said that "the board turned its back on the chance to right an egregious wrong."

The *Tennessean,* and others that were so certain about what the board should have done, had the advantage of hindsight. While this historian believes there is no question that Frank was an innocent man, the fact is that his case was much more complex than those who have read about it afterward recognize. One should not dismiss the impact of Jim Conley's performance on the witness stand or the electrifying effects of the innuendoes and charges in the courtroom that Frank might have engaged in improper sexual activities with the young people who worked in the pencil factory. Aside from the defendant's partisans, most people who heard the evidence or read about it in the newspapers during the summer of 1913 accepted its truthfulness. No reporter who attended the proceedings daily ever wrote of Frank's innocence. Long after the trial

ended, O. B. Keeler and Herbert Asbury, newspapermen who covered the case, still regarded him as guilty; Harold Ross, another writer and later the founding editor of *The New Yorker,* stated merely that the "evidence did not prove [Frank] guilty beyond that 'reasonable doubt' required by law."

Another factor is the ineptitude of Frank's counsel. They failed to expose the inaccuracies in Conley's testimony, and they blundered by asking him to discuss occasions when Frank had allegedly entertained young women. This opened the door for a great deal of titillating but irrelevant material and allowed Dorsey to bring in witnesses to corroborate Conley's accusations. The defense attorneys demonstrated their limitations once more by ignoring relevant constitutional questions in their original appeal to the Georgia Supreme Court. Thus a reinvestigation of the case in the 1950s led one observer to write that "the defense of Leo Frank was one of the most ill-conducted in the history of Georgia jurisprudence."

Still another consideration is the environment in which the trial took place. Today judicial standards have been tightened, and it is unlikely that any court proceedings would be conducted in so hostile an atmosphere as that in which Frank met his doom. But that does not necessarily outweigh the effect of the witnesses' testimony and the subsequent cross-examinations. To be sure, many of the jurors feared going against popular opinion, but perhaps they might have reached an identical judgment in a hermetically sealed chamber.

There is no reason to doubt that Alonzo Mann's affidavit is accurate. Had he ignored his mother's advice and gone to the police with his information right away, Conley would surely have been arrested, the police and district attorney would not have concentrated their efforts on finding Frank guilty, and the crime would most likely have been quickly solved. But by the time the trial began, in July 1913, Mann's testimony might hardly have even seemed important.

When reviewing the case, one need not be so one-sided as to ignore the very real gut reactions that Atlantans had to Mary Phagan's murder, the trial, and Leo Frank. Prejudice did exist in Atlanta, some people did lie at the trial, and anti-Semitism did contribute to the verdict. There were also contradictions in the case that people could not understand. Rational persons believed Conley's tale, and there is no denying that the janitor made a tremendously good impression on the stand. A reporter listening to him wrote that "if so much as 5 per cent" of his story was true, it would suffice to convict Frank.

The struggle to exonerate Leo Frank continued, and in March 1986 the state Board of Pardons and Paroles reversed itself and granted a pardon. It had been granted, said the accompanying document, "in recognition of the state's failure to protect the person of Leo Frank and thereby preserve his opportunity of continued legal appeal of his conviction, and in recognition of the state's failure to bring his killers to justice, and as an effort to heal old wounds."

Not, that is, because Frank was innocent.

In the late 1980s a Georgia citizen, firmly convinced of Frank's guilt, vehemently underscored the point in a letter to the Marietta *Daily Journal*: "The pardon expressly does not relieve Mr. Frank of his conviction or of his guilt. Rather, it simply restored to him his civil rights, permitting him to vote and serve on juries, activities which, presumably, at this date are meaningless."

Meaningless they may be. Still, Leo Frank's unquiet spirit continues to vex the conscience of many Georgians eighty-one years after he died on an oak tree in Marietta.

Leonard Dinnerstein is a professor of history and the director of Judaic Studies at the University of Arizona. His books include The Leonard Frank Case *(available in paperback from the University of Georgia Press),* America and the Survivors of the Holocaust, *and* Antisemitism in America.

Margaret Sanger

Her crusade to legalize birth control spurred the movement for women's liberation

By Gloria Steinem

"The movement she started will grow to be, a hundred years from now, the most influential of all time," predicted futurist and historian H. G. Wells in 1931. "When the history of our civilization is written, it will be a biological history, and Margaret Sanger will be its heroine."

BORN Sept. 14, 1879, in Corning, N.Y.

1914 Launches The Woman Rebel, a feminist monthly that advocates birth control; is indicted for inciting violence and promoting obscenity

1916 Opens the U.S.'s first family-planning clinic, in Brooklyn, N.Y.; is later jailed for 30 days

1921 Founds the American Birth Control League, the precursor to the Planned Parenthood Federation

DIED Sept. 6, 1966, in Tucson, Ariz.

UPI/CORBIS-BETTMANN

Facing trial in 1916 for violating obscenity laws

Though this prophecy of nearly 70 years ago credited one woman with the power that actually came from a wide and deep movement of women, no one person deserves it more. Now that reproductive freedom is becoming accepted and conservative groups are fighting to maintain control over women's bodies as the means of reproduction, Sanger's revolution may be even more controversial than during her 50-year career of national and international battles. Her experience can teach us many lessons.

She taught us, first, to look at the world as if women mattered. Born into an Irish working-class family, Margaret witnessed her mother's slow death, worn out after 18 pregnancies and 11 live births. While working as a practical nurse and midwife in the poorest neighborhoods of New York City in the years before World War I, she saw women deprived of their health, sexuality and ability to care for children already born. Contraceptive information was so suppressed by clergy-influenced, physician-accepted laws that it was a criminal offense to send it through the mail. Yet the educated had access to such information and could use subterfuge to buy "French" products, which were really condoms and other barrier methods, and "feminine hy-

giene" products, which were really spermicides.

It was this injustice that inspired Sanger to defy church and state. In a series of articles called "What Every Girl Should Know," then in her own newspaper *The Woman Rebel* and finally through neighborhood clinics that dispensed woman-controlled forms of birth control (a phrase she coined), Sanger put information and power into the hands of women.

While in Europe for a year to avoid severe criminal penalties, partly due to her political radicalism, partly for violating postal obscenity laws, she learned more about contraception, the politics of sexuality and the commonality of women's experience. Her case was dismissed after her return to the States. Sanger continued to push legal and social boundaries by initiating sex counseling, founding the American Birth Control League (which became, in 1942, the Planned Parenthood Federation of America) and organizing the first international population conference. Eventually her work would extend as far as Japan and India, where organizations she helped start still flourish.

Sanger was past 80 when she saw the first marketing of a contraceptive pill, which she had helped develop. But legal change was slow. It took until 1965, a year before her death, for the Supreme Court to strike down a Connecticut law that prohibited the use of contraception, even by married couples. Extended to unmarried couples only in 1972, this constitutionally guaranteed right to pri-

"She made people accept that women had the right to control their own destinies."

Grandson **ALEXANDER SANGER,** head of Planned Parenthood of New York City

vacy would become as important to women's equality as the vote. In 1973 the right to privacy was extended to the abortion decision of a woman and her physician, thus making abortion a safe and legal alternative—unlike the $5 illegal butcheries of Sanger's day.

One can imagine Sanger's response to the current anti-choice lobby and congressional leadership that opposes abortion, sex education in schools, and federally funded contraceptive programs that would make abortion less necessary; that supports ownership of young women's bodies through parental-consent laws; that limits poor women's choices by denying Medicaid funding; and that holds hostage the entire U.S. billion-dollar debt to the United Nations in the hope of attaching an antiabortion rider. As in her day, the question seems to be less about what gets decided than who has the power to make the decision.

One can also imagine her response to pro-life rhetoric being used to justify an average of one clinic bombing or arson per month—sometimes the same clinics Sanger helped found—and the murder of six clinic staff members, the attempted murder of 15 others, and assault and battery against 104 more. In each case, the justification is that potential fetal life is more important than a living woman's health or freedom.

What are mistakes in our era that parallel those of Sanger's? There is still an effort to distort her goal of giving women control over their bodies by attributing such quotes to Sanger as "More children from the fit, less from the unfit—that is the chief issue of birth control." Sanger didn't say those words; in fact, she condemned them as a eugenicist argument for "cradle competition." To her, poor mental development was largely the result of poverty, overpopulation and the lack of attention to children. She correctly foresaw racism as the nation's major challenge, conducted surveys that countered stereotypes regarding the black community and birth control, and established clinics in the rural South with the help of such African-American leaders as W. E. B. Du Bois and Mary McLeod Bethune.

Nonetheless, expediency caused Sanger to distance herself from her radical past; for instance, she used soft phrases such as "family planning" instead of her original, more pointed argument that the poor were being manipulated into producing an endless supply of cheap labor. She also adopted the mainstream eugenics language of the day, partly as a tactic, since many eugenicists opposed birth control on the grounds that the educated would use it more. Though her own work was directed toward voluntary birth control and public health programs, her use of eugenics language probably helped justify sterilization abuse. Her misjudgments should cause us to wonder what parallel errors we are making now and to question any tactics that fail to embody the ends we hope to achieve.

Sanger led by example. Her brave and joyous life included fulfilling work, three children, two husbands, many lovers and an international network of friends and colleagues. She was charismatic and sometimes quixotic, but she never abandoned her focus on women's freedom and its larger implications for social justice (an inspiration that continues through Ellen Chesler's excellent biography, *Woman of Valor: Margaret Sanger and the Birth Control Movement in America*). Indeed, she lived as if she and everyone else had the right to control her or his own life. By word and deed, she pioneered the most radical, humane and transforming political movement of the century.

Gloria Steinem is a co-founder of Ms. *magazine and author of* Revolution from Within

Alcohol in American History

National binges have alternated with enforced abstinence for 200 years, but there may be hope for moderation

David F. Musto

David F. Musto, a professor of child psychiatry and history of medicine at Yale University, has studied attitudes toward alcohol and other drugs since the 1960s. He received a B.A. in classical languages from the University of Washington in 1956, an M.A. in the history of science and medicine from Yale in 1961, and an M.D. from Washington in 1963. He has been a member of the alcohol policy panel of the National Academy of Sciences and the Connecticut Drug and Alcohol Commission. Musto spent his medical internship at the Pennsylvania Hospital in Philadelphia, where the pioneering temperance author Benjamin Rush was an attending physician in the late 18th century.

The young American ship of state floated on a sea of distilled spirits. In the period immediately after the American Revolution, a generally favorable view of alcoholic beverages coincided with rising levels of consumption that far exceeded any in modern times. By the early decades of the 19th century, Americans drank roughly three times as much alcohol as they do in the 1990s.

The country also had its abstemious side. Even as consumption of alcohol was reaching unprecedented levels, an awareness of the dangers of drink began to emerge, and the first American temperance movement took hold. At its peak in 1855, 13 of 40 states and territories had

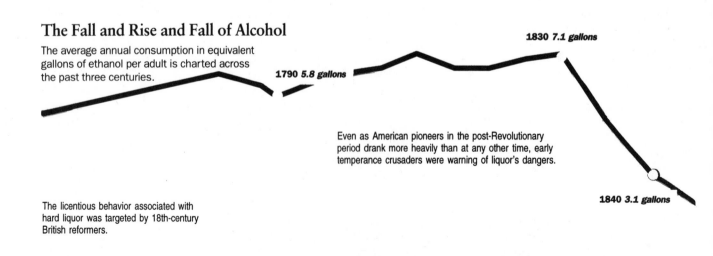

The Fall and Rise and Fall of Alcohol

The average annual consumption in equivalent gallons of ethanol per adult is charted across the past three centuries.

1790 *5.8 gallons*

1830 *7.1 gallons*

1840 *3.1 gallons*

Even as American pioneers in the post-Revolutionary period drank more heavily than at any other time, early temperance crusaders were warning of liquor's dangers.

The licentious behavior associated with hard liquor was targeted by 18th-century British reformers.

1700　　　　　　　　　　　　　1800

London Gin Epidemic, 1710–1750　　*Revolutionary War, 1775–1783*　　*War of 1812*　　*Opening of Erie Canal, 1825*

adopted legal prohibition. By the 1870s, public opinion had turned back, and liquor was flowing freely again; then, around the turn of the century, a movement for abstinence gained steam, culminating in the 13-year experiment of Prohibition that began in 1920.

Over the history of the U.S., popular attitudes and legal responses to the consumption of alcohol and other mood-altering substances have oscillated from toleration to a peak of disapproval and back again in cycles roughly 70 years long. Although other nations appear to have embraced the virtues of moderation, the U.S. continues to swing slowly back and forth between extremes.

The length of these trends may explain why most people are unaware of our repetitive history. Few contemporary Americans concerned about the abuse of illegal drugs, for example, know that opiate use was also a burning issue in the first decades of the 20th century, just as few of today's nutrition and exercise enthusiasts know about their health-minded predecessors from the same period. Furthermore, a phenomenon analogous to political correctness seems to control discourse on alcohol and other "vices"; when drinking is on the rise and most believe that liquor poses little risk to life and health, temperance advocates are derided as ignorant and puritanical;

in the end stage of a temperance movement, brewers, distillers, sellers and drinkers all come under harsh attack. Citizens may come of age with little knowledge of the contrary experiences of their forebears. Even rigorous studies that contradict current wisdom may be ignored—data showing both the damaging and beneficial effects of alcohol appear equally susceptible to suppression, depending on the era.

It now appears that a third era of temperance is under way in the U.S. Alcohol consumption peaked around 1980 and has since fallen by about 15 percent. The biggest drop has been in distilled spirits, but wine use has also waned. Beer sales have fallen less, but nonalcoholic brews—replicas of Prohibition's "near beer"—have been rising in popularity.

The shift in attitude is apparent in the cyclic movement of the legal drinking age. In 1971 the 26th Amendment to the Constitution—the most rapidly ratified in the nation's history—lowered the voting age to 18. Soon after, many state legislatures lowered the drinking age to conform to the voting age. Around 1980, however, states started rolling back the drinking age to 21. Surprisingly, the action was praised even among the 18- to 20-year-olds it affected. In 1984 the U.S. government, which cannot itself

mandate a national drinking age, threatened to withhold federal highway funds from any state or territory that did not raise its drinking age to 21. Within a short time every state and the District of Columbia were in compliance. Puerto Rico has been the only holdout.

ALCOHOL, DRIVING AND YOUTH

Drunk driving is the most recent catalyst for public activism against alcohol abuse. At the end of the 1970s, two groups appeared with the goal of combating alcohol-related accidents: Remove Intoxicated Drivers (RID) on the East Coast and Mothers Against Drunk Driving (MADD) in California. Both groups attacked weak drunk-driving laws and judicial laxness, especially in cases where drivers may have been repeatedly arrested for drunk driving—including some who had killed others in crashes—but never imprisoned.

Across the nation RID and MADD have strengthened the drunk-driving laws. Although sometimes at odds with each other, both have successfully lobbied for laws reducing the legal threshold of intoxication, increasing the likelihood of incarceration and suspending drivers' licenses without a hearing if

Women were at the forefront of the second wave of antialcohol movements. The issue helped to legitimize their participation in political life, because alcohol abuse impinged on the family sphere to which women had been relegated.

Beverage manufacturers, especially brewers, tried to fight back against temperance movements by portraying their product as a healthy part of the national culture.

1860 *2.1 gallons*

1890 *2.1 gallons*

1850

1880

Maine temperance law, 1851   Civil War, 1861–1865   WCTU founded, 1874 their blood alcohol levels exceed a state's legal limit, typically about 0.1 percent.

In 1981 Students Against Driving Drunk (SADD) was established to improve the safety of high school students. The group promotes a contract between parents and their children in which the children agree to call for transportation if they have been drinking, and the parents agree to provide it. As a result, however, RID and MADD have accused SADD of sanctioning youthful drinking rather than trying to eliminate it.

Political action has reinforced the prevailing public beliefs. In 1988 Congress set up the Office of Substance Abuse Prevention (OSAP) under the auspices of the Department of Health and Human Services. The OSAP provided what it called "editorial guidelines" to encourage media to adopt new ways of describing drug and alcohol use. Instead of referring to "responsible use" of alcohol, for example, the office suggested that newspapers and magazines should speak simply of "use, since there is a risk associated with all use." This language suggests that there is no safe threshold of consumption—a view also espoused by the American Temperance Society in the 1840s and the Anti-Saloon League early in this century. The OSAP also evaluated information on al-

cohol and drugs intended for distribution to schools and communities. It asserted that "materials recommending a designated driver should be rated unacceptable. They encourage heavy alcohol use by implying it is okay to drink to intoxication as long as you don't drive."

Another example of changing attitudes is the history of beliefs about alcohol's effects on fetal development. In the early 1930s, after Prohibition had ended, Charles R. Stockard of Cornell University, a leading authority on embryology, published animal studies that suggested minimal effects on fetal development. At about the same time, Harold T. Hyman of the Columbia University College of Physicians and Surgeons reviewed human experiments and found that "the habitual use of alcohol in moderate amounts by the normal human adult appears to be without any permanent organic effect deleterious in character."

FETAL ALCOHOL SYNDROME

Then, in the 1970s, researchers at the University of Washington described what they called fetal alcohol syndrome, a set of physical and mental abnormalities in children born to women who im-

bibed during pregnancy. At first, the syndrome appeared to require very heavy consumption, but after further investigation these researchers have come to assert that even a tiny amount of alcohol can cause the disorder. Drinks consumed at the earliest stage of embryonic development, when a woman may have no idea that she is pregnant, can be a particularly potent teratogen. Since 1989, all alcoholic beverages must bear a warning label for pregnant women from the U.S. Surgeon General's office.

Societal reaction to these findings has resulted in strong condemnation of women who drink any alcohol at all while pregnant. In a celebrated Seattle case in 1991, a woman nine months and a couple of weeks pregnant (who had abstained from alcohol during that time) decided to have a drink with her meal in a restaurant. Most embryologists agree that a single drink at such a late stage of pregnancy produces minimal risk. The waiters, however, repeatedly cautioned her against it; she became angry; the waiters lost their jobs. When the story became known, letters appeared in a local newspaper questioning her fitness as a mother. One University of Washington embryology expert even suggested that pregnant women should no longer be served alcohol in public.

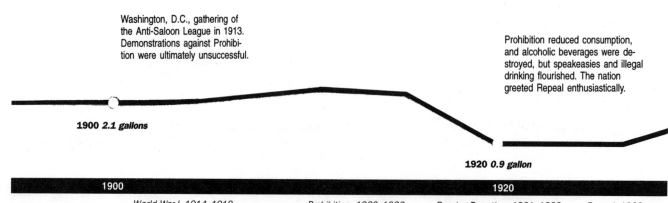

Washington, D.C., gathering of the Anti-Saloon League in 1913. Demonstrations against Prohibition were ultimately unsuccessful.

Prohibition reduced consumption, and alcoholic beverages were destroyed, but speakeasies and illegal drinking flourished. The nation greeted Repeal enthusiastically.

1900 *2.1 gallons*

1920 *0.9 gallon*

1900

1920

World War I, 1914–1918   *Prohibition, 1920–1933*   *Roaring Twenties, 1921–1929*   *Repeal, 1933*

The current worry over the effect of small amounts of alcohol during pregnancy is particularly interesting because belief in alcohol's ability to damage the fetus is a hallmark of American temperance movements in this and the past century. Indeed, as far back as 1726, during the English "gin epidemic," the College of Physicians of London issued a formal warning that parents drinking spirits were committing "a great and growing evil which was, too often, a cause of weak, feeble, and distempered children." There is little question that fetal alcohol syndrome is a real phenomenon, but the explosion in diagnosed cases in conjunction with changing social attitudes merits closer scrutiny.

THE FIRST TEMPERANCE MOVEMENT

Like today's antialcohol movement, earlier campaigns started with temperance and only later began pushing abstinence. In 1785 Benjamin Rush of Philadelphia, celebrated physician and inveterate reformer, became America's most prominent advocate of limited alcohol use. Tens of thousands of copies of his booklet, *An Inquiry into the Effects of Ardent Spirits upon the Human Mind and Body,* were distributed throughout the young nation. Like many of his compatriots, Rush censured spirits while accepting the beneficent effects of milder beverages. His "moral thermometer" introduced a striking visual tool to illustrate the graduated effects of beer and wine (health and wealth) and spirits (intemperance, vice and disease). When reformers "took the pledge" in the early years of the 19th century, it was a pledge to abstain from distilled spirits, not all alcoholic beverages.

The same kind of distinction had been made almost a century earlier in England, during an antispirits crusade in response to the gin epidemic. Rapidly increasing consumption of cheap distilled spirits swamped London during the first half of the 18th century. Gin was blamed for a dramatic rise in deaths and a falling birth rate. William Hogarth's powerful prints *Gin Lane* and *Beer Street* were designed to contrast the desolation caused by gin with the healthy prosperity enjoyed by beer drinkers. Despite the exhortations of Rush and others, until the 1830s most Americans believed that strong alcoholic drinks imparted vitality and health, easing hard work, warding off fevers and other illnesses, and relieving colds and snakebite. Soldiers and sailors took a daily ration of rum, and whiskey had a ceremonial role for marking any social event from a family gathering to an ordination. Even as concern grew, so did the distilling business. Annual consumption peaked around 1830 at an estimated 7.1 gallons of alcohol per adult.

TOTAL ABSTENTION

The creation of the Massachusetts Society for the Suppression of Intemperance in 1812 heralded the first organized antidrinking crusade on a state level. Through the inspiration and determination of one of the most dynamic writers and speakers of the century, the Reverend Lyman Beecher, the tide began to turn in earnest. That same year the annual meeting of the Connecticut Congregational Church received a report on the enormous rise in drinking and concluded, regretfully, that nothing could be done about it. An outraged Beecher demanded that a new report be written, then produced one himself overnight. He called for a crusade against alcohol. In 1826 Beecher limned the specifics of his argument in his epochal *Six Sermons on Intemperance.*

Beecher's words swept hundreds of thousands into America's first temperance movement. One of his signal contributions was to throw out compromise—how can

First Lady Betty Ford was later a founder of alcohol and drug clinics.

Victims Wall put up by Mothers Against Drunk Driving in Washington, D.C., in 1990 displayed photographs of people who died in alcohol-related crashes.

Soldiers, dry during the first world war, drank during the second.

1980 *2.76 gallons*

1940 *1.56 gallons*

| 1940 | 1990 |

World War II, 1939–1945   MADD founded, 1980   Federal support for age 21 drinking law, 1984   Warning labels on alcoholic beverages, 1989 you compromise with a poison? He extended the condemnation of spirits to all alcohol-containing beverages and denounced "prudent use."

"It is not enough," Beecher declaimed, "to erect the flag ahead, to mark the spot where the drunkard dies. It must be planted at the entrance of his course, proclaiming in waving capitals—THIS IS THE WAY TO DEATH!!" Beecher's argument that abstinence is the inevitable final stage of temperance gradually won dominance. In 1836 the American Temperance Society (founded in 1826) officially changed its definition of temperance to abstinence.

Not until 1851 did Maine pass its groundbreaking prohibition law but after that, things moved quickly. By 1855 about a third of Americans lived under democratically achieved laws that prohibited the sale of alcohol. Alcohol consumption fell to less than a third of its pretemperance level and has never again reached the heights of the early republic.

THE WOMAN'S CRUSADE

As the first temperance movement was reaching its peak, another moral debate claimed national attention: slavery. Proabstinence forces began to lose their political strength, especially during the Civil War, when the federal government raised money by means of an excise tax on liquor. Starting in the 1860s, some states repealed their prohibitions, courts in others found the statutes unconstitutional, and prohibition laws in yet other states and territories fell into disuse.

Nevertheless, important antialcohol events continued. The most dramatic, the Woman's Crusade, began in Ohio in 1873. Large groups gathered and employed hymn singing and prayers to sway onlookers against saloons. Out of this movement evolved the Women's Christian Temperance Union (WCTU). Although it is now associated only with prohibition in the popular mind, during the union's prime it pushed for far broader reforms: its platform included equal legal rights for women, the right of women to vote, the institution of kindergartens and an attack on tobacco smoking.

Opposition to alcohol legitimized women's participation in national political life. Because women had been relegated to defense of the home, they could reasonably argue that they had a duty to oppose alcohol and saloons—which were efficiently separating men from their paychecks and turning them into drunken menaces to their families.

In each era of reform, people have tried to influence the education of children and to portray alcohol in a new, presumably more correct light. Today the federal Center for Substance Abuse Prevention (CSAP, the successor to the OSAP) works through prevention materials distributed to schools, but the champion of early efforts was the WCTU's Department of Scientific Temperance Instruction. It successfully fought for mandatory temperance lessons in the public schools and oversaw the writing of approved texts. Pupils would learn, among other things, that "the majority of beer drinkers die of dropsy"; "when alcohol passes down the throat it burns off the skin, leaving it bare and burning"; and "alcohol clogs the brain and turns the liver quickly from yellow to green to black."

The WCTU's multifarious agenda hampered its effectiveness, though, and in 1895 national leadership of the antialcohol movement was seized by the

Down the Memory Hole

Deeply held attitudes can rewrite popular history. An 1848 lithograph of George Washington saying farewell to his officers shows the father of his country drinking a toast with his compatriots. In the 1876 edition the wineglasses and bottle are gone. If teetotalism was the only moral lifestyle, Washington could not possibly be a drinker.

Indeed, late in the first temperance movement, the American Tract Society "reprinted" Philadelphia physician Benjamin Rush's essay against distilled spirits but abruptly truncated the text before his praise of wine and beer. On the other side, many people today may find it more comfortable to remember First Lady Eleanor Roosevelt, for example, as a compassionate social reformer than as an ardent supporter of Prohibition.

N. CURRIER (LEFT) and CURRIER & IVES (RIGHT), *MUSEUM OF THE CITY OF NEW YORK*

Anti-Saloon League, which went on to become the most successful single-issue group in American history. At first, the new organization had as its ostensible goal only abolition of the saloon, a social cesspool that had already elicited wide public outcry. As sentiment against alcohol escalated, however, so did the league's intentions, and finally it aimed at national prohibition.

In 1917, aided by a more general national push for health and fitness, what would become the 18th Amendment passed in both houses of Congress by a two-thirds majority. Two years later it became part of the Constitution, coming into effect in January 1920. In the span of one generation, antialcohol campaigns had reached a point where prohibition seemed reasonable to a political majority of Americans. Although brewers and vintners had attempted to portray their products as wholesome, they could not escape the rising tide against intoxicating beverages of any kind.

The first temperance movement had rallied a broad segment of society alarmed at excessive drinking of spirits; only later did the concern move to alcohol in general. Similarly, this second temperance movement initially focused on that widely criticized feature of urban life, the saloon, and then gradually took aim at all drinking.

THE GREAT EXPERIMENT

Prohibition lasted almost 14 years. On the positive side, the incidence of liver cirrhosis reached an all-time low: the death rate from the condition fell to half its 1907 peak and did not start to increase again until the amendment was repealed. On the negative side, Prohibition was a blatant failure at permanently convincing a large majority of Americans that alcohol was intrinsically de-

structive, and it made a significant contribution to the growth of already entrenched criminal organizations. These factors—combined after 1929 with the specious hope that revival of the alcoholic beverage industry would help lift the nation out of the Great Depression—all brought about the overwhelming national rejection of Prohibition in 1933.

As we look at the ways in which the U.S. has addressed issues related to alcohol, we might ask whether prohibition is the inevitable—if brief—culmination of temperance movements. Is our Puritan tradition of uncompromising moral stances still supplying righteous energy to the battle against alcohol? During the 1920s, when many nations of the Western world turned against alcohol, a sustained campaign in the Netherlands led by the workers' movement and religious groups reduced alcohol consumption by 1930 to a very low level, but without legal prohibition. Likewise in Britain: the antialcohol movement reduced consumption even though it did not result in legal bans. Apparently, each nation has its own style of control.

Underlying the U.S. travail with alcohol is the persistence of a sharp dichotomy in the way we perceive it: alcohol is either very good or very bad. Those who oppose alcohol doubt that it might have any value in the diet; those who support it deny any positive effect of prohibition. Compromise seems unthinkable for either side.

Dealing with alcohol on a practical level while maintaining either a totally favorable or totally condemnatory attitude is fraught with trouble. The backlash to Prohibition made discussion of the ill effects associated with alcohol extremely difficult, because those worried about drinking problems would often be labeled as straitlaced prudes. Not until another 50 years had passed and new generations had emerged did grass-roots

movements such as RID and MADD arise and, without apology, promote new laws against drinking. Yet public acceptance of such restrictions on alcohol consumption has a natural limit that can be exceeded only with great danger to the temperance movement itself: that is the lesson of Prohibition.

During the past 15 years, groups such as RID, MADD and the CSAP, aided by advances in medical understanding, have been transforming the image of alcohol into a somber picture heretofore unknown to the current cohort of Americans. This reframing may bring about a healthy rebalancing of our perception of alcohol. But how far will this trend go?

Can we find a stance toward drink that will be workable in the long term? Or will we again achieve an extreme but unsustainable position that will create a lengthy, destructive backlash? There are some signs of moderation—in particular, recent pronouncements by the U.S. Department of Agriculture that it should be considered permissible for men and women to consume a glass of wine a day to reduce their risk of heart disease—but it is still unclear whether the U.S. will be able to apply history's lessons.

FURTHER READING

DELIVER US FROM EVIL: AN INTERPRETATION OF AMERICAN PROHIBITION. Norman H. Clark. W. W. Norton and Company, 1976.

THE ALCOHOLIC REPUBLIC: AN AMERICAN TRADITION. W. J. Rorabaugh. Oxford University Press, 1979.

TEMPERANCE AND PROHIBITION IN AMERICA: A HISTORICAL OVERVIEW. Paul Aaron and David Musto in *Alcohol and Public Policy: Beyond the Shadow of Prohibition.* Edited by M. Moore and D. Gerstein. National Academy Press, 1981.

DRINKING IN AMERICA: A HISTORY. Mark E. Lender and James K. Martin. Free Press, 1987.

THE TURNING POINT: REPEALING PROHIBITION, Chapter 2. DRINKING, Chapter 3. In *Bad Habits,* by John Burnham. New York University Press, 1993.

F. Scott Fitzgerald

By Edward Oxford *Dashing, brilliant, and self-destructive, author F. Scott Fitzgerald led a life that epitomized the Jazz Age that he wrote about in his acclaimed novels and short stories.*

I remember riding in a taxi one afternoon between very tall buildings under a mauve and rosy sky." F. Scott Fitzgerald wrote of his first days in New York City. "I began to bawl because I had everything I wanted and knew I would never be so happy again."

It was the 1920s—the Jazz Age—a time that F. Scott Fitzgerald would celebrate, try to capture in his writings, and eventually come to symbolize. Like the "Roaring Twenties" themselves—which started with high expectations following the Great War but which ended with the stock market crash of 1929—Fitzgerald found success, along with a desperate struggle to sustain it. He impressed the nation with his ability to convey the image and the energy of this razzle-dazzle era, only to become an ironic witness to the age's—and his own—demise.

Self-absorbed, alcoholic, still questing, the flamboyant Scott, who wrote so tellingly of the "sad young men" of the days that followed World War I, died in 1940 at the age of 44, as new war clouds gathered over the world. Often characterized as the drunken writer, ruined novelist, or spoiled genius, this quicksilver personality was to become, through his sometimes superb fiction, an unforgettable figure in American letters—one of the most colorful, important, and cherished American authors of the twentieth century.

Francis Scott Key Fitzgerald was born on September 24, 1896, in his parents' rented apartment on the fringe of a well-to-do neighborhood in St. Paul, Minnesota. Named for the author of the "Star Spangled Banner," a distant relative of his father's, Scott, as he was known, fantasized as a youngster that he was of royal lineage. It seemed fitting, in his view of himself, that he should be blessed with wealth, and his life graced with ease. Destiny however, did not deem him quite so deserving.

Fortunate to be accepted into Princeton University's class of 1917, Fitzgerald was not at all a scholar's scholar; rather, he was more a collegian's collegian. "He thrilled to the poetry of Princeton," biographer Andrew Turnbull noted, "to the colorful crowds at the football games, to the snatches of song drifting across the campus, to the mellow lamplight back of Nassau Hall. . . ."

Fitzgerald both found and lost himself at Princeton. He became something of a *littérateur,* writing pieces for the university's literary magazine and frothy lyrics for Triangle Club musicals. But the more he pursued campus glory the more his studies suffered. Once, when a professor threatened to fail him, Fitzgerald retorted: "Sir, you can't do that, I'm a writer!"

By his junior year, a chastened Fitzgerald was required to withdraw from the university "for scholastic deficiencies." Although he returned to the school in September 1916, he had to accept the bitter realization that there would be "no badges of pride, no medals after all." Even so, he would ever revere Princeton as a place "that preserves so much of what is fair, gracious, charming and honorable in American life."

With the outbreak of World War I, Fitzgerald pictured himself a war hero and planned to volunteer for service. Since admission to officers' training required that he be 21 years of age, he remained at Princeton until his birthday in 1917, then earned a commission as a second lieutenant in the United States Army.

But just as studies interfered with his writing interests at Princeton, so marches and drills got in the way of the novel he was trying to write—a book about "my generation in America"—while in the army. Convinced that he would not live through the war should he make it into combat, he ground out chapters in the officers' club, then completed the manuscript during a furlough spent at Princeton. Entitled *The Romantic Egotist,* Fitzgerald's first novel impressed the editor of Charles Scribner's Sons publishers, but was politely turned down.

While stationed near Montgomery, Alabama, Lieutenant Fitzgerald met Zelda Sayre at a country club dance on a "firefly evening" in the summer of 1918. Vivacious, provocative, and unpredictable, Zelda was, as she put it, a *femme fatale* "without a single feeling of inferiority or shyness, or doubt." Scott, who was unaware of the history of mental instability in her mother's family, found Zelda mesmerizing.

The more Scott pursued Zelda, the less certain she seemed about the prospect of marrying him. When he left the

From *American History,* December 1996, pp. 44-49, 63. © 1996 by Cowles Magazine, Inc. Reprinted through the courtesy of Cowles Magazines, publishers of *American History.*

army never having found the glory he had aspired to on the battlefield, she demurred "because he had no money and could make no money." In a letter, Zelda advised him: "I'd just hate to live a sordid, colorless existence, because you'd soon love me less and less."

Fitzgerald determined to win Zelda by writing a successful novel. Retreating to a room at his parents' home, he bore down, reshaped the novel he had written while in uniform, and produced *This Side of Paradise,* a book that captured the postwar disillusionment of his generation. The work's hero, the thinly disguised author himself, dreamed youthful dreams in the never-never land of campus life. He was part of a generation "grown-up to find all Gods dead, all wars fought, and all faiths in man shaken." Scribner's published *This Side of Paradise* in March 1920, selling out the first run within 24 hours. "A Novel About Flappers for Philosophers," as Scott's own ad-line read, it ushered in the "Jazz Age" and heralded the arrival of a 23-year-old star upon the American literary scene.

A week after *This Side of Paradise* appeared, Zelda and Scott were married. America had set out upon "the gaudiest spree in history" and a glittering future beckoned. There, on the garish stage-center of New York, the golden couple basked in the bright light of acclaim. Like aristocratic bohemians, Scott and Zelda drank, went to parties, and made the gossip columns. They tried to outdo one another in their zaniness—Scott tore his shirt off in a theater, Zelda rode on the hood of a taxi; he jumped into one public fountain, she into another.

"They complemented each other like gin and vermouth in a martini," wrote one chronicler. Erratic, self-admiring, and often inebriated, they came to personify the times. They lived to seek out "useless pleasure-giving pursuits." The Fitzgeralds interupted their free-wheeling lifestyle, however, in the fall of 1921, to prepare for the arrival of a baby. Amidst the relative tranquility of St. Paul, their daughter, Frances Scott Fitzgerald, was born on October 26, 1921.

"Scottie" was a pretty, bright girl, and her father delighted in teaching her

all sorts of new things. Zelda, though somewhat indifferent to the chores of motherhood, sincerely enjoyed spending time with her daughter. Scott proved to be a strict parent and later recalled that he brought Scottie up "hard as nails." He provided her with a first-rate education, and she became strong and independent minded at an early age. Given her parents' lifestyle however, Scottie as a youngster, spent much time with nannies and friends of her parents.

"Parties are a form of suicide," Fitzgerald said, yet he and Zelda could not get enough of them. The couple's antics caused them to resemble, said one friend, "the Marx Brothers at a cotillion." Their drinking became so bad that a friend commented: "God knows where the two of them are going to end up."

Out of such turmoil came Fitzgerald's *The Beautiful and Damned.* Published in March 1922, the novel etched the decline and fall of a vain young couple from the privileged life of the beautiful to the degradation of the damned. It vividly reflected the downward drift of Scott and Zelda's own lives. As one epigrammatic line put it: "The victor belongs to the spoils."

That autumn, they settled in Great Neck, on Long Island's north-shore "Gold Coast." Scott and Zelda cavorted back and forth between parties in Great Neck and in Manhattan in his second-hand Rolls-Royce. Against the backdrop of the grand estates, the glittering couple of American letters became tireless, if tedious, court-jesters. At *soirées* the incorrigible Scott would crawl under tables, hack off his tie with a kitchen knife, or try to eat soup with a fork. He and Zelda blithely drove his car into a pond. It was all, in Fitzgerald's words, "Very alcoholic and chaotic."

Moving to the French Riviera in 1924 to get away from the chaos—and themselves—the couple stayed clear of drink while Scott toiled at what was to become a masterpiece: *The Great Gatsby.* Zelda, meanwhile, had a romantic dalliance with a French aviator. Although the Fitzgeralds' marriage weathered that interlude, it never again was the same.

Fitzgerald's next novel—*Tender Is the Night*—did not come easily. Starting

work in 1925, he labored over the draft in starts-and-stops for nine years. During that time, life for the no-longer-shimmering couple turned into a running "cat-and-dog" fight. Zelda complained that Scott was "constantly drunk." Once, he bloodied her nose.

Perhaps in an effort to earn fame in her own right, Zelda turned to ballet, obsessively dancing in a vain attempt, especially given her age, to become a first-rate ballerina. Then, she began to show signs of falling apart, suffering dizzy spells, hearing strange noises, and sensing vibrations from people she met. While driving in Cannes, France, Zelda tried to veer her car off a cliff. Another time, she sprawled in front of a parked car and said, "Scott, drive over me." In a flower shop, she thought that the lilies were talking to her.

Soon after the 1929 Crash on Wall Street, Zelda experienced the first of three devastating mental breakdowns. As America reeled under the Depression, Fitzgerald lived in the somber shadow of Zelda's schizophrenia. She would endure a dozen stays—sometimes for weeks, sometimes months—in mental institutions in Europe and the United States. It became the view of psychiatrists that she could never again permanently take her place back "in the world."

Zelda's looks faded. Her face hardened, becoming wraith-like. "Isn't it terrible," she said to Scott, "When you have one little corner of your brain that needs fixing?" While in confinement, Zelda wrote *Save Me the Waltz,* an autobiographical novel in which she paraphrased their tempestuous marriage. Hallucinations, depression, mental anguish, suicide attemps—the dazed Zelda lived out the horror of it all.

At last, after 17 drafts, Scott completed *Tender Is the Night.* Finally published in April 1934, the poignant work reflected, through fictional alter-egos, Zelda's breakdown and Scott's own decline. The book intrigued some reviewers, but garnered only modest success. As the Depression deepened, Americans had become far more interested in the "havenots" than the "haves."

"Waste and horror," Fitzgerald wrote of his life, "what I might have been and

AN AMERICAN CLASSIC

The Great Gatsby, the best known and most enduringly popular of F. Scott Fitzgerald's novels, first appeared on April 10, 1925. An elegant, silkenly-woven, bittersweet tale of the well-to-do, of illusions, of love unrequited, the book has become an American classic.

Fitzgerald began planning the novel as early as 1922, telling Maxwell Perkins, his editor at Scribner's: "I want to write something new—something extraordinary and beautiful and simple and intricately patterned." A short story he wrote that year—*Winter Dreams*—about a poor boy's love for a rich girl, presaged the novel.

As with so many of his writings, Fitzgerald mirrored his own yearnings and lost hopes in *The Great Gatsby*. The brief, finely etched work tells of the self-made Jay Gatsby's foredoomed striving to recapture the love of Daisy Buchanan, an upper-class woman. The love-stricken Gatsby paid the price for living too long with a dream that could not be realized.

The novel reflected the Great Neck, Long Island, settings Fitzgerald knew while he and Zelda lived there from the fall of 1922 until the spring of 1924. His deft sketches of the "Gold Coast:"—the colossal mansions, languid women, blue lawns, crimson rooms, men in white flannel suits, crystal glasses, orchestras playing in the moonlight—would form vivid backgrounds for the tale's unfolding. And there, as though by fortune's hand, Fitzgerald met a shadowy bootlegger by the name of Max von Gerlach. Given to using the expression "old sport," it quite likely was Gerlach who provided the crucial prototype for the enigmatic Jay Gatsby.

Although he started working on the book in the summer of 1923 at Great Neck, Fitzgerald did most of the writing on the French Riviera from April 1924 to February 1925. At the time, he thought that "the whole basis of this novel was the loss of illusions that give such color to the world so that you don't care whether things are true or false as long as they partake of the magical glory."

At first, the impressionistic, nine-chapter novel found few readers. In its publication year of 1925, the book sold but 25,000 copies, earning a dismayed Fitzgerald barely enough to cover the advances he had drawn against it. Fifteen years later at the time of his death, copies from its second printing were still stacked in the publisher's warehouse. But in the 1940s, 17 new editions were published. During World War II, more than 150,000 copies were distributed to servicemen in an Armed Forces Edition. And since 1950, the book has been translated into 33 languages.

The Great Gatsby, turned into dramatic form by Owen Davis in 1926, had a Broadway run of 112 performances. That same year saw the silent movie version, with Warner Baxter as Gatsby and Lois Wilson as Daisy. A second film version, made in 1949, featured Alan Ladd and Betty Field. In 1974, a third starred Robert Redford and Mia Farrow. Along the way the Gatsby theme would inspire a 1958 television adaptation, a university musical, and even clothing and coiffure styles.

Professor Matthew J. Bruccoli, pre-eminent Fitzgerald biographer and scholar, states: "Much of the endurance of *The Great Gatsby* results from its investigation of the American Dream as Fitzgerald enlarged a Horatio Alger story into a meditation on the New World myth. He was profoundly moved by the innocence and generosity he perceived in American history—what he would refer to as 'a willingness of heart.' . . . The reverberating meanings of the fable have never been depleted."

---

done—that is lost, spent, gone, dissipated, unrecapturable." He drank, had sporadic affairs, and tried to hold onto his ebbing creative strength. He wrote in his notebook: "I left my capacity for hoping on the little roads that led to Zelda's sanitarium." Nonetheless, in his way, Scott continued to hold onto the memory of—and love for—the woman she had been.

By 1936, Fitzgerald's dreams were in ruins. His wife was mentally ill, his health was fading, and he was deeply in debt. He smoked heavily, ate poorly and, as ever, drank far too much. He used pills to put himself to sleep and to wake himself up. In *The Crack-Up*, a startling three-part magazine series, he stripped himself bare in print, announcing to the world that he was spiritually and artistically bankrupt. "There was not an 'I' anymore," he wrote.

Money, or Fitzgerald's inability to hang onto it, was a constant problem. In one year, for example, he earned $36,000—twenty times as much as the average American worker—yet was unable to sustain his lifestyle. He insisted on providing the best, most expensive care for Zelda, and an excellent private education for Scottie. He was forced to live off the proceeds from his short stories and the constant advances drawn against pieces yet to be written.

In mid-1937, Fitzgerald, owing thousands of dollars, made his third and last assault on the motion-picture citadel, heading to Hollywood as a highly-paid screenwriter. He had tried in the past to show the film studios a thing or two about scriptwriting, but displayed scant command of the movie medium. He toiled anew at a number of scripts, but still lacked the filmic touch, managing to earn but one screen credit, for *Three Comrades*. Director Billy Wilder said of Scott's efforts: "It was like asking a sculptor to be a plumber."

During his more than three years in Hollywood, columnist Sheilah Graham became his companion and lover. They lived a somewhat quiet life together, and he was sober most of the time. When he was drunk, however, he would rant and sometimes become violent.

In a final effort, Fitzgerald summoned enough power of will to begin another novel. In October 1939, his nerves frazzled and his heart burdened with a sense of sadness, he began work on *The Last Tycoon*. The book would build around the fictionalized figure of Monroe Stahr, based on the character of Irving Thalberg, an almost mythic Hollywood producer. Scott saw his protagonist as the last of the American heroes.

For more than a year, he followed his plot outline. In a letter to Zelda he said: "I am deep in the novel, living in it, and it makes me happy. . . ." By late fall 1940, Fitzgerald had written some 44,000 words, roughly two-thirds of the project that he had in mind. *The Last Tycoon,* however, was to remain an unfinished portrait.

"I was drunk for many years," Fitzgerald had once jotted prophetically in his notebook, "and then I died." The end for the once-luminous literary figure came quietly, as if an afterthought to so garish, erratic, and self-defeating a life. He simply fell to the floor while reading the *Princeton Alumni Weekly* on the afternoon of December 21, 1940. Struck by a massive heart attack, F. Scott Fitzgerald was dead at the relatively young age of 44.

The world took small note of his passing. His daughter Scottie, now a 19-year old student at Vassar College, and twenty or so friends attended his funeral service in Rockville, Maryland, the town where Fitzgerald's ancestors were buried. Zelda was not well enough to take part, and Sheilah Graham, for the sake of propriety, absented herself.

In the years following her husband's death, Zelda lived with her mother in Montgomery, Alabama, and occasionally spent time with Scottie, who had since married and moved to New York. In times of travail, she would return to a mental hospital in Asheville, North Carolina. As time passed, Zelda became fervently religious. To a friend she wrote: "To be rejected of God is to be prey of the Devil."

At about midnight on March 10, 1948, fire broke out in the main hospital building where Zelda was sleeping, trapping and killing nine women on the top floor. Zelda was one of them. She was buried alongside her husband in Rockville.

F. Scott Fitzgerald had reason to believe that he had outlived his success. At the time he died, his books were not selling well. Since his death, however, more than ten million copies of his novels have been sold, *The Great Gatsby* being the most popular among them.

Of Fitzgerald, author John O'Hara once declared: "All he was was our best novelist, one of our best novella-ists, and one of our finest writers of short stories." In critical circles, Fitzgerald's place is considered secure, along with Ernest Hemingway and William Faulkner, as one of the "Big Three" American authors of the first half of the twentieth century.

His brief life, glittering and raucous, was a tragic one. A legend in his own time, living at the edge of delight, Fitzgerald wrote eloquently of soul-weary young men and beautiful women in quest of their fantasies. And he and Zelda came to symbolize the glamour—and the heartbreak—of self-indulgence.

New York-based writer Edward Oxford is a frequent contributor to American History.

When White Hoods Were in Flower

Bernard A. Weisberger

This month's historical reflections are inspired by the presidential candidacy of David Duke, a former Imperial Wizard of the Ku Klux Klan, whose elevation to at least marginal respectability reminds me uncomfortably of a time when the Klan was functioning openly and above-ground and was a very palpable force in American politics.

The "original" Knights of the Ku Klux Klan, the "invisible empire" of hooded nightriders immortalized in *The Birth of a Nation* and *Gone with the Wind,* got its start in 1866 in the defeated former Confederacy. Whatever its exact origins, its purpose soon became to drive freed blacks and their Northern allies away from the polling places and back into a state of economic and political subservience. It "persuaded" by fires, floggings, and lynchings. Forget the romantic mush; it was an outlawed terrorist organization, designed to undo Reconstruction. And with its help, Reconstruction was undone. But so, by 1872, was the Klan. However, in 1915 it underwent a second ten- to fifteen-year incarnation, of which more in a moment. That is the main story here.

During the 1950s a third, "new" Klan—or perhaps several successive new Klans—emerged, in reaction to the legal dismantling of Jim Crow, sometimes called the Second Reconstruction. Like the original KKK, the groups functioned in the South, and they were responsible for bombings and the gunshot murders of at least five civil rights workers. Post-1970 Klans have had a large, changing, Cold War–influenced list of enemies, allies, and strategies. All have led a furtive existence under legal surveillance and almost universal repudiation.

But it wasn't so with that "middle" Klan that lived in the atmosphere of World War I and the 1920s. That one targeted Catholics, Jews, and foreigners as well as blacks. In so doing, it expanded its base beyond Dixie and had more national influence than is pleasant to think about.

The evidence? How about a parade of forty thousand robed and proud-of-it Klansmen down Pennsylvania Avenue in Washington, D.C.? Or a state—Indiana—whose KKK "Grand Dragon" held a political IOU—one of many—from the mayor of Indianapolis promising to appoint no person to the Board of Public Works without his endorsement? Or a Democratic National Convention of 1924 that split down the middle of a vote to condemn the Klan by name, with just over half the delegates refusing?

This new Klan was the creation of Alabama-born "Colonel" William J. Simmons, who resuscitated fading memories of the original Knights in a Thanksgiving Day cross-burning ceremony atop Stone Mountain, Georgia, in 1915. Its credo not only pledged members to be "true to the faithful maintenance of White Supremacy" but restricted the membership to "native born American citizens who believe in the tenets of the Christian religion and owe no allegiance . . . to any foreign Government, nation, political institution, sect, people or person." The "person" was the Pope, and the new KKK tapped into a long-standing tradition of nativism that went back at least as far as the American or Know-Nothing party of the 1850s, which flared transiently in the cloudy political skies just before the Civil War.

Simmons kept and improved on the primal Klan's ritual mumbo jumbo, including secret initiations and an array of officeholders with titles like Imperial Wizard, Exalted Cyclopes, and Grand Goblin. He struck an alliance with a publicist named Edward Clarke who helped devise a deft recruiting scheme. Recruiters called Kleagles signed up members for local chapters (Klaverns) at ten dollars a head. The Kleagle kept four dollars; one dollar went to the state's King Kleagle, fifty cents to the Grand Goblin, and so on up the chain of command, with two dollars to Simmons himself.

For many native-born, white, Gentile Americans, joiners by nature, the new Klan became a special lodge, like the Elks, the Rotarians, or Woodmen of the World, for which Simmons had been a field organizer. There were four million Klansmen by 1924, according to some estimates, in a population that turned out only about thirty million voters in that year's presidential election. So it became prudent for some politicians, President Harding included, to join the KKK or at least seek its support. According to Wyn C. Wade, author of *The Fiery Cross,* one of the latest books on the Klan, the number of municipal officials elected nationwide by Klan votes has yet to be counted. The organization likewise had input in the choice of more than a dozen senators and eleven governors.

The Klan's greatest victories were in Indiana, whose Grand Dragon, purple-robed David C. Stephenson, was a gifted publicist who organized a women's auxiliary and staged barbecues and picnics, which he visited by dropping from the sky in an airplane with gilded wings. He made enough on the regalia and literature concessions to live in princely style, with lots of clandestine booze and women available. And he endorsed a slate of state candidates that swept Indiana's Republican Convention in 1924 and followed Calvin Coolidge to victory in the fall. Stephenson's dreams of the future for himself included a Senate seat and perhaps even the White House.

What made these astonishing successes possible? Was the whole country gripped by a fever of hatred? Yes and no. Racism and xenophobia actually were enjoying a favorable climate. The KKK's rebirth in 1915 coincided with the success of *The Birth of a Nation,* which depicted the original Klan as a necessity to save Southern civilization from barbaric blacks egged on by Radical Republican plunderers. This was not much of an exaggeration of the "official" version of Reconstruction then embalmed in scholarly histories, but D. W. Griffith's cinematic skills burned it into the popular mind.

At the same time, a wave of immigration from Southern and Eastern Europe troubled "old stock" American. In 1924 the immigration laws were rewritten specifically to keep out such indigestible Catholic and Jewish hordes, as they were considered.

Then there was the experience of World War I, in which "100 percent Americanism" was enforced by vigilante groups and by the government, armed with Espionage and Sedition acts. Following that, the Bolshevik Revolution inaugurated a Red scare that brought a frantic search for "agitators" to arrest or deport.

All these forces predisposed potential Klan members to accept its exclusionary message without much analysis—and to overlook incidents of violence. But there was more. Thousands of fundamentalist Christians, beleaguered and bewildered by the Progressive Era victories of evolution and the social gospel—not to mention jazz, gin, and short skirts—saw the Klan as the savior of oldtime religion. The KKK played to their anxiety by supporting Prohibition and the teaching of religion in the schools. Had the Moral Majority then been in existence, it might have absorbed some who instead became Klan followers.

In the 1920s the KKK expanded its base beyond Dixie and had far more national influence than is pleasant to think about.

It was the onrush of change, the shakeups brought by radio and film and the auto, that spooked so many Americans. My friend David Chalmers, author of *Hooded Americanism,* put it neatly to me by phone. "They couldn't blame Henry Ford or Charles Steinmetz [the socialist engineering genius of the General Electric Company], but happily they found 'the dago on the Tiber' " instead.

But change could not be held back for long. In the mid-twenties the Klan's strength dropped off dramatically, to forty-five thousand by 1930. There were many reasons. One was internal feuding among Klan leaders over control of the organization's assets. Another was the exposure of Klan-led bombings, beatings, threats, and atrocities by courageous newspapers like the Indianapolis *Times,* the Memphis *Commercial Appeal,* and the Columbus (Georgia) *Enquirer-Sun.* They resisted boycotts and other forms of pressure in the heart of the enemy's country and told the truth. So did many courageous politicians who repudiated the votes of bigotry. Revelations that some Klan officials were given to liquor, loot, and lechery also defaced the "knightly" image. The biggest scandal of all sent Grand Dragon Stephenson to jail for the brutal rape of Madge Oberholtzer, a young state employee, who afterward committed suicide. Stephenson, outraged that the Indiana authorities did not set him above the law, avenged himself by squealing on his political puppets and ruining their subsequent careers.

And over time the second Klan was repudiated because it collided with the fundamental American values of inclusiveness and pluralism. The trouble is that it also expressed equally durable American attitudes: the ongoing quest for an unalloyed "Americanism," the perverse pressure to conform to a single majority standard, and the tendency to substitute mob "justice" for the unsatisfying ambiguities of legal verdicts.

It seems that current historians, unencumbered by having lived through the period's hostilities, are more inclined to explain than to condemn the Klan of the twenties. Most of its members, they suggest, were tradition-bound outsiders to the emerging new urban money culture, more frightened than vicious. I am unpersuaded, even while acknowledging that "good" people can join "bad" associations out of understandable frustrations. But the Klan could not be separated from its hateful implications then, and the Klan spirit cannot be so separated now, however prettified, sanitized, and shorn of wacky costumes and titles. Scapegoating of "the other," assurances that "we" must safeguard our system, our heritage, and our values from "them"—these notions inevitably carry implications of violence and repression.

Yet under certain conditions they can become widespread, unless watched and guarded against. As the evidence presented shows, it has happened. Here. And not so long ago.

Unit Selections

Key Points to Consider

❖ How had the financial situation in the United States grown so desperate that President Franklin Roosevelt declared a bank holiday? How well did his action stem the crisis?

❖ Based on the articles in this unit, discuss the character and personality of both Franklin and Eleanor Roosevelt.

❖ How did the United States government mobilize the economy for total war? What means were used to persuade Americans to support a war that was being fought thousands of miles away?

❖ Discuss the article on the use of atomic bombs against Japan. What alternatives did President Harry Truman believe were available? Do you agree or disagree with this choice? Why?

 **Links**   # www.dushkin.com/online/

These sites are annotated on pages 4 and 5.

By the end of the 1920s stock market prices had soared to unprecedented heights, but on October 24, 1929, the market crashed. "Black Thursday" set off an avalanche of selling as holders dumped their shares at whatever price they could get. Despite many efforts to shore up confidence, prices continued to go down in the months following.

President Herbert Hoover tried to restore confidence by assuring the public that the economy of America was sound and that there was no reason business should not go on as usual. But businessmen as well as stockholders were worried about the future. To protect themselves, they laid off workers, cut back on inventory, and put off previous plans to expand. But their actions had the collective result of making the situation worse.

Hoover endorsed more federal programs than had any of his predecessors, but they failed to stop the downward slide; Hoover became the most widely detested man in America. In the presidential election of 1932, the discredited Hoover lost by a landslide to Democratic candidate Franklin D. Roosevelt.

Unlike Hoover, Roosevelt was willing to act boldly and on a large scale. His "first 100 days" in office resulted in the passage of an unprecedented number of measures designed to promote recovery and to restore confidence. "Bang! Went the Doors of Every Bank in America," by James Chiles, describes the financial crisis that led to Roosevelt's proclamation of a bank "holiday" only 2 days after he assumed office. Gerald Parshall's "A Monumental Man" provides a portrait of Roosevelt the man: his appearance, his confidence, his ability to persuade.

Eleanor Roosevelt was America's most influential "first lady" with no close second. Her story is recounted in "Eleanor Roosevelt," by Doris Kearns Goodwin. Her marriage to Franklin was no love story, especially when she discovered that he was involved with another woman. Their marriage continued, but Eleanor began developing her own interests. She served as Roosevelt's "eyes and ears" and his conscience. They made an effective team: Franklin the pragmatic politician not overly concerned with moral issues, Eleanor the moral uplifter. Eleanor was wrong in saying "the story is over" when Franklin died, for her stature and influence actually increased in later years.

Roosevelt's "New Deal" mitigated the effects of the Depression but did not end it. That came with the onset of war in Europe and America's preparedness program. Roosevelt believed that the United States ought to cooperate with other nations to stop aggression, but he had to contend with a Congress and public that was deeply influenced by isolationists. After war broke out, Roosevelt took steps to transfer 50 overage destroyers to Great Britain and, later, he pushed through Congress a lend-lease program that provided aid for nations fighting the Axis (Germany, Italy, Japan). Alarmed at Japan's attempt to conquer China, Roosevelt tried to use economic pressure to get Japan to back off. His efforts only stiffened the will of Japanese hard-liners who planned and carried out the raid on Pearl Harbor on December 7, 1941.

Pearl Harbor and Germany's declaration of war against the United States united Americans in their determination to win the war. For the next 6 months, the Japanese ran rampant as they inflicted a string of defeats in the Pacific. The tide of Japanese expansion was halted during the summer of 1942 by the naval battles at the Coral Sea and at Midway. The United States launched its first offensive operations on Guadalcanal in the Solomon Islands. American military and industrial might eventually ensured Japan's ultimate defeat.

James Wensyel, in "Home Front," argues that the war was "fought and won on the assembly line as much as on the battle line." Gearing up to fight a total war, the United States mobilized its physical and human resources to produce a cascade of tanks, planes, guns, and other war equipment. Massive propaganda campaigns were launched to get people behind the war effort, and during the latter stages of the war, the United States was producing more war materials than Germany, Japan, and Italy combined.

Roosevelt and his military advisers agreed that the European theater should receive top priority. Offensive operations against the Germans and Italians began when U.S. forces invaded North Africa in November 1942. Still, the main effort against Germany was delayed until June 6, 1944, when Allied forces invaded the French beaches at Normandy. But, even as German troops were retreating, Hitler began planning a major counteroffensive that he hoped would split the Allied forces in two. In "Our Greatest Land Battle," Edward Oxford describes what Americans came to call the "Battle of the Bulg," and its aftermath. After more months of fighting, with Germany caught between the western Allies and the Soviet armies advancing from the east, Adolf Hitler committed suicide and Germany finally surrendered on May 8, 1945.

Meanwhile, American forces in the Pacific were steadily advancing toward the Japanese homeland. Capture of the Mariana Islands enabled the United States to mount massive air attacks against Japanese cities, and naval actions progressively strangled Japan's war machine. Some historians have argued that President Harry S. Truman could have attained a Japanese surrender by the summer of 1945 if only he had assured them that they could retain their sacred emperor. That is incorrect. Japan's will to resist still ran strong, as the bloody battles of Iwo Jima and Okinawa during the first half of 1945 had shown. Robert Maddox claims, in "The Biggest Decision: Why We Had to Drop the Atomic Bomb," that Truman used atomic weapons to end a bloody war that would have been far bloodier for the United States if an invasion had been necessary.

Bang! went the doors of every bank in America

Cashless, we carried on with nothing to fear but fear itself; by the time FDR opened them again, something called the New Deal was hard upon us

By James R. Chiles

James Chiles recently wrote about the rowdy goings-on in the U.S. Congress during the early 1800s.

On March 1, 1933, Mark Massey had everything he needed for a profitable day: a plan, a gun and a bank to rob. The one he had his eye on was the Community Bank of Arkadelphia, Arkansas. Small-town banks had been easy pickings for daylight robbers all through the late '20s and early '30s. Lurking in the woods on the edge of town, he probably felt sure this stickup would be a piece of cake.

What Massey didn't plan on was a scene right out of *It's a Wonderful Life*: a bank jammed with desperate depositors trying to get their money out. Earlier that day, the bank's managers had taken advantage of a new state law designed to save banks from ruin by limiting withdrawals. Now wild-eyed Arkadelphians were trying to withdraw what cash they could. There were so many people, Massey couldn't cover them all with his gun, so he tried to herd the whole crowd into the bank's washroom—and failed. One customer slipped out and brought back the sheriff. "I never got a break in my life," Massey later complained from the hoosegow.

That day bank customers all over America were feeling pretty much like Massey. In Michigan two weeks before, the governor had shut down his state's banks to head off a likely financial collapse in the city of Detroit. A shock wave of raw panic had spread outward from the nation's industrial center. The country had become more or less used to bank closings; there had been 10,000 or so during the previous decade. But now all that looked like some sort of slow-fused warm-up. Even the flimsiest rumor was enough to set off a killing run on the strongest bank; the final banking explosion seemed, and in fact was, only days away.

In our era of wall-to-wall credit cards and guarantees that protect depositors, it's hard to convey the sheer panic that a nationwide bank run could cause in a time with none of those supports. In impact on the national psyche, the recent savings and loan scandals do not compare. In 1933 a depositor would lose as much as half of his life savings if other customers got to tellers' windows first and the bank ran out of cash and had to close its doors. Runs led to forced liquidations that made banks dump assets onto a market already crumpling under the weight of unwanted stocks, bonds

A 1933 cartoon blamed zealous bank examiners for the credit shortage.

and real estate. The U.S. Secret Service had just formed a "rumor patrol"; its purpose was to investigate all seditious whispers and sternly warn citizens that bad-mouthing a bank was a felony offense.

Major banks tried to hold the line. But by March 1933, even the huge banks of New York and Chicago couldn't resist the pressure. Two days after Mark Massey's aborted bank robbery, state and local government funds were tied up in dozens of closed banks. March 3, as it happened, was also the day before the inauguration of a new President, Franklin Delano Roosevelt. "Action, and action now," he had promised during his 1932 campaign against Herbert Hoover. Driven by a national crisis, he was about to make history by telling millions of Americans via the magic voice of radio, that "the only thing we have to fear is fear itself." He was about to close the nation's banks—all 18,000 of them—and that was only the beginning. The country was a third of the way into the Great Depression, an event that still casts a shadow over America's fiscal policies and collective conscience. After FDR got through, the country's financial system would never be the same again.

For starters, during seven historic days, Americans found themselves trying to get by without benefit of cash, credit or confidence in the stability of their country's currency.

The sudden lack of cash proved an astonishment; newspapers were soon reveling in stories of a nation with its pockets turned inside out. In a throwback to the days of wampum, a Rexall drugstore in California painted clamshells with coin denominations and used them as change. A Detroit department store offered three suits, three pairs of shoes and a dress in exchange for a 500-pound hog. Bootleggers in Toledo announced they would accept substitute currency being printed by the city. Airline companies (there were only a handful) optimistically suggested that travelers without cash could ship themselves C.O.D. and rely on relatives at the other end to pay the freight. The country was delighted to hear that John D. Rockefeller couldn't pay his servants—something he always did in cash—and had to ask them to wait a few days. Iowa State Senator Ora Husted arrived at the state capital toting a side of pork and 12 dozen eggs with which to pay his bills.

Beginning with FDR's inauguration and winding up with the reopening of some banks on March 13, new Democrats at the U.S. Department of the Treasury were teamed up with holdovers from Herbert Hoover's administration to

figure out a quick way to check the health of every bank in America. Said Raymond Moley, one of FDR's advisers, "We were just a bunch of men trying to save the banking system." In fact, they were about to help the country get round a crucial corner on the long road back to recovery from the 1929 crash.

The Great Depression had not looked so great when it began. To be sure, the drop in stock value after the October 1929 Wall Street crash was astonishing—a sum approaching the national cost of fighting World War I was lost to investors in a few weeks. But people with money in the market back then tended to be wealthy: there was nothing like the widespread investment of today. Besides, milk still arrived at the doorstep every morning in clean glass bottles; trains still ran on schedule. Banks opened as they always had, five weekdays plus Saturday morning. Within months political leaders announced brightly that the country was turning the corner; business was adjusting nicely. Financial panics in the past, after all, had usually come and gone once speculators had absorbed their losses.

This one stayed on. Now and then upticks in the market made hopes soar, but economic indicators kept tipping back to new record lows. Nobody could agree on why. Republicans claimed crashes always came because of the spendthrift politicians in Washington. In 1932 the government was running at a deficit of something like $2.7 million a day. Democrats piled all the blame they could on President Hoover. He had once been the most honored man in the world. His relief organization in postwar Europe had saved some 15 million people from starvation. "I wish we could make him President of the United States," FDR had said of Hoover in 1920. "There could not be a better one."

Now he was reviled by his countrymen. In 1932 Hoover had done what he could. He created the Reconstruction Finance Corporation, which would lend billions in pump-priming money to all sorts of enterprises, including banks. But it wasn't enough. Shantytowns of tin and wood kept spreading, and became "Hoovervilles." Homeless folk on park benches tried to keep warm with

newspapers, known as "Hoover blankets." People laughed over the story of the hitchhiker who zoomed across the country in five days by displaying the sign, "Give me a lift or I'll vote for Hoover." Trying to find ways to end the Depression, Hoover often worked 18 hours at a stretch; during that time he lost 25 pounds and his hair turned white. But deficit financing was anathema to him as to most economists then; he was committed to free enterprise and self-help and the goal of a balanced budget, and the situation seemed to have outrun those remedies.

For months on end, every week brought new stories of suffering and fear. As early as April 1932, a quarter of rural Mississippi was up for auction. In the 1920s America's railroad companies had bought 1,300 locomotives a year. In 1932 they didn't buy a single one. By some estimates, one out of three willing American workers couldn't find a job. Out of the 14,000 residents of Donora, Pennsylvania, a steel town, exactly 277 had a job. Sawmill workers were making 5 cents an hour and were lucky to get it.

Within a year of the 1929 crash, a series of rural Midwestern banks failed, foreshadowing the spectacular collapse of the big, official-sounding but privately owned Bank of the United States. It closed two weeks before Christmas in 1930, trapping deposits from a half-million customers.

In these days of federally insured banks, Yuletide broadcasts showing Jimmy Stewart trying to save Bedford Falls from Lionel Barrymore are as close as we get to the infectious terror of a full-blown bank run, with frenzied depositors trying to yank out their savings all at once. Back then many banks were small and underfinanced, with no branches to draw on. It didn't take much to bring one down. Even bigger banks found it hard to handle runs because most of their money was spread around in loans that couldn't be quickly converted to cash. Runs on local banks usually lasted only a day or two, sometimes just hours, so a banker's best course was to get hold of as much cash as he could and try to slow down the processing of withdrawals, meanwhile reassuring customers that the bank would make it through the panic.

That wasn't so easy. The reputation of bankers, never exactly glowing, had been taking a terrible beating. A Minnesota Congressman, Francis Shoemaker, went to jail for calling one banker a robber of widows and orphans. The drunken president of a bank in the St. Louis suburbs pulled out a revolver and took a shot at an examiner who had come to check over the books; the bank, it turned out, had strengthened its balance sheet with forged loans. Father Charles Coughlin, the radical radio priest, regularly accused "banksters" of robbing just about everybody. The government, he insisted, needed to nationalize all the banks. "Don't tell my mother what I'm doing," a banker in one Depression-era joke exclaimed. "She thinks I'm playing the piano in a sporting house."

Some banks favored an in-your-face show of confidence. During a run in Van Buren, Arkansas, a bank took to paying its depositors in silver coins: "Bring your own bag to take home the balance." After trying to drag away 50 pounds of savings, some customers gave up. Seeing a run looming, the First Security Bank of Boise, Idaho, hung a welcome sign over the door: "If You Want Your Money Come and Get it." Meanwhile, the bank urgently wired to Salt Lake City for $500,000 in cash. The run stopped before the cash arrived by plane.

Depositors sometimes reacted bizarrely to such ploys even after getting their money back. At Boise's First Security, one woman took out $75,000 in cash, then returned it the next day. "If you've got my money, I guess I really don't want it," another person standing in line told the teller. "But if you haven't got it, then by heaven, I want it now and in full!"

One draconian method was to get all the local banks to close at the same time—which required considerable courage and political cooperation. Faced with bank panic spilling over from Champaign, Illinois, the lead-ers of sister city Urbana got the town's bankers to agree to a shutdown. Only then did they find out that if a bank decided on its own to lock its doors, the state deemed this a "bank failure" and might move in, either to close the bank permanently or to drastically reorganize it. Then somebody realized that all banks close on legal holidays, and nobody complains about it. So on January 19, 1932, Urbana's mayor declared a five-day holiday. All the city's banks and most businesses were to close while teams of volunteers spread out to wrestle local depositors into signing a no-withdrawal pledge. It worked, and the term "bank holiday" became popular. The so-called Urbana Plan spread to other cities in Illinois and Iowa, but it wasn't always successful.

In any case, depositor pledges were only a stopgap; they didn't get to the real problem: lack of cash, lack of commerce and a galloping deficit in public confidence. It was a vicious circle. Loan payments to banks fell behind as Depression layoffs and wage cuts squeezed borrowers; when banks foreclosed, they found that collateral accepted before the crash—securities and houses alike—had plummeted in value. Nationally, banks were foreclosing on a thousand homes a day.

As 1933 dawned, many Americans felt that the banking crisis with all its interconnected problems was part of a colossal national failure that perhaps could not be fixed without resorting to violence or dictatorship. Newspaper cartoonists called the enemy "General Depression," sketching it like a scraggly, sinister generalissimo. But if this was war, America seemed to be on the losing side. "I have no remedy in mind," the president of U.S. Steel told a Senate committee. Hitler was even then confirming his grip on Germany; American newspapers quoted Mussolini's suggestions that what America needed was a "lone guiding mind." Perhaps a violent uprising or dictatorship lay just around the corner.

Farmers came closest to fomenting a real revolution.

By 1932, people all through the farm belt were burning corn in their furnaces; it had become cheaper than coal. Mis-souri chicken farmers often got as little as 3 cents a dozen for their eggs. In January 1933, an Iowa farmer named August Weger sent five calves via rail to Chicago. Instead of a check he got back a bill for $1.98; the selling price of the livestock couldn't cover the cost of shipping and feed. But taxes and mortgage payments didn't drop with prices.

"Farmers are ready to do anything," the president of the Wisconsin Farmers' Union told a Senate committee. "I almost hate to express it, but I honestly believe that if some of them could buy airplanes, they would come down here to Washington to blow you fellows all up."

The toughest agricultural group was the Farmers' Holiday Association, led by firebrand Milo Reno, an ex-preacher who blamed everything on "Eastern interests and international bankers." Reno's forces began blocking highways that led to rural market towns, using spiked logs and backed by farmers toting wooden clubs and sometimes shotguns. They let cars through but turned back trucks carrying produce. After stopping a dairy truck in 1932, Holiday protesters in Iowa slathered butter over U.S. Highway 75; passing vehicles would hit the patch and slide smoothly into a ditch.

Law enforcement officials were helpless. Near Sioux City, Iowa, farmers easily took away the sheriff's badge and gun and tossed them into a cornfield. In Council Bluffs, Iowa, after dozens of men were arrested, a thousand farmers marched on the jail and got the prisoners out.

Farmers began shutting down foreclosure sales. In January 1933, a thousand angry farmers showed up in minus-22 weather at the sale of a farm near Willmar, Minnesota. The sale was postponed. Sometimes angry mobs of farmworkers simply took over. In those circumstances, sales often became penny auctions with the mob threatening violence to anyone who bid more than pocket change. At a sale in Woodbury County, Iowa, neighbors helped things along by cutting the phone line and keeping bids from the audience down to a total of $11.75. Then they forced the holder of the mortgage to sign a note accepting that amount as settlement.

As it often does, violence seemed to work. By February 1933, many mortgage holders were backing off. Some states had even passed laws to suspend all farm and home foreclosures until conditions got better.

Halting foreclosures, however, hit the banks hard, because they couldn't collect on loans and were facing foreclosures of their own in the form of runs by depositors. Eventually banks found themselves stuck with millions of America's homes and farms, but there was nobody to sell them to.

What the farmers really wanted was for the government to artificially reverse the price decline. "Reflation, or revolution," was the cry. As Inauguration Day approached, Hoover wanted Roosevelt to promise that as President he would swear allegiance to the gold standard and balance the federal budget, figuring that would restore investor confidence. FDR refused. As he saw it, budget cutting and helping business with loans wasn't going to restore the country's confidence.

Though he did not save time as he might have by working with Hoover before the inauguration, his adviser Raymond Moley and his new Treasury Secretary designate, William Woodin, had already teamed up with Hoover's Treasury staff at the Federal Reserve Board. They were trying to convince the governors of Illinois and New York to close their banks by state action. Both

did so; withdrawals from New York City banks had reached $440 million a week, a loss that could not long be sustained.

The gifted impresario of America's banking salvation proved to be the 64-year-old Woodin. A man of many parts, he had done day labor in a foundry after college, then headed for Europe to study musical composition. He also composed symphonies and children's songs in his spare time. Before becoming Secretary of the Treasury, he had been a successful manufacturer of railroad equipment and held directorships in 21 companies. Democrats trusted him because he had been one of FDR's early financial backers. The night before the inauguration, the National Symphony Orchestra performed his piece "On the Prairie" in Washington; Woodin was too deep in meetings with FDR at the Mayflower Hotel to go. He had forged a close friendship with Hoover's Assistant Secretary of the Treasury, Arthur Ballantine, who agreed to stay on and help out temporarily, on condition that nobody would be hired to fill Treasury Department posts without a joint say-so between Woodin and Ballantine. Woodin agreed.

On Saturday, March 4, in the last minutes before motoring off to be sworn in, FDR met with Woodin and agreed on what was to be done. In his inaugural speech it was the phrase about having nothing to fear but fear itself that lodged in the public memory.

The short-term cure Roosevelt proposed was to have banking—and debt—take a federal holiday all over America. The closings ordered were stricter than anything that most states had tried: rather than cutting back on withdrawals, FDR's proclamation cut them off almost entirely. Meanwhile, banks could accept deposits and could cash Treasury checks.

To justify this high-handed proclamation, FDR cited the "Trading with the Enemy Act." An old law, passed in 1917 as a wartime measure, it said nothing whatever about shutting down banks, but it did give the President the power to stop the export or hoarding of gold and currency in times of national emergency. This was quite a stretch, legally, but FDR figured the bank holiday idea would hold up if Congress immediately passed a law approving what he had done.

The great bank holiday began on Monday, March 6. Wealthy folk, particularly, had been predicting food riots and mass assaults on bank vaults. After all, they gloomed, during the draft riots of 1863, police had lost control of whole sections of New York City for days at a time. "Fearing a possible siege, many of us bought a great deal of canned food and stored it in our cellars," a resident of Muncie, Indiana, had recalled. "One family I know bought enough for more than five years."

But within a day, it was clear that something different was going on. After months of worrying about what other depositors were up to, most people welcomed rule by proclamation—and the national holiday as well. *Business Week* went so far as to tell its readers: " . . . a little to our astonishment we find that we are still here and that we can still eat and sleep and work and smile. We can deal with an open crisis; we could not fight a shadow."

Even staunch Republican newspapers, perhaps inspired by a few moves by FDR to cut federal spending, raved about his first days in office. "Honor to President Roosevelt who, more than any man, is responsible for the wondrous change in the nation's outlook and its prospects!" said the Hearst's *New York American.* FDR was showing "bald

Desperate Midwestern farmers, like these stopping a cattle truck in Sioux City, Iowa, tried to improve prices by keeping goods from the market.

courage and unselfish leadership," said the *Boston Transcript.* Even *The Chicago Daily Tribune,* which shortly before had been blaming the whole Depression on Democrats in general and excess government spending in particular, joined the chorus.

Only a three-day closing had been planned, but FDR's emergency banking bill provided that it could last as long as necessary. A survey by a Massachusetts newspaper showed the average family had $18.23 in cash on hand when the banks closed. People began raiding their children's piggy banks and dusting off coin collections. Hoarders dug around in attics and rolltop desks for gold and silver coins and old, oversize bills that had been out of circulation for years.

Travelers caught away from home had to hunt up friends for meals, a loan or a place to sleep. The papers were full of stories about how FDR's bank holiday was bulldozing through class distinctions. Executives of one New York corporation hocked their jewelry and watches to raise $3,000; then each employee, from the company president to the shipping clerk, was given exactly $10 to live on. Finding himself in need of bus fare to Connecticut, a New York banker ended up borrowing it from a newsboy.

People who had managed to cash out their deposits in large bills before the holiday found that change was in such short supply, businesses wouldn't accept fifties, twenties or even five-dollar bills for small purchases. After a customer offered up a five-dollar bill for a 75-cent meal in western Arkansas, the waitress told him, "The meal is on us and don't bring five-dollar bills around here." The Commodore Hotel in New York sent a messenger around to nearby churches to exchange big bills for the change in their collection plates. Roseland, a famous Manhattan dance hall that charged 10 cents for a turn around the floor, accepted IOUs from customers—but only if they could produce a bankbook.

Barter produced the best bank holiday stories. Stopped for a traffic violation in Stuttgart, Arkansas, a truck driver paid his fine with two bags of rice and drove on. Ten bushels of wheat bought

a year's subscription to the Lewistown, Montana, *Democrat-News.* Ticket sales at movie theaters fell to half their pre-holiday levels and Hollywood studios shut down. The Minneapolis Symphony gave free concerts; in Chicago you could get to see the Irish Players for a couple of new potatoes. "I see no reason why there should not be a new theatrical season," deadpanned Robert Benchley, "providing my proposed plan for using pressed figs and dates as money goes into effect fairly soon."

The *New York Daily News* sponsored a boxing tournament and advertised admission on a barter basis. The normal price was 50 cents; by the time the sluggers got under way, the organizers had issued tickets in return for false teeth, golf knickers, mattresses, spark plugs, baseball bats, balls, Bibles, underwear and jigsaw puzzles. Swappable food offerings included salami, franks and a big box of egg noodles.

This holiday atmosphere couldn't last, especially in cities like Detroit, which had already been bankless for four weeks before FDR's holiday started. Out of 1,400 city employees there, a thousand couldn't cash their checks. After some people fainted on the job from hunger, Detroit put municipal

employees on welfare rolls so they could draw on whatever federal cash had escaped the bank closures. "Everybody's broke," merchants reported. Stores had bountiful collections of IOUs and uncashed checks, but no money to pay wholesalers.

Before it could lift the holiday, FDR's brand-new administration had to answer two questions: Which banks were sound enough to reopen? And what would the reopened ones use for money in case panicking depositors showed up to pull out their savings? On the first problem, Woodin decided to dispatch a legion of federal and state bank examiners charged with sorting the nation's banks into three groups: class A banks could open the week beginning March 13; class B needed some changes first; class C would be closed for good. With 18,000 banks to check, Woodin's examiners were given just five days to do the job.

Because the federal government was nearly out of cash itself, it couldn't ease the cash shortage by lending banks its own money. Bankers at first favored creating a torrent of scrip, such as was already circulating in a few cities like Nashville and Atlanta.

In a sign of the times, a National Guardsman, called out to keep order, threatened an embattled farmer protesting a foreclosure.

New York banks quickly ordered $250 million in multicolored "emergency certificates." Scrip was essentially a set of printed IOUs handed out by someone who promised to redeem them for cash after the emergency. The issuer might be a county government, a local industry that paid workers with it, or a hotel like the posh Huntington in Pasadena, California. The rich and famous staying there—the former Speaker of the House, a princess from Denmark, East Coast bankers—lined up to get their share of $2,000 worth of scrip to pay for meals, shoeshines, cigars and tips.

Apart from paper, ersatz cash took some odd forms. There were magnesium coins in Michigan and plywood rectangles in Tenino, Washington. Four merchants in Clear Lake, Iowa, opened a Corn Bank that issued 25 cents' worth of scrip per bushel for thousands of bushels of corn that farmers obligingly dumped into giant cribs set up on city streets.

But Woodin decided that using scrip nationwide would cause more problems than it solved, mainly because a national economy couldn't cope with hundreds of currencies of uncertain worth. It was he who arranged for the federal government to print up a great many more Federal Reserve Bank Notes. This was a federal currency guaranteed by the government, but by the time Woodin and Roosevelt were through, the notes would not be backed by gold or silver as had been the case before. To get Federal Reserve Bank Notes, banks had to put up their own assets.

On Thursday, March 9, four days into the national holiday, Congress swiftly passed an emergency bill to prepare for reopening the banks. "The house is burning down, and the President of the United States says this is the way to put out the fire," said House Republican floor leader Bertrand Snell. The measure moved so fast that Representatives didn't even wait to look at a printed copy before voting. Roosevelt signed the bill in the White House the same night, in a library still cluttered with unshelved books and unhung pictures from the move-in. Next day the Bureau of Engraving began cranking out $2 billion in new banknotes—fives, tens, twenties, fifties, hundreds. The cash began arriving by the planeload at 12 Federal Reserve banks around the country. Roosevelt explained the bank crisis—and how he proposed to set things right—to 60 million radio listeners.

"Mr. Roosevelt stepped to the microphone last night and knocked another home run," said Will Rogers the next day. "He made everybody understand it, even the bankers."

In what surely ranks as the most abrupt reversal of opinion in this century, Americans responded to the lifting of the bank holiday not by pulling the new currency out of banks but by dumping what hoarded money they had back in. By the end of that first day most of the nation's banks were running again; in New York, all but nine had reopened. The New York Stock Exchange took one of the biggest price jumps in its history. Shoppers returned to stores in a rush. The federal government issued a new series of Treasury Certificates and found more buyers for them than it could handle.

Hoarded gold had been coming back to banks at a furious rate even before the bank holiday ended, because the Treasury Department had warned during the first week of the holiday that it would soon start printing the names of those who had recently taken gold or gold certificates out of banks. Rumors added fuel to the fear: maybe the government would confiscate all gold; maybe it would fine people twice the value. In a single day, 3,000 New Yorkers turned in their gold. In April, the United States went off the gold standard permanently; in June it created the Federal Deposit Insurance Corporation, which to this day guarantees private deposits against bank failure. The Federal Emergency Relief Administration came next, offering immediate help to some 15 million people out of work. In 1934 the Gold Reserve Act prohibited the private ownership of gold bullion and discontinued the use of gold coins in commerce. It also allowed Roosevelt to change the official price of gold here and thereby devalue the U.S. dollar abroad. Early in 1935 came the Social Security Act. It has been amended six times since, but originally involved only a guaranteed minimum income for working people after they retired. In 1936, for the first time in almost 60 years, not a single national bank closed.

The Great Depression was far from over, but FDR's monetary experiment had worked. The New Deal had begun, though with what long-term effects on America's economy, history has yet to decide.

A Monumental Man

FDR's chiseled features defined an American epoch

By Gerald Parshall

Franklin Roosevelt made no small plans—except for his own commemoration. The first Roosevelt memorial, now all but forgotten, was installed outside the National Archievs building in 1965. A marble slab about the size of Roosevelt's desk, it was scaled to its subject's wishes. The new Roosevelt memorial now being completed in Washington is scaled to its subject's significance: Some 4,500 tons of granite went into it. Designer Lawrence Halprin laid out a wall that meanders over 7.5 acres, forming four outdoor rooms, each devoted to one of FDR's terms in the White House and each open on one side to a stunning vista of the Tidal Basin. Waterfalls, reflecting pools, and sculptures are set along what is likely to become one of the most popular walks in the nation's capital. The entry building contains a photograph of FDR in his wheelchair and a replica of the chair itself. The memorial's time line includes these words: "1921, STRICKEN WITH POLIOMYELITIS—HE NEVER AGAIN WALKED UNAIDED." *But because no statue depicts him in his wheelchair, the dedication ceremony on May 2 faces a threatened protest by the disabled. Controversy often surrounded Roosevelt in life; his spirit should feel right at home.*

THE POWER OF HIS SMILE

Today, we carry the face of Franklin Roosevelt in our pockets and purses—it is stamped on more than 18 billion dimes. From 1933 to 1945, Americans carried it in their hearts. It was stamped on their consciousness, looking out from every newspaper and newsreel, FDR's smile as bright as the headlight on a steam locomotive. Roosevelt's portrait hung in bus stations, in barber shops, in kitchens, in parlors, in Dust Bowl shacks—and in Winston Churchill's bedchamber in wartime London. It was the face of hope and freedom for the masses. Even among the "economic royalists," the haters of "that man in the White House," the portrait could stir emotion—as a dartboard.

In 1911, when the 28-year-old Roosevelt was newly elected to the New York Senate, the *New York Times* found him "a young man with the finely chiseled face of a Roman patrician" who "could make a fortune on the stage and set the matinee girl's heart throbbing with subtle and happy emotion." Tammany Hall Democrats, however, weren't swooning. They noted the freshman's habit of tossing his head back and peering down his nose (on which he wore pince-nez like Theodore Roosevelt, a fifth cousin) and read in it a squire's disdain for grubby city boys. The quirk persisted but acquired a new meaning decades later, when FDR wrestled with unprecedented domestic and foreign crises. His upturned chin and eyes, along with his cigarette holder, itself tilted toward the heavens, became symbols of indomitable determination to triumph over adversity—his own and the country's.

It was, indeed, the face of a great actor, a living sculpture continuously reshaped by the artist. The knowing twinkle. The arched eyebrow. The eloquent grimace. Roosevelt was a master of misdirection. He could lie without blinking, disarm enemies with infectious bonhomie, and make a bore feel like the most fascinating fellow on Earth. Officials with rival agendas often came away from the Oval Office equally sure that they alone had the president's ear.

From *U.S. News & World Report*, April 28, 1997, pp. 59-61, 64. © 1997 by U.S. News & World Report. Reprinted by permission.

"Never let your left hand know what your right is doing," FDR once confided to a cabinet member. Idealism and duplicity fused behind his smile, buttressing one another like the two sides of a Roosevelt dime.

THE WARMTH OF HIS WORDS

He was one of the greatest orators of his time but suffered from stage fright. While he waited on the dais, Franklin Roosevelt fidgeted, shuffled the pages of his speech, chain-smoked, and doused the butterflies in his stomach with gulps of water. At last, they let him start—"My friends. . . ." In a New York minute, his nervousness was gone and the audience under his spell. His voice—languid one moment, theatrical the next—dripped with Groton, Harvard, and centuries of blue blood. Yet no president has ever communicated better with ordinary people.

A Roosevelt speech sounded spontaneous, straight from the heart, effortless—effects that took much effort to achieve. Some speeches went through a dozen drafts, with speech writers laboring at the big table in the Cabinet Room until 3 a.m. Roosevelt then revised mercilessly—shortening sentences, substituting words with fewer syllables, polishing similes—until his own muscular style emerged. Sometimes, he wrote a speech entirely by himself. He used a yellow legal pad to draft his first inaugural address, which rang with one of the most effective buck-up lines in history: "The only thing we have to fear is fear itself." He dictated to his secretary most of the Pearl Harbor message he delivered to Congress. He edited himself, changing "a date which will live in world history" to "a date which will live in infamy."

Roosevelt held two press conferences a week right in the Oval Office. Relaxed and jocular, he gently decreed what could and could not be printed. He talked to reporters, John Dos Passos remembered, in a fatherly voice "like the

ATLANTA CHANCE—FRANKLIN D. ROOSEVELT LIBRARY
REVISIONIST. FDR rewrote his speeches until they sang.

voice of a principal in a first-rate boy's school." Likewise, Roosevelt's "fireside chats" on the radio reverberated with paternal intimacy. He had a flair for homely analogies, such as equating Lend-Lease aid to Britian with loaning your neighbor a garden hose to put out a house fire. Who wouldn't do that? Speaking into the microphone, he gestured and smiled as if the audience would somehow sense what it could not see. Millions shushed the children and turned up the radio. They ached for leadership and "Doctor New Deal"—soon to become "Doctor Win the War"—was making a house call.

THE SPLENDOR OF HIS STRIDE

At the 1936 Democratic National Convention, Franklin Roosevelt fell down as he moved across the podium to address the delegates. He was quickly pulled up again, his withered legs bruised but unbroken. No newspaper stories or radio reports mentioned this incident—and for good reason. It hadn't happened. America was in denial. Prejudice against "cripples" was widespread. The nation wanted no reminders that it was following a man who could not walk.

From the earliest days of the polio that ravaged his legs in 1921, denial had been Roosevelt's way of coping. He

spoke of his infirmity with no one, not even with members of his family. For seven years, almost every day, he took his crutches, tried—and failed—to reach the end of his Hyde Park driveway. He could not walk. But how he ran. Campaigning animatedly from open cars and the rear platform of trains, he was elected governor of New York twice and president of the United States four times. No crutches were seen and no wheelchair. His steel leg braces were painted black to blend with his socks; he wore extra long trousers. The Secret Service built ramps all over Washington, D.C., to give his limousine close access to his destinations. FDR jerkily "walked" the final distance by holding on to one of his sons with his left arm and supporting his right side with a cane. Newsreel cameras stopped; press photographers took a breather. If an amateur was spotted attempting to get a picture, the Secret Service swiftly closed in and exposed the film.

"FDR's splendid deception," historian Hugh Gallagher dubbed the little conspiracy in his book of that title. It worked so well that most Americans never knew of Roosevelt's disability, or they repressed what they did know. Such was the national amnesia, cartoonists even drew him jumping. FDR dropped the ruse for only one group. Military amputee wards were filled with men brooding about what fate had done to their futures. A high official sometimes came calling. The severely wounded GIs recognized the visitor immediately—no face was more famous—and his arrival brought an exhilarating revelation. Down the aisles came the nemesis of Hitler and Hirohito, his wheelchair in full view and looking like a royal chariot.

THE MAINSPRING OF HIS MIND

When the British monarch visited America in 1939, Franklin Roosevelt greeted him with unaccustomed familiarity. He served him hot dogs at a Hyde Park picnic and addressed him not as "your majesty" but as "George." "Why don't my ministers talk to me as the president did tonight?" an enchanted George VI remarked to a member of his entourage. "I felt exactly as though a father were giving me his most careful and wise advice." It was Roosevelt's genius to treat kings like commoners and commoners like kings. And both loved him for it.

His monumental self-assurance was bred in the bone. His mother, Sara, had reared him, her only child, to believe he had a fixed place in the center of the cosmos like other Roosevelts. She—and the example set by cousin Theodore—imparted another formative lesson: Privileged people have a duty to do good. Noblesse oblige, Christianity, and the golden rule made up the moral core of the aristocrat who became both the Democrat of the century and the democrat of the century.

Critics called him a socialist and a "traitor to his class." History would call him the savior of capitalism, the pragmatist who saved free enterprise from very possibly disappearing into the abyss and taking democracy with it. It seemed evident to him that only government could curb or cushion the worst excesses of industrialism. But, at bottom, he was less a thinker than a doer. Luckily, like gardeners and governesses, intellectuals could be hired. Roosevelt hired a brain trust and pumped it for ideas to which he applied this test: Will it work? If one program belly-flopped, he cheerfully tried another. "A second-class intellect," Justice Oliver Wendell Holmes pegged him. "But a first-class temperament."

For all his amiability, FDR knew with Machiavelli that self-seekers abound this side of paradise. Navigating perilous domestic and foreign waters by dead reckoning, he often felt compelled to be a shameless schemer. He hid his intentions, manipulated people, set aides to contrary tasks—all to keep control of the game in trustworthy hands (his own). Charm and high purposes palliated the pure ether of his arrogance. Franklin Roosevelt was hip-deep in the muck of politics and power, but his eyes were always on the stars.

Eleanor Roosevelt

America's most influential First Lady blazed paths for women and led the battle for social justice everywhere

By Doris Kearns Goodwin

When Eleanor Roosevelt journeyed to New York City a week after her husband's funeral in April 1945, a cluster of reporters were waiting at the door of her Washington Square apartment. "The story is over," she said simply, assuming that her words and opinions would no longer be of interest once her husband was dead and she was no longer First Lady. She could not have been more mistaken. As the years have passed, Eleanor Roosevelt's influence and stature have continued to grow. Today she remains a powerful inspiration to leaders in both the civil rights and women's movements.

Eleanor shattered the ceremonial mold in which the role of the First Lady had traditionally been fashioned, and reshaped it around her own skills and her deep commitment to social reform. She gave a voice to people who did not have access to power. She was the first woman to speak in front of a national convention, to write a syndicated column, to earn money as a lecturer, to be a radio commentator and to hold regular press conferences.

The path to this unique position of power had not been easy. The only daughter of an alcoholic father and a beautiful but aloof mother who was openly disappointed by Eleanor's lack of a pretty face, Eleanor was plagued by insecurity and shyness. An early marriage to her handsome fifth cousin once removed, Franklin Roosevelt, increased her insecurity and took away her one source of confidence: her work in a New York City settlement house. "For 10 years, I was always just getting over having a baby or about to have another one," she later lamented, "so my occupations were considerably restricted."

> ### "The bottom dropped out of my own particular world. I faced myself, my surroundings, my world honestly for the first time."
>
> **ELEANOR ROOSEVELT,**
> **on discovering her husband's affair**

But 13 years after her marriage, and after bearing six children, Eleanor resumed the search for her identity. The voyage began with a shock: the discovery in 1918 of love letters revealing that Franklin was involved with Lucy Mercer. "The bottom dropped out of my own particular world," she later said. "I faced myself, my surroundings, my world, honestly for the first time." There

was talk of divorce, but when Franklin promised never to see Lucy again, the marriage continued. For Eleanor a new path had opened, a possibility of standing apart from Franklin. No longer would she define herself solely in terms of his wants and needs. A new relationship was forged, on terms wholly different from the old.

She turned her energies to a variety of reformist organizations, joining a cir-

POPPERFOTO—ARCHIVE PHOTOS

Eleanor, right, "never smiled" as a child

From *Time*, April 13, 1998, pp. 123-125. © 1998 by Time Inc. Magazine Company. Reprinted by permission.

"Can't you muzzle that wife of yours? . . . Do you have lace on your panties for allowing her to speak out so much? . . . Why can't she stay home and tend to her knitting?"

QUESTIONS put to F.D.R.

about his wife's unrelenting outspokenness on political issues

cle of postsuffrage feminists dedicated to the abolition of child labor, the establishment of a minimum wage and the passage of legislation to protect workers. In the process she discovered that she had talents—for public speaking, for organizing, for articulating social problems. She formed an extraordinary constellation of lifelong female friends, who helped to assuage an enduring sense of loneliness. When Franklin was paralyzed by polio in 1921, her political activism became an even more vital force. She became Franklin's eyes and ears," traveling the country gathering the grassroots knowledge he needed to understand the people he governed.

They made an exceptional team. She was more earnest, less devious, less patient, less fun, more uncompromisingly moral; he possessed the more trustworthy political talent, the more finely tuned sense of timing, the better feel for the citizenry, the smarter understanding of how to get things done. But they were linked by indissoluble bonds. Together they mobilized the American people to effect enduring changes in the political and social landscape of the nation.

Nowhere was Eleanor's influence greater than in civil rights. In her travels around the country, she developed a sophisticated understanding of race relations. When she first began inspecting New Deal programs in the South, she was stunned to find that blacks were being systematically discriminated against at every turn. Citing statistics to back up her story, she would interrupt her husband at any time, barging into his cocktail hour when he wanted only to relax, cross-examining him at dinner, handing him memos to read late at night. But her confrontational style compelled him to sign a series of Executive Orders barring discrimination in the administration of vari-

ous New Deal projects. From that point on, African Americans' share in the New Deal work projects expanded, and Eleanor's independent legacy began to grow.

She understood, for instance, the importance of symbolism in fighting discrimination. In 1938, while attending the Southern Conference for Human Welfare in Birmingham, Ala., she refused to abide by a segregation ordinance that required her to sit in the white section of the auditorium, apart from her black friends. The following year, she publicly resigned from the Daughters of the American Revolution after it barred the black singer Marian Anderson from its auditorium.

During World War II, Eleanor remained an uncompromising voice on civil rights, insisting that America could not fight racism abroad while tolerating it at home. Progress was slow, but her continuing intervention led to broadened opportunities for blacks in the factories and shipyards at home and in the armed forces overseas.

Eleanor's positions on civil rights were far in advance of her time: 10 years before the Supreme Court rejected the "separate but equal" doctrine, Eleanor argued that equal facilities were not enough: "The basic fact of segregation, which warps and twists the lives of our Negro population, [is] itself discriminatory."

There were other warps and twists that caught her eye. Long before the contemporary women's movement provided ideological arguments for women's rights, Eleanor instinctively challenged institutions that failed to provide equal opportunity for women. As First Lady, she held more than 300 press conferences that she cleverly restricted

to women journalists, knowing that news organizations all over the country would be forced to hire their first female reporter in order to have access to the First Lady.

Through her speeches and her columns, she provided a powerful voice in the campaign to recruit women workers to the factories during the war. "If I were of debutante age, I would go into a factory, where I could learn a skill and be useful," Eleanor told young women, cautioning them against marrying too hastily before they had a chance to expand their horizons. She was instrumental in securing the first government funds ever allotted for the building of child-care centers. And when women workers were unceremoniously fired as the war came to an end, she fought to stem the tide. She argued on principle that everyone who wanted to work had a right to be productive, and she railed against the closing of the child-care centers as a shortsighted response to a fundamental social need. What the women workers needed, she said, was the courage to ask for their rights with a loud voice.

For her own part, she never let the intense criticism that she encountered silence her. "If I . . . worried about mudslinging, I would have been dead long ago." Yet she insisted that she was not a feminist. She did not believe, she maintained, that "women should be judged, when it comes to appointing them or electing them, purely because they are women." She wanted to see the country "get away from considering a man or woman from the point of view of religion, color or sex." But the story of her life—her insistence on her right to an identity of her own apart from her husband and her family, her constant struggle against depression and insecurity, her ability to turn her vulnerabilities into strengths—provides an enduring example of a feminist who transcended the dictates of her times to become one of the century's most powerful and effective advocates for social justice.

Doris Kearns Goodwin is a Pulitzerprizewinning author, historian and political analyst

Home Front

World War II was fought and won on the assembly line as much as on the battle line. The nation's massive war effort involved and affected the lives of all Americans.

James W. Wensyel

James W. "Skip" Wensyel, a previous contributor to American History *magazine, is a retired Army colonel and a licensed battlefield guide at Gettysburg National Military Park.*

As Americans turned the pages of their calendars at the beginning of December 1941, the United States was slowly emerging from the Great Depression that had crippled the nation for nearly a decade. The economy to be sure, was still soft, with more than 5 million Americans unemployed and 7.5 million workers earning less than 40 cents per hour. But when you could remember (as the author did) a Christmas when your parents, having only $3.50 to spend on food and presents for their four boys, compromised by wrapping oranges as gifts, it was a lot better than people had known for a long time.

For the first time in years most Americans had enough food on their tables and some change to jingle in their pockets. Retail sales were rising to $54 million in 1941 from $10 million the previous year. The national median income was $2,000, which bought a lot when a new car cost about $1,000 and a pound of good steak could be had for 23 cents.

But despite the signs of economic recovery Americans had good reason to be concerned about the future. For three years the United States had been able to remain aloof from the war that was sweeping across Europe. Now, however,

LIBRARY OF CONGRESS.

President Franklin D. Roosevelt's call for a declaration of war in response to Japan's December 7, 1941 attack on Hawaii was a summons to action for every citizen. Drawn together in unanimity of purpose, Americans on the home front mobilized themselves and their resources for a full commitment to the men on the fighting lines.

From *American History,* June 1995, pp. 44-63, 77, 78, 81 © by Cowles Magazine, Inc. Reprinted through the courtesy of Cowles Magazines, publishers of *American History.*

WE ARE NOW IN THIS WAR
We are all in it all the way

Every single man, woman and child is a partner in the most tremendous undertaking of our American history. We must share together the bad news and the good news, the defeats and the victories – the changing fortunes of war.

(President Roosevelt, Address to the Nation, December 9, 1941)

in its ninth year under the leadership of President Franklin D. Roosevelt, the U.S. found itself drawn ever closer to the European conflict and into a confrontation with Japan in the Pacific as well. In 1940 Congress enacted the Selective Service and Training Act that saw more than sixteen million American men between the ages of twenty-one and thirty-six registered for military service. Under the provisions of the Lend-Lease Act passed by Congress in March 1941, the U.S. was providing war matériel, as well as food and medicine, to Great Britain. And to protect the convoys carrying those desperately needed supplies to Europe, we had armed our merchant ships, and the Navy was attacking German U-boats.

The world situation notwithstanding, most Americans greeted December 7, 1941 as a typical peaceful Sunday. Throughout the country families relaxed over their newspapers, attended church, washed their cars, or planned their Christmas shopping (department stores were closed for the Sabbath). With a little money that year, it promised to be a wonderful Christmas.

By evening, however, everything had changed. The suddenness, ferocity and

To unite Americans and build their determination to win the war, the Office of War Information distributed millions of posters. Wherever they went, people on the home front were exhorted to support the armed forces, join the defense industry, avoid waste, buy war bonds, and keep quiet.

BUY WAR BONDS

EVERY FIRE IS SABOTAGE TODAY !

FIRE PREVENTION WEEK Oct. 4-10

THIS IS THE ENEMY

ALL: MISCELLANEOUS MAN.

surprise of the Japanese attack against the big U.S. Navy base and military airfields on the island of Oahu, Hawaii, left Americans confused, shocked, and stunned. For those old enough to understand, the name, the date, the act itself would be indelibly seared in their memories as if cameras had clicked in their minds and frozen "Pearl Harbor" there for all time.

Following news of the attack, Americans from Maine to Oregon waited for President Roosevelt to speak. Party affiliation and political philosophy no longer mattered. He was the president, and all Americans looked to their chief executive (and trusted him) to lead the nation in this time of crisis. In Washington, D.C., hundreds instinctively walked to the White House, where FDR was meeting with his Cabinet. Standing quietly before the darkened Executive Mansion, they began to sing, softly at first but then more strongly, *God Bless America* and other patriotic songs.

Shortly after noon on December 8, in an address to a joint session of Congress and the nation, President Roosevelt condemned the Japanese attack and requested an immediate declaration of war. The Senate complied, voting 82 to 0 for war against Japan. The House of Representatives, with one exception (Congresswoman Jeanette Rankin of Montana) concurred.

Three days later, Germany and Italy, supporting their Japanese ally, declared war against the United States. The waiting was over; in joining the fight against the Axis powers, America was now committed to a global conflict the likes of which had never before been seen.

With America at war, life on the home front began to change almost immediately. Robert Albert, then living near Fort MacArthur in San Pedro, California, remembers that even as the president addressed Congress, "things started moving fast for the military. We looked out to see Army vehicles blocking the streets to the beach below. "Barricades of coiled barbed wire

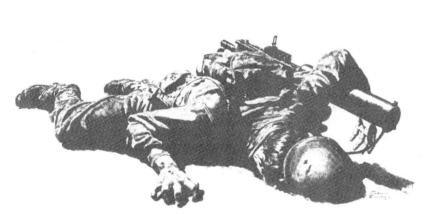

What did *you* do today
... for Freedom?

Today, at the front, he died ... Today, what did *you* do?

Next time you see a list of dead and wounded, ask yourself:

"What have *I* done today for freedom?

What can I do tomorrow that will *save* the lives of

men like this and help them win the war?"

ALL: MISCELLANEOUS MAN.

had been erected to prevent passage. Soldiers were everywhere."

Christmas 1941 was a somber holiday. Families were being separated, and a great many Americans already were fighting in the Pacific. On December 24, Britain's Prime Minister Winston Churchill paid a surprise visit to America and the White House. While watching the annual lighting of the great Christmas tree, he remarked, "I spend this anniversary and festival far from my family. And yet I cannot truthfully say that I feel far from home."

FDR proclaimed New Year's Day 1942 a National Day of Prayer, and Americans greeted the new year with absolute confidence in victory. Signs of that certainty were everywhere. A street banner in Yuma, Arizona, proclaimed "TO HELL WITH JAPAN AND ALL HER FRIENDS." In an Alabama town a notice appeared in the window of Joe's Country Lunch: "Maybe you don't know there's a war on. Have gone to see what it's all about. Meanwhile good luck and best wishes until we all come home—Joe."

Even our ice cream treats—with such names as "Blackout Sundae," "Commando Sundae," and "Paratroop Sundae—it goes down easy"—reflected Americans' newfound patriotism. Some popular tunes, like *Jingle, Jangle, Jingle* or *Deep in the Heart of Texas,* reflected that same cheerfulness, but others— *White Christmas, Don't Get Around Much Anymore, I Left My Heart At The Stage Door Canteen,* and *You'd Be So Nice To Come Home To*—revealed the nationwide undercurrent of pensiveness and loneliness that would deepen as the war dragged on.

Anger at everything Japanese was not limited to adults. At fourteen years and a robust 115 pounds, this author tried to persuade Army recruiters to give me a uniform. Their friendly "Thanks, but no thanks," was repeated every month until I reached seventeen. And in Newburgh, New York, a nine-year-old girl (now my wife) was scolded for smashing her Japanese toy piano to pieces.

With the exception of Lieutenant Colonel Jimmy Doolittle's daring April 18 bombing raid on Japanese cities from the aircraft carrier *Hornet,* war news was not encouraging in 1942. At home, oil slicks from torpedoed merchant ships appeared on beaches from Cape Cod to the Gulf of Mexico. German submarine "wolf packs" lay a few miles offshore, preying on merchant ships silhouetted against the coastal lights. When bodies and debris began to float ashore, the Navy sealed off beaches to restrict news of the grim battle they were waging (and at that point losing) on our doorstep.

Americans had some of their first war heroes in Captain Colin P. Kelly, Jr., a B17 pilot who died while bombing a Japanese warship off the Philippines, and Second Lieutenant Alexander R. Nininger, Jr., posthumously awarded the Medal of Honor for his courage during fighting on the Bataan Peninsula. Church attendance grew as it would throughout the war, and more and more homes displayed blue-star emblems. As the war went on, gold stars would replace many of the blue ones, signifying the loss of another loved one.

For some, especially children, this change from blue to gold did more than anything else to bring home the horrible reality of war. Dianne Price's grandfather "had placed a small rectangular silk flag, emblazoned by three blue stars on a white background in our front window in honor of his three sons in the Army. After Uncle Eddy was killed, I remember a blue star was changed to gold. Grandma was never the same after that. My uncle's young wife was a basket case for a long time and my mother, who was trying to buoy everyone else up, almost had a nervous breakdown. For myself, I hated the war now I had seen, firsthand, how bad it could hurt."

As America prepared to send its armed forces abroad, so too did it begin to take precautions for the security of the home front. The Office of Civilian Defense (OCD) enlisted more than 12 million volunteers and organized most communities down to the block level, adding such expressions as "block warden," "blackout," and "dim-out" to our wartime vocabulary. Volunteers studied aircraft identification silhouettes and stored sandbags, helmets, flashlights, buckets, and hoses for use in the event of an air raid. In mock attacks Civil Air Patrol planes dropped flour-filled dummy bombs or wardens threw firecrackers to simulate exploding shells. Medical volunteers treated masses of ketchup-stained Boy Scout "casualties."

Residents hung opaque blackout curtains in their windows and when an alert sounded, carefully drew them and waited by candlelight or flashlight for the "all clear." Air raid wardens, official-looking in their white helmets and arm bands, meant business. If a light showed, the person responsible was sure to hear about it.

Air-raid drills "were a source of entertainment" for nine-year-old Cornelius Lynch and his three siblings. "It was always exciting to have the house pitch black, particularly if it coincided with the broadcast of *Inner Sanctum* or *Lights Out* on the radio. I found those programs scary-fun enough when the lights were on." Not all children shared that sense of excitement, however. For Louise Butler, near Washington, D.C., the wartime measures instilled fear. "The Germans were bombing other countries and sinking ships. It was logical to us that they would attempt to bomb our nation's capital. We knew that we weren't just exercising childish imagination because the government made us all wear dog tags stamped with name, address, and a long number so that in case of injury our parents would be notified we were in the hospital. In case of death they would know they were burying the right child."

Civil defense volunteer Eva Schillingburg recalls an air-raid drill in Baltimore: "It was very dark. I could not see where I was walking. My memory of the sidewalk guided me. How weird to be on a street in the city with no lights, no sound."

Initially some cities and towns had to improvise air-raid signals. Sepulveda, California, used a century-old cast-iron bell. Reading, Pennsylvania, used car horns beeping out the Morse Code "V", for Victory. Bell Telephone Laboratories developed a device to be used countrywide. This "Victory Siren" proved so ear-shattering, how-

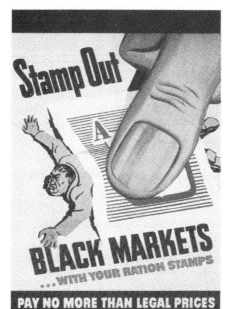

When consumer goods began to become scarce, rationing was established under the Office of Price Administration to insure distribution of items on an equitable basis and to prevent runaway inflation. And, to supplement the nation's food supply, Americans planted "Victory Gardens" in almost any available plot of earth.

was organized in his Pennsylvania hometown, fourteen-year-old Uzal Ent volunteered as a messenger. "I was proud of my white helmet and arm band, which proclaimed me a member of Civil Defense. In the darkness and solitude of my lonely post [during alerts], I fantasized German bombers attacking, and how I would act—very bravely of course."

The greatest potential danger to American security was thought to be German or Japanese saboteurs or intelligence agents within the United States. In June 1942 a German submarine landed four agents near Amagansett, Long Island. Several days later four more made it ashore near Ponte Vedra Beach, Florida. All spoke excellent English. When caught, the saboteurs were carrying U.S. currency bombs, timing devices, incendiary pistols, magnesium flares, and a long list of targets— factories, bridges, railroads, terminals, power plants, and dams. Apprehended before they could carry out any of the planned attacks, the infiltrators were tried in secrecy and found guilty of espionage. Six were executed; the remaining two received thirty-year sentences.

Concern about foreign agents led the FBI to round up thousands of Japanese, German, and Italian aliens and Ameri-

ever, that some communities refused to install it.

All across America, civilian defense seemed to be an area where Americans, anxious to help, could contribute to the war effort. A meeting to recruit OCD volunteers in Hannibal, Missouri, packed the armory with four thousand applicants, while another fifteen thousand waited outside. When the mayor of Northport, Alabama, galloped through the streets on horseback calling for volunteers, eighty percent of the town's 2,500 residents responded.

The Ground Observer Corps (GOC), another branch of the OCD, attracted 600,000 plane spotters who manned posts up to three hundred miles inland, reporting every aircraft observed. Spotters at the twenty-four-hours-a-day posts included men, women, and children. In Nebraska three ladies, each over seventy, took turns serving as their town's "plane spotter" every day of the war.

The Civil Air Patrol (CAP) of the OCD recruited 100,000 private pilots who used their own aircraft to fly antisubmarine patrols, search for downed aircraft, tow targets, watch for fires, and carry critical food and medicine. By July 1942, CAP planes on antisubmarine patrols were armed with bombs,

and by 1945 they had attacked fifty-seven U-boats, actually sinking a few.

OCD volunteers also organized block projects, explained government programs, sold war savings stamps, surveyed housing needs, recruited for the armed forces and for industry, distributed anti-black-market pledges, encouraged Victory Gardens and salvage campaigns, and performed many other useful services. When the Civil Defense

BE A VICTORY FARM VOLUNTEER
For information see   OF THE U. S. CROP CORPS

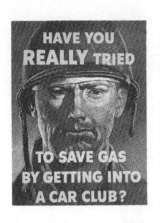

ALL: MISCELLANEOUS MAN.

To conserve irreplaceable cars and rubber, the government regulated tire ownership, reduced the speed limit, and restricted driving by rationing gasoline. With the needs of the military given priority on public transportation, civilian travelers endured long waits, crowded conditions, and altered schedules.

can citizens of the same ethnic backgrounds. Most German and Italian Americans were able to resume normal lives within a year, but 127,000 Japanese men, women, and children (many of whom were second- or third-generation American citizens) were—in accordance with Executive Order 9066 signed by President Roosevelt—given forty-eight hours to settle their affairs and report to designated collecting stations. "A Jap's a Jap," declared Army General John L. DeWitt, "it makes no difference whether he's an American or not."

Each internee was allowed to carry two suitcases and a duffel bag to one of the ten hastily built camps. By late 1942 most were permitted to leave the camps if they could find destinations inland, away from the Pacific coast, that would receive them. Two Japanese families moved to Leon Wahlbrink's town of St. Charles, Missouri. Their children, Itsu and Sammy "were surprisingly well accepted by their classmates and suddenly Japanese became different than 'Japs.'"

Life in the guarded internment camps was bleak, crowded, and disheartening, and most internees never regained the homes, businesses, and property they had been forced to abandon. Despite all this no Japanese American was charged with espionage or sabotage during the war, and some eight thousand *Nisei* served with great valor in American infantry units.

Perhaps the most important way that Americans on the home front contributed to the war effort was by producing the arms and equipment Allied forces needed to win the war. FDR set ambitious production goals for 1942: 60,000 airplanes, 48,000 tanks, 20,000 anti-aircraft guns. Although these totals were not reached, American industry learned from its mistakes and for the most part met or exceeded the even higher quotas set for 1943. By war's end Americans had produced a staggering total of almost 300,000 planes, 87,000 ships and landing craft, more than 100,000 tanks and self-propelled guns, 47 million tons of artillery shells, and 44 billion rounds of small-arms ammunition.

To achieve such goals, it became necessary to centralize coordination of personnel, equipment, facilities, raw materials, and industrial information. From January 1942 to September 1944, responsibility for this enormous undertaking fell to Donald M. Nelson, a Sears, Roebuck executive picked to head the War Production Board (WPB). With thousands of employees and volunteers, Nelson oversaw the war efforts of 13 million workers at 185,999 factories nationwide.

By May 1942 Nelson had 16,000 new plants operating around-the-clock shifts, and thousands of older factories had been converted to war industries. Former canneries now made parts for

merchant ships; cotton-processing plants produced guns; bedspread manufacturers turned out mosquito netting; a soft drink company loaded shells with explosives; a shoe manufacturer forged cannon; and a former burial-vault builder now specialized in one-hundred-pound bombs.

Some of these almost miraculous changes were wrought by industrialists like Henry J. Kaiser and Henry Ford. With no previous experience in shipbuilding (he called ships' bows "front ends"), Kaiser introduced mass production and prefabrication techniques. In 1941 it took eight months to produce a Liberty ship, a version of a British tramp steamer that became our premier cargo carrier. Within two years, Kaiser cut that time to fourteen days. A record time was set when workers at his Richmond, California, plant assembled the *Robert E. Peary* in less than five days.

One of the largest defense plants in the U.S. was built by Henry Ford at Willow Run outside Detroit for the manufacture of B-24 Liberator bombers. Completed in six months, the $65-million plant consisted of a single building a half-mile long and nearly a quarter-mile wide. Raw materials were fed from railroad sidings and loading ramps at one end of the building and joined with assembled components en route to the far side of the plant, where completed B-24s rolled out onto a runway to be flight-tested.

The Willow Run facility encountered difficulties caused by repeated design changes in the complex aircraft; absenteeism among the employees forced to commute more than twenty miles from Detroit in an era of gas and tire rationing; and a general shortage of workers that was exacerbated by Ford's strict regulations and his refusal to hire women for factory positions. During its first year, Willow Run produced only one bomber a day, leading critics to dub the facility "Willit Run?" By 1944, however, streamlining increased production to one bomber every sixty-three minutes. By war's end, 8,685 planes had rolled off the Willow Run assembly line.

The shortage of workers [a]ffected all businesses. A sign on a diner read "Be polite to our waitresses. They are harder to get than customers." A newspaper advertised: "Wanted: Registered druggist; young or old, deaf or dumb. Must have license and walk without crutches. Apply Clover Leaf Drug Store."

One solution to the problem was the opening of previously male-only positions to women. Initially there was resistance; during the first six months after the bombing of Pearl Harbor, of the 750,000 women who applied for jobs in the defense industry only about 80,000 were hired. Necessity however, soon forced manufacturers to put aside their prejudices, and advertisements courting prospective women employees appeared, proclaiming "If you can drive a car, you can run a machine" or "If you've followed recipes exactly in making cakes, you can learn to load shells."

Single women, widows, wives, and those whose husbands were away at war responded in great numbers. In Marietta, Georgia, the eighty-year-old widow of Confederate General James Longstreet joined the 8:00 A.M. shift at the Bell Aircraft Company. By 1945 about 16.5 million women comprised 36 percent of the labor force.

"By late 1943 acute labor shortages meant that even a short, skinny sixteen-year-old girl with an eighth-grade education was employable," recalls Pennsylvanian Sonya Jason, who coated glider wings at a Heinz factory in Pittsburgh. Later Sonya moved to the state capital at Harrisburg, where she and coworkers "fought home-front battles—rent-gouging landladies, amorous girl-starved servicemen, shortages of everything, fatigue and boredom—all for $25 for a six-day week."

Some companies hired leading fashion designers such as Lily Dache to create uniforms for their women workers. These creations were not well received; American women did not like being told what to wear. When Vought-Sikorsky tried to ban sweaters at its aircraft plant, "Rosie the Riveters" ignored such restrictions. Other companies tried to do away with the popular "Veronica Lake" hairdo (long tresses covering one eye),

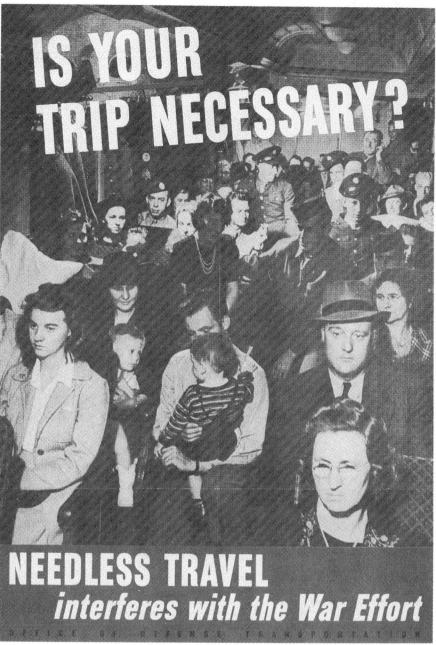

IS YOUR TRIP NECESSARY?

NEEDLESS TRAVEL
interferes with the War Effort

MISCELLANEOUS MAN.

LIBRARY OF CONGRESS.

127

Metal items were salvaged enthusiastically by Americans of all ages for recycling into tanks, guns, and ammunition. The successful scrap drives resulted in huge heaps of "junk"; hard-pressed to keep up with the collection, the government nevertheless put it all to good use.

but some female workers persisted until the movie star, as a patriotic gesture, altered her own hairstyle. Most companies simply asked that women workers wear "practical" clothing: slacks, sturdy shoes, hair in bandannas or net snoods.

Women proved their worth, and their presence usually improved working conditions for everyone through cleaner, better cafeterias and rest rooms; labor-saving lifts; and increased safety precautions. They also seemed to loaf less on the job and were less concerned with jockeying for the boss's favor. Despite their performance, however, women were not paid as much for their labor as their male counterparts, earning about forty percent of the salaries paid to men for the same work.

Like women, blacks seeking employment in the defense industry faced prejudice based on stereotypes. When the U.S. entered the war, most defense jobs were virtually closed to African Americans; one aircraft company for example, had ten black workers among 33,000 employees. When blacks threatened to stage a massive protest march on Washington in 1941, President Roosevelt issued Executive Order 8802 banning discrimination on the basis of race in the defense industry. To enforce the ban, the Fair Employment Practices Commission was established. Although successful in resolving some complaints, the commission lacked the enforcement authority necessary to bring about desegregation in defense plants. More blacks were hired and more acquired desirable job skills, but the overall economic situation of African Americans continued to lag far behind that of whites. The situation exploded into riots in several American cities in 1943 and led to a renewed activism that presaged the civil rights movement of the 1950s and '60s.

The national shortage of workers also resulted in the hiring of children under the age of sixteen in contravention of child labor laws, with an attendant rise in rates of truancy and school dropouts. In 1943, Lockheed Aircraft hired 1,500 boys as riveters, draftsmen, and electricians. For most youngsters, however, employment took the form of lesser jobs in drugstores, restaurants, or dime stores that had been vacated by adults now working in the defense industry.

Dorothy Martell, a young teacher at the time, saw her classes grow in size as male teachers entered the services. Then some of her older students "quit school and went to work in factories in Pittsburgh. One student came to visit me, showed me his paycheck and noted that he was making more than I was. Furthermore, he told me that he had some influence and could get me a job if I wanted it."

As Americans followed jobs to their sources or loved ones to military bases, we became a transient society and certain areas of the country experienced sudden and enormous growth. Particularly congested were the shipyard centers of Mobile, Alabama; Hampton Roads, Virginia; San Diego, California; and Charleston, South Carolina, whose populations rose anywhere from thirty-eight to more than sixty-four percent.

The most obvious problem associated with this influx of new residents was finding adequate housing. Many of San Francisco's two million newcomers slept in garages on mattresses spread out on cement floors. Near San Pablo, a California Navy base, a family of four adults and seven children made do with two cots and a full-sized bed in an eight-by-ten-foot wooden shack. "Bomber City" near Ford's Willow Run plant housed 14,000 workers in trailers, dormitories, and prefabricated family units. At some sites, workers paid 25 cents to sleep in a "hot bed" during an eight-hour shift, then stood in long lines at restaurants and used shower or restroom facilities wherever they could find them.

The situation in the nation's capital typified the housing problem. In less than a year, twenty-seven prefabricated office buildings sprang up in the city. The Pentagon, the huge nerve center of the armed forces, followed. Almost

300,000 new government workers staffed these facilities. Housing for the newcomers was nearly non-existent. Since hotels limited stays to three days, many people made the rounds from one to another, never sure where they would rest that night. Hospitals induced childbirth when a room was vacant lest one not be available when the mother's time came.

Many wives followed their husbands to military training camps and then to ports of embarkation. Care-worn and often disheveled, with crying babies and heavy suitcases, they appeared at bus and train stations, endured outrageous rents, and cooked on portable stoves, all for the few hours they might have with their loved ones. When Sue Williams and her mother joined her stepfather, then a serviceman stationed in Charlotte, North Carolina, they lived in quarters that "consisted of one room and a closet-kitchen containing a table and a hot plate. My mother thought she should buy some food and cook a meal. Checking her purse, she found $1.50 and no ration stamps. This was Friday. Payday was Monday. She decided to go to the grocery store and beg, borrow or steal. Our family lived for three days on dehydrated potato soup and a loaf of bread."

During 1940–45, the number of families headed at least temporarily by women jumped from 770,000 to more than 2.7 million. Anthropologist Margaret Mead observed that when American men returned from the war they would find women "more interchangeable with men than they used to be, better able to fix a tire, or mend a faucet or fix an electrical connection, or preside at a meeting, or keep a treasurer's account, or organize a political campaign than when they went away."

With fathers and older brothers in uniform and mothers working, children were cared for by friends, grandparents, or often simply fended for themselves. With no daycare facilities, mothers left children wherever they could, providing as stable an environment as possible under the circumstances.

School children were very patriotic. They kept war maps; proudly displayed bits of uniforms; wore unit patches on

their sleeves; read comic books such as "Spy Smasher," "GI Joe," or "Don Winslow of the Navy;" and used allowances to buy 10- and 25-cent defense stamps. "We fought the war daily in school," remembers Joseph Gregory, then a boy in Laurel Run, Pennsylvania. "Our tablets would be filled with aerial 'dog fights' which, to be sure, the sons of the emperor would always lose. My classmates and I must have downed three hundred Japanese Zeros each and at least that many German Messerschmidts without any of us even getting scratched."

Students took part in school air-raid drills, crouching beneath desks in the approved fashion until the "all clear" buzzer sounded. Young patriots picked streets, back yards, and attics clean of paper, tinfoil, rubber, iron, and tin cans (with the ends removed and the cans flattened) for scrap drives. In Robert Jollay's school in Dayton, Ohio, all the children "learned to KNIT! From the first to sixth grade, we knitted small, varied colored squares. These squares, which measured six by six inches, we were told, were sent to a central location and made into blankets for the troops. I've often wondered what became of my squares."

Even before Pearl Harbor, as the United States provided matériel for its allies and Americans raised funds for Bundles for Britain, the nation felt the war's effects on the availability of various commodities that originated in countries no longer open for trade. The U.S. entrance into the war and the consequent needs of the military and defense industry caused additional shortages of hundreds of ordinary items ranging from batteries, lawn mowers, and cigarettes to bobby pins, diapers, and soap. Paper match books vanished; so did zippers, only recently introduced in clothing.

The federal government established the Office of Price Administration (OPA) in April 1941 to oversee the marketplace so that goods in short supply could, through rationing, be made available to consumers on an equitable basis and to regulate prices in order to prevent runaway inflation. The OPA began by controlling raw materials used in manufacturing, then expanded to rationing many consumer goods.

On the local level, the OPA was represented by 5,500 ration boards staffed by volunteers, whose number eventually grew to 30,000. These boards issued "War Ration Book One" to consumers in May 1942. The ration stamps in each book represented "points" that were needed to buy the restricted items. Each individual received sixty-four red stamps (for meat, fish, and dairy products) and forty-eight blue Stamps (for processed foods) each month.

The number of points needed for a particular product varied with the scar-

LIBRARY OF CONGRESS.

MISCELLANEOUS MAN.

Americans helped to finance the war by buying $135 billion in war savings bonds. School children bought savings stamps that, when they filled an album, were redeemable for a $25 bond.

city of goods. Applesauce, for example, required ten blue points or stamps in March 1943 and twenty-five twelve months later; grapefruit juice, during the same period, went from twenty-three blue points to just four.

Housewives had the bewildering task of putting their family's ration stamps to best use, finding grocery stores stocking the items they needed, and arriving there with purses stuffed with the right number and kind of stamps. According to George Kaulbach, who lived in Atlanta with his family during the war years, "If someone needed an extra pair of shoes, meat and sugar coupons were offered in exchange. Everyone swapped for gas stamps. Some who did not use them sold them for a sporty price. All this was illegal, but it happened."

Sugar, the first item rationed, remained scarce until 1946 (newsman Walter Winchell whimsically wrote "Roses are Red/Violets are Blue/Sugar is Sweet, Remember?"). Each person was permitted to buy eight ounces of the sweetener a week, but grocers often did not have sugar in stock, causing housewives to find substitutes in saccharin, corn syrup, honey or molasses.

Meat rationing began on March 29, 1943 with each person allowed twenty-eight ounces per week. The number of points required varied with the type of meat and cut, as well as with its availability.

Butter was especially precious. A half-pound, when one could get it, might cost a week's supply of red stamps. It was something Louise Butler really missed. Then one day her mother returned from the store with a whole pound of the spread. "I slipped away with it to a hiding place behind the sofa. I ate just a little, and then a little more until it was half gone, three-quarters gone, and finally all gone. Mother never could figure out whom to blame. Every morning I was tortured by remorse as the family went without."

An artificially colored margarine developed as a substitute took the form of white lard-like cakes that came with an envelope of vegetable food coloring. When kneaded into the spread, the margarine might pass for anemic butter: unfortunately it still tasted like lard.

"If you were blind, you didn't need the coloring because it didn't [a]ffect the taste," recalls George Kaulbach. "For the rest of us it was a necessity. Who wants to coat their toast with white grease?"

Coffee rationing, begun in November 1942, eased the following summer when South American supplies became available. The one pound authorized to each person was supposed to last for five weeks. Hotels stopped giving refills, and railroad diners did not serve coffee at all, except for breakfast. One woman, caught with a large supply she had gathered before rationing began, explained to authorities that "I'm just stocking up before the hoarders get it all."

Probably the biggest inconvenience caused by rationing on the home front came with the restrictions placed on the use of Americans' beloved automobiles. On February 2, 1942 the last wartime civilian automobile (a Ford) authorized by the OPA came off a Detroit assembly line. Americans had to be made to drive less, and cars had to last longer. Rubber, a product of territories occupied by Japan, and vitally important for the tires of both military and civilian vehicles, was especially scarce. A speed limit of thirty-five miles per hour was enacted to save wear and tear on the tires, and a massive scrap drive to recycle used rubber began.

The OPA cut tire production for civilian use from 4 million to 35,000 a month. No one was supposed to own more than four tires; anyone with extras was expected to turn them in. To prolong tire use drivers tried recapping and sometimes wrapped plastic, paper, or cornsilk between a worn inner tube and the tire itself. Eventually a synthetic rubber was developed, easing the shortage.

The unpopular notion of gasoline rationing to cut down on car use was introduced in certain areas as early as the spring of 1942, but took effect nationally in December of that year. Each car and truck was assigned a colored sticker emblazoned with a large letter to be affixed to its windshield. The letter indicated the quantity of gasoline the vehicle's driver could buy each week.

Hasten the Homecoming

BUY VICTORY BONDS

LIBRARY OF CONGRESS.

Back to Elm Street, U. S. A.

Back from the business of killing — to the business of living! ... and despair and

traded in their freedom for promises of security — for brightly painted pictures of a "planned economy" under an all-wise, all-powerful government.

Greater incentives must be provided, so that workers can make more money, by making more goods for more people.

Mr. Private Citizen must be allowed to make money — and be free to invest it in business ventures of his own — or of others.

... of that sort of thing ... ...have they

MISCELLANEOUS MAN.

An "A" sticker, the one most Americans received, authorized the purchase of from three to five gallons per week. "B" stickers went to war workers, entitling them to exactly as much as they needed to get back and forth to work; those who required automobiles for their jobs but could not estimate precisely how much driving they would have to do (doctors, clergymen, and telegram deliverers) were issued a "C" sticker. Almost unlimited fuel went to emergency vehicles with "E" stickers, trucks marked with a "T", and a few civilians who qualified for an "X" sticker. No sticker, however, could guarantee that there would be any gasoline to buy. Long lines of thirsty automobiles could often be seen trailing gas delivery trucks to their destinations.

The need to conserve rubber, fuel, and metal also [a]ffected commercial transportation. Travel by airline, for those not in uniform, became a nonoption. And with increased pressure on buses and trains, comfort while traveling became a distant memory. It was nothing to have to sit on a suitcase or stand for an eight-hour trip. Sue Williams was a child when she and her mother headed out by train from Bloomington, Illinois, to join her stepfather in Charlotte, North Carolina. "Train schedules and seating were dictated by military needs, and there was no guarantee that a train would go when or where it was scheduled, or that it would ever go," she remembers. "Our route should have been Bloomington-Cincinnati-Charlotte, switching trains at Cincinnati. It turned out to be Bloomington-Cincinnati-Washington-Richmond-Charlotte, with three switches and double the time."

To save electricity all Americans turned their clocks ahead one hour on February 2, 1942, put-

More than three years after Pearl Harbor, the cherished dream of all Americans—the safe return home of loved ones—finally became a reality for most following V-E Day on May 8, 1945 and then V-J Day on August 15. Victory and peace had now been won—at the cost of 320,000 war dead and through the commitment of tens of millions of other men and women both in and out of uniform.

ting the country on War Time. Fuel oil and coal rationing cut consumption for heating by one-third as folks at home donned sweaters in the evening, went to bed early and set thermostats at sixty-five degrees.

By February 1943 clothing, too, was becoming scarce. Each person was allowed two pairs of shoes a year, but most families pooled stamps to buy shoes for growing children. To conserve cloth, tailors fashioned "Victory Suits" with short jackets, narrow lapels, no vests, and one pair of trousers (no cuffs).

As a further means of combating shortages of rubber, paper, and critical metals, Americans held scrap drives. Everywhere there were reminders: a poster proclaiming "Slap the Japs with Scrap;" Bing Crosby singing "Junk Will Win the War" (not his best effort); or an old jalopy on its way to be recycled bearing the sign, "Praise the Lord, I'll Soon Be Ammunition."

Children turned in masses of tinfoil, tin cans, and old overshoes (scrap rubber was worth a penny a pound at most gas stations). A youngster in Maywood, Illinois—told that a P-51 fighter plane required 1,069 square feet of paper packaging for overseas shipment—collected one hundred tons of scrap paper.

Leon Wahlbrink, while in the first grade, got enthused about scrap drives. "All of us who collected scrap got to wear an arm band," he recalls. "I could not have been prouder to wear a Marine dress-uniform. On more than one Satur-

day I pulled my red wagon around town and proudly picked up scrap metal on the curb in front of people's homes."

Billy Kerr's high school in Baytown (then Goose Creek), Texas, had a nice Civil War bronze cannon mounted on a pedestal. "Unfortunately this historical memento went into, and served as the centerpiece of, a special brass, copper, and bronze scrap drive which also featured old razor blade injectors, wire, water faucets, and all sorts of weird copper-containing items that only high school students could possibly locate."

Housewives—made aware that one pound of kitchen fat provided enough glycerine for a pound of black powder, which then equated to six artillery shells or fifty .30-caliber bullets—took what they had saved to the local butcher, who sometimes sweetened their reward with red ration stamps.

To increase the nation's food supply, Americans cultivated "Victory Gardens" wherever the ground would hold them—the Portland, Oregon zoo; Boston common; a downtown parking lot in New Orleans; Chicago's Arlington Race Track—in tracts ranging from eight-by-ten-feet backyard plots to hundreds of acres behind defense plants. The 20.5 million Victory Gardens cultivated in 1943 provided more than thirty percent of all the vegetables grown in America that year. Growing food was something the ordinary citizen felt good about—a tangible and tasty way to help the war effort.

There was some black marketing in rationed goods, but most home-front Americans played pretty straight. Sometimes they became angrier at "stoopers"—store owners who always seemed able to stoop behind their counters and come up with a scarce item for favored customers—than at black marketeers.

Americans—once again reaping the benefits of a healthy economy—also helped to finance the war. A five-percent surcharge, dubbed a "Victory Tax," was added to each wage-earner's federal income tax. To put more funds immediately at the government's disposal, employers were required to withhold taxes from workers' pay instead of allowing them to make a

single payment each March. In addition to helping the national treasury these measures cut down on individual spending and thus prevented inflation from getting out of control, a real danger during such an economic boom.

To further reduce the enormous debt incurred by the nation during the war, the government began the sale of war bonds. Sold in denominations ranging from $25 (ten-year maturity on the $18.75 purchase price) to $10,000, the bonds brought $135 billion into the national treasury.

War heroes, entertainers, and other popular figures on the home front helped to sell the bonds. Actress Betty Grable donated her nylons to the top bidder at a bond rally; Man O' War's horseshoes rewarded another; comedian Jack Benny's $75 violin brought a $1-million bid; and starlet Hedy Lamarr promised to reward any buyer of $25,000 worth of bonds with a kiss. Singer Kate Smith outdid all rivals when she sold $40 million in bonds during a sixteen-hour radio marathon.

The media and the entertainment industry played an important role in keeping the American public informed and in a positive frame of mind during the war years. In June 1942 President Roosevelt created the Office of War Information (OWI), charging it to "tell the people as much about the war as possible, as fast as possible, and with as few contradictions as possible." There was a lot of home-grown propaganda in the media's offerings but, all in all, reports from the battle lines were accurate and reached the public quickly. By 1944 CBS was devoting thirty percent of its air time to war news, and NBC's news coverage had grown from 1939's 3.6 percent to better than 20 percent. FDR himelf used radio, in a series of "fireside chats," to keep Americans informed of the war's progress.

American newspapers and radio had more than seven hundred reporters and correspondents stationed overseas at a given time; more than four hundred covered the D-Day Normandy landings. "Geography may not have been in the curriculum for those of us in the primary grades," recalls Leon Wahlbrink, "but I can guarantee that we learned it. Each day the newspapers printed maps of the war zones, and the front pages were covered with stories of the war's progress. Hans V. Kaltenborn, Gabriel Heater, and Edward R. Murrow were heard broadcasting war news every day. The programs originating from the battle areas made an indelible mark on my young mind."

The most popular American correspondent was Ernie Pyle, a slight (110 pounds), balding man in his forties who found his stories, not in generals' headquarters or Pentagon offices, but among the ranks of the beleaguered foot soldiers he accompanied into battle. Pyle's newspaper column appeared six times a week in 310 newspapers for an audience of more than 12 million readers. His writings brought the war home, perhaps even more clearly than today's television journalism, because he not only pictured war but made the reader *feel* it and *think* about it. He marched with the troops from Africa to Sicily to Italy to France; then he went to the Pacific theater—and was killed on the tiny atoll of Ie Shima near Okinawa. Over his grave his fellow soldiers placed a headstone: "On this spot the 77th Infantry Division lost a buddy, Ernie Pyle, 18 April 1945."

On newspaper "funny pages," comic-strip heroes went to war too. The Army had Privates Joe Palooka and Snuffy Smith. The Air Corps had Terry of "Terry and the Pirates" and Smilin' Jack. The Navy had Don Winslow and Dick Tracy (special duty with Naval Intelligence when he was not battling such criminals as Pruneface, 88 Keys, Brow or Flattop on the home front). Tillie the Toiler joined the WAACS, and Fritzie Ritz (of "Nancy") and Winnie Winkle took their places on assembly lines.

During the last months of the war, an irresistible cartoon—a bulb-nosed, scant-haired, wide-eyed man peering over some kind of wall, always with the simple message "Kilroy was Here"—appeared on the combat front and on virtually every public surface at home. The ubiquitous character epitomized the spirit of the American GI at war—omnipotent, irreverent, and *there*.

The OWI tried to guide Hollywood's movie-making efforts by suggesting that they not condemn *all* Germans and Japanese; show farm boys remaining on the farm instead of enlisting (food production was critical to the war effort); and not portray Chinese in menial positions, Englishmen living lavishly or GIs as cocky, bumptious, and undisciplined. Producers bought some of OWI's guidance, but ignored most of it.

The movie industry provided films with both recreational and propaganda value, as well as military and industrial training films. John O'Neill recalls that "on Saturday afternoons we would go to the movies and watch John Wayne and the Fighting Seabees capture an island to build an airstrip for our pilots. Then we watched a short, patriotic film urging us to buy War Bonds. 'Buy a Bond to Buy a Bomber and Send Your Name to War' was the slogan they used."

In retrospect, wartime films seem to have inspired us to fight the Nazis because they were the aggressor and had to be fought, but to seek the utter destruction of the Japanese because we hated what they had done to us at Pearl Harbor, Wake Island, and Bataan. Early movies did not dwell on the extent of America's losses at Pearl Harbor and seldom showed U.S. war dead. Some— *The Story of G.I. Joe* and *Guadalcanal Diary* among them—were good motion pictures, but mainly war movies such as *Mrs. Miniver, Thirty Seconds Over Tokyo, The Purple Heart, Objective Burma,* and *Wake island* were intended to arouse the nation's patriotism and will to win.

Movie stars and other celebrities also helped the war effort by entertaining servicemen at United Service Organization (USO) canteens across the country. The USO's three thousand canteens provided a club-like atmosphere for those away from home. When Vice President Harry S. Truman showed up to play for the troops at the canteen in the National Press Club building in Washington; D.C., his performance was enhanced by the presence of Hollywood star Lauren Bacall perched atop the piano. At the "Stage Door Canteen," in the basement of New York's Forty-Fourth Street Theater, Broadway stars entertained, danced with servicemen, or helped by washing dishes, pouring coffee, or just chatting with those who stopped by. Hollywood's canteen attracted stars and starlets under the watchful eye of its first director, actress Bette Davis.

Music was a major source of enjoyment or comfort to war-weary Americans. There were patriotic songs—"Praise the Lord and Pass the Ammunition" "Remember Pearl Harbor," and Irving Berlin's "This is the Army, Mr. Jones"; sentimental favorites such as "Don't Sit Under the Apple Tree," and "Don't Get Around Much Anymore," which reflected the loneliness of loved ones separated by the war; and specially crafted numbers, most very short-lived, supporting such home front phenomena as bond drives ("Cash for Your Trash"), Victory Gardens ("Get Out and Dig, Dig, Dig"), and women defense workers ("Rosie the Riveter").

Despite the war, sports remained popular on the home front. When baseball commissioner Judge Kennesaw Mountain Landis addressed the question of cancelling professional baseball for the duration of the war, President Roosevelt replied that the sport was a "definite recreational asset to at least 20 million [Americans] and that in my judgment is thoroughly worthwhile."

Most professional athletes traded their team uniforms for new ones in the military but ball clubs fielded less skilled, draft-deferred players in their place. The St. Louis Browns signed Pete Gray, a one-armed outfielder who batted .218 during a seventy-seven-game season. One sports writer lamented that rosters of players were as full of unknown names as YMCA hotel registers. There were other problems to be overcome— night baseball was banned in many cities; rail travel from city to city was difficult; and baseballs were in short supply (eventually we accepted a different composition ball, but then argued whether hitters got an unfair advantage from the new ball).

Nonetheless, more than 4 million fans attended major-league baseball games in 1942, and Americans continued to support the game throughout the war years. In New York City the Yankees, Giants, and Dodgers played a three-team exhibition game to sell war bonds. Each team batted six times against rotating opponents. The score: Dodgers 5, Yankees 1, Giants 0; Uncle Sam $56.5 million.

More than six hundred players from the ten-team National Football League went into military service. The league continued during the war, but, due to the shortage of players, teams—the Philadelphia Eagles and the Pittsburgh Steelers in 1943, the Brooklyn Tigers and the new Boston Yanks in 1945—were forced to merge squads. College football, dominated by West Point's Army team, included service teams from such facilities as the Great Lakes Naval Training Center near Chicago and California's March Field among their ranks.

When Franklin D. Roosevelt won an unprecedented fourth term as president in November 1944, comedian Bob Hope teased, "I've always voted for Roosevelt as president; my *father* always voted for Roosevelt as president."

As that year drew to a close, more and more living room windows displayed service flags. Now however, because there had been many Western Union messengers bearing telegrams beginning "The War Department regrets to inform you . . . ," many of the blue stars had been replaced by gold. At Christmas Mrs. Belle Ellzey of Texas, who lost her son, Lieutenant John G. Ellzey, in France expressed the feelings of many an American mother: "I am so very homesick for him. It is Christmas—and . . . I cannot write to him, putting my tears into words, for my eyes stay strangely dry."

Finally by the spring of 1945 it was clear that the war would soon be over. But it was too soon to celebrate. On April 12 Americans were stunned to learn that President Roosevelt, having suffered a massive cerebral hemorrhage while at his "Little White House" near Warm Springs, Georgia, was dead.

The news flashed across the country with great force. Businesses closed. Theaters emptied. Traffic slowed to a halt. Newspaper "extras" hit the streets. All military units in the country were put on alert. A New York City cab driver stopped, parked, and cried, "It just doesn't seem possible." A hastily-closed shop in Pittsburgh bore the simple sign "He died." In Washington, a soldier probably spoke for most Americans when he confided, "I felt as if I knew him—and I felt as if he liked me."

For three days and nights radio programming was suspended, except for news broadcasts and religious music. After appropriate national ceremonies in Washington, Roosevelt's body was returned to his home in Hyde Park, New York, for burial. On a Sunday morning the funeral train chugged its way up the shore of the Hudson River past West Point and through Beacon, where the young girl who, four years before, had been scolded for breaking her Japanese toy piano, held her mother's hand and promised to always remember that day.

Less than a month later, on May 8, 1945, Germany officially surrendered, ending the war in Europe. The news touched off a frenzied celebration in the United States. Schools, offices, and defense plants emptied, and streets were filled with jubilant revelers who sounded whatever noisemakers they had. In St. Charles, Missouri, Leon Wahlbrink rushed off to join in the town's impromptu parade as "horns honked, church bells pealed, factory whistles went full blast for hours. It was a grand and glorious day."

Three months later, on the other side of the world, Japan surrendered. Three years, eight months, and seven days after the attack on Pearl Harbor, the war was over at a cost of more than a million American casualties.

The surviving soldiers, sailors, and airmen came home. They seemed older, a bit tense, impatient to do at once everything they had dreamed about during the past four years. And their language was pretty salty at times. Soon however, they picked up most of their prewar ways. Home-front emergency defense organizations were disbanded. Defense workers gave up (or were laid off from) wartime jobs, moving over to give the veterans their places.

"Perhaps my most significant memory from the early forties," sums up Cornelius Lynch, "is that overnight the world around me had changed dramatically and significantly. . . . For me, it was part of growing up but I realize now that it was more than simply a childhood I had left behind; it was another age."

The war, which had eradicated the last vestiges of the Great Depression and marked the U.S. as an economic and military superpower, also significantly altered Americans' perceptions of how things should be. Previously held assumptions about a "woman's place" or an African American's ability to get a job done would never again go unchallenged. "Female clothing became feminine [in the postwar years,] and veterans wanted their women to return home and stay there," says Sonya Jason, "but the genie could not be squeezed back into the bottle. Few of us who experienced the satisfaction of doing a demanding job and earning our own money could ever again be content to be dependent on anyone else, even the man we loved."

The American people had demonstrated a remarkable unanimity of purpose during almost four years of war. Although they never wavered in the belief that the Allies would prevail, Americans realized early on that winning would not be easy. But almost everyone, it seemed, felt a personal sense of responsibility to get the job done. On the home front, citizens pretty much did what their leaders asked—and a bit more. "To a boy growing from age six to ten, World War II, with all its horrors, was a romantic period," recalls Leon Wahlbrink. "I was fortunate that it did not tragically touch my most immediate family. Maybe it was just me at my young age, but the war seemed to be a time of unparalleled heroes and patriotism. We were proud to be Americans."

Fifty years later, the ranks of World War II veterans (both those in uniform and those who maintained the home front) have thinned. We wear bifocals now and aren't quite so concerned about the extra pounds and the receding hair (too late to worry about that) as we were when we were younger. Some of those who once wore uniforms still squeeze into them to fire rifle volleys at funerals or Veterans' Day rallies, while home-front veterans preserve their memories in other ways. But all of us remain very concerned about our country. May that characteristic of Americans never change.

The editors wish to express their appreciation to the numerous individuals who shared their home-front memories as part of this article.

Our Greatest Land Battle

BY EDWARD OXFORD   Fifty years ago, amid the snow, blood, and death of Belgium's Ardennes forest, 600,000 American soldiers defeated a half-million Germans in the Battle of the Bulge—the largest engagement involving the U.S. army in World War II.

American soldiers manning an eighty-five-mile stretch of rugged, heavily wooded countryside along the Belgian-Luxembourg-German border were jolted awake in the predawn hours of December 16, 1944, by the thunder of mortar, rocket, and artillery fire. When the barrage finally ended, the Americans peered from their foxholes to see strange lights playing against the low-hanging clouds and reflecting onto the forest floor to reveal ghostly figures advancing among the trees. The bewildered GIs didn't know what to make of it.

The Americans were holding the northern sector of a five-hundred-mile line that extended across France and Belgium all the way from the Swiss border to the North Sea. During the six months since the Allied invasion of Normandy they had driven east in an effort to push the German Army across the Rhine and establish a foothold on the far side of the river. The Allies had been stopped short of their objective and suffered significant losses, especially in the bloody hard-fought offensive of the Hürtgen Forest, but they had inflicted an even higher toll on the enemy.

As the Americans paused just short of Germany's vaunted West Wall—also known as the Siegfried Line—to rest their battle-worn veterans and train newcomers, they did not suspect that the enemy was capable of anything but defensive action. For days, and in many cases weeks, more than eighty thousand soldiers of the 14th Cavalry Group, the 9th Armored Division, and four U.S. infantry divisions—the 4th, 28th, 99th, and 106th—had marked time along the mist-ridden battlefront.

Almost incredibly, spearheads of the "beaten" German Army were thrusting into U.S. lines.

During these pre-Christmas days, all seemed relatively secure. Film star Marlene Dietrich, heading a USO troupe, performed to the raucous applause of GIs. Numbers of men wangled three-day passes to Paris. One soldier wrote home: "As long as I stay where I am now I'll be safe."

But, in the half-light of that Saturday's dawn, the enemy soldiers advancing in the reflected glow of searchlights were very much alive and threatening. U.S. rifleman Bernard Macay saw "hundreds of Germans against the skyline as they came over the hill, right at us." American troops on the front lines opened up with rifle, machine-gun, and

NATIONAL ARCHIVES.

mortar fire. Their first response, though earnest, was sporadic, uncoordinated, and confused. Almost incredibly spearheads of German Führer Adolf Hitler's "beaten" German Army were thrusting into U.S. lines.

The Battle of the Bulge, with fire and fury, had begun.

Somehow in the heart of Ardennes darkness, Hitler had discerned a glimmer of hope. Just as Allied commanders judged the rugged countryside unsuitable for an attack route into Germany so also did they disregard it as a likely approach for an enemy counteroffensive.

In the fifth year of devastating war, Hitler's "Thousand-Year" Third Reich was under siege. The Germans had fought hard, but Allied troops, quite like their leaders, felt a sense of momentum as they moved relentlessly through France and the Low Countries toward the Rhine. On the Eastern Front, Russian forces hammered the Germans with equal fury. By day and by night, air raids continued to turn the Fatherland's cities and factories into ruins. German ground forces had by this time suffered more than four million casualties, nearly half of them in the summer of 1944. Yet

even an attempt on his life by his own officers in July had failed to break the Führer's determination to continue the war.

Refusing to listen to his military advisors, Hitler decided to draw upon the best of his remaining men and matériel in a do-or-die attempt to turn back the Allied onslaught. Under the cover of mist and snow, German forces would strike through a weak sector on the Allied front in the Ardennes, cross the Meuse River sixty miles to the West, and press on another sixty miles to capture the vital Channel port of Antwerp. They would, thereby, split the American and British forces—and their alliance as well—inflicting so many losses that, conceivably the Allies would sue for peace.

There was a grim, if fatalistic, logic to Hitler's plan. Unconditional surrender was unthinkable, and Germany could not survive by fighting a defensive war. The one route left was through the Ardennes. As a German adage put the choice: "Better an end in horror than a horror without end."

During the three months since Hitler revealed his scheme, the Germans east of the Ardennes had moved with remarkable stealth to ready thirty assault

divisions. Although they fell short of that goal by two divisions, they had moved some 300,000 men, 1,900 artillery pieces, and nearly 1,000 tanks and armored vehicles into place. The operation was deceptively code-named "*Wacht am Rhein*" ("Watch on the Rhine").

Incredibly, the large-scale preparation went barely noticed by Allied intelligence. The Germans had begun to suspect that "Enigma," their code system, might be vulnerable to Allied codebreakers (which, throughout the war, it was). Hitler therefore directed that orders relating to the crucial Ardennes attack be sent by motorcycle rather than by radio. "Ultra," the Allied intelligence derived from cracking Enigma, dried up in that sector.

U.S. Army historian Hugh M. Cole has called the prelude to the Ardennes action "a gross failure by Allied ground and air intelligence. . . . The Allies had looked in a mirror for the enemy and seen there only the reflection of their own intentions." Bent upon attacking Germany they did not conceive that the enemy might strike back at them—much as the Germans, attacking at Stalingrad in 1942, had assumed that the Russians could not possibly attack *them*.

NATIONAL ARCHIVES.

NATIONAL ARCHIVES.

than two thousand casualties in the first four days of fighting. As the nearby 2nd Division deftly slipped battalions forward through the 99th to burrow into enemy forces, the two groups together formed an unbreakable barrier.

At the southern end of the German assault, the veteran U.S. 4th Infantry Division put up a fierce holding action at the village of Berdorf. Their steadfast refusal to budge held the enemy within two miles of their starting point and blocked their access to any of the main roads through the town.

At the center, however, the Fifth Panzer Army made penetrations with stealth and speed. On the thickly forested Schnee Eifel ridge, Panzer tank forces surrounded two regiments of the green 106th Division, subjecting them for three days to a numbing assault. Promised airdrops of supplies, the beleaguered units attempted to move out on December 18. But the relief drops never materialized. Nearly out of food, water, medical supplies, and ammunition, and facing vastly superior firepower, the regiments crumpled on December 19. In a kind of European "Bataan," seven to eight thousand men—the largest number of Americans ever captured in a single action—were taken prisoner by the Germans.

At his headquarters in Paris, Supreme Allied Commander General Dwight D. Eisenhower pondered the breakthrough. General Omar Bradley, whose command encompassed the Ardennes sector, first thought the assault to be a "spoiling attack" aimed at hindering the planned advance of the U.S. First and Third Armies in the region. Eisenhower, however, sensed major trouble: the massive attack had ominous momentum.

In this time of peril, Eisenhower held just about as much strategic power as Hitler himself did. He had full authority to put countermeasures into action at once. In a matter of days, he was to pour a quarter of a million men and thousands of tanks and artillery pieces into the Ardennes—a strike-back no other army in history has ever matched.

Concerned by the enormity of the German salient, Eisenhower imposed a news blackout on the battle action. It would be days before Americans on the

The top Allied commanders themselves accepted this analysis. Overconfidence, which led them to accept a paper-thin Ardennes line as a "legitimate risk," was to bring their forces to the brink of catastrophe.

Not until December 12, at Hitler's western command bunker north of Frankfurt, were his lower-echelon officers given the final details of the attack. The Fifth and Sixth SS Panzer Armies would make the main strike into Belgium, while the Seventh Army protected their southern flank. "This battle is to decide whether we shall live or die," the Führer exhorted his commanders: "I want all my soldiers to fight hard and without pity.... The enemy must be beaten—now or never!"

Hitler cannily scheduled the offensive for November to allow bad weather to set in, so as to cloak his ground attack from the view of Allied fighters and bombers. Logistical problems, however,

necessitated delaying the assault until mid-December. As Hitler had hoped, at least for the first few days fog did keep the Allied planes grounded.

At 5:30 A.M. on December 16 the German barrage began. The firing continued for more than an hour, aiming for U.S. command posts, communications centers, and encampments. Soon, from out of the gloom, came the German foot-soldiers bathed in the eerie glow of searchlights. Thousands of GIs, many in combat for the first time, battled for their lives. Short of ammunition, without air support, and dazed by the devastating artillery fire, disciplined infantry assaults, and deadly tank attacks, some faltered. But the orders were to "hold fast." "In other words," wrote Sergeant Henry Giles in his diary "get killed but don't fall back."

In the north, the Sixth SS Panzer Army met unexpected trouble when the untried U.S. 99th Infantry Division offered stiff resistance, at a cost of more home front found out what their sons, brothers, and husbands on the battlefront had learned firsthand: the Western Front's biggest ground battle had broken out in the Ardennes.

The Germans had driven a wedge between the First and Ninth U.S. Armies in the North and the Third Army under General George S. Patton in the South. Faced with that emergency, Eisenhower was forced to make the difficult decision to divide General Omar Bradley's command of these armies, giving charge of the First and Ninth Armies to British Field Marshal Bernard L. Montgomery and leaving Bradley in command of the Third. Among the American officers it was not a popular decision, but it had the added effect that Eisenhower had hoped for; it brought the British XXX Corps into the fray to back up the troops sent to block key bridges from the German advance.

Eisenhower's strategy overall was to hold the "shoulders" of the penetration—limiting the width of the breakthrough so that he could counterattack the flanks, hem in the Panzer columns so that they could not maneuver, and put a choke-hold on the breakthrough.

As the battle intensified, a dozen units were deployed to hold the northern edge of the salient.* In the very first hours, the 101st Airborne raced by truck through the night to reach Bastogne, a strategic crossroads town with seven paved roads radiating from its center, that lay directly in the path of the Fifth Panzer Army's advance. At the full tide of battle, thirty-two U.S. divisions would take part in the action.

By December 20, the Sixth Panzer Army had advanced only about five miles, but its First Panzer Division had driven forward twenty miles. The Fifth Panzer Army

*These, ranging roughly east to west through the First Army sector commanded by General Courtney Hodges, would include: the 9th, 2nd, 99th, 1st, and 30th Infantry divisions; the 82nd Airborne; the 7th and 3rd Armored; the 75th, 84th, and 83rd Infantry; and the 2nd Armored. General George Patton's Third Army pressed up from the south. Here would be arrayed the 4th, 9th, and 5th Infantry divisions; the 10th Armored, the 80th, and 26th Infantry; the 6th, 4th, 9th, and 11th Armored; the 17th Airborne; and the 87th Infantry.

In one of the worst atrocities of the Western Front, SS troops murdered eighty-six American prisoners of war in a field near Malmédy.

---

fared well, slashing more than fifteen miles ahead on a wide front and threatening the key crossroads town of Bastogne.

Though German advance forces quickly overran American outposts, with every new mile they found the going tougher. They fell behind their schedule, and—fatefully—their tanks began to run low on fuel.

GIs found themselves in a foot-by-foot fight for hills, villages, and woods. They struggled through mud and rain with their M-1 rifles slung on their shoulders; pockets stuffed with grenades, cigarettes, and candle stubs; sheets of toilet paper tucked inside their helmets. Some stuffed newspapers into their overcoats for warmth. Private Lester Atwell wrote: "Their chapped hands split open, their lips cracked, their feet froze. They had colds, frostbite, trench foot, pneumonia. After trudging miles through deep snow along they came, their faces pinched, astonished, mottled. The young looked old."

Driving captured jeeps, English-speaking German troops wearing U.S. Military Police armbands and GI field jackets and trousers over their uniforms began to infiltrate key road junctions. Many of these dissemblers were German-Americans who had lived in the United States before the war. They misdirected U.S. vehicles, turned signposts the wrong way and hung red ribbons to signify—falsely—that roads were mined.

Thousands of jumpy GIs played cat-and-mouse with one another as they tried to search out the roving saboteurs. At gunpoint, genuine MPs would ask American soldiers such questions as: "What's the capital of Illinois?" "Who are 'dem Bums'?" . . . "What's the name

of Roosevelt's dog?" One U.S. general was put under guard when he mistakenly said the Chicago Cubs were an American League team.

Although their masquerade quickly came undone, the impostors managed to set off a scare throughout the American forces. Eighteen of those captured were executed by U.S. firing squads.

Hitler's hopes rode highest on SS Lieutenant Colonel Joachim Peiper, his handpicked choice to spearhead the Panzer drive through the American line. A believer in brutality, Peiper urged his commanders to "fight in the SS spirit."

On Sunday afternoon, December 17, in a field near Malmédy, SS troops under Peiper's command engaged in a particularly heinous episode of *blutraush*—killing frenzy. They had captured some 130 men of the U.S. 285th Field Artillery Observation Battalion and ordered them into rows, hands above their heads. According to later war-crimes testimony, SS soldiers moved among the prisoners, confiscating their rings, wallets, and cigarettes. A German officer then gave the command: *"Machen alles kaput!"* ("Kill them all!") German troops opened up with machine gun and pistol fire on the helpless Americans. Terrified GIs ran in all directions. Private James Mattera recalls: "SS soldiers came to men who were still alive and they shot them in the head." The executioners kicked some downed men in their faces, striking others with rifle butts. One man's eyes were gouged out.

Later that day, the unburied, bullet-ridden bodies of eighty-six soldiers were found in the bloodstained field. A few wounded but still living, survived by pretending to be dead. Forty or so others escaped into the woodlands.

The Malmédy Massacre undoubtedly strengthened the resolve of American soldiers—not just to stop the Germans but to beat them severely on the field of battle.* Gunners hammered at Peiper's

*This massacre was only one of many confirmed acts of brutality laid at Peiper's feet. All told, he was found responsible for ordering the murder of more than 350 American prisoners of war and 111 Belgian civilians along his line of march.

tanks. Engineers blew up bridges to thwart his advance. Major Paul J. Solis, commander of an armored infantry detachment sent to defend Stavelot, ignited thousands of gallons of fuel at a gasoline dump to form a barrier against him. By December 21, out of fuel, ammunition, and hope, Peiper ignominiously led eight hundred survivors of his original force of five thousand back toward Germany on foot.

Throughout the Ardennes, U.S. tanks and infantrymen did bitter battle against the more-heavily-armored German Mark IV, Panther, and Tiger tanks. "Our Sherman tanks would lie in wait, and hit those big tanks in the back, where their armor could be pierced," First Sergeant Bill Wagner recalls. "It was the only way to stop them. "In only three minutes, tank gunner Gerald Nelson knocked out three enemy tanks with three shots. Private Bernard Michin, firing a bazooka from only ten yards away hit and destroyed a Tiger; the blast left him blind for eight hours. In a dusk attack, a Sherman commanded by Lieutenant Charles Power set three Panthers afire. Sergeant Settimio Tiberio hunkered low when a Tiger tank rolled right over his foxhole and lived to tell of it.

Temperatures dipped below freezing, with intermittent snow, hanging mists, and ground fog. GIs went to sleep in overcoats and woke up encased in a film of ice. Water froze in canteens. C-rations became blocks of ice. Corporal Howard Peterson remembers: "To get out of the cold we crawled into a pigpen; soldiers and pigs—we all smelled the same." "It went down near zero one night," recalls infantryman Joseph Kiss. "By dawn I had half a foot of snow on top of me. We were dirty, wet, and tired. I saw some men cry. The Germans would yell at us to give up. But we never did." Sergeant Nat Youngblood tells of a twelve-year-old Belgian farm girl, scarved and bundled, plodding through snowdrifts to bring hot coffee to U.S. soldiers burrowed in foxholes. "I'll never forget her young face. 'Good morning,' she said to me. 'Coffee, sir?' "

For days, furious action centered around Bastogne. Here troopers of the 101st Airborne Division, along with soldiers from other units, formed an island of Americans in a sea of Germans. The 18,000 defenders fought in every direction at once, holding a sixteen-mile perimeter against more than twice their number. In relentless waves, German tanks and troops strove to smash into "the hole in the doughnut."

U.S. field guns dropped a "dam of fire" around the perimeter. Mud slowed and just about stopped the advancing tanks. As German infantry ran forward shouting, the Americans cut them down. The attackers kept on coming, climbing over bodies of their comrades before being killed themselves.

Midday on December 22, Brigadier General Anthony McAuliffe, commander of the besieged 101st, received an ultimatum to surrender or risk the annihilation of his troops. McAuliffe, who had earlier received word that part of Patton's Third Army was on their way to Bastogne, responded with his memorable, one-syllable reply: "Nuts!"

Hell-bent upon the rescue of Bastogne, tanks of the 4th Armored Division of Patton's Third Army went into high gear alongside infantry, punching up from the south. In their remarkable dash toward the besieged town, the Third Army moved farther and engaged more enemy divisions in less time then any other army in the history of the United States. As Patton had said to Eisenhower: "This time the German has stuck his hand in a meat grinder—and I've got hold of the handle."

"Hitler's weather," a blanket of fog and cloud, continued to cloak the battleground. Allied airpower, poised to strike, could but bide its time. Forlorn U.S. soldiers looked to the sky in vain.

Finally, at dawn on December 23, a cold front moved through, sweeping the clouds away. U.S. Army Air Force P-51 Mustangs, P-47 Thunderbolts, P-38 Lightnings, and B-26 Marauders, along with Royal Air Force Typhoons swarmed down on the Germans. The besieged troops at Bastogne received their first airdrop of badly needed supplies. At American-held Malmédy, however, a number of U.S. troops and Belgian civilians were killed when mistakenly bombed by the Ninth Air Force on three consecutive nights.

Come Christmas morning, with German forces closing in on Bastogne, paratroopers shook hands with one another in a farewell gesture. Hour after hour, enemy soldiers bore in upon them, full-circle. In one particularly dramatic showdown, beleaguered Americans knocked out eighteen German tanks and cut to ribbons waves of white-clad Panzer grenadiers. By nightfall, the paratroopers—with cooks and mechanics and clerks fighting alongside them—still held the rim. Their Christmas present came the next day. In the fast-fading afternoon light of the 26th, the first of Patton's tanks broke into Bastogne.

For Hitler, Bastogne became the crucial symbol—the place that *must* be taken. Even into the New Year, his Panzers hit Bastogne with as many as fifteen attacks a day—but could not break the ring. A German victory here was not to be.

The price, for both sides at Bastogne, was high. Some 7,000 Germans and 3,500 Americans were killed or wounded fighting for the village.

Spellbinding though the Bastogne action was, scores of bloody thrusts and ripostes—death-duels waged by tanks, artillery and foot-soldiers—were fought throughout the Ardennes woodlands. For the battle-worn "dogface," misery was the order of the day. "We would attack each pitch-black morning," says Corporal Mitchell Kaidy. "If we slept, it was sitting up—fitfully, shallowly, cradling our rifles and hand grenades like babies." Private First Class Thor Ronnigen remembers "dead Germans toppling into our foxholes." "There were shapes in the snow and we would fire and fire," recalls Private Charles Oxford, brother of the author of this article. "A shell-burst got me at one point. When they carried me out, my feet were frostbitten."

"The Germans came through after the moon had set," said Corporal William Fowler. "I fired my machine gun. I could hear them holler, begging for mercy when they were hit." At a roadblock, paratrooper Roger Carqueville stopped a hurrying jeep: "I stuck an M-1 at the driver's ear and asked him for the password. Turned out he was a chaplain.

I figured I wasn't going to make it through the scrap, so I asked him to hear my confession. Which he did, right in the middle of the road."

The battle map of the Ardennes action took on a whirlwind look—lines of advance and withdrawal, loops and counter-loops, swirls and twists as the contenders stalked, entrapped, and pounded one another. There was no pattern to it all—just ferocity in the mist.

German tank columns could push forward only as far as their fast-dwindling fuel sustained them. Their hope of "living off" captured fuel supplies, though sporadically realized, proved futile. The tide of advance, sector by sector, had begun to crest.

As of Christmas morning, German tanks had smashed to within sight of the Meuse River—the high-point of their advance, some sixty miles from their starting line. But the column ran short of fuel and hit a hardening wall of U.S. armor and infantry. This far, fate ruled— and no farther.

When the shock of American armor failed to produce breakthroughs, infantrymen moved through deep snow on foot to get at enemy positions.

That day and the next, the Battle of the Bulge reached its climax. In and about Celles, the U.S. 2nd Armored Division caught the Second Panzer Division, out of fuel, dead in its tracks. American armor, artillery and infantry, strongly supported by fighter-bombers, ripped into the enemy. In "a great slaughter," they inflicted more than 2,000 casualties on the Germans, de-stroying 80 tanks, 450 other vehicles, and 80 assault guns caught on the road—losses fivefold those suffered by the Americans. The westernmost German spearhead had been decapitated.

Villages were taken, lost, retaken. In one night action, a single American artillery battalion fired eleven thousand rounds at enemy tanks. Two companies of 82nd Airborne paratroopers made a gallant, straight-ahead attack against German positions to take Cheneux. There, Corporal George Graves witnessed "bloody GI clothes. Dead bodies everywhere. Living troops hugging the ground."

The arrows of the Allied advance began to swing eastward. With clearing skies, U.S. fighter-bombers struck at enemy positions in more than five hundred sorties a day. German field commanders ordered gradual pullbacks. GIs drove through bitter enemy resistance, storms, and knee-deep snow to take back pieces of lost ground.

NATIONAL ARCHIVES.

Headlines back home told of the turnaround: "First Army Drives Ahead in Sleet" . . . "Third Army Gains" . . . "Ice, Mud and Fog Slow Tanks" . . . "Germans Battle Back" . . . "Americans Cut Into Bulge" . . . As the Germans had been fierce on the attack, so were they every bit as fierce in their withdrawal. Steadily collapsing the "Bulge" about themselves, they exacted heavy casualties for every foot of frozen earth.

Even in the face of disaster, many German troops remained loyal to the spirit of the *Fahneneid,* the ancient oath of the Teutonic knights that swore them to serve their leader to the death. A young SS Panzer commander had stated: "The snow must turn red with American blood. We will throw them from our homeland. It is a holy task."

Americans by the thousands found unceremonious death in the Ardennes. "I was a new replacement," recalls Private Harmon Horowitz. "One of the seasoned BAR guys said, 'Kid, stay close to me.' Two days later I saw him blown apart by a mortar shell." One soldier remembered a wounded GI, "perhaps twenty years old, with frightened eyes. The medic couldn't give him blood plasma; it was frozen. The soldier died in a barn." "Our squad had eight men," relates Private First Class Leslie Shellhase. "Within days, three had been killed—and five, counting me, had been wounded." Captain Frances Slanger, after working a string of eighteen-hour days as a nurse in a field hospital, got some time off. While she rested in her tent, an 88-millimeter shell burst overhead. She was buried in her green fatigues.

When the shock of American armor failed to produce breakthroughs, infantrymen moved through deep snow on foot, among wooded hills and steep defiles and along serpentine rivers, working past felled trees, mines, and anti-tank guns to get at enemy positions.

Hitler unleashed one last surprise. On January 1, 1945, almost a thousand German fighter planes swept in over the Western Front at treetop level. By midday they had struck twenty-seven Allied airbases in Belgium, France, and the Netherlands, destroying or damaging nearly three hundred planes. But in so

NATIONAL ARCHIVES.

Fifty years ago, Theodore O. Simpson was a corporal with a "Pack 75 mm" battery in the 319 Glider Field Artillery Battalion of the 82nd Airborne Division. Simpson's vivid recollections of the Battle of the Bulge could fairly represent the memories [of] any of the 600,000 Americans who took part in that physically punishing and hard-fought campaign:

What I mainly remember are the still-shivering experiences of life in the "fridge" . . . never knowing (nor particularly caring) where we were at any given moment, but rather, just swapping one set of woods, hills, mined valleys, for another.

Sleeping bags with frozen zippers. (Bad, when one has contracted diarrhea from small metal flakings that cracked away from inner walls of a canteen after being heated over the campfire to melt water inside.)

Changing fire zones and positions continuously. Guns always firing. Dropping with fatigue into trail pits dug for the howitzers and sleeping soundly despite middle-of-the-night "fire missions" when one's sleeping body was two feet from a barking cannon.

Mounds of bodies under a merciful wrapping of snow. Piles of O.D. body bags beside the morning chow line. Contorted positions of the frozen dead. Singing shrapnel headed earthward from just above our heads as larger artillery units, behind, experimented with new "posit fuzes."

Eyes burning with campfire smoke. Accumulating body dirt. No baths. Always the deep, penetrating cold. Snipers in the woods. Infrequent but blessed letters from home. One reassuring feeling: *everyone* was there—tanks, big guns, infantry, engineers, etc.

Death reminders in every direction. A frozen hand reaching from the snow. A ruptured helmet lying alone. A German wallet beside its former owner's mutilated body—spilling letters, pictures from home.

Tangled tanks and jeeps afire. Watching smoke bubble peacefully from a Belgian home on the hillside—and wondering why they were comfortably ensconced while we were out here trying to save their country.

Vicious artillery counter-battery attacks until one or the other contender was silent. Day after frozen day dragging by, with little comfort or hope.

Fifty years later, I still do not care much for snow, frozen woods, or unexplained mounds on the frosted white ground.

NATIONAL ARCHIVES.

Battle of the Ardennes has been the most decisive of the Second World War," stated Charles MacDonald, U.S. Army historian. "It was the most important feat of arms in the history of the United States Army."

British Prime Minister Sir Winston Churchill, addressing the House of Commons following the Battle of the Bulge, declared: "This is undoubtedly the greatest American battle of the war and will, I believe, be regarded as an ever-famous American victory."

The battle sealed Germany's fate. Casualties and prisoners exceeded 100,000 men—losses Germany could no longer make good.

The battle of the Ardennes lasted forty-three days and cost the United States nine times as many casualties as D-Day. Of 600,000 Americans who fought there, more than 80,000 became casualties: some 10,276 killed; 47,493 wounded; and 23,218 captured or missing. As well, U.S. forces lost about 700 tanks and tank destroyers and some 600 planes. British casualties totalled 1,400 men.

But the battle had sealed Germany's fate. Estimates of troop losses exceeded a staggering 100,000 men—with more than 10,000 killed, 50,000 wounded, and 40,000 captured—losses Germany could no longer make good. Some 800 tanks and assault guns were destroyed. And the Luftwaffe, in a near-death gasp, lost more than 800 aircraft, leaving Germany with virtually no air force.

The Ardennes campaign was a classic example of Hitler's willingness to expect the impossible—as though to will victory would be to win it. In so doing, he not only overestimated the strength of his own forces but also undervalued

doing, they lost about three hundred of their own planes, along with irreplaceable pilots.

By the second week of the new year, the issue had been decided. On January 16, patrols of the U.S. First and Third Armies linked up at Houffalize, closing off much of the Bulge. It would take another eight days to push the German troops back to their starting point. From blue skies on January 22, U.S. pilots devastated retreating German columns. By January 28, the last trace of the Bulge had disappeared.

Battle brought poignance. Captain Sally Zumaris-McKinney remembers "American soldiers shot to pieces, or frozen, or sick—just kids, some of

them." Joining his battalion's mortician under cover of fire to recover bodies, Sergeant Edward Bergh came upon that of his best buddy. An infantryman relates: "One night we found shelter inside a church. It had been shattered by shellfire. It was quiet there. I prayed near the altar, then went to sleep before it."

A million men had been caught up in desperate fighting during a six-week period in forested, mountainous, frozen terrain of five hundred square miles. Out of it all emerged the memorable figure of the foot-slogging American GI—stoic, hard-eyed, and of abiding strength. He typified the whole array of U.S. soldiers—tankers, engineers, artillery men, drivers, clerks—who, each in his own way had fought the desperate fight. "The

the resolve of the American soldier.* The Germans, fierce though their determination was, failed to reach Antwerp; failed to destroy large pockets of trapped U.S. units; failed to get a single tank across the Meuse River. Thirty-two American and four British divisions had battled twenty-eight German divisions to a standstill, and then had driven them back into Germany.

Hitler's last, desperate gamble had, for a brief, astonishing time, seemed about to succeed. It did, in fact, upset the Allied timetable for the invasion of Germany—but at a crushing cost to his

---

*Nearly a score of American soldiers, displaying valor beyond the call of duty in the Ardennes, were awarded the Medal of Honor.

own manpower and armor. Soon the Allies would be at the Rhine.

The vast drama of the Ardennes ended, for Hitler's armies, in disillusion and disaster. "Rivers of men and machines flowed slowly toward the Fatherland," wrote historian John Toland. "Trucks, tanks and self-propelled guns rumbled east over icy roads and trails clogged with snow-drifts. Each refugee of the Battle of the Bulge brought home a story of doom, of overwhelming Allied might and of a terrible weapon forged in the Ardennes: the American fighting man."

Those who would seek Hitler's monument in those woods of death had but to look around them. Scattered upon

the snow-mantled landscape rested shattered tanks, broken artillery pieces, charred vehicles. Corpses of German soldiers lay white and stiff, their weapons on the frozen earth about them.

As a German grenadier made his way out of a burning village, he scrawled on the side of a battered German scout car: "*Aus Der Traum.*" "The Dream is Over."

New York writer Edward Oxford has contributed more than two dozen articles to American History. *His last contribution—on the World War II draft—appeared in the September/October issue.*

The Biggest Decision: Why We Had to Drop the Atomic Bomb

Robert James Maddox

Robert James Maddox teaches American history at Pennsylvania State University. His Weapons for Victory: Hiroshima Fifty Years Later *is published by the University of Missouri Press (1995).*

On the morning of August 6, 1945, the American B-29 *Enola Gay* dropped an atomic bomb on the Japanese city of Hiroshima. Three days later another B-29, *Bock's Car,* released one over Nagasaki. Both caused enormous casualties and physical destruction. These two cataclysmic events have preyed upon the American conscience ever since. The furor over the Smithsonian Institution's *Enola Gay* exhibit and over the mushroom-cloud postage stamp last autumn are merely the most obvious examples. Harry S. Truman and other officials claimed that the bombs caused Japan to surrender, thereby avoiding a bloody invasion. Critics have accused them of at best failing to explore alternatives, at worst of using the bombs primarily to make the Soviet Union "more manageable" rather than to defeat a Japan they knew already was on the verge of capitulation.

By any rational calculation Japan was a beaten nation by the summer of 1945. Conventional bombing had reduced many of its cities to rubble, blockade had strangled its importation of vitally needed materials, and its navy had sustained such heavy losses as to be powerless to interfere with the invasion everyone knew was coming. By late June advancing American forces had completed the conquest of Okinawa, which lay only 350 miles from the southernmost Japanese home island of Kyushu. They now stood poised for the final onslaught.

OKINAWA provided a preview of what an invasion of the home islands would entail. Rational calculations did not determine Japan's position.

Rational calculations did not determine Japan's position. Although a peace faction within the government wished to end the war—provided certain conditions were met—militants were prepared to fight on regardless of consequences. They claimed to welcome an invasion of the home islands, promising to inflict such hideous casualties that the United States would retreat from its announced policy of unconditional surrender. The militarists held effective power over the government and were capable of defying the emperor, as they had in the past, on the ground that his civilian advisers were misleading him.

Okinawa provided a preview of what invasion of the home islands would entail. Since April 1 the Japanese had fought with a ferocity that mocked any notion that their will to resist was eroding. They had inflicted nearly 50,000 casualties on the invaders, many resulting from the first large-scale use of kamikazes. They also had dispatched the superbattleship *Yamato* on a suicide mission to Okinawa, where, after attacking American ships offshore, it was to plunge ashore to become a huge, doomed steel fortress. *Yamato* was sunk shortly after leaving port, but its mission symbolized Japan's willingness to sacrifice everything in an apparently hopeless cause.

The Japanese could be expected to defend their sacred homeland with even greater fervor, and kamikazes flying at short range promised to be even more devastating than at Okinawa. The Japanese had more than 2,000,000 troops in the home islands, were training millions of irregulars, and for some time had been conserving aircraft that might have been used to protect Japanese cities against American bombers.

Reports from Tokyo indicated that Japan meant to fight the war to a finish. On June 8 an imperial conference adopted "The Fundamental Policy to Be Followed Henceforth in the Conduct of

From *American Heritage,* May/June 1995, pp. 70-74, 76-77 © 1995 by Forbes, Inc. Reprinted by permission of *American Heritage* magazine, a division of Forbes, Inc.

the War," which pledged to "prosecute the war to the bitter end in order to uphold the national polity, protect the imperial land, and accomplish the objectives for which we went to war." Truman had no reason to believe that the proclamation meant anything other than what it said.

Against this background, while fighting on Okinawa still continued, the President had his naval chief of staff, Adm. William D. Leahy, notify the Joint Chiefs of Staff (JCS) and the Secretaries of War and Navy that a meeting would be held at the White House on June 18. The night before the conference Truman wrote in his diary that "I have to decide Japanese strategy—shall we invade Japan proper or shall we bomb and blockade? That is my hardest decision to date. But I'll make it when I have all the facts."

Truman met with the chiefs at three-thirty in the afternoon. Present were Army Chief of Staff Gen. George C. Marshall, Army Air Force's Gen. Ira C. Eaker (sitting in for the Army Air Force's chief of staff, Henry H. Arnold, who was on an inspection tour of installations in the Pacific), Navy Chief of Staff Adm. Ernest J. King, Leahy (also a member of the JCS), Secretary of the Navy James Forrestal, Secretary of War Henry L. Stimson, and Assistant Secretary of War John J. McCloy. Truman opened the meeting, then asked Marshall for his views. Marshall was the dominant figure on the JCS. He was Truman's most trusted military adviser, as he had been President Franklin D. Roosevelt's.

Marshall reported that the chiefs, supported by the Pacific commanders Gen. Douglas MacArthur and Adm. Chester W. Nimitz, agreed that an invasion of Kyushu "appears to be the least costly worthwhile operation following Okinawa." Lodgment in Kyushu, he said, was necessary to make blockade and bombardment more effective and to serve as a staging area for the invasion of Japan's main island of Honshu. The chiefs recommended a target date of November 1 for the first phase, code-named Olympic, because delay would give the Japanese more time to prepare

and because bad weather might postpone the invasion "and hence the end of the war" for up to six months. Marshall said that in his opinion, Olympic was "the only course to pursue." The chiefs also proposed that Operation Cornet be launched against Honshu on March 1, 1946.

Leahy's memorandum calling the meeting had asked for casualty projections which that invasion might be expected to produce. Marshall stated that campaigns in the Pacific had been so diverse "it is considered wrong" to make total estimates. All he would say was that casualties during the first thirty days on Kyushu should not exceed those sustained in taking Luzon in the Philippines—31,000 men killed, wounded, or missing in action. "It is a grim fact," Marshall said, "that there is not an easy, bloodless way to victory in war." Leahy estimated a higher casualty rate similar to Okinawa, and King guessed somewhere in between.

King and Eaker, speaking for the Navy and the Army Air Forces respectively, endorsed Marshall's proposals. King said that he had become convinced that Kyushu was "the key to the success of any siege operations." He recommended that "we should do Kyushu now" and begin preparations for invading Honshu. Eaker "agreed completely" with Marshall. He said he had just received a message from Arnold also expressing "complete agreement." Air Force plans called for the use of forty groups of heavy bombers, which "could not be deployed without the use of airfields on Kyushu." Stimson and Forrestal concurred.

Truman summed up. He considered "the Kyushu plan all right from the military standpoint" and directed the chiefs to "go ahead with it." He said he "had hoped that there was a possibility of preventing an Okinawa from one end of Japan to the other," but "he was clear on the situation now" and was "quite sure" the chiefs should proceed with the plan. Just before the meeting adjourned, McCloy raised the possibility of avoiding an invasion by warning the Japanese that the United States would employ atomic weapons if there were no surren-

der. The ensuing discussion was inconclusive because the first test was a month away and no one could be sure the weapons would work.

In his memoirs Truman claimed that using atomic bombs prevented an invasion that would have cost 500,000 American lives. Other officials mentioned the same or even higher figures. Critics have assailed such statements as gross exaggerations designed to forestall scrutiny of Truman's real motives. They have given wide publicity to a report prepared by the Joint War Plans Committee (JWPC) for the chiefs' meeting with Truman. The committee estimated that the invasion of Kyushu, followed by that of Honshu, as the chiefs proposed, would cost approximately 40,000 dead, 150,000 wounded, and 3,500 missing in action for a total of 193,500 casualties.

That those responsible for a decision should exaggerate the consequences of alternatives is commonplace. Some who cite the JWPC report profess to see more sinister motives, insisting that such "low" casualty projections call into question the very idea that atomic bombs were used to avoid heavy losses. By discrediting that justification as a cover-up, they seek to bolster their contention that the bombs really were used to permit the employment of "atomic diplomacy" against the Soviet Union.

The notion that 193,500 anticipated casualties were too insignificant to have caused Truman to resort to atomic bombs might seem bizarre to anyone other than an academic, but let it pass. Those who have cited the JWPC report in countless op-ed pieces in newspapers and in magazine articles have created a myth by omitting key considerations: First, the report itself is studded with qualifications that casualties "are not subject to accurate estimate" and that the projection "is admittedly only an educated guess." Second, the figures never were conveyed to Truman. They were excised at high military echelons, which is why Marshall cited only estimates for the first thirty days on Kyushu. And indeed, subsequent Japanese troop buildups on Kyushu rendered the JWPC estimates totally irrelevent by the time the first atomic bomb was dropped.

Another myth that has attained wide attention is that at least several of Truman's top military advisers later informed him that using atomic bombs against Japan would be militarily unnecessary or immoral, or both. There is no persuasive evidence that any of them did so. None of the Joint Chiefs ever made such a claim, although one inventive author has tried to make it appear that Leahy did by braiding together several unrelated passages from the admiral's memoirs. Actually, two days after Hiroshima, Truman told aides that Leahy had "said up to the last that it wouldn't go off."

Neither MacArthur nor Nimitz ever communicated to Truman any change of mind about the need for invasion or expressed reservations about using the bombs. When first informed about their imminent use only days before Hiroshima, MacArthur responded with a lecture on the future of atomic warfare and even after Hiroshima strongly recommended that the invasion go forward. Nimitz, from whose jurisdiction the atomic strikes would be launched, was notified in early 1945. "This sounds fine," he told the courier, "but this is only February. Can't we get one sooner?" Nimitz later would join Air Force generals Carl D. Spaatz, Nathan Twining, and Curtis LeMay in recommending that a third bomb be dropped on Tokyo.

Only Dwight D. Eisenhower later claimed to have remonstrated against the use of the bomb. In his *Crusade in Europe,* published in 1948, he wrote that when Secretary Stimson informed him during the Potsdam Conference of plans to use the bomb, he replied that he hoped "we would never have to use such a thing against any enemy," because he did not want the United States to be the first to use such a weapon. He added, "My views were merely personal and immediate reactions; they were not based on any analysis of the subject."

Eisenhower's recollections grew more colorful as the years went on. A later account of his meeting with Stimson had it taking place at Ike's headquarters in Frankfurt on the very day news arrived of the successful atomic test in New Mexico. "We'd had a nice

evening at headquarters in Germany," he remembered. Then, after dinner, "Stimson got this cable saying that the bomb had been perfected and was ready to be

MYTH HOLDS that several of Truman's top military advisers begged him not to use the bomb. In fact, there is no persuasive evidence that any of them did.

dropped. The cable was in code . . . 'the lamb is born' or some damn thing like that." In this version Eisenhower claimed to have protested vehemently that "the Japanese were ready to surrender and it wasn't necessary to hit them with that awful thing." "Well," Eisenhower concluded, "the old gentleman got furious."

The best that can be said about Eisenhower's memory is that it had become flawed by the passage of time. Stimson was in Potsdam and Eisenhower in Frankfurt on July 16, when word came of the successful test. Aside from a brief conversation at a flag-raising ceremony in Berlin on July 20, the only other time they met was at Ike's headquarters on July 27. By then orders already had been sent to the Pacific to use the bombs if Japan had not yet surrendered. Notes made by one of Stimson's aides indicate that there was a discussion of atomic bombs, but there is no mention of any protest on Eisenhower's part. Even if there had been, two factors must be kept in mind. Eisenhower had commanded Allied forces in Europe, and his opinion on how close Japan was to surrender would have carried no special weight. More important, Stimson left for home immediately after the meeting and could not have person-

ally conveyed Ike's sentiments to the President, who did not return to Washington until after Hiroshima.

On July 8 the Combined Intelligence Committee submitted to the American and British Combined Chiefs of Staff a report entitled "Estimate of the Enemy Situation." The committee predicted that as Japan's position continued to deteriorate, it might "make a serious effort to use the USSR [then a neutral] as a mediator in ending the war." Tokyo also would put out "intermittent peace feelers" to "weaken the determination of the United Nations to fight to the bitter end, or to create inter-allied dissension." While the Japanese people would be willing to make large concessions to end the war, "For a surrender to be acceptable to the Japanese army, it would be necessary for the military leaders to believe that it would not entail discrediting warrior tradition and that it would permit the ultimate resurgence of a military Japan."

Small wonder that American officials remained unimpressed when Japan proceeded to do exactly what the committee predicted. On July 12 Japanese Foreign Minister Shigenori Togo instructed Ambassador Naotaki Sato in Moscow to inform the Soviets that the emperor wished to send a personal envoy, Prince Fuminaro Konoye, in an attempt "to restore peace with all possible speed." Although he realized Konoye could not reach Moscow before the Soviet leader Joseph Stalin and Foreign Minister V. M. Molotov left to attend a Big Three meeting scheduled to begin in Potsdam on the fifteenth, Togo sought to have negotiations begin as soon as they returned.

American officials had long since been able to read Japanese diplomatic traffic through a process known as the MAGIC intercepts. Army intelligence (G-2) prepared for General Marshall its interpretation of Togo's message the next day. The report listed several possible constructions, the most probable being that the Japanese "governing clique" was making a coordinated effort to "stave off defeat" through Soviet intervention and an "appeal to war weariness in the United States." The report added that Undersecretary of State Joseph C. Grew, who had spent ten years in Japan as ambassador, "agrees with these conclusions."

Some have claimed that Togo's overture to the Soviet Union, together with attempts by some minor Japanese officials in Switzerland and other neutral countries to get peace talks started through the Office of Strategic Services (OSS), constituted clear evidence that the Japanese were near surrender. Their sole prerequisite was retention of their sacred emperor, whose unique cultural/religious status within the Japanese polity they would not compromise. If only the United States had extended assurances about the emperor, according to this view, much bloodshed and the atomic bombs would have been unnecessary.

A careful reading of the MAGIC intercepts of subsequent exchanges between Togo and Sato provides no evidence that retention of the emperor was the sole obstacle to peace. What they show instead is that the Japanese Foreign Office was trying to cut a deal through the Soviet Union that would have permitted Japan to retain its political system and its prewar empire intact. Even the most lenient American official could not have countenanced such a settlement.

Togo on July 17 informed Sato that "we are not asking the Russians' mediation in *anything like unconditional surrender* [emphasis added]." During the following weeks Sato pleaded with his superiors to abandon hope of Soviet intercession and to approach the United States directly to find out what peace terms would be offered. "There is . . . no alternative but immediate unconditional surrender," he cabled on July 31, and he bluntly informed Togo that "your way of looking at things and the actual situation in the Eastern Area may be seen to be absolutely contradictory." The Foreign Ministry ignored his pleas and continued to seek Soviet help even after Hiroshima.

"Peace feelers" by Japanese officials abroad seemed no more promising from the American point of view. Although several of the consular personnel and military attachés engaged in these activities claimed important connections at home, none produced verification. Had the Japanese government sought only an assurance about the emperor, all it had to do was grant one of these men authority to begin talks through the OSS. Its failure to do so led American officials to assume that those involved were either well-meaning individuals acting alone or that they were being orchestrated by Tokyo. Grew characterized such "peace feelers" as "familiar weapons of psychological warfare" designed to "divide the Allies."

By late July the casualty projection of 31,000 that Marshall had given Truman at the June 18 strategy meeting had become meaningless.

Some American officials, such as Stimson and Grew, nonetheless wanted to signal the Japanese that they might retain the emperorship in the form of a constitutional monarchy. Such an assurance might remove the last stumbling block to surrender, if not when it was issued, then later. Only an imperial rescript would bring about an orderly surrender, they argued, without which Japanese forces would fight to the last man regardless of what the government in Tokyo did. Besides, the emperor could serve as a stabilizing factor during the transition to peacetime.

There were many arguments against an American initiative. Some opposed retaining such an undemocratic institution on principle and because they feared it might later serve as a rallying point for future militarism. Should that happen, as one assistant Secretary of State put it, "those lives already spent will have been sacrificed in vain, and lives will be lost again in the future." Japanese hard-liners were certain to exploit an overture as evidence that losses sustained at Okinawa had weakened American resolve and to argue that continued resistance would bring further concessions. Stalin, who earlier had told an American envoy that he favored abolishing the emperorship because the ineffectual Hirohito might be succeeded by "an energetic and vigorous figure who could cause trouble," was just as certain to interpret it as a treacherous effort to end the war before the Soviets could share in the spoils.

There were domestic considerations as well. Roosevelt had announced the unconditional surrender policy in early 1943, and it since had become a slogan of the war. He also had advocated that peoples everywhere should have the right to choose their own form of government, and Truman had publicly pledged to carry out his predecessor's legacies. For him to have formally *guaranteed* continuance of the emperorship, as opposed to merely accepting it on American terms pending free elections, as he later did, would have constituted a blatant repudiation of his own promises.

Nor was that all. Regardless of the emperor's actual role in Japanese aggression, which is still debated, much wartime propaganda had encouraged Americans to regard Hirohito as no less a war criminal than Adolf Hitler or Benito Mussolini. Although Truman said on several occasions that he had no objection to retaining the emperor, he understandably refused to make the first move. The ultimatum he issued from Potsdam on July 26 did not refer specifically to the emperorship. All it said was that occupation forces would be removed after "a peaceful and responsible" government had been established according to the "freely expressed will of the Japanese people." When the Japanese rejected the ultimatum rather than at last inquire whether they might retain the emperor, Truman permitted the plans for using the bombs to go forward.

Reliance on MAGIC intercepts and the "peace feelers" to gauge how near Japan was to surrender is misleading in any case. The army, not the Foreign Office, controlled the situation. Intercepts of Japanese military communications, designated ULTRA, provided no reason to believe the army was even considering surrender. Japanese Imperial Headquarters had correctly guessed that the next operation after Okinawa would be Kyushu and was making every effort to bolster its defenses there.

General Marshall reported on July 24 that there were "approximately 500,000 troops in Kyushu" and that more were on the way. ULTRA identified new units arriving almost daily. MacArthur's G-2 reported on July 29 that "this threatening development, if not checked, may grow to a point where we attack on a ratio of one (1) to one (1) which is not the recipe for victory." By the time the first atomic bomb fell, ULTRA indicated that there were 560,000 troops in southern Kyushu (the actual figure was closer to 900,000), and projections for November 1 placed the number at 680,000. A report, for medical purposes, of July 31 estimated that total battle and non-battle casualties might run as high as 394,859 *for the Kyushu operation alone.* This figure did not include those men expected to be killed outright, for obviously they would require no medical attention. Marshall regarded Japanese defenses as so formidable that even after Hiroshima he asked MacArthur to consider alternate landing sites and began contemplating the use of atomic bombs as tactical weapons to support the invasion.

The thirty-day casualty projection of 31,000 Marshall had given Truman at the June 18 strategy meeting had become meaningless. It had been based on the assumption that the Japanese had about 350,000 defenders in Kyushu and that naval and air interdiction would preclude significant reinforcement. But the Japanese buildup since that time meant that the defenders would have nearly twice the number of troops available by "X-day" than earlier assumed. The assertion that apprehensions about casualties are insufficient to explain Truman's use of the bombs, therefore, cannot be taken seri-

ously. On the contrary, as Winston Churchill wrote after a conversation with him at Potsdam, Truman was tormented by "the terrible responsibilities that rested upon him in regard to the unlimited effusions of American blood."

Some historians have argued that while the first bomb *might* have been required to achieve Japanese surrender, dropping the second constituted a needless barbarism. The record shows otherwise. American officials believed more than one bomb would be necessary because they assumed Japanese hard-liners would minimize the first explosion or attempt to explain it away as some sort of natural catastrophe, precisely what they did. The Japanese minister of war, for instance, at first refused even to admit that the Hiroshima bomb was atomic. A few hours after Nagasaki he told the cabinet that "the Americans appeared to have one hundred atomic bombs . . . they could drop three per day. The next target might well be Tokyo."

Even after both bombs had fallen and Russia entered the war, Japanese militants insisted on such lenient peace terms that moderates knew there was no sense even transmitting them to the United States. Hirohito had to intervene personally on two occasions during the next few days to induce hard-liners to abandon their conditions and to accept the American stipulation that the emperor's authority "shall be subject to the Supreme Commander of the Allied Powers." That the militarists would have accepted such a settlement before the bombs is farfetched, to say the least.

Some writers have argued that the cumulative effects of battlefield defeats, conventional bombing, and naval blockade already had defeated Japan. Even

without extending assurances about the emperor, all the United States had to do was wait. The most frequently cited basis for this contention is the *United States Strategic Bombing Survey,* published in 1946, which stated that Japan would have surrendered by November 1 "even if the atomic bombs had not been dropped, even if Russia had not entered the war, and even if no invasion had been planned or contemplated." Recent scholarship by the historian Robert P. Newman and others has demonstrated that the survey was "cooked" by those who prepared it to arrive at such a conclusion. No matter. This or any other document based on information available only after the war ended is irrelevant with regard to what Truman could have known at the time.

What often goes unremarked is that when the bombs were dropped, fighting was still going on in the Philippines, China, and elsewhere. Every day that the war continued thousands of prisoners of war had to live and die in abysmal conditions, and there were rumors that the Japanese intended to slaughter them if the homeland was invaded. Truman was Commander in Chief of the American armed forces, and he had a duty to the men under his command not shared by those sitting in moral judgment decades later. Available evidence points to the conclusion that he acted for the reason he said he did: to end a bloody war that would have become far bloodier had invasion proved necessary. One can only imagine what would have happened if tens of thousands of American boys had died or been wounded on Japanese soil and then it had become known that Truman had chosen not to use weapons that might have ended the war months sooner.

Unit 5

Unit Selections

Key Points to Consider

❖ The G.I. Bill has been described as one of the most revolutionary pieces of legislation in American history. Discuss the changes it helped to bring about.

❖ What conditions in Europe caused the Truman administration to devise the Marshall Plan. How did it operate, and what were its accomplishments?

❖ The Korean War has not received the attention that some other military conflicts have. What was its significance?

❖ Evaluate Martin Luther King's career. What does the author mean in his article by referring to King's "half-forgotten dream"?

❖ Does the author of "Scenes from the '60s" offer a persuasive account of the radicals he knew? Why or why not?

❖ After reviewing the article on Watergate and the one on the 1970s, discuss what, if any, legacies of that decade are still with us.

 **Links** — **www.dushkin.com/online/**

These sites are annotated on pages 4 and 5.

President Franklin D. Roosevelt sought to build a working relationship with Soviet leader Josef Stalin throughout World War II. Roosevelt believed that the wartime collaboration had to continue if a lasting peace were to be achieved. At the Yalta Conference of February 1945, a series of agreements were made that Roosevelt hoped would provide the basis for continued cooperation. Subsequent disputes over interpretation of these agreements raised doubts in Roosevelt's mind that Stalin was acting in good faith.

Roosevelt died on April 12, 1945. His successor, Harry S. Truman, assumed the presidency with little knowledge of Roosevelt's thinking. Truman had to rely on discussions with the advisers he inherited and his own reading of messages passed between Roosevelt and the Soviets. Truman attempted to carry out what he believed were Roosevelt's intentions: be firm with the Soviets, but continue to seek accommodation. He came to believe that Molotov was trying to sabotage U.S.–Soviet relations and that the best way to reach agreements was to negotiate directly with Soviet leader Stalin. This he did at the Potsdam Conference during the summer of 1945. He came away from the talks believing that Stalin was a hard bargainer but one who could be trusted.

Events during the late summer and early autumn eroded Truman's hopes that the Soviets genuinely wanted to get along. A host of issues finally persuaded Truman that it was time to stop "babying" the Soviets. A militant public speech by Stalin, which one American referred to as the "declaration of World War III," appeared to confirm this view. Increasingly hostile relations led to what became known as the "cold war," during which each side increasingly came to regard the other as an enemy rather than merely an adversary.

Meanwhile the United States had to cope with the problems of conversion to a peacetime economy. Demobilization of the armed forces proved especially vexing as the public clamored to have servicemen and servicewomen brought home and discharged as quickly as possible. When the administration seemed to be moving too slowly, the threat "no boats, no votes" became popular. Race riots, labor strife, and inflation also marred the immediate postwar period. One of the brighter spots was provided by the Serviceman's Readjustment Act of 1944, better known as "The G.I. Bill." Michael Haydock's article of that name tells how this revolutionary legislation provided millions of ex-servicepersons with educations that would have been impossible to afford without it.

There was social ferment as well. Many blacks had served in the armed forces or worked in defense industries. They had encountered segregation in the military and unequal treatment in civilian jobs. Professional sports at that time was kept "lily white." "Baseball's Noble Experiment," by William Kashatus, describes how Brooklyn Dodger president Branch Rickey maneuvered to break down

the color line in baseball. Jackie Robinson, a former army officer, was chosen to be the test case as much for his mental toughness as for his physical skills. Robinson proved more than equal to the challenge. He carved out a distinguished career and opened the doors for other black players.

Relations with the Soviets continued to deteriorate. Soviet threats against Greece and Turkey led to the Truman Doctrine in 1947, which placed the United States on the side of nations threatened with overt aggression or internal subversion. "From Plan to Practice: The Context and Consequences of the Marshall Plan" provides an account of an even more ambitious effort to prevent economic chaos in Europe.

In 1950, only 5 years after the end of World War II, the United States found itself at war again. The North Korean invasion of the South in June of that year appeared to American leaders as a Soviet-inspired probe to test Western resolve. Failure to halt aggression there, according to Bernard Weisberger's "Echoes of a Distant War," would embolden the Soviets to strike elsewhere just as Hitler had done in the 1930s.

Dwight D. Eisenhower was elected president in 1952. A truce ending the Korean War was hammered out the following year, but the cold war continued with a vengeance. Eisenhower and his secretary of state, John Foster Dulles, had come into office promising to "roll back the Iron Curtain" and to "free captive peoples." They did neither. More and more the entire globe was viewed as an arena of competition between the forces of Communism and the Free World ("free" meant free of Communism; some of the nations included were headed by repressive dictatorships). However, the United States appeared secure behind its nuclear arsenal and technological superiority. In the article, "Sputnik," Stephen Bates describes how news that the Soviets had successfully launched a space satellite shattered these assumptions and raised the specter that the Soviets might be able to destroy the United States.

Two essays in this unit deal with the turbulent 1960s. In "Martin Luther King's Half-Forgotten Dream," Peter Ling places particular emphasis upon the last years of this inspiring civil rights leader's life. Radicals of the 1960s are often depicted in the most glowing terms, as courageous young people battling the "establishment" to bring about social justice and an end to the Vietnam War. David Horowitz presents a glimpse of the darker side of "the movement" in "Scenes from the '60s: One Radical's Story."

Richard M. Nixon won reelection in 1972 in a landslide. But "The Legacy of Watergate," by Andrew Phillips, describes how the Watergate affair gradually unfolded into a major scandal that caused Nixon's resignation. Nicholas Lemann, in "How the Seventies Changed America," denies that the 1970s was merely a "loser decade" following the high drama of the 1960s. He believes that some of the problems and issues of the 1970s still have not been resolved.

From the Cold War to the 1990s

The G.I. Bill

By Michael D. Haydock *More than 2,250,000 American veterans of WWII received at least part of their college education as a result of legislation known as "The G.I. Bill."*

By the time the last American World War II veteran was graduated in 1956, the United States was richer by 450,000 engineers; 238,000 teachers; 91,000 scientists; 67,000 doctors; 22,000 dentists; and more than a million other college-trained men and women, thanks largely to the Servicemen's Readjustment Act of 1944, universally known as "the G.I. Bill." This landmark legislation helped steer a country geared to winning a globe-spanning war—with roughly 8 million citizens in uniform in 1945 and 22 million involved in war production—smoothly back into a peacetime economy; led to lasting changes in America's system of higher education; and turned uncertainty into opportunity for thousands of war veterans.

The idea of aiding veterans grew partially out of economic concerns. With World War II winding down, many foresaw the day when millions of servicemen and -women would begin reentering the job market. Government officials wished to find a way to ensure against anything akin to the 1932 march on Washington, D.C., by 15,000 disgruntled World War I veterans, who were suffering from the ravages of the Great Depression. This "Bonus Army" sought immediate credit for the certificates they had received upon being discharged years earlier. These notes were not scheduled to mature until 1945, but the impoverished men who had risked their lives for their country felt they deserved immediate assistance.

The main inspiration for the G.I. Bill, however, was a sincere desire to assist returnees. The American Legion, which would become a primary force in guiding the legislation through Congress, declared that "Veterans earned certain rights to which they are entitled. Gratuities do not enter the picture."

In his "fireside chat" to the nation on July 28, 1943, President Franklin D. Roosevelt made his first mention of the veterans' benefits that should follow the war and touched on the more practical aspects of the problem. With the suffering of the Depression vivid in his memory, Roosevelt declared that American veterans "must not be demobilized into an environment of inflation and unemployment, to a place on a bread line or on a corner selling apples." He suggested government-financed education and training as one facet of veterans' benefits that should be implemented.

The president's concern was echoed in the halls of Congress, where Republican Representative Hamilton Fish of New York, a staunch conservative and frequent foe of Roosevelt's, nevertheless agreed that veterans could not "come home and sell apples as they did after the last war, because if that is all they are offered, I believe we would have chaotic and revolutionary conditions in America."

By November 1943, more than a score of Congressmen were sponsoring bills relating to "veterans' rights." The Senate passed its version of the G.I. Bill in March 1944; the House of Representatives followed suit in May. The compromise bill, ready for the president's signature soon after the June 6 Allied invasion of Normandy was fi-

nally signed into law at the White House on June 22, 1944, with members of Congress and various veterans groups in attendance.

But with the war not yet over, most future candidates for veterans' relief went about their business that day, unaware that their futures may have been altered by what was going on in the nation's capital.

The Keenan twins, for example, were at work in a base hospital in England. The second youngest in a first generation, Irish-American family of a dozen siblings, Ellen and Teresa had trained as nurses before the war and enlisted in the Army Nurse Corps in 1942. Their patients, unaware there were two Miss Keenans working on different shifts, referred to them as "that nurse who never sleeps."

An infantryman with the 20th Armored Division, John Rigas was in France when President Roosevelt signed what was officially designated Public Law 346. Rigas had landed in Europe days earlier with his fellow soldiers to begin the drive that would place the American force deep in Bavaria at the end of the war.

Don Balfour, honorably discharged because of his poor eyesight, was working hard to pay for his classes at Georgetown University in Washington, D.C., where he served as the editor of the school paper, *The Hatchet*.

The G.I. Bill entitled anyone with ninety days of service to one year of higher education. Each additional month of active duty earned a month of schooling, up to a maximum

From *American History*, September/October 1996, pp. 53-56, 68-70. © 1996 by Cowles Magazine, Inc. Reprinted through the courtesy of Cowles Magazines, publishers of *American History*.

As members of Congress and representatives of various veterans groups watched, President Franklin D. Roosevelt signed the Servicemen's Readjustment Act—otherwise known as "the G.I. Bill"—into law on June 22, 1944. Among the motives inspiring the legislation was the desire to spare the veterans and the nation the economic hardships that accompanied the return, years before, of those who fought in World War I.

of 48 months. The law set a $500 per year limit for tuition, fees, and supplies, at a time when the cost of top schools ranged from $350 to $450. Single veterans could claim a subsistence allowance of $50 per month, while those who were married drew $75. By 1948, inflation had pushed these limits to $75 for those who were single and $105 for anyone with two dependents.

Initially few thought that the program would have much impact. When the War Department conducted several surveys concerning the number of service personnel who intended to enter college after the war, the results were not encouraging. Before the adoption of the bill, the Research Branch of the Morale Service Division concluded, after canvassing a representative cross-section, that only seven percent of those eligible intended to return to school or college after the war and that a government subsidy would increase that number only to eight per cent. A 1945 poll confidently predicted that "a minimum of eight percent and a maximum of twelve percent of all veterans of Army service in World War II will attend full-time school or college." The surveys also concluded that married men, those over 24, and those who had been in college prior to their entry into the military and had now been away from school for more than a year would be "quite unlikely to return to a school." An article entitled "G.I.'s Reject Education," which appeared in the *Saturday Evening Post*, concluded that as beneficial as the G.I. Bill seemed to be, it had one conspicuous drawback: "The guys aren't buying it."

Don Balfour did not see the *Post* article, but he learned of the passage of the law and thought it would make a good story for *The Hatchet*. He called on a vocational officer at the Veterans Administration one day after President Roosevelt had signed the bill. Part way through the interview Balfour asked if he could sign up for benefits. By August, his Georgetown tuition was being covered by the G.I. Bill.

Some members of the educational establishment expressed doubts and concerns about veterans arriving on their campuses in any great number. Robert M. Hutchens, President of the University of Chicago, described what he characterized as the threat to American education in *Colliers* magazine in December 1944. "Colleges and universities," he wrote, "will find themselves converted into educational hobo jungles. . . . [E]ducation is not a device for coping with mass unemployment." Harvard University's president, James B. Conant, lamented that the G.I. Bill failed "to distinguish between those who can profit most from advanced education and those who cannot" and expressed fear that "we may find the least capable among the war generation . . . flooding the facilities for advanced education."

A few educators believed that their added maturity and greater sense of purpose and social consciousness would make the returnees exceptional students, but most viewed their presence on campus with anxiety. Some predicted that the veterans would, as a result of their military experience, reject discipline, rebel against authority, lack initiative, and suffer from restlessness and hostility. "No man can fight in a war," wrote Professor Willard Waller of Columbia University, "without being changed by that experience. Veterans come home, but they come home angry." The fact was, however, that no one knew what to expect. No war in history had involved such numbers, and no nation had ever virtually guaranteed each returning veteran a free college education.

During the first year of the program, 8,200 ex-servicemen and -women enrolled in college; by November 1945, the number had swelled to 88,000. But the real deluge came with the discharge of millions of military personnel in the fall and winter of 1945–46. By late 1946, total college enrollment in the United States, for the first time, exceeded two million, 48.7 percent of whom were veterans attending under the G.I. Bill.

At Rutgers University in New Jersey, the student population grew from a prewar high of 7,000 to nearly 16,000. At California's Stanford University, where the admissions office rejected two students for each one accepted, enrollment climbed almost fifty percent. Rensselaer Polytechnic Institute (RPI) in Troy, New York, saw a rise of 132 percent to 3,308; John Rigas, having fought his way across Europe, was among their number. At Lehigh University in the forested hills just outside the steel town of Bethlehem, Pennsylvania, the 940 veterans on the campus far outnumbered the 396 "civilians."

In addition to the established institutions, veterans could choose to attend one of the new schools that seemingly sprang to life overnight, often on the sites of former military bases. Congress amended a 1940 act that created housing for defense workers to allow the facilities to be turned over to returning veterans. In August 1945, Congress went further, approving the use of surplus war-related buildings for educational purposes.

New York's famed Plattsburg Barracks, established as a fortification during the War of 1812, now took on new life as Champlain College, with an immediate enrollment of 1,101—ninety percent of whom were veterans. Mohawk College in Rome, New York was established on the grounds of the former Rhodes General Military Hospital and enrolled 1,314 students during its first year. And the Sampson Naval Training Center in the state's Finger Lakes region became Sampson College, with 2,825 students.

Out West, the University of California at Berkeley gained 17 buildings, totalling more than 185,000 square feet of floor space, under the federal program. Nationwide, the U.S. Office of Education estimated that the Veterans Educational Facilities Program, as Congress had named it, supplied 78 percent of the space that colleges urgently needed.

As the veterans began to crowd onto campuses across the nation there were, naturally enough, instances of "culture clash." Lehigh's freshmen had been required, since before anyone could remember, to wear brown socks, a brown tie, and a beanie. Those who did not don such attire could expect punishment from the Junior Vigilante Committee.

But, when veterans at Lehigh chose to ignore the tradition, it was a rash upperclassman indeed who attempted to force a brown dink onto the skull of a man who might have fought on Iwo Jima or on the beaches of Normandy. The school paper, which was still controlled by "civilians," ran an editorial pointing out the advantages offered by hazing, paddling, and wearing beanies. Few of the veterans bothered to respond; none took up wearing beanies.

All across the country colleges scrambled to meet the needs of the returning veterans. Lack of classroom space, teacher shortages, and inadequate housing for the students, all became immediate problems. At the University of Pittsburgh, there were so many students that classes had to be held on both a day and a night schedule. At Iowa State University too, classes began at 7:30 A.M. and went until 10:30 at night. The University of Florida, where enrollment jumped 155 percent, conducted a 61-hour academic week.

The wives of Ohio State faculty members were enlisted to aid their spouses in teaching, and Iowa's College of Liberal Arts hired 91 new instructors, more than a third of them with no previous teaching experience and most under 32 years of age. When a Harvard professor of philosophy, who normally

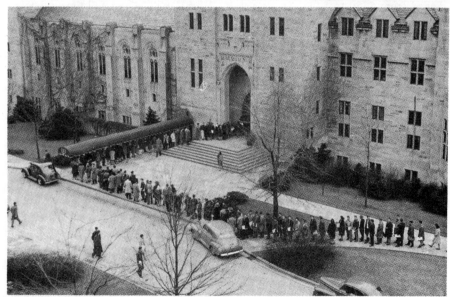

INDIANA UNIVERSITY PHOTOGRAPHIC SERVICES

The response of the returnees to the G.I. Bill overwhelmed many colleges, which saw their student population swell dramatically almost overnight. Scenes such as these were typical as veterans fought long lines to purchase supplies or register for classes.

Finding ways to house the increased student population—especially those who were married and had families—presented the biggest challenge for many schools. Although few veterans resorted to tents (top), many did find themselves living in military-surplus Quonset (center) and Nissen huts or trailers (bottom).

UNIVERSITY OF WISCONSIN-MADISON

UNIVERSITY OF KENTUCKY LIBRARY

INDIANA UNIVERSITY PHOTOGRAPHIC SERVICES

instructed groups of ten, found his classroom overflowing, he promptly left, thinking that he had somehow wandered into a required "Freshman English" course.

Military surplus Quonset and Nissen huts, used both for additional classroom space and for student housing until more permanent quarters could be built, soon dotted the nation's campuses. Before the arrival of these structures, students camped out in gyms, auditoriums, and any other space not already occupied. Having known far worse living conditions, the veterans did not complain.

At RPI, the more permanent residential quarters initially took the form of one hundred units of prefabricated housing obtained from the federal government. The commitment to build these structures was announced in February 1946. Only a month later, the list of RPI families looking for housing had grown to 250; the construction program was expanded.

Because the concept of married students was new to most of the colleges, their presence on campus created unique problems. The schools rose to the challenge by supplying both on- and off-campus family housing. They also set up day care centers and pediatric health clinics for the children.

Campus life presented unique challenges for the married students as well. Barbara Gunn, wife of a veteran studying at the University of Oregon, and a student herself, neatly summed up the experience when she wrote: "For my husband Rex and me, and many like us, college has been anything but a shelter from real life—it's been a baby crib squeezed into one corner, diapers drying over the furnace, and grocery bills instead of prom tickets." Barbara and Rex—24 years old and a 4-year veteran of the Pacific Theater—had signed up for veterans' housing during his freshman year. But the waiting list was long, and they never did get in.

Instead, just before their baby was born almost two years later, the Gunns managed to rent a one-bedroom house in Eugene for $45 a month—no small feat in a city where the population had grown from 35,000 in 1940 to 86,000 by the war's end. The house was a large step up from the one-room, converted workshop that the couple had occupied earlier, where the cooking was done on a hot plate, the heat came from a cast iron stove, and the bath facilities were out the back door and thirty steps down a gravel path.

By the time Barbara and Rex Gunn were graduated, the influx of veterans onto the campuses of the nation had reached its peak and was beginning to ebb. In 1947, more than a million of the college students in the United States—49.2 percent—were veterans. They took an active role in the campus community and made their presence felt on the athletic field as well. The halfback of the University of Michigan's 1947 championship football team was Bob Chappuis, a top contender for that year's Heisman Trophy. A few years earlier, during his 21st mission as an aerial gunner, Chappuis had bailed out of his crippled airplane over Italy. The 1947 Heisman eventually went to Johnny Lujack, a quarterback for the University of Notre Dame who had returned to school after three years in the Navy.

By 1948, when the number of veterans in college had slipped to 975,000, there was a growing consensus among educators that the veterans were the hardest working, most serious, and best students that the campuses had ever seen. "The G.I.'s," an education editor for *The New York Times* wrote late in 1947, "are hogging the honor rolls and the Dean's lists."

A professor at Lehigh spoke for most of his colleagues when he stated: "The civilian kids consider most of us doddering imbeciles. But the veterans seem to be impressed with our knowledge. They are old enough to realize that they know very little." He added that "They are the most responsive and receptive students Lehigh has ever had." One non-veteran student at Lehigh complained that the veterans "work so hard, we have to slave to keep up."

Even President Conant of Harvard changed his mind about veterans as students. In an article in *Life* magazine, he admitted that, "for seriousness, perceptiveness, steadiness, and all other undergraduate virtues," the former soldiers and sailors were "the best in Harvard's history." At Columbia University in '47, none of the 7,826 veterans in attendance was in serious academic difficulty. Such performances were the norm on campuses across the country.

Criticisms of the G.I. Bill for alleged abuses were few, but, as with any program of this size—more than $14 billion was eventually expended on it—there were some transgressions. Virtually all problems, however, occurred in education and training on the "trade," not the college, level. Numerous vocational schools had sprung into existence seemingly overnight. Until Congress tightened the restrictions on vocational/technical training in 1949, much of what was offered in some 5,635 such institutions was useless to those enrolled.

In 1948, while living in a cramped studio apartment on Riverside Drive in New York City, the Keenan twins began their studies at Columbia University. Thanks to credits that the school granted for their nurse's training and for courses they had taken in the Army, they received their degrees in 1950. They went on to Catholic University in Washington, D.C., for postgraduate work, earning master's degrees in education. The sisters were among the more than 64,000 women veterans to gain degrees under the G.I. Bill.

John Rigas received his degree in management engineering from RPI in 1950. The yearbook photograph taken of his graduating class includes the wives and children of the veterans. Grouped in the front, next to their gowned husbands and fathers, these family members dominate the picture. Dr. L. W. Houston, then president of the college, is pictured near the center of the photo, holding one of the youngest of the babies in his arms. Instead of looking at the camera, he is smiling down at the child.

The G.I. Bill and the veterans it helped to educate have been the subject of many studies by educators and statisticians in recent years. The findings consistently show that twenty percent of these graduates would never have been able to attend college had it not been for the bill.

By the time the provisions of the original G.I. Bill expired in 1952, roughly 15 percent—some 2.25 million—of the veterans eligible for its benefits had passed through institutions of higher learning. A study conducted by the Veterans Administration, with the assistance of the Departments of Labor and Commerce, revealed in 1965 that the G.I. Bill had substantially increased the earning power of those who had availed themselves of the opportunities it provided, and in the process, it generated an estimated $1 billion in additional income tax revenue. In less than twenty years, the federal government had recouped more than the original $14 billion cost of the program.

In 1969, Paul Cunningham, a reporter on NBC's *Today* show and a veteran who attended college under the G.I. Bill, spoke affectionately of the legislation on the 25th anniversary of its passage. The occasion, he said, recalled "images like olive-drab sweaters dyed blue or maroon, a lapel button—what we called a 'ruptured duck'—young wives standing in mud to hang up baby clothes outside a Quonset hut. What it did for this country may never be reckoned . . . except we know it changed the entire concept of adult education. . . . Some had suggested, he noted, that a memorial to the G.I. Bill be established. That, Cunningham concluded, might be good. "It might remind us that once in a while we do something right."

Michael D. Haydock, recently retired as a code enforcer, now works as a consultant and freelance writer, whose articles have appeared in Military History, Buffalo Spree, *and* Army Times.

Baseball's *Noble* Experiment

When former Negro Leaguer Jackie Robinson took his place in the Brooklyn Dodgers' starting lineup on April 15, 1947, he initiated a major change not only in sports, but in American society as a whole.

by William Kashatus

On August 28, 1945, Jackie Robinson, the star shortstop of the Negro Leagues' Kansas City Monarchs, arrived at the executive offices of the Brooklyn Dodgers Baseball Club. Invited on the pretense that Branch Rickey, since 1942 a part owner of the club as well as its president and general manager, was seeking top black talent in order to create a Negro League team of his own, Robinson approached the meeting with great reluctance. Deep down he wanted to break the color barrier that existed in professional baseball, not discuss the possibility of playing for yet another all-black team. Little did he realize that Rickey shared his dream.

A shrewd, talkative man who had dedicated his life to baseball, the 64-year-old Rickey was secretly plotting a sweeping revolution within the national pastime. He believed that integration of the major leagues would be good for the country as well as for the game. Financial gain was only part of his motive—it was also a matter of moral principle. Rickey a devout Methodist, disdained the bigoted attitudes of the white baseball establishment.

Greeting Robinson with a vigorous handshake, Rickey wasted no time in revealing his true intentions. "The truth is," he confessed, "I'm interested in you as a candidate for the Brooklyn Dodgers. I think you can play in the major leagues. How do you feel about it?"

The young ball player was speechless. He had taught himself to be cynical toward all baseball-club owners, especially white ones, in order to prevent any personal disillusionment.

"What about it? You think you can play for Montreal?" demanded the stocky beetle-browed executive.

Robinson, awestruck, managed to say "yes." He knew that the Montreal Royals was the Dodgers' top minor-league team and that if he made good there, he had an excellent chance to crack the majors. "I just want to be treated fairly" he added. You will not be treated fairly!" Rickey snapped. " 'Nigger' will be a compliment!"

For the next three hours, Rickey interrogated the star shortstop. With great dramatic flair, he role-played every conceivable scenario that would confront the first player to break baseball's color barrier: first he was a bigoted sportswriter who only wrote lies about Robinson's performance; next he was a Southern hotel manager refusing room and board; then, a racist major leaguer looking for a fight; and after that a waiter throwing Robinson out of a "for whites only" diner. In every scenario, Rickey cursed Robinson and threatened him, verbally degrading him in every way imaginable. The Dodger general manager's performance was so convincing, Robinson later said, that "I found myself chain-gripping my fingers behind my back."

When he was through, Rickey told Robinson that he knew he was "a fine ballplayer. But what I need," he added, "is more than a great player. I need a man that will take abuse and insults for his race. And what I don't know is whether you have the guts!"

Robinson struggled to keep his temper. He was insulted by the implication that he was a coward. "Mr. Rickey," he retorted, "do you want a Negro who's afraid to fight back?"

"No!" Rickey barked, "I want a ballplayer with guts enough *not* to fight back. We can't *fight* our way through this. There's virtually nobody on our side. No owners, no umpires, virtually no newspapermen. And I'm afraid that many fans will be hostile too. They'll taunt you and goad you. They'll do anything to make you react. They'll try to provoke a race riot in the ball park."

From *American History,* March/April 1997, pp. 32-37, 56-57. © 1997 by Cowles Magazine, Inc. Reprinted through the courtesy of Cowles Magazines, publishers of *American History.*

UPI/CORBIS-BETTMANN

In 1945, after a careful search for just the right man to do the job, Branch Rickey, president, general manager, and part owner of the Brooklyn Dodgers, bucked the long segregationist history of major-league baseball by signing Jack Roosevelt (Jackie) Robinson to play in the Dodger organization. At the time he signed with the Dodgers, Jackie was a shortstop with the Kansas City Monarchs of the Negro Leagues. During his ten seasons with the Dodgers, Robinson played under three managers—Burt Shotten, Chuck Dressen, and Walt Alston.

inferior public schools, health care, and public lodging, as well as discriminatory voter registration procedures that kept many of them disenfranchised.

For the nearly one million African Americans who had served in the armed forces during World War II, the contradiction inherent in their fight against totalitarianism abroad while enduring segregation at home was insufferable. No longer willing to knuckle under to Jim Crow this young generation of black Americans was determined to secure full political and social equality. Many migrated to Northern cities, where they found better jobs, better schooling, and freedom from landlord control. Together with their white allies, these Northern blacks would lay the foundations of the momentous civil rights campaign of the 1950s and '60s. And Jackie Robinson became their hero.

To be sure, Robinson's challenge to baseball's whites-only policy was a formidable one. Blacks had been expelled from the major leagues when segregation was established by the 1896 Supreme Court ruling in *Plessy v. Ferguson.*** Racist attitudes were reinforced

As he listened, Robinson became transfixed by the Dodger president. He felt his sincerity his deep, quiet strength, and his sense of moral justice. "We can only win," concluded Rickey, "if we can convince the world that I'm doing this because you're a great ballplayer and a fine gentleman. You will symbolize a crucial cause. One incident, just one incident, can set it back twenty years."

"Mr. Rickey," Robinson finally said, "I think I can play ball in Montreal. I think I can play ball in Brooklyn. . . . If you want to take this gamble, I will promise you there will be no incident."

The agreement was sealed by a handshake. Jackie Robinson and Branch Rickey had launched a noble experiment to integrate major-league baseball. Two

years later, in 1947, when Robinson actually broke the color barrier, winning rookie-of-the-year honors with the Dodgers, he raised the hopes and expectations of millions of black Americans who believed that deeply rooted patterns of discrimination could be changed.

In 1945, segregation was the most distinguishing characteristic of American race relations. More than half of the nation's 15 million African Americans still lived in the South, amidst a society that sanctioned the principle of "equal but separate." A rigid system of state and local ordinances enforced strict separation of the races in schools, restaurants, movie theaters, and even restrooms. For blacks, these so-called "Jim Crow laws"* meant

---

* Originally used in connection with legislation enacted in Southern states during the nineteenth century to separate the races on public transportation, the term "Jim Crow law" eventually applied to all statutes that enforced segregation.

** The 1896 decision of the Supreme Court in *Plessy v. Ferguson* upheld a Louisiana law that required railroads in that state to provide "equal but separate accommodations for the white and colored races." It was this "equal but separate" doctrine that made the discriminatory practices of this century legal in the United States. The Court essentially reversed itself in its 1954 *Brown v. Board of Education of Topeka, Kansas* decision, effectively ending legal segregation.

BASEBALL HALL OF FAME LIBRARY

A versatile athlete, Robinson earned varsity letters in four sports, including track (above, left, while a student at the University of California at Los Angeles. As a lieutenant in the U.S. Army during World War II (above, right), Robinson faced a court-martial for refusing to move to the back of a military bus; he was acquitted and honorably discharged.

by the significant numbers of white Southerners who played in the majors, as well as by the extensive minor-league system that existed in the South. When blacks established their own Negro Leagues, white journalists, as well as historians, ignored them.

Despite the periodic efforts of some white club owners to circumvent the racist policies and sign exceptional Negro Leaguers, the majors continued to bar blacks through the end of World War II. Baseball Commissioner Judge Kenesaw Mountain Landis ensured the sport's segregationist policies by thwarting all efforts to sign blacks, while publicly stating that "There is no rule, formal or informal, or any understanding—unwritten, subterranean, or sub-anything—against the hiring of Negro players by the teams of organized baseball." Not until Landis died in 1944, however, did baseball open the door for integration.

The new commissioner, Albert "Happy" Chandler, was adamant in de-fending the "freedom of blacks," especially those who served in the war, to "make it in major league baseball." Chandler's support for integration earned for him the open hostility of the owners of 15 of the 16 major-league clubs, the exception being the Dodgers and Branch Rickey.

Publicly, Rickey never revealed his intentions of breaking the color barrier. Instead, he announced to the baseball world that he was going to organize a team to be known as the "Brown Dodgers" or the "Brown Bombers" as part of a new all-black "United States League." His scouts combed baseball leagues across the country, as well as in Cuba, Mexico, Puerto Rico, and Venezuela, for black prospects. What Rickey really wanted to find was a talented, college-educated ballplayer who would be able to contradict the popular myth of black ignorance. His search narrowed to Jack Roosevelt Robinson, then an infielder for the Kansas City Monarchs.

Born on January 31, 1919, in Cairo, Georgia, Jackie was the grandson of a slave and the fifth child of a sharecropper who deserted his family Raised by his mother in a white, middle-class neighborhood in Pasadena, California, Jackie and his brothers and sister were verbally ridiculed and frequently pelted with rocks by local children. Rather than endure the humiliation, the boys formed a gang and began to return fire.

What saved the young Jackie from more serious trouble and even crime was his exceptional athletic ability. Robinson's high school career was distinguished by remarkable success in football, baseball, basketball, and track. His versatility earned him an athletic scholarship, first to Pasadena Junior College and later to the University of California at Los Angeles, where he earned varsity letters in four different sports and All American honors in football.

Drafted into the Army in the spring of 1942, Robinson applied to be admitted to Officers' Candidate School, but was denied admission because of his race. His application was eventually approved, however, thanks to the help of boxing champion Joe Louis, who was stationed with Jackie at Fort Riley, Kansas. Commissioned a second lieutenant, Robinson continued during the next few years to defy discriminatory practices within the military. When, in July 1944, he refused to move to the rear of a military bus at Fort Hood, Texas, Robinson was charged with insubordination and court-martialed. But the case against him was weak—the Army had recently issued orders against such segregation—and a good lawyer won his acquittal. Although he received an honorable discharge in November 1944, Robinson's time in the military had left him feeling vulnerable and uncertain about the future.

Shortly after his discharge, the Kansas City Monarchs, one of the most talented of baseball's Negro League teams, offered Robinson a contract for four hundred dollars a month. While with the Monarchs, Robinson established himself as a fine defensive shortstop with impressive base stealing and hitting abilities. But he hated barnstorming through the South, with its Jim Crow restaurants and hotels, and frequently allowed his temper to get the better of him.

Some teammates thought Jackie too impatient with the segregationist treatment of blacks. Others admired him for his determination to take a stand against racism. Yet Robinson never saw himself as a crusader for civil rights as much as an athlete who had grown disillusioned with his chosen career. "When I look back at what I had to go through," he recalled years later, "I can only marvel at the many black players who stuck it out for years in the Jim Crow leagues because they had nowhere to go. The black press, some liberal sportswriters and even a few politicians were banging away at those Jim Crow barriers in baseball, but I never expected the walls to come tumbling down in my lifetime. I began to wonder why I should dedicate my life to a career where the boundaries of progress were set by racial discrimination."

Although many white fans eagerly sought Robinson's autograph, others did their best to make his life miserable by heckling, shouting insults, and making threats. Among the many pieces of hate mail Jackie received was a letter threatening his life if he played in Cincinnati's Crosley Field in May 1947; Robinson not only played, he hit a home run. At the end of the '47 season, J. G. Taylor Spink, publisher of *Sporting News,* presented Robinson with the magazine's award as "Rookie of the Year" in the National League.

There were indications, however, that the tide was turning in favor of integration. On April 16, 1945, Robinson was invited along with two other Negro League stars—Marvin Williams of the Philadelphia Stars and the Cleveland Buckeyes' Sam Jethroe—to try-out for the Boston Red Sox. Manager Joe Cronin was especially impressed with the Monarchs' shortstop, but still passed on the opportunity to sign him. Nevertheless, the try out brought Robinson to the attention of Clyde Sukeforth, the chief scout of the Brooklyn Dodgers. Convinced of Robinson's exceptional playing ability and personal determination, Sukeforth set the stage for the memorable August meeting between Robinson and Rickey.

Robinson had no illusions about the purpose of his agreement with the Dodgers. He realized that Rickey's altruism was tempered by a profit motive, and yet he admired the moral courage of the Dodger president. "Mr. Rickey knew that achieving racial equality in baseball would be terribly difficult," Robinson remembered. "There would be deep resentment, determined opposition and perhaps even racial violence. But he was convinced that he was morally right and he shrewdly sensed that making the game a truly national one would have healthy financial results." Rickey was absolutely correct on both counts.

The Dodgers' October 23, 1945, announcement that Robinson had signed a contract for six hundred dollars a month* to play for their top minor-league club at Montreal was greeted with great hostility by baseball's white establishment. Rickey was accused of being "a carpetbagger who, under the guise of helping, is in truth using the Negro for his own self-interest." Criticism even came from the Negro League owners who feared, not without reason, that Robinson's signing would lead to declining fan interest in their clubs. The Monarchs were especially angered by the signing and went so far as to threaten a lawsuit against the Dodgers for tampering with a player who was already under contract.

UPI/CORBIS-BETTMANN

---

* Robinson also received a bonus of $3,500.

With Rachel's Support

When Jackie Robinson met with Branch Rickey in August 1945, the Dodgers' general manager asked him if he had a girlfriend, and was pleased when Jackie told him that he was engaged to be married. As he had made abundantly clear to Robinson that day, Rickey was aware that the first black player in the major leagues would face a terrible ordeal, and he clearly believed that he should not face it alone.

In her recent book, *Jackie Robinson: An Intimate Portrait*, Rachel Robinson writes that it was at the start of the '47 season that she and Jackie first realized "how important we were to black America and how much we symbolized its hunger for opportunity and its determination to make dreams long deferred possible." If Jackie failed to make the grade as a player, or if the pressures became so great that he decided to pull out of Rickey's "noble experiment," the hopes of all the nation's blacks would be done enormous, if not irreparable, harm. It was a tremendous burden to have to bear, and it belonged not only to Jackie, but also to his family.

Rachel Isum had met her future husband in 1940 while they were both students at UCLA, where she earned a degree in nursing. Engaged in 1941, they endured long separations during World War II, and in 1945, as Jackie traveled with the Kansas City Monarchs. Finally, in February 1946—just before Jackie was due to report to Daytona Beach, Florida, to try to earn a place with the Montreal Royals—they were married.

Both Jackie and Rachel had known racial bigotry and discrimination in Southern California, where they grew up, but they realized that they would face something much more difficult in the institutionalized segregation of the 1940s South. During that first trip to Florida, they experienced repeated humiliations that were, according to Rachel, "merely a foreshadowing of trials to come." As the Royals played exhibition games in other Florida cities, Jackie got a taste of how many Americans viewed his presence in professional baseball.

Following spring training, Jackie joined the Royals in Montreal, where the couple found a much more receptive environment. Although Jackie still faced racism during road trips, the Robinsons' year in Canada was fondly remembered as a respite that helped them prepare for the real test that came when he moved on to the Dodgers in 1947.

As players and fans in cities around the National League tormented Jackie, Rachel was forced to sit "through name calling, jeers, and vicious baiting in a furious silence." For his part, the Dodgers' rookie infielder, who had promised Rickey that he would turn the other cheek, "found that the most powerful form of retaliation against prejudice was his excellent play." But after the '48 season, Robinson called off his deal with Rickey. He would no longer submit quietly to insults, discrimination, and abuses. Able at last to release some of the pent-up pressure and emotion, Robinson became a more confident player; in 1949, he won the National League batting championship with a .349 average and received a trophy ironically named for Kenesaw Mountain Landis, the man who tried to keep blacks out of baseball.

By mid-November the criticism became so hostile that Rickey's own family pleaded with him to abandon his crusade for fear that it would destroy his health. The Dodger president refused, speaking only of the excitement and competitive advantage that black players would bring to Brooklyn baseball, while downplaying the moral significance he attached to integration. "The greatest untapped reservoir of raw material in the history of the game is the black race," he contended. "The Negroes will make us winners for years to come and for that I will happily bear being called a 'bleeding heart' and a 'do-gooder' and all that humanitarian rot."

Robinson's first test came during the 1946 preseason, even before he debuted with the Montreal Royals. Rickey named Mississippian Clay Hopper, who had worked for him since 1929, to manage the Royals. There were reports, probably true, that Hopper begged Rickey to reconsider giving him this assignment. But Rickey's careful handling of Robinson's jump to the big leagues would seem to suggest that he believed that having a Southerner at the helm of the Montreal club would head off some dissension among the players and that he trusted Hopper to handle any situations that might arise.

Throughout the '46 season, Robinson endured racist remarks from fans and opposing players and humiliating treatment in the South. By season's end, the constant pressure and abuse had taken its toll—his hair began to gray he suffered with chronic stomach trouble, and some thought he was on the brink of a nervous breakdown. Finding himself unable to eat or sleep, he went to a doctor; who concluded that he was suffering from stress. "You're not having a nervous breakdown," the physician told him. "You're under a lot of stress. Stay home and don't read any newspapers, and don't go to the ballpark for a week." Jackie, his wife Rachel remembered, stayed home for one day. The problem, she said, came from his not being able to fight back." It was, as Rickey had warned him, "the cross that you must bear."

Despite the tension and distractions, Robinson managed to hit for an impressive .349 average and led the Montreal Royals to victory over the Louisville Colonels in the Little World Series. After the final game in that championship series, grateful Royals fans hoisted Robinson onto their shoulders and carried him to the locker room. Hopper shook his shortstop's hand and said: "You're a real ballplayer and a gentleman. It's been wonderful having you on the team." Robinson had made his first convert.

Because Robinson's success with Montreal had been so impressive, Rickey assumed that all the Dodgers would demand his promotion to the majors for the 1947 season. "After all," he reasoned, "Robinson could mean a pennant, and ball players are not averse to cashing World Series checks."

To promote and protect his young black star, Rickey made some additional moves. First, in order to avoid Jim Crow restrictions, he held spring training in Havana, Cuba, instead of Florida. Next, he moved Robinson, an experienced shortstop and second baseman, to first base, where he would be spared physical contact with opposing players who might try to injure him deliberately.

Finally, Rickey scheduled a seven-game series between the Dodgers and the Royals in order to showcase Robinson's talent. "I want you to be a whirling demon against the Dodgers in this series," Rickey told Robinson. "You have to be so good that the Dodger players themselves are going to want you on their club. . . . I want you to hit that ball. I want you to get on base and run wild. Steal their pants off. Be the most conspicuous player on the field. The newspapermen from New York will send good stories back about you and help mold favorable public opinion."

Robinson more than obliged, batting .625 and stealing seven bases in the series. But instead of helping him, the performance served only to alienate him from his future teammates, many of whom were Southerners. Alabamian Dixie Walker drafted a petition stating that the players who signed would prefer to be traded than to play with a black teammate. While the team was playing exhibition games in Panama, Walker proceeded to gather signatures from Dodger teammates. Harold "Pee Wee" Reese, although a Kentuckian, refused to sign. It was a tremendously courageous act on his part because, as the team's shortstop, Reese had more to lose than any other Dodger. "If he can take my job," Reese insisted, "he's entitled to it."

When Dodger manager Leo Durocher learned of the petition, he was furious. He had asked Rickey to bring Robinson up to Brooklyn during the previous year's pennant drive. At a late-night team meeting, according to Harold Parrott, the Dodger road secretary, Durocher told Walker and the other petitioners that "I don't care if the guy is yellow or black, or if he has stripes like a zebra. I'm the manager of this team and I say he plays. What's more, I say he can make us all rich. . . . An' if any of you can't use the money, I'll see that you're traded."*

---

* Walker, one of a handful of players who asked to be traded, eventually went to the Pittsburgh Pirates, but not until after the '47 season. Durocher, himself, was suspended from baseball before the '47 season and never had the opportunity to manage Robinson.

The rebellion squelched, Rickey announced on April 10, 1947, that Jackie Robinson had officially been signed to play first base for the Brooklyn Dodgers. The noble experiment was in full swing.

Of all the major-league cities, Brooklyn, with its ethnically diverse and racially mixed neighborhoods, was just the place to break the color barrier. Despite their reputation as "perennial losers"—since the franchise's establishment in 1883, no Brooklyn team had won a World Series—the Dodgers enjoyed an enduring love affair with their fans. This warm affinity was fostered, in part, by their cramped but colorful ballpark, Ebbets Field, located in the Flatbush section of Brooklyn. The double-decked grandstand stood only along the foul lines, allowing the fans a special intimacy with the players. "If you were in a box seat," said broadcaster Red Barber, "you were so close you were practically an infielder." Aside from the patchwork collection of local advertisements in left field; the large, black scoreboard in right; and the tone-deaf "Dodger Symphony Band" that roamed the grandstand, nothing came between the Dodgers and their die-hard fans.

When Robinson made his first appearance as a Dodger on April 15, 1947, more than 26,000 fans packed Ebbets Field; reportedly some 14,000 of those were African Americans. The afternoon was cold and rainy and Robinson went hitless. Nonetheless, the sight of a black man on a major-league diamond during a regular season game moved the crowd so deeply that they cheered the Dodgers on to a 5–3 victory over the Boston Braves. Every move the 28-year-old rookie made seemed to be greeted with the chant: "Jackie! Jackie! Jackie!" It seemed as if baseball had finally shed its three-quarters of a century of hypocrisy to become truly deserving of the title "national pastime."

When the Philadelphia Phillies arrived in Brooklyn a week later, however, all hopes that integration would come peaceably were shattered. In one of the lowest moments ever in baseball history the Phillies, led by their Southern manager, Ben Chapman, launched a tirade of racial epithets during the pregame batting practice. And the jeering did not let up throughout the entire three-game series.

Two weeks later, when the Dodgers traveled to the so-called "City of Brotherly Love," Chapman and his Phillies picked up where they had left off, warning the Dodger players that they would contract diseases if they touched Robinson and indulging in even more personal racial slurs. Robinson's less-than-stellar hitting in the series only added to the Phillies' contention that he did not belong in the majors and was a ploy to attract blacks to Dodger games and make more money for Rickey.

BASEBALL HALL OF FAME LIBRARY

By the 1948 season, Robinson was no longer the only black player in the majors. African Americans brought up by Rickey that year included catcher Roy Campanella, (above) who would be voted the National League's Most Valuable Player three times.

After the second game of the series, angry Dodger fans launched a full-scale protest with the National League's president, Ford Frick, who responded by ordering Chapman and the Phillies to stop their verbal assault immediately. In fact, Chapman probably would have lost his job over the incident, if Robinson had not agreed to pose with him for a conciliatory newspaper photograph. Under duress, the Phillies' manager agreed to stand next to the Dodger rookie. "Ben extended his hand," Harold Parrott recalled, "smiling broadly as if they had been buddy-buddy for a lifetime. Robinson reached out and grasped it. The flicker of a smile crept across his face

BASEBALL HALL OF FAME LIBRARY

After his baseball career ended, Robinson became even more deeply involved in the Civil Rights Movement, supporting the work of leaders such as Dr. Martin Luther King, Jr., (above). Jackie and his family took part in the 1963 March on Washington that featured King's stirring "I Have a Dream" speech.

as the photographer snapped away getting several shots."

Years later Robinson admitted that the incessant abuse during those games with the Phillies almost led him to the breaking point. As he described it: "For one wild and rage-crazed minute I thought, 'To hell with Mr. Rickey's noble experiment. It's clear that it won't succeed.... What a glorious, cleansing thing it would be to let go.' To hell with the image of the patient black freak I was supposed to create. I could throw down my bat, stride over to the Phillies dugout, grab one of those white sons of bitches and smash his teeth in with my despised black fist. Then I could walk away from it and I'd never become a sports star. But my son could tell his son some day what his daddy could have been if he hadn't been too much of a man."

The experience with the Phillies revealed the shocking severity of the racism that existed in baseball. At the same time, however, Robinson's tremendous restraint in the face of such ugly prejudice served to rally his teammates around him and the cause of integration. Eddie Stanky one of those who had signed the petition against Robinson joining the team, became so angered by the Phillies' relentless abuse that he challenged them to "yell at somebody

who can answer back." Soon after, before a game in Cincinnati, the Reds' players taunted Pee Wee Reese about playing with a black teammate. The Dodger shortstop walked over to Robinson and, in a firm show of support, placed his arm around the first baseman's shoulders.

As the season unfolded, Dodger support for Robinson strengthened in response to the admirable way he handled all the adversity. Opposing pitchers threw at his head and ribs, while infielders would spit in his face if he was involved in a close play on the base paths. And the hate mail was unending. But through it all, Robinson persevered. He even managed to keep a sense of humor. Before one game in Cincinnati, when the Dodgers learned that their first baseman's life had been threatened, one teammate suggested that all the players wear Robinson's uniform number "42" on their backs to confuse the assailant. "Okay with me," responded the rookie. "Paint your faces black and run pigeon-toed too!"

Even the white baseball establishment began to embrace the Dodger infielder. In May of 1947, when Ford Frick learned of the St. Louis Cardinals' intention to instigate a league-wide strike by walking off the ball diamond

in a scheduled game against the integrated Dodgers, he vowed to suspend the ringleaders if they carried out their plan. "... I don't care if I wreck the National League for five years," he declared. "This is the United States of America, and one citizen has as much right to play as another. The National League will go down the line with Robinson whatever the consequence." The conspiracy died on the spot.

When the season ended, the *Sporting News,* which had gone on record earlier as opposing the integration of baseball because "There is not a single Negro player with major league possibilities," named Robinson the National League's "Rookie of the Year" for his impressive performance that season—29 stolen bases, 12 home runs, 42 successful bunt hits, and a .297 batting average.

Those efforts helped the Dodgers to capture a pennant, and on September 23, jubilant Brooklyn fans cheered their first baseman with a "Jackie Robinson Day" at Ebbets Field. In addition to a new car and other gifts, Robinson received tributes for his contribution to racial equal-

Jackie Robinson's death in October 1972 deeply affected African Americans and baseball fans across the country. As his funeral cortege made its way to his final resting place in Cypress Hills Cemetery in Brooklyn, the camera captured one mourner, shown in the foreground, offering Robinson a black-power salute.

BASEBALL HALL OF FAME LIBRARY

ity. Song-and-dance man Bill "Bojangles" Robinson, one of the guest speakers, told the crowd: "I'm 69 years old but never thought I'd live to see the day when I'd stand face-to-face with Ty Cobb in Technicolor."

The Dodgers forced the New York Yankees to a seventh and deciding game in the World Series. And when all was said and done, no amount of hate mail or verbal and psychological abuse could tarnish the indisputable fact that Jackie Robinson was an exceptional baseball player. He belonged in the major leagues.

Robinson's greatest accomplishment, however, was the inspiration that he provided for other African Americans, both in and out of baseball. Thousands of blacks came to watch him play setting new attendance records in such cities as Chicago and Pittsburgh. Even in St. Louis, Cincinnati, and Philadelphia, where the opposing teams were the most hostile toward the Dodger rookie, black fans would arrive on chartered buses called "Jackie Robinson Specials," having traveled hundreds of miles just to see him play.

Ed Charles, a black youngster from the Deep South who went on to play in the major leagues himself, remembered the thrill of seeing his childhood hero for the first time. "I sat in the segregated section of the ball park and watched Jackie," he said. "And I finally believed what I read in the papers—that one of us had made it. When the game was over we kids followed Jackie to the train station. When the train pulled out, we ran down the tracks listening for the sounds as far as we could. And when we couldn't hear it any longer, we stopped and put our ears to the track so we could feel the vibrations of that train

carrying Jackie Robinson. We wanted to be part of him as long as we could."

Indeed, Robinson had jolted the national consciousness in a profound way. Until 1947 all of baseball's heroes had been white men. Suddenly there was a black baseball star who could hit, bunt, steal, and field with the best of them. His style of play was nothing new in the Negro Leagues, but in the white majors, it was innovative and exciting. Robinson made things happen on the base paths. If he got on first, he stole second. If he could not steal third, he would distract the pitcher by dancing off second in order to advance. And then he would steal home. The name of the game was to score runs without a hit, something quite different from the "power hitting" strategy that had characterized major-league baseball. During the next decade, this new style of play would become known as "Dodger Baseball."

Before the '47 season was over, Branch Rickey had signed 16 additional Negro Leaguers, including catcher and future three-time "Most Valuable Player" Roy Campanella; pitcher Don Newcombe, who in 1956 would win 27 games; and second baseman Jim Gilham, like Robinson always a threat to steal a base. Together with Robinson and such white stars as Pee Wee Reese, Edwin "Duke" Snider, Gil Hodges, and Carl Erskine, these men would form the nucleus of a team that would capture six pennants and, at long last, in 1955, a world championship, before the Dodgers left Brooklyn for the West Coast at the end of the 1957 season. By 1959, every team in major-league baseball was integrated, one of every five players being of African-American descent.

When Rickey talked of trading Robinson to the New York Giants after the '56 season, the pioneering ballplayer chose to retire at the age of 38. His career totals, which included 1,518 hits, more than 200 stolen bases, and a lifetime batting average of .311, earned him a place in the National Baseball Hall of Fame in 1962, the first African American so honored. He continued to fight actively for civil rights long after his baseball career had ended, supporting Dr. Martin Luther King, Jr., and his call for the peaceful integration of American society.

Despite his tremendous accomplishments on and off the baseball field, Jackie Robinson, with characteristic humility never gave himself much credit. A year before his untimely death in 1972, he reflected on his struggle to break baseballs color barrier. "I was proud," Robinson admitted, "yet I was uneasy. Proud to be in the hurricane eye of a significant breakthrough and to be used to prove that a sport can't be called 'national' if blacks are barred from it But uneasy because I knew that I was still a black man in a white world. And so I continue to ask myself 'what have I really done for my people?' "

The answer was evident to everyone but him; for by appealing to the moral conscience of the nation, Jackie Robinson had given a young generation of blacks a chance at the "American Dream" and in the process taught many white Americans to respect others regardless of the color of their skin.

William Kashatus is a school teacher and freelance writer who lives in Philadelphia.

From Plan to Practice

The context and consequences of the Marshall Plan

by Charles S. Maier

When secretary of state George C. Marshall delivered his lapidary Commencement address under the Harvard elms on June 5, 1947, the concept he outlined was hardly a finished "plan." Still, it summarized weeks of intensive discussion and position papers at the State Department and other government agencies.

Political and economic developments seemed grave for many reasons. Marshall had returned dismayed from the Moscow foreign ministers' conference in April 1947. Although the victorious allies had pledged in 1945 to administer occupied Germany as a unit, mutual suspicions and conflicting agendas were sealing off their respective zones. In Moscow, both the Western allies and the Soviets seemed to approach agreement, then dug in their heels, preferring to assure the development they wanted at least in their own parts of the country rather than to gamble on losing influence over the whole.

The disputes were complicated: Americans feared the burden of reparation exactions that Russia felt had already been agreed to, and London and Washington were also concerned that the Soviets aspired to dominate the agencies that would administer a unified Germany. In addition, the Western allies, observing the increasingly repressive grip of the Communist-dominated Socialist Unity Party in the eastern zone of occupation, were unwilling to risk any such result in their regions. Meanwhile, the German economy was mired

in shortages, flight from a vastly depreciated currency, stalled reconstruction, and a breakdown of urban-rural exchange. These stresses were leading to hunger protests and a continuing decline of the already vastly diminished production of mines and factories.

Nor was Germany the only region in distress. European trade had barely revived since the war. After a promising resumption of production in 1946, the delicate postwar economy appeared snarled in bottlenecks and demoralization. The 1946 harvest had been meager; the severe winter that followed had frozen the rivers on which barges normally transported much of the coal needed to generate electricity and run factories. Reconstruction required products from the United States; the Europeans did not have the dollars to purchase this material.

In the same months, East-West ideological divisions became ever more intractable. Russians and Americans had failed to reach agreement on the control of atomic energy; they had exchanged bitter messages on the control of postwar Iran; most dismaying, the East European countries that Soviet troops had occupied were forced into satellite status as Communist people's parties or spurious political fronts tightened their control over government, industry, and the press. In the West, Communist and non-Communist parties ended the coalition governments that they had formed in the immediate aftermath of liberation. The fading politicians, labor leaders, and intellectuals who still wanly hoped

to bridge the deepening split were consigned to irrelevance and excluded from influence in the West; in the East, they were silenced, exiled, or imprisoned.

In March 1947, Washington agreed to assume Britain's role in supplying and in fact organizing the Greek government's fight against Communist guerrillas. As the president explained in what became known as the Truman Doctrine, the United States was prepared to extend aid to any government fighting subversive movements. The resounding declaration was designed for American political realities. The midterm elections of 1946 had returned a Republican Congress. Some GOP conservatives feared embroilment in Europe, but the majority of the party was prepared to support an anticommunist, bipartisan foreign policy. The "vital center"—to cite the expression of then Harvard historian Arthur Schlesinger Jr. '38—would rally to define an anticommunist liberalism. Nonetheless, the Truman Doctrine was not an instrument for combating the discontents in Western Europe. Could not Americans offer something more positive and hopeful?

This was the challenge to which Marshall and his assistants responded in the six weeks between Moscow and Harvard Yard. The new policy planning staff under George Kennan coordinated ideas; everyone in the relevant agencies was soon eager to claim paternity, as Charles Kindleberger—then dealing with German and Austrian economic affairs in the State Department and for decades

From *Harvard Magazine*, May/June 1997, pp. 40-43. © 1997 by Charles S. Maier. Reprinted by permission.

thereafter a vigorous economist and historian at MIT—pointed out in a humorous note on the origins of the plan. The concept that emerged was simple but innovative: Washington must make a multiyear commitment of foreign aid to those European governments that would respond cooperatively, in order to alleviate the dollar shortage, catalyze recovery, and preclude any reversion to authoritarian solutions.

The new assistance program, eventually christened the European Recovery Program (ERP), differed from the substantial aid provided ever since the end of the war. The United States had been extending roughly $5 billion in aid each year (from a peacetime GNP rising toward $200 billion) under the auspices of the United Nations Relief and Rehabilitation Agency (UNRRA); the funds went to countries in eastern as well as western Europe, to Egypt, and to its own occupation forces. Washington had also extended or facilitated key loans to Britain and France. But Congress grew increasingly restive about these expensive stopgap infusions. Some UNRRA supplies flowed to Communist countries that became more and more hostile, or went toward relief measures that did not seem to promote any revival of production. The new program would target investment and reconstruction; it would include what today we call technology transfer, and involve advisers in economic modernization. Advocates stressed the ERP was not merely an anticommunist expedient, but an effort to encourage Europe to emulate the modern production methods that the United States had mobilized so successfully in fighting World War II.

From Marshall's speech onward, the Europeans were summoned to cooperate among themselves in assigning priorities—although the United States would sign a pact with each. The political astuteness of the project lay in its open-handed offer. No country was to be excluded: if the East European Communist regimes were willing to open their economies to scrutiny and cooperative trade practices—and undoubtedly to American investors and products—they could allegedly share in the resources. Did Marshall and his advisers really expect this result? Could they have per-

suaded Congress to authorize such assistance? Skepticism was warranted. But perhaps the Marshall Plan might persuade Moscow to move toward a more cooperative course, such as had seemed possible at the end of the war. If not, the onus for the break would be on the Soviets, and a critical mass of the West European working middle classes, desirous of sharing in American aid, would rally around non-Communist leaders.

Not all these developments could be envisaged as part of a coherent strategy in early June 1947. But the key concepts were all implicit: sustained aid targeted for investment, growth, and balance-of-payments viability—not just for relief; aid proffered to a potentially integrated economic region, not just to individual countries; aid that would stress productivity and cooperation between capital and labor and would encourage Europeans to emulate the productive political economy of the United States.

Subsequent developments would shape the final outcome. Although Soviet foreign minister Vyacheslav Molotov briefly attended the initial Paris conference of recipients in July, the Russians and the regimes they controlled soon withdrew. Moscow's leaders summoned foreign Communist parties together in September and warned them to prepare for a long period of hostile confrontation. The Communist parties of France and Italy soon engaged in a series of provocative and unsuccessful strikes to protest their recent exclusion from governing coalitions. In effect, Europe's Communists retreated into a political ghetto at Moscow's behest rather than risk losing their militant identity. They accepted the risk of isolating themselves rather than accept the risks of détente. The Czech government, still democratic and still a coalition, dared to remain in Paris for another few months until Soviet pressure compelled it to withdraw. The concession did not placate Moscow, and Communist factory committees and political leaders forced a dictatorial regime upon the country in February 1948. This final extension of Communist control helped to overcome remaining hesitation on the part of the American Congress to fund the recovery program.

Americans designed an innovative structure: an independent aid agency in Washington, the European Cooperation Administration (ECA), under former Studebaker Corporation president Paul Hoffman, who headed the effort, coordinated economic planning,and solicited the yearly appropriations from Congress. Former Lend-Lease administrator and Soviet ambassador Averell Harriman (followed in 1950 by future Harvard law professor Milton Katz '27, J.D. '31) headed the Paris ERP headquarters as special representative in Europe, and coordinated the country aid missions attached to each American embassy. Each country had to prepare recovery plans and have them approved by the new Organization for European Economic Cooperation (founded in 1948) and by the Americans. The amount allocated depended upon the projected balance of payments deficit; need, not virtuous austerity, opened Washington's purse. Once the European planners received approval for the matériel sought from the United States, the ECA bought the goods from American suppliers—steel and industrial raw materials, industrial components, wheat, foodstuffs, and tobacco—and delivered them across the Atlantic. The recipient governments then in effect sold the goods for local currency, termed "counterpart," to the national agencies or industries that had sought them. Marshall Plan officials retained a voice in approving the use of local counterpart funds. The French, for example, allocated their counterpart francs to Jean Monnet's national planning commission for specific infrastructure projects; the British won approval to reduce government debt, which in turn freed private capital for market-oriented investment.

In general, American advisers found it difficult simply to oppose the counterpart projects for which Europeans might plead; aside from vetoing the occasional rank pork-barrel proposal, it was hard to impose alternatives. Still, U.S. advisers could play constructive roles in collaborating on local development strategies; Hollis Chenery, Ph.D. '50, later to teach in the Harvard economics department, was instrumental in planning for Italy's Mezzogiorno region. The young economists who staffed ERP agencies had learned the new Keynesian doctrines just before the war. They appreciated large and integrated markets, but understood that sometimes government spending was required to help markets function. World War II had further demonstrated that governments could plan purposeful economic activity and mobilize productive resources.

How decisive an economic and political impact did the Marshall Plan exert over its four-year existence? By 1951, when, in the wake of the Korean War, the U.S. transformed the assistance program into the Mutual Security Administration, Americans had supplied about $14 billion in aid, probably between 1 and 2 percent of our gross national product for the period—roughly five times the proportional share we now allocate to foreign assistance. In the first two years of the program, American aid provided a major share of German and Italian gross capital formation; then it fell, as in Britain and France, to a much smaller share. In quantitative terms, Europeans were soon accumulating their own capital. Nonetheless, Washington's assistance satisfied key needs and was targeted to eliminate critical shortages. Assistance in dollars allowed Europeans to invest without trying to remedy their balance of payments drastically through deflation and austerity. This meant that economic recovery did not have to be financed out of general wage levels. Working-class voters (at least outside France and Italy, where strong communist political cultures still thrived) could thus be rallied by politicians who offered gradualist social-democratic alternatives and remained friendly to the West.

Would Europe have "gone Communist" without the Marshall Plan? No, but the mean and dispirited politics of the late 1930s might well have returned. The Marshall Plan made it easier to inaugurate a quarter century of ebullient economic growth; it provided incentives for closer regional integration (especially the decisive European Payments Union of 1950, which Washington helped to finance); and worked to stabilize the consensual welfare-state politics that prevailed until the 1970s.

Such an outcome was hardly foreordained. Europeans and Americans had trapped themselves in destructive policies in the 1930s with catastrophic consequences. They could have done so again. But in the late 1940s, Americans and Europeans made constructive choices. Fifty years later, that moment in Harvard Yard gives us a lot to ponder. What policies will unleash innovative energies, transforming bleak prospects and dangerous impasses into opportunity? How do we recover that sense of public purpose, that confidence in our institutions?

Charles S. Maier '60, Ph.D. '67, Krupp Foundation professor of European studies and director of the Minda de Gunzburg Center for European Studies, is the editor of The Marshall Plan and Germany *(1991) and other works on twentieth-century European history, including the forthcoming* Dissolution: The Crisis of Communism and the End of East Germany. *He and Joseph S. Nye Jr., dean of the Kennedy School of Government, have organized a symposium at Harvard on June 3 and 4 to celebrate the fiftieth anniversary of the Marshall Plan.*

Echoes of a Distant War

The half-remembered Korean conflict was full of surprises,
and nearly all of them were unpleasant

Bernard A. Weisberger

Korea is in the news again, and it's ugly news. North Korea may or may not have the capability to make nuclear weapons, and North Korea's aging dictator, Kim Il Sung, is unwilling to let international inspectors find out. The United Nations is talking of sanctions. The United States is pointedly scheduling military maneuvers with the army of the Republic of South Korea. Some of the media's self-chosen secretaries of state summon us, from their word processors, to sturdy firmness. Others warn that the unpredictable Kim should not be cornered, lest he provoke a second Korean War.

I don't know if that last is an impossible scenario. But the mere idea gives me the feeling of being trapped in a re-run. Nearly five years after the Cold War ended, we are talking about possible renewed hostilities with a chief character from its early phases. Kim is the oldest surviving Communist boss. He goes back beyond an era already ancient—the days of Khrushchev; Eisenhower, Adenauer, de Gaulle, Ho Chi Minh—to an almost paleolithic time when World War II strongmen like Truman, Stalin, and Chiang Kai-shek still walked the stage.

A great many people know nothing whatever about the original Korean War. It is a barely commemorated conflict, buried between the heroics of World War II, the "good war," and the torments of Vietnam, the bad one, which we lost.

And it partakes of both traditions. It started as a neat epilogue to the great war against fascist aggression and ended as a curtain raiser to the frustrations of an age of limited power. It was full of surprises, almost all of them unpleasant.

To begin at the beginning, North and South Korea, like East and West Germany, were political fictions created by the post-1945 failure of the wartime Soviet-U.S. alliance. Korea was a single nation, divided into temporary Soviet and American occupation zones pending a final peace treaty with Japan, which had seized and annexed Korea.

The little peninsula was a rich prize, half of which fell into Stalin's lap cheaply in August of 1945, when the U.S.S.R. entered the war against Japan in its final days. Moscow's forces got to occupy Manchuria and northern Korea and help themselves to "reparations" from both places. In Korea the Soviets also dominated the political reorganization that was supposedly the prelude to all-Korean elections that would at last set up a free, single, democratic Korea. Kim Il Sung, a veteran of Korea's Communist underground, emerged at this time. He was thought by Americans to be a totally obedient Stalin puppet, but so was every Communist leader in those days—a somewhat simplistic assessment, as events showed.

In South Korea the reawakening of independent political life brought back a long-exiled figure, Dr. Syngman Rhee, who was seventy years old at the war's end. Rhee was a veteran nationalist, jailed and tortured by the Japanese in his youth. He was a popular autocrat whose limited brand of "democracy" had America's blessing, and when he won elections held in the South, Washington helped him build an army for his Republic of Korea and then withdrew its forces. The U.S.S.R. did likewise with Kim, whom it endowed with the leadership of the People's Democratic Republic of Korea. By 1950 Kim and Rhee—their man and ours—were glaring at each other from their respective capitals, Pyongyang and Seoul. Each wished passionately to depose the other "puppet" and unify Korea under his own rule. There were border clashes and provocations, threats (unpleasantly like those we are hearing today) and clear indications that either would use force if he could get his patron's backing.

But it was Kim who struck first. On June 25, 1950, his tanks rolled across the thirty-eighth parallel, which marked the border between South and North, and gave the world the first of a series of shocks. Number one was the attack itself, seemingly a crude act of aggression in imitation of Japan's grab of Manchuria, Mussolini's attack on Ethiopia, or Hitler's march into Austria. This searing parallel to the 1930s led American public opinion almost universally

From *American Heritage*, July/August 1994, pp. 28, 30, © 1994 by Forbes, Inc. Reprinted by permission of *American Heritage* magazine, a division of Forbes, Inc.

and instantly to agree that action was needed. *This* time international outlawry would be stopped in its tracks. And right at hand was the United Nations, the precise agency for calling in the international cops. The United States got a resolution authorizing "police action" rushed through the Security Council. The war thereby became technically a UN operation, though 90 percent of the forces, and the overall commander, Gen. Douglas MacArthur, were furnished by the Republic of Korea and the United States.

Now came the second great shock. The air and naval forces that President Truman immediately ordered to support the South Koreans were not enough to stop the invasion. Ground troops were needed, and MacArthur could deploy only his occupation forces, softened by years of garrison duty. Fed piecemeal into action, they were quickly overrun by North Korean divisions. By the end of August the soldiery of a "tiny" Asian nation had penned the UN forces in a perimeter around the port of Pusan and seemed on the verge of driving them completely off the peninsula.

Then a thunderclap for our side. MacArthur had assembled an amphibious force from the reinforcements pouring into Japan, and on September 15 it landed at Inchon, on Korea's western coast, in a dramatic high-risk attack against strong positions in tricky tides—a gamble that, to MacArthur's delight, was brilliantly successful. Now it was the enemy that faced cutoff and entrapment. The North Koreans retreated pell-mell; inside two weeks Seoul was back in UN hands, and American troops were surging northward above the thirty-eighth parallel, for the United Nations had authorized the then-untouchable MacArthur (though not without debate) not only to restore the status quo but to overrun North Korea and punish the aggressor.

That set up shock number three. The Chinese Communists, who had been in power since 1949, when Chiang Kai-shek and his Nationalist army were driven off the mainland and onto Taiwan, let it be known through neutrals that they would not tolerate a UN armed

presence on their common border with North Korea, the Yalu River. MacArthur, who fancied himself a master of "Oriental" psychology, persuaded Washington to ignore these warnings and pushed on. At the end of October 1950 Chinese infantry entered the fighting against the Americans in force, although technically there was no state of war between Peking and Washington or Peking and Seoul. Within days the divided and outnumbered American and ROK forces were enveloped and driven into a bitter winter retreat. As the new year opened, Seoul fell to the Communists again. MacArthur then set the stage for the next scene.

For the general, who had spent the preceding fifteen years in Asia, the war with China, declared or not, was real and had to be pursued to victory. He wanted American bombers to hit Chinese and North Korean bases and "sanctuaries" in Manchuria and also wished to have Chiang's army sea-lifted from Taiwan to Korea. In the Cold War atmosphere these ideas were attractive to many Americans, but not to Truman and the Joint Chiefs of Staff. Preoccupied with confronting Stalin in Europe, they wanted no part of consuming land battles in Asia. MacArthur pushed his public quarrel with Washington up to, if not over, the edge of insubordination.

The American public dealt with the frustration of a victoryless war by forgetting the whole episode.

But he was up against another rock-like, if less flamboyant, individual in Truman. Politician though he was, the President was immovable when he thought he had the Constitution on his side. And so the fourth great shock: On April 11, 1951, Truman fired MacArthur amid a firestorm of public fury. MacArthur's dismissal was a turning point. After ten months of violent pendulum swings, the war settled into a new kind

of conflict. None of the major powers wanted a full-scale engagement in Korea. What was needed was a peace of some kind with neither victory nor defeat. In July of 1951 truce talks began. They lasted for two years.

And in that time the real and most terrible Korean War was fought. The battle line stabilized more or less near the thirty-eighth parallel, and the fighting became a nasty and brutish affair, reminiscent of World War I, of small advances against strongly fortified positions with names like Pork Chop Hill and the Iron Triangle. Each gain cost hundreds, sometimes thousands, of lives. When final truce terms were approved on July 27, 1953 (over the strong objections of Rhee, and possibly Kim too), there was no exultation but mainly a kind of grim relief. Little was changed, except that a U.S. security treaty with Seoul pledged us to the future defense of the ROK against any attack, so as to leave no tempting doubt.

The American public, grudgingly forced to accept a victoryless war, seems to have dealt with frustration by forgetting the whole episode. There is just now under way a memorial in Washington to the thirty-three thousand Americans who died in Korea. Its returning veterans got no parades; they got a platter of benefits sharply reduced from that provided for the warriors of 1941–45. The United Nations, rather than being perceived as the force that had stopped aggression, fell into disrepute with some Americans for its failure to destroy North Korea. The United States settled into an era of diminished expectations of world perfection. Perhaps not diminished enough: The Korean War seems not to have prepared the public mind fully for the limits to power encountered later in Vietnam.

I don't wish to sound dismissive or to trivialize the vast suffering of soldiers and civilians on all sides. One could argue that the war was "won" to the extent that it may have discouraged further adventurism. Still, I wish it were possible to worry less about the surprises that a still divided Korea may bring us in the years to come.

SPUTNIK

***Forty years ago this month the Soviet Union orbited a
"man-made moon" whose derisive chirp persuaded Americans
they'd already lost a race that had barely begun***

By Edwin Diamond and Stephen Bates

It wasn't the best of times, but it wasn't the worst of times either. Although a mild recession had cooled down the post–Korean War economy, many families were living comfortable lives in the autumn of 1957. There were 170 million Americans now, and more of them had taken a vacation that summer than ever before, just like the swells out in Southampton.

To be sure, there was turbulence in the air. Three years after *Brown* v. *Board of Education* had struck down school segregation, the governor of Arkansas, Orval Faubus, defied a federal judge's integration order. Reluctantly, President Dwight D. Eisenhower dispatched the 101st Airborne to enforce the Constitution at Little Rock's Central High School. Slowly, though, the walls of segregation were falling. In July of that long-ago summer, Althea Gibson of Harlem, U.S.A., scored a first. A decade after Jackie Robinson had broken the baseball color line, Gibson won the Wimbledon tennis singles championship and curtsied to the Queen of England.

No Americans were fighting abroad in 1957, though tens of thousands of GIs were deployed in Cold War hot spots from divided Berlin to the Korean demilitarized zone. The Americans and the Russians were methodically testing bigger and "dirtier" (more radioactive fallout) nuclear bombs while perfecting

UPI/CORBIS-BETTMANN

intercontinental missile systems to deliver them. But Nikita Khrushchev, the new Number One Red (as the newspapers referred to him), was talking peaceful competition between socialism and the Free World (as the same papers referred to our side), and summitry, not shooting, seemed to be the prospect between the United States and the U.S.S.R.

Everything in fact appeared to be converging on a broad consensual middle, a prospect that evoked varying responses. What enthusiasts touted as serene abundance (the Republicans had just produced a film called *These Peaceful and Prosperous Years*), critics scorned as soulless conformity and complacency—from Holden Caulfield's contempt for "phonies" to *The Man in the Gray Flannel Suit's* self-doubt.

Then, early in the evening of October 4, the sky seemed to fall, literally, on the American edifice. At 6:30 P.M. EST the Associated Press moved a bulletin: Moscow Radio had announced that "the Soviet Union has launched an earth satellite." Later in the evening NBC interrupted regular programming to give more details of the "man-made moon" and to play its high-pitched radio signal "as recorded by RCA engineers." The next morning's *New York Times* and *Washington Post* both gave three-line eight-column banners to the feat, the kind of headline reserved for a Pearl Harbor or a D-day. The editors of *Newsweek* scrapped their planned feature on Detroit's new line of cars (trashing 1,309,990 cover copies—twenty tons of paper). The new cover showed an artist's conception of the Soviet satellite *Sputnik* (Russian for "fellow traveler"). Inside, the weekly explained "The Red Conquest," "The Meaning to the World," and, ominously, "Why We Are Lagging."

Overnight the self-assured center began coming apart. Inventive, free-enterprise America, home of Edison and the Wright brothers, Levittown and "modern laborsaving kitchen appliances," was being overtaken—surpassed?—by a backward, to-

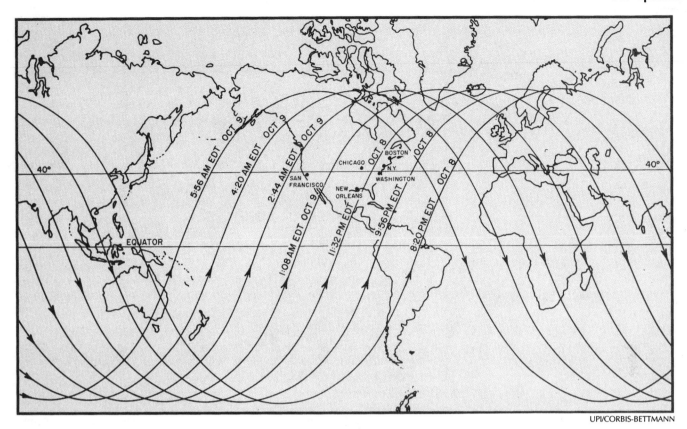

UPI/CORBIS-BETTMANN

Four days after the launch the U.S. Naval Research Laboratory released a chart of *Sputnik*'s course for October 8 and 9.

talitarian, *Communist* nation. And the shock to can-do pride was the least of it. A missile gap apparently yawned, with the Soviets pulling decisively

---

Sputnik, said Ike, "does not raise my apprehensions, not one iota." The reporters were, to put it mildly, skeptical.

---

ahead in the ultimate nuclear weapons, ICBMs. Democrats in Congress charged that amiable Ike's mid-register budgetary caution had jeopardized U.S. military prowess. It seemed that the energetic five-star architect of victory in the Big War had turned into a Burning Tree Country Club slacker (one cartoonist showed *Sputnik* whizzing past a golf ball), a myopic Pangloss, a President Magoo.

Sen. Stuart Symington of Missouri, a potential Democratic presidential candidate in 1960, demanded that the President call a special session of Congress to address the *Sputnik* crisis. Ike refused; he even declined to deliver a televised speech addressing the nation's apprehensions, so as not to appear "alarmist." Instead he chose to hold a news conference on October 9, five days after the Soviet announcement. It was, in the view of Eisenhower's biographer Stephen Ambrose, one of the most hostile Q&A sessions of Ike's Presidency. Eisenhower repeatedly maintained that *Sputnik* was in essence meaningless. "As far as the satellite itself is concerned," he said, "that does not raise my apprehensions, not one iota."

The reporters were, to put it mildly, skeptical. If the Soviets could orbit a satellite, they could fire a nuclear warhead across the ocean at Washington; if the Americans couldn't orbit a satellite, they couldn't shoot a warhead inside Soviet boundaries. Or so experts were telling journalists, and journalists were telling the public. War planners had been confident that the United States could

fight off a nuclear strike launched by Soviet long-range bombers, but if Soviet *missiles* could reach the United States, as *Sputnik* hinted, then perhaps our way of life *was* doomed. *Life* magazine presented "The Case for Being Panicky."

Readers were persuaded. Soon Gallup found that half of all Americans believed the Soviets held the lead "in the development of missiles and long-distance rockets." By early 1958 more than a third of Americans thought that the Soviets "could wipe out most cities in the United States in a matter of a few hours with their new rockets and missiles." One out of three Americans also expected the outbreak of World War III by the early 1960s.

The news grew gloomier. In early November, just in time for the celebration of the fortieth anniversary of the Russian Revolution, the Soviets announced the launch of a second *Sputnik*, this one carrying Laika, the orbiting dog. No matter that Laika had a one-way ticket; the capsule accommodated enough oxygen to keep her alive for ten days (because a thermal-control system failed, she didn't last even that long).

First dogs, and soon, the Soviets hinted, men. "What will Americans find on the other side of the moon?" went the joke. "Russians."

The Soviets began hinting at plans for manned spaceflights. "What will Americans find on the other side of the moon?" went the joke. "Russians."

In reality the United States was winning both the arms race and the nascent space race. There was indeed a "missile gap," but the lead belonged to the Americans. Ike, it turned out, knew something the rest of us didn't.

Sputnik, like so many 1950s developments in military technology, had its roots in World War II. Hours after the satellite was launched, a U.S. military official complained, "We've got the wrong Germans!" He was mistaken. Most of "their" German rocket scientists—the Peenemünde group captured by the Soviets at the end of the war—had been repatriated. The four-hundred-thousand-pound three-stage rocket that launched *Sputnik* may have been an elaboration of the successful German V-2 design, but it was homegrown.

The best known of "our" Germans, those who had fled west to avoid capture by the Russians, was a civilian scientist for the U.S. Army Redstone missile command in Huntsville, Alabama, named Wernher von Braun. Smooth, handsome in a Hollywood-heavy sort of way, von Braun had been trying for years to get the government to make satellites a priority. His 1954 report "A Minimum Satellite Vehicle" outlined a plan for orbiting an American satellite by 1956. "It is only logical to assume that other countries could do the same," von Braun wrote, adding (emphasis in original): "*It would be a blow to U.S. Prestige if we did not do it first.*" He sought one hundred thousand dollars to start an

Army satellite program. The request was turned down.

Instead the administration divvied up the tasks—and the pork—of missile development. In that 1950s spirit of compromise, every service got a piece of the action (as did the contractors allied with each service—Martin, Northrop, Convair, Aero-Jet General). Even though von Braun and the Army were far ahead in testing rocket designs, the Defense Department gave the Navy the satellite assignment. A new Navy Vanguard rocket would be developed to lift a four-pound satellite and its modest telemetry into orbit. At the same time, the Army would continue to develop the Jupiter intermediate-range ballistic missile, while the Air Force would work on its Atlas and Titan intercontinental ballistic missiles. Eisenhower didn't warm to the idea of a "missile czar," on the model of Gen. Leslie Groves during the Manhattan Project, to knock Army, Navy, and Air Force heads together; each service forged ahead independently of the others.

On July 31, 1955, American scientists, with the blessing of the White House, announced that the United States would launch a satellite during the International Geophysical Year (IGY), a resolutely peaceful eighteen-month (July 1957 through the end of 1958) multinational investigation of the planet and its resources. Within days of the American announcement, Soviet scientists revealed that they, too, were readying a satellite, also to be launched during IGY. American experts scoffed.

While the Navy worked to meet the IGY goal, von Braun's Army team launched a four-stage rocket on September 20, 1956. It reached a speed of 13,000 miles per hour and a record-setting altitude of 682 miles. The last stage might have been capable of achieving orbit, but because the Navy was in charge of satellites, the nose cone was filled with sand.

To Eisenhower and one faction of his allies, *Sputnik* was noise signifying nothing. The President said, "We never considered ourselves to be in a race." The White House adviser Sherman Adams declared that the United States had no interest in "an outer-space bas-

ketball game." In *The New Republic* Richard Strout dryly saw a parallel to Ike's above-the-fray re-election campaign of 1956: "Mr. Eisenhower appeared prepared to treat the satellite as though it were Adlai Stevenson."

But some politicians took to badmouthing one another. A few Republicans, including Ike's Vice President, Richard M. Nixon, blamed Harry S. Truman, by then nearly five years out of office. Truman responded by writing a long article blaming Eisenhower and lamenting this "sorry chapter in the story of our defense." Distributed by the North American Newspaper Alliance, the article made its way to the front page of *The New York Times.* Evoking the memory of the "atomic spy couple," Julius and Ethel Rosenberg, *U.S. News & World Report* suggested that skulduggery explained the Soviet feat: "Did Russia Steal Satellite Secret from U.S.?"

Others faulted progressive educators, who, the critics claimed, had concentrated on children's feelings to the detriment of hard knowledge. *Life* devoted five issues to the "Crisis in Education," arguing in one article that the spartan Soviet system was producing students better equipped to cope with the Space Age. *Why Johnny Can't Read* rocketed up the bestseller lists. In an October 31 news conference, Eisenhower, while remaining unruffled by *Sputnik*'s military implications, declared himself "shocked" to learn the magnitude of the nation's education shortcomings. The following year he backed the National Defense Education Act, which funded laboratories and textbooks in public schools as well as loans for college-bound students—the federal government's first major steps into education. Like interstate highways, schooling had become a matter of national defense, endorsed by both the Republican White House and the Democratic-controlled Congress. The former Harvard president James Bryant Conant urged parents to tell children, "For your own sake and for the sake of the nation, do your homework."

Still others contended that the Soviets' lead in space reflected a deteriorating American spirit. Peace and prosperity, according to this line of argument, had produced an indolent self-satisfaction. "Our goal has become a life of amiable sloth," wrote the journalist Thomas Griffith. To the sharp-tongued playwright and Republican loyalist Clare Boothe Luce, *Sputnik*'s beeps represented "an intercontinental outer-space raspberry" aimed at American pretensions of superiority. *Sputnik*, then, might serve as a warning shot that would force "bland, gray-suited" America to contemplate national interest instead of self-interest. "We needed *Sputnik*," Adlai Stevenson said, calling the satellite "sure proof that God has not despaired of us."

As television recorded the scene, Vanguard's first-stage rocket roared, spewed flame and smoke—and rose all of four feet.

Vice President Nixon recognized that the White House efforts to shrug off *Sputnik* were failing miserably. He deemed Adams's basketball remark "wrong in substance and disastrous in terms of public opinion." In a San Francisco speech the Vice President staked out his own ground, saying that "we could make no greater mistake than to brush off this event as a scientific stunt of more significance to the man in the moon than to men on earth." Privately Nixon urged Eisenhower to say that money was no object in the contest of freedom against slavery. Ignoring the advice, Ike instead cautioned against any "hasty and extraordinary effort under the impetus of sudden fear."

Nixon wasn't the only Republican up in arms. In early November a panel of defense experts delivered its previously commissioned report to Ike's National Security Council. The work of such Establishment bulwarks as John McCloy and Paul Nitze, the report argued that

the United States could be "critically vulnerable" to a missile attack by the end of 1959, with likely casualties of up to 50 percent. Even if the Soviets chose not to wage cataclysmic war, the report suggested, they could conquer space, maybe militarize the moon. The panel's bottom line: Continued American security required *major* increases in the military budget, to be achieved by deficit spending. Called the Gaither Report (after the group's chair, the Ford Foundation's head, H. Rowan Gaither, Jr.), the document was leaked to *The New York Times* and the *Washington Post*. In his magisterial memoir *Danger and Survival*, McGeorge Bundy writes that Ike came to feel he'd been hit by a "double barrelled shock"—*Sputnik* and Gaither.

But the worst blast came a few weeks later. Along with portraying the *Sputnik*s as meaningless, the administration had been telling reporters that the United States was about to launch a satellite of its own. The Navy was still in charge of the program, though von Braun and the Army were quietly at work too. The day after *Sputnik I*'s launch, von Braun had told Defense Secretary Neil McElroy that the Navy rocket "will never make it," whereas the Army rocketeers could launch a satellite in sixty days. McElroy took it under advisement. A month later, amid the aftershocks of *Sputnik II,* von Braun was told to get to work.

The Navy's Vanguard program was also on an accelerated countdown. The original schedule called for a dozen meticulous test runs, each one involving additional hardware and equipment. Not until number seven was a full-scale "earnest try" for orbit to be attempted. But with two *Sputnik*s in orbit, as *Newsweek* put it, "the Vanguard test rocket with its grapefruit-sized satellite suddenly became the U.S. answer to the Soviet challenge."

For four excruciating days beginning on December 2, the formerly sleepy (and off-limits) Cape Canaveral test site on Florida's Atlantic coast became media central. The Vanguard launch team sweated through a series of postponements that Navy spokesmen attributed to, at one time or another, "balky" guidance systems, "minor electrical troubles," and "sticky

LOX" (liquid oxygen) valves. One countdown was aborted because of the "weariness of overworked technicians." Because this was nominally IGY "science," reporters received extraordinary cooperation: two Air Force flatbed trailers for photographers, schedules of launch times, viewing points on the beach outside the Cape gates.

Finally, at 11:45 A.M. on December 6, a rocket propulsion engineer flipped the firing toggle. As television recorded the scene, Vanguard's first-stage rocket roared, spewed flame and smoke, rose four feet—and fell back onto the steel launching pad and tumbled to the ground, exploding in a spectacular fireball. The satellite cargo, thrown clear, was damaged but still beeping. For Eisenhower, recovering from a late November stroke, the news couldn't get much worse. Headline writers around the world outdid each other: "Flopnik," "Stay-putnik," "Dudnik." A Russian delegate to the United Nations asked his American colleagues if they would be interested in applying for aid "under the Soviet program of technical assistance to backward nations."

Through it all Ike remained bafflingly calm—because he knew that Sputnik *actually represented some good news.*

Ike, his popularity plummeting (it had gone from almost 80 percent in late 1956 to just 50 percent in late 1957), bent a bit. His post-*Sputnik* budget increased military expenditures, a rise that mandated, in Eisenhower's words, "at least a token reduction in the 'butter' side of government," so spending on urban development and hospitals was cut. Still, the parsimonious President had little use for space exploration. "Look," he told his cabinet, "I'd like to know what's on the other side of the moon, but I won't pay to find out this year." Even so, he signed legislation creating NASA in 1958.

Through it all, though, while Ike bent, he never broke. He remained mostly, and bafflingly, unflappable in the eyes of many Americans. He had his reasons. He knew that *Sputnik* actually represented some good news. While it showed that the Soviets were ahead in rocketry thrust, it also showed that they were well behind in miniaturizing communications technology (the beeping *Sputnik I* weighed 184 pounds). Moreover, *Sputnik* settled practically a lingering question of international law: How high does a nation's airspace reach? That issue would have considerable bearing on the spy satellites then under development, a space venture that *did* interest Eisenhower. "The Russians," Assistant Defense Secretary Donald Quarles told the President, "have in fact done us a good turn, unintentionally, in establishing the concept of freedom of international space."

Most important, Ike knew that the Russians were behind the United States militarily—so far behind on warhead production and ICBM development that a surprise attack on the United States would be suicidal. Since 1956 Ike had been seeing photographs taken by supersecret U-2 spy planes. These photos revealed the Soviet disadvantage in ICBMs and tellingly, they didn't show any preparations for a first strike. "We can still destroy Russia," Eisenhower told his cabinet. "We know it."

But the U-2 information was top secret. The Gaither Report authors didn't know about it. Neither did a thirty-four-year-old Harvard professor named Henry Kissinger, author of a sky-is-falling report for the Rockefeller Brothers Fund that was heavily publicized in early 1958, as brother Nelson positioned himself for 1960 presidential politics

(when Nelson appeared on "Today" on NBC, Dave Garroway offered to send a free copy of the report to anyone who requested it. More than two hundred thousand people asked). Ike couldn't reveal the U-2 flights without disclosing American violations of Soviet airspace; at the altitudes at which the U-2s were flying, international law was very clear. This could jeopardize his attempts to achieve accommodation with Khrushchev over such flash points as Berlin and nuclear testing. (It later turned out that the Soviets already knew of the U-2 overflights but didn't have the missiles to shoot them down—yet.) Ike also didn't want to push the Soviets to escalate their military spending, as any revelation of American superiority would likely do. So mostly he tried to persuade the public to trust him on the basis of his own military record.

Historians tend to give Eisenhower high marks for *Sputnik*. In Stephen Ambrose's view, Ike's calm response to the Soviet satellite was "one of his finest hours," saving his country countless billions of dollars. In his book *Grand Expectations,* James Patterson agrees, noting that Ike presided over major gains in the U.S. nuclear capacity and did so quietly enough to allay Soviet fears.

Historians, though, do fault Ike for failing to grasp the public relations implications of *Sputnik.* The National Security Council recommended a greater emphasis on space-related projects "which, while having scientific or military value, are designed to achieve a favorable worldwide psychological impact," but Eisenhower responded coolly. As he later said, "I don't believe in spectaculars." When von Braun's Army team successfully launched the first American satellite (which weighed just thirty-one pounds) on January 31, 1958, Eisenhower downplayed what others were portraying as a great American triumph.

Ike instructed his aides, "Let's not make too great a hullabaloo over this."

History's verdict on Ike came slowly. Even after the U-2 flights became known, the Alsop brothers, columnists Joseph and Stewart, argued that because the photography was limited, it was not all that trustworthy. U-2 spy photography, they said, was confined to major Soviet railroad lines that would service ICBM launch complexes and thus skipped large parts of the Soviet land expanse. Later, by the time John Kennedy was in the Oval Office—propelled to some extent by all the talk of the space and missile gaps—U.S. spy satellites covered all of the Soviet Union. These photos, in the summer of 1961, confirmed that there was indeed a missile gap all along—in America's favor. Mac Bundy, a key player in the Kennedy White House, recalls the Soviet missile threat being steadily de-escalated from hundreds of ICBMs during the late 1950s to around thirty-five by the mid-1960s. The Alsops eventually confessed their error.

Such was the self-defeating effect of Soviet secrecy: In the absence of facts about Russian ICBMs, many Americans responded out of fear. By the late 1960s the American nuclear triad ensured invulnerability, reliability, and massive retaliatory capacity. By the 1990s the Communist state had collapsed, amid evidence that the Soviets had spent themselves into poverty trying to keep up in all the various races.

Edwin Diamond, who died in July, taught at New York University. His book White House to Your House: Media and Politics in Virtual America *(M.I.T. Press) was issued in May in a paperback edition with a new epilogue. Stephen Bates is the literary editor of the* Wilson Quarterly. *Their article on the ancient history of the Internet ran in the October 1995 issue.*

Martin Luther King's Half-Forgotten Dream

Peter Ling argues that, by adulating King for his work in the Civil Rights campaigns, we have misrepresented the complexity of those struggles and ignored some of the equally challenging campaigns of his last years.

Martin Luther King is the only African-American honoured by a national public holiday. Thirty years after his assassination in Memphis, Tennessee, the Martin Luther King remembered on such occasions is overwhelmingly the orator of 1963 who mesmerised a nation from the steps of the Lincoln Memorial with the declaration 'I Have a Dream'. One of the first national events broadcast live and in full, the March on Washington, has provided sound-bites that have been used again and again. Alongside the images of President Kennedy's assassination in the same year, the King speech has become far more of an icon than a simple historical document.

In recent years, however, historians have become unhappy with the distorting effect of the King legacy. The first sign of this discomfort, which reflects the misgivings of veterans of the Civil Rights movement, was the insistence that the movement was far more than Martin Luther King, Jr and that its achievements should not be ascribed to one man, however charismatic. More recently, this criticism has been enlarged by those scholars who have focused on the local struggles within which King was an occasional and sometimes marginal player. This has been particularly the case in studies of civil rights activism in Mississippi and Louisiana. For specialist historians, the television montage of the movement, which has King in the lead role of a thirteen- or fourteen-year epic from 1954–55 to 1968, because of its emphasis on the 'war reports' from Montgomery in 1955–56 to the Selma-to-Montgomery march of 1965, fails to capture vital aspects of what made the movement possible and successful.

As recently as 1995, Charles Payne in his award-winning account of the movement in Mississippi could argue persuasively that 'The issues that were invisible to the media and to the current generation of Black activists are still almost as invisible to scholars'. The King-centric popular literature, which scholars like Payne find especially culpable, is guilty not only of neglecting other actors in the civil rights struggle but of emphasising the first ten years of King's public ministry over the years that followed. There is a need to explore in more detail King's later campaigns from 1966 to 1968.

Looked at closely, King's successful national role was episodic and short-lived. The media did catapult the young preacher into the global spotlight in 1956 as the Montgomery Bus Boycott intensified. But, as the best scholar of King's Southern Christian Leadership Conference, Adam Fairclough, admits, the organisations's early years from 1957 to 1959 were 'fallow years'. A near fatal attack on King himself by a deranged black woman is commonly overlooked as one of the reasons why he had failed to develop a leadership programme by 1960. Yet there is some merit in the gripes of the Student Non-violent Coordinating Committee (SNCC) veterans that it was their initiatives in the form of the sit-ins of 1960, the Freedom Ride to Mississippi in 1961, and the voter registration attempts in the Magnolia state that did more to shape the movement than did any action of the Southern Christian Leadership Conference. By 1962, for some hard-core activists, King seemed more a media figure than a true leader, getting headlines and donations largely for talk rather than actions.

It is worth noting the time span of just over six years between the settlement of the Montgomery Bus Boycott in December 1956 and the dramatic Birmingham campaign of April–May 1963 to underline the brevity of King's period of critical national influence that followed. This peaked in August 1965 with the passage of the Voting Rights Act and fell away steadily during 1966 with the setbacks of his Chicago campaign and the media's interest in the new protest slogan of 'Black Power'. Even if one stretches King's influence at the national level to February 1967, when his public denunciation of US involvement in Vietnam permanently closed the doors of President Johnson's Oval Office to him, his most powerful period was shorter than a single presidential term and considerably shorter than the public career that preceded it.

At the outset of his period of significant influence King had written the 'Letter from Birmingham Jail' in which he explained why he had led the protest campaign in Alabama's largest city. He explained his strategy of non-violent direct action as being organised 'to create such a crisis and foster such a tension that a community which has constantly refused to negotiate is forced to confront the issue'. Such a creative tension was necessary to compel change since 'freedom is never voluntarily given up by the oppressor'. Much of the Letter was devoted to explaining the importance of protest to a white moderate audience alarmed by the spectre of social disorder. Such people had to understand the difference between laws that guaranteed justice and a legal system that preserved order. If was the inaction of people of so-called good will, King argued, rather than the activities of racial extremists that sustained segregation and racial discrimination. This emphasis on the political significance of the guilty bystander became even more central to King's thinking in the years after 1966 when he addressed the economies of racism and militarism.

It is misleading to portray the Civil Rights movement as exclusively a southern struggle intent on ending desegregation and disenfranchisement in the South. In the early 1960s national leaders like the trade unionist A. Philip Randolph and black figures within northern radical circles recognised dangerous trends in employment, education and housing discrimination. The famous March on Washington was officially a march for jobs and freedom and, in addition to crowds attracted to the fiery separatist rhetoric of Malcolm X, there were major protest campaigns in Boston, Chicago and other northern cities well before 28 blacks died in the Watts disturbances in August 1965. Nonetheless, King was as ill-prepared to launch an effective assault on ghetto problems in 1966 as he had been to orchestrate

an attack on legal segregation in the South in 1957. But, given his belief that a failure to act against a social evil made one complicit in its perpetuation, he had no choice but to offer a programme, especially when it appeared that other sources of non-violent leadership, notably SNCC and the Congress of Racial Equality, were no longer committed to non-violence.

Chronology

1955 December 5th: King as head of the Montgomery Improvement Association leads bus boycott.

1956 December 21st: boycott ends after the city's bus segregation is declared illegal.

1957 February: Southern Christian Leadership Conference (SCLC) is founded with King as president.

1958 September 20th: King is stabbed in the chest at a book-signing in Harlem.

1960 February: Beginning in Greensboro, North Carolina, lunch counter sit-ins spread across the South. April: Student Non-violent Coordinating Committee (SNCC) established at an SCLC sponsored conference.

1961 February: John F. Kennedy is inaugurated as president.
May–June: Freedom Rides are begun by Congress of Racial Equality (CORE) and continued by SNCC, SNCC begins voter registration in hard-core districts in Mississippi.

1962 Unsuccessful campaign in Albany, Georgia.

1963 April–May: King leads demonstration in Birmingham, Alabama. While imprisoned he writes 'Letter from the Birmingham Jail'. TV cameras show police brutality.
August 28th: King delivers 'I Have a Dream' speech at March on Washington.
November 22nd: President Kennedy is assassinated in Dallas, Texas.

1964 June–September: The Freedom Summer voter registration project in Mississippi.
July 2nd: The Civil Rights Act outlawing segregation becomes law.
August 7th: Gulf of Tonkin resolutions allow US troop escalation in Vietnam.
December 10th: King receives the Nobel Peace Prize.

1965 January–March: Escalating protests over right to vote in Selma, Alabama.
February 21st: Malcolm X is assassinated.
March 15th: President Johnson calls for voting rights legislation.
August 6th: Johnson signs the Voting Rights Act.
August 11th–16th: Violent disorder in the Watts district of Los Angeles.

1966 Troop numbers in Vietnam escalate from 184,000 to 385,000.
January–August: SCLC campaign in Chicago.
June: New SNCC chairman Stokely Carmichael popularises the slogan 'Black Power' during a mass march through Mississippi. King expresses misgivings.
July: CORE endorses 'Black Power'; NAACP condemns it.
December: SNCC votes to exclude white members.

1967 February: King denounces US involvement in Vietnam.
April 4th: King preaches against Vietnam at Riverside church, New York. He next participates in a huge anti-war demonstration—larger than the 1963 March.
July: Major ghetto disturbances in Newark, Detroit and elsewhere.
August: King attends Chicago conference on a 'New Politics', but is heckled and booed.
November: Carl Stokes elected as first black mayor of Cleveland.
December: Marion Wright proposes interracial anti-poverty campaign in Washington.

1968 January 31st: Tet offensive shakes US hopes of victory in Vietnam.
February: King is warned that plans for the 'Poor People's Campaign' are faltering.
March 18th: King agrees to lead a march by striking Memphis sanitation workers. After this is marred by violence, he feels compelled to return to lead a non-violent march.
April 4th: King is assassinated while standing on the balcony at the Lorraine Motel in Memphis.
May–June: Ralph Abernathy leads the Poor People's Campaign in Washington.

By the same token, while King recognised that speaking out against the Johnson administration's policy in Vietnam would attract enormous criticism, he could not remain silent without giving sustenance to a gross evil. Biographers report how he was deeply shaken by pictures of Vietnamese casualties of the intensified bombing campaign and decided that in conscience he had to speak out. At New York City's Riverside Church on April 4th, 1967, King denounced his own country as 'the greatest purveyor of violence in the world today'. Linking the deepening crisis in America's ghettos with the escalating military expenditures in Vietnam, he warned the bombs that were dropped in Vietnam would explode at home. 'The security we profess to seek in foreign adventures,' he warned the crowds at an anti-war rally at the United Nations building later that month, 'we will lose in our decaying cities'. Giving credence to this warning, major civil disturbances in Newark, Detroit and other cities that summer resulted in massive destruction of property, injuries and deaths.

In this desperate context, King agreed to attend the National Conference for a New Politics in Chicago in August 1967, which was supposed to provide a programme for radical social change. Previously derided by militants for maintaining links with the political establishment, King indicated that SCLC planned to end its affiliation with the Democratic Party. Speaking in a manner not heard from a national African-American figure since anti-Communist attacks silenced the socialist educator W.E.B. Du Bois and the signer Paul Robeson in the early 1950s, King denounced capitalism and urged a guaranteed minimum income. The West, he added, should not oppose but should support Third World revolutions. Deaf to King's radicalism, many in the audience of New Left activists and Black Power militants jeered or walked away. Rejected by the self-declared revolutionaries, and alienated from the Cold War liberals who dominated the Democratic Party, King searched for a new strategy. His public standing was so dubious that black electoral candidates like Carl Stokes, who was elected mayor of Cleveland in 1967, preferred to downplay King's role in their campaigns.

King had never been a master strategist. Others had launched the Montgomery Bus Boycott, the Birmingham and Selma movement, and some of his young lieutenants, notably former sit-in student James Bevel, were more adept tactically. It was Bevel who had recognised the value of recruiting children to march in Birmingham and who urged the use of 'coercive' non-violence to prevent the existing social order from conducting 'business as usual'. Predictably, therefore, the idea for the Poor People's Campaign (to pressurise the federal government to withdraw from war in Vietnam and to intensify instead the War on Poverty), although built logically on the philosophy of non-violent direct action enunciated in the 'Letter from Birmingham Jail', was the brainchild of Marion Wright, a black lawyer with strong ties to the Mississippi movement. Ironically, the plan to have the nation's poor converge on Washington for a campaign of non-violent direct action was also far more similar to A. Philip Randolph's original March on Washington movement of 1941 (which protested at African-Americans being excluded from defence employment) than was the 1963 event that had confirmed King's pre-eminence as a race leader. Like the earlier set piece campaigns of SCLC, it would seek to induce sufficient creative tension to compel Congressional action. As King told a BBC correspondent only a week before his assassination in 1968, 'We're going to escalate non-violence and seek to make it as dramatic, as attention-getting, as anything we did in Birmingham or Selma, without destroying life or property in the process.'

In the event King did not live to see the Poor People's Campaign and its failure can at least partly be attributed to the organisational confusion that followed his sudden death.

However, the campaign marked a significant departure from his previous campaigns. Unlike Birmingham or Selma or even Chicago, it did not seek to build on existing local protest activities in their home bases but to take local movements onto the national stage by moving them to the capital. In doing so, SCLC organisers underestimated the resources needed to sustain such a transplanted community. When the campaign occurred, Resurrection City, as the Poor People encampment was called, absorbed much of SCLC's energy.

Whereas earlier campaigns had tried to use the leverage of a federal political system to bring national power to bear against local state and city power, the Poor People's Campaign targeted the Federal Government in the expectation that the disruption of normal practice and the pressure from a sympathetic public audience would revise the Congressional agenda and re-shape policy. The peculiar status of the District of Columbia as the creature of Congress facilitated this focus on the Federal Government, but complicated public perceptions. Non-violent demonstrators were no longer confronting authorities in somebody else's community but in every American's capital city. In previous campaigns, the tension between national embarrassment and local resentment had tended to favour peaceful demonstrators but in 1968, in a context of increasing insecurity and conservatism, they operated mainly against the movement.

The Poor People's Campaign also repeated the same tactical errors that had helped to frustrate the Chicago campaign of 1966 in that it had too many targets. By concentrating on the right to vote in Selma, the SCLC had dramatised the need for federal voting rights legislation. It was unrealistic to suppose that a militant Poor People's Movement could be organised in nine months so as to command sufficient resources to compel the Federal Government to reverse established policy in many different areas. To those who argue that King might have provided sounder guidance in this respect than did his successor, Ralph Abernathy, one can respond that the last year of King's life was characterised by an escalation of his goals rather than a shrewd selection of immediate aims. His decision to go to the aid of the striking Memphis sanitation workers in March 1968 was symptomatic of this tendency. In 1966 the SCLC had struggled to manage the difficulties of handling many local groups in Chicago, yet in 1968, at a time when the factionalism within the movement had intensified, it proposed to unite an even more diverse coalition.

So, what does a focus on the 1966–68 period rather than the 1963–65 period of King's career reveal about him? One argument would be that it provides a vantage point from which to see the weaknesses within his leadership. In essence, he repeated mistakes. He needed to learn more about the ghetto before he could attack it, just as he had needed to know more about the rural Deep South before he could organise effective campaigns there. He needed to adapt his repertoire of non-violent tactics, which had relied heavily on the cumulative and interactive impact of economic pressure and media censure, to a new terrain and new objectives. Despite the pressures from unfulfilled expectations and worsening economic and political indicators, King needed to have more realistic tactical objectives. As he himself told a press conference in 1967, he needed a victory, even a limited one, to retain credibility in the context of rival calls for separatism.

The ultimate charge in such a critique is one of *hubris*. King believed that he was the only one who could address the ghetto crisis non-violently and, with equal fervour, he believed that the Nobel Prize and his own Christian ministry had made him an anointed international champion for peace. This led him to dissipate his own and SCLC's energies outside of the South and the immediate needs of African-Americans in that region. At a time when effective implementation of the Civil Rights Act of

1964 and the voting Rights Act of 1965 provided the potential for a genuine political reconstruction, SCLC continued to devote much of its depleted resources to Chicago and King himself was prepared to sacrifice his access to the President by his pronouncements on foreign policy.

The criticisms against King seem largely to boil down to a condemnation of the philosophy of non-violent direct action. Consistent with his axiom that 'Injustice anywhere is a threat to justice everywhere', King believed that he had to provide an alternative to urban conflagration as a means of signalling the plight of inner-city dwellers. Similarly, being convinced that evil was sustained more by the inaction of others than by the deeds of the wicked, he felt unable to stay silent while the United States pursued a foreign policy that entailed wanton warfare against a people who had not attacked the United States. Rather than lamenting the failure of King to mobilise enough support to end the war in Vietnam or to shift government priorities back to the issues of social and economic justice, it seems more useful to reflect on the accuracy of his analysis.

Was he wrong to stress that uneven distribution of wealth was crucial to the persistence of racial inequality? At a time when indices suggest that the gulf between rich and poor, black and white, is widening in the United States, one would have to accept his diagnosis. If the South that emerged after the Voting Rights Act did not fulfil the hopes of those who dreamed of a more egalitarian

and more tolerant America, was this not due more to the failure to re-educate white southerners than to a failure of African-American leadership? Similarly, if King's calls for America to make the elimination of poverty its priority failed to prevent the impoverishment of the unskilled working classes since the 1960s, surely this was due to a lack of moral commitment not from King, but from so many of his contemporaries? Thirty years after his death, King's concept of the guilty bystander still points us to the injustices that we support by our inaction. We each make history—by the causes we pursue, but much more commonly by the many times we stand aside.

FOR FURTHER READING:

Charles Payne, *I've Got the Light of Freedom: The Organizing Tradition and the Mississippi Freedom Struggle* (University of California, 1995); Adam Fairclough, *To Redeem the Soul of America: The Southern Christian Leadership Conference and Martin Luther King, Jr* (University of Georgia Press, 1987); James M. Washington, ed., *A Testament of Hope: The Essential Writings and Speeches of Martin Luther King, Jr* (Harper Collins, 1986); David J. Garrow, *Bearing the Cross: Martin Luther King, Jr. and the Southern Christian Leadership Conference* (Jonathan Cape, 1986); Taylor Branch, *Parting the Waters: America in the King Years, 1954–1963* (Touchstone, 1989); Robert Cook, *Sweet Land of Liberty? The African-American Struggle for Civil Rights in the Twentieth Century* (Longman, 1998).

Peter Ling is Senior Lecturer in American Studies at the University of Nottingham and is currently writing a book on political education in the Civil Rights movement.

Scenes from the '60s

One Radical's Story

David Horowitz, who grew up in New York City as the son of two lifelong Communists, was a founding member of the New Left. During the 1960s he was a prominent editor of Ramparts, *the leading radical journal. In his memoir* Radical Son, *just published by The Free Press, Horowitz provides a stark record of radical life in the '60s. Following are some firsthand snapshots from his book. They depict the Black Panthers, Tom Hayden, the Weathermen, the sex and drug revolutions, and other aspects of the '60s "Movement" as they really were.*

by David Horowitz

BERKELEY'S NEW WORLD

As a grad student, I had been active in the New Left that was forming at Berkeley in the late '50s and early '60s, but I moved my family to Europe in 1962. When we returned to Berkeley in January 1968, the change was everywhere evident. Peace symbols and crystal pendants had become the emblems of religious conviction. Clothes were tie-dyed and bucolic, colors psychedelic, and hair long. To liberate themselves from the old sexual order, women were going bra-less, a protest whose immediate effect was to raise the libidinal pulses of everyday life. At the south end of campus, hippie craftsmen had transformed Telegraph Avenue into a street fair, where musicians and jugglers "doing their thing" attracted crowds for the tradesmen. It all had the air of a medieval pastoral, like the Forest of Arden in Shakespeare's *As You Like It,* where there were no menacing creatures, or hungers that could not be satisfied.

When I took my son Jonathan to hear a band called Purple Earthquake, I had my first encounter with electric instruments in a live setting. Booming through huge amplified speakers, the sound produced an effect something like entering a new dimension. I looked around at the dreamy faces of the audience. They were wearing the insignias and uniforms of the new counterculture that had blossomed while we were gone, and I experienced an unmistakable, strong kinship with them: A *new world is possible.*

As principal architect of the Port Huron Statement in 1962, Tom Hayden had helped launch Students for a Democratic Society (SDS), which soon became the largest student organization of the New Left. When he called for a demonstration at the 1968 Democratic national convention to protest the Vietnam War, everybody knew it meant a confrontation with the Chicago police that could prove bloody. *Ramparts* editor-in-chief Warren Hinckle decided to participate by publishing a "wall paper," as Mao's Red Guards had done during the cultural revolution in China.

During the riots that followed the assassination of Martin Luther King, Chicago's Mayor Daley had recently ordered his police to shoot looters. A radical street protest would put people's lives at risk. Because of such considerations, Hayden's plans attracted only two or three thousand people to Lincoln Park. But that was enough to generate trouble—Hayden's real agenda.

The ensuing melee changed the shape of American politics. The now-famous pictures of demonstrators being bloodied by police, and the chaos on the convention floor, destroyed the presidential chances of Hubert Humphrey and moved the Democratic party dramatically to the left. Four years later, Hayden and the protesters provided the push and the party rule changes that pushed the antiwar candidacy of George McGovern and propelled the party's left wing into power.

Reprinted from *The American Enterprise,* May/June 1997, pp. 28-32. *The American Enterprise,* a Washington-based magazine of politics, business, and culture.

When the dust cleared in Chicago, Hayden and seven other radicals, including the Black Panthers' Bobby Seale, were indicted for conspiring to create a riot. During the trial, the defendants created a near-riot in the courtroom itself. Seale was so obstructive that the judge ordered him bound and gagged. The picture of a black man in chains was a made-to-order script for the radical melodrama. One of the conspirators, Jerry Rubin, admitted a decade later that the organizers had lured activists to Chicago hoping to create the riot that eventually took place. This fit with the general strategy Hayden had laid out in private discussions with me. When people's heads are cracked by police, he said more than once, it "radicalizes them." The trick was to maneuver the idealistic and unsuspecting into situations that would achieve this result.

Sid Peck, a member of MOBE, the pacifist group that issued the call to the Chicago demonstration, later told me with some bitterness that Hayden had been "extremely deceptive" in outlining his agenda for the gathering, assuring everyone that his intentions were nonviolent. Hayden's duplicity continued throughout the event, causing the radical historian Staughton Lynd to comment that "on Monday, Wednesday, and Friday [Hayden] was a National Liberation Front guerrilla, and on Tuesday, Thursday, and Saturday, he . . . was on the left wing of the Democratic party." Anyone who knew Tom knew that the bomb-thrower was the real Hayden.

Having secured pacifist cover, Hayden then went to the most radical elements in the Left—those who actively advocated violence as a political tactic—and proposed that they provoke a conflict with the police who would be at the demonstration. According to Hayden's own retrospective account, he warned one group in New York that "they should come to Chicago prepared to shed their blood," and he told his co-organizer, Rennie Davis, that he expected 25 people to die. He recruited the Yippies, a group organized by Abbie Hoffman and Jerry Rubin, who alarmed Chicago officials by immediately threatening to put LSD in the Chicago water supply.

Hayden also met before the convention with the Weatherman faction of SDS, which had issued a call for "armed struggle" in American cities. As one of the Weather leaders told me later, Hayden proposed to them that "It might be useful if someone were to fire-bomb police cars."

At the event, Hayden gave Bobby Seale a platform in Lincoln Park, and Seale addressed the crowd with the suggestive exhortation that "If a pig comes up to us and starts swinging a billy club, and you check around and you got your piece, you got to down that pig in defense of yourself. We're gonna barbecue us some pork!" Once the violence started, Hayden defiantly incited the crowd to "make sure that if blood is going to flow, it will flow all over the city."

HOMELIFE

While an editor at *Ramparts,* I discovered I liked working at home near my wife, Elissa, and around the children, despite the distractions. And I spent weekends at parks, playgrounds, zoos, and other children's entertainments, while my *Ramparts* colleagues were at political meetings or hanging out in rock clubs. The plants, animals, and children with which Elissa had filled our lives answered a need in me. Her focus was life-centered, present-oriented, and outside herself. This provided a discipline and counterpoint to my own impulses, which were interior, intellectual, and relentlessly toward the future.

When I conveyed the news of our third pregnancy to my father, his reaction was unexpectedly negative. "You've broken the mold," he said cryptically. It took me a while to decipher what he meant. Roz Baxandall, a historian of the Left and a friend, observed that in our parents' generation no progressive had more than two offspring. In the '20s, U.S. Communist Party members considered it reactionary to have any children, since they would be obstacles to the revolutionary mission. When years passed and there was no revolution, people became frustrated and began to start families. But even then, two children were regarded as a practical limit. More than two indicated a lack of

political focus, a surrender to the forces of self-indulgence.

But even the chores generated by our toddlers and pets, which sometimes seemed endless, created a bond between Elissa and I. I felt integral to the fabric of the life we had created, and not only in emotional ways. Elissa did not know, for example, how to drive—and wouldn't learn. Yet we lived a mile from any stores, and driving was a necessity. In this and other practical ways she made me indispensable. As a result, I was also needed in a traditional sense as the man of the house. The idea was politically retrograde, but it resulted from Elissa's choices.

Like a dutiful Leftist, I pressed my wife to attend a "consciousness-raising" women's group that included Berkeley's feminist elite when this became a radical fashion. To distinguish their radical outlook from merely liberal groups, they called their agenda "women's liberation." Elissa came home from the first session in a state of agitation, vowing never to return. "They hate me because I'm a mother," was all she said. Years later I learned that they had berated her for allowing me to "oppress" her by "making" her assume the housewifely role. I also found that within a year of the group's formation, every marriage in it had dissolved.

Michael Lerner, later popular with the Clintons, told me "You have to take LSD. Until you've dropped acid, you don't know what socialism is."

Few of my radical colleagues had much connection to family or real community. A friend with a Freudian bent observed of *Ramparts* editor Bob Scheer that he "projected onto the socialist future the human connection he had failed to achieve in his own life." I had the same intuition about Tom Hayden, who was not on speaking terms with his fa-

David Horowitz (right and *Ramparts* colleagues hold a news conference in 1973 to announce the magazine's publication of classified defense information, which he hoped would help America "lose the war."

ther, and seemed to have no fixed home address. But it was the radical Michael Lerner—later famous for his "politics of meaning" which attracted the Clintons' admiration during their first term in the White House—who illustrated the syndrome best. The cake at his first wedding was inscribed with a Weatherman slogan: *Smash Monogamy.* Soon he and his wife had a child, and the young family went east. When the couple separated shortly thereafter, mother and son went to live in Boston. Lerner, however, returned to Berkeley. "Michael," I said, "how can you leave your son in the east to come to Berkeley? He needs you." Without hesitation, Lerner answered: "David, you don't understand. I have to be here. Berkeley is the center of the world-historical spirit."

Lerner also made me understand that drugs were central to the consciousness of the Movement. On discovering that I had never taken LSD, he was incredulous: "You have to take LSD. Until you've dropped acid, you don't know what socialism is."

Elissa and I anxiously watched many of our friends' children fall to drugs and other destructive influences around them. The permissive attitude toward marijuana took a particular toll. Harmless as it may have seemed to adult radicals, its impact on adolescents was difficult to control. Many a youngster in our circle who

"tripped out" on marijuana went on to harder drugs, or psychosis, and never came back. The responsibility for other, more vulnerable, lives separated us from our childless peers.

AN AMERICAN VIETCONG

When Bernadine Dohrn became president of SDS in 1968 she announced that she was "a revolutionary Communist." With calculated pride, her vice president, Billy Ayers, declared that he had not read a book in a year. In the Movement, anti-intellectualism was becoming a revolutionary badge of honor. Shortly after their election, these new leaders dissolved SDS into the "Weathermen," Dohrn's political cult which preached a Marxist version of race war. They issued a manifesto inspired by the Maoist doctrine of "people's war" and predicted the coming of a global Armageddon in which the Third World would take revenge on "Amerika" by "bringing the war home." American radicals could atone for their "white skin privilege" by serving as a fifth column inside the enemy camp.

Weathermen and the Black Panthers were the vanguards of the hour. Even Hayden, one of the few radical leaders able to engage serious ideas, had surrendered to the "Vietnam Metaphor"—the prism through which the New Left had

come to interpret all events. In articles for the *Berkeley Barb,* he called the Panthers "America's Vietcong" and advocated guerrilla warfare and the creation of "liberated zones" in American cities through armed force. He established a Berkeley Liberation School with its own "Minister of Defense" who trained students in the use of weapons and explosives. At one point, Hayden and his activists even conducted a training session in an emergency clinic in Los Baños, posing as doctors and paramedics, practicing on unsuspecting patients.

"Fascism is coming," Hayden announced on a visit to our *Ramparts* offices. "By the end of the year they're going to put us all in jail." About this time, Michael Lerner suggested I should buy a gun. "Michael," I said in disbelief, "The people aren't with us. You couldn't even describe a scenario in which there was a shoot-out with the police that we could win." Hardly pausing, he said, "Then you have to buy a hand gun and give it to someone else for use in assassinations."

On election eve the year before, the Peace and Freedom Party had nominated Eldridge Cleaver and Jerry Rubin for its presidential ticket. They held a "Pre-Erection Day" (*sic*) celebration in the Berkeley Community Theater, and Rubin came on stage wheeling a live pig in a shopping cart. This was "Pigasus," the Yippie mascot, he informed the crowd. Then he announced he was turning over his vice-presidential spot on the ticket to the pig, and lit up a joint. Eldridge took the microphone and began a rant in which he said the Left had to unite with the Machine Gun Kellys and John Dillingers of the world. He talked about "p*ssy power" and said that he would kill San Francisco Mayor Alioto and his children and grandchildren.

MOB JUSTICE

Without a formal hierarchy at *Ramparts,* every issue that came up had to be debated. The need to justify decisions was not only time-consuming for us, but at times cruel to others, as I discovered when we attempted to reduce the mailroom budget at *Ramparts* and were met with a political revolt. The mailroom was staffed by members of Newsreel, a "collective" of radicals who had made promotional films for the Black Panthers and the Vietcong. They had no respect for our publication. The revolution's pecking order had again shifted to the left, and we could not overcome the view that *Ramparts* was part of the power structure that needed to be overthrown.

Originally, we hired just one Newsreeler to do the mailroom work, but he took on more and more part-time help, featherbedding for his revolutionary comrades. When the mailroom budget exceeded that of the editorial department, we decided that things had gone far enough and that we had to cut their hours. But no appeals to the common good made any impression. The Newsreelers saw *Ramparts* as their gravy train rather than their cause, and refused any cuts at all. To them, we were the ruling class and they our rebellious peons.

Because every decision had to be justified collectively, we assembled the entire staff and in an all-day session hammered at the recalcitrants' deficiencies and derelictions, summoning other staff members to testify against them. The session went on for eight hours, escalating as the embattled mailroom crew resisted. Their obstinacy made it necessary to expand the charges and sharpen their personal edge. What had begun as a move to institute economies that would save all our jobs turned into a prosecution. Accusations of laziness, dishonesty, and exploitation of fellow workers were hurled at the hapless defendants. In the end, they were made to feel so bad about what they had done that firing them was almost a mercy. This episode was a collectively supported, brutal exercise, necessary for us to prevail, but it made me recognize the utility and compassion that lay in the principle of hierarchy we had cast aside.

Meanwhile, as we ran out of funds at *Ramparts,* we developed schemes which were border-line criminal, but which the reigning rhetoric of the Left encouraged us to think of as civil disobedience. We had printed an excerpt from Abbie Hoffman's anarchist bible *Steal This Book* in which he argued that "ripping off the system was a revolutionary act. Abbie outlined various scams and

justified them as prefigurings of the communist future in which everything would be free. His idea was that people should take according to their needs. But like most radicals, including Marx himself, he gave no thought as to how things would be provided. Our own solution at the magazine was to put half the *Ramparts* staff on unemployment, so that they could collect their "paychecks" from the government. When the government allowance expired, we would put them back on the payroll and lay off the rest.

LIFE AND DEATH WITH THE PANTHERS

Inside the Black Panthers, Huey Newton had created a group of enforcers he called the Squad. He used it to intimidate Black Panther members, who were subject to beatings with bullwhips and chains for disciplinary infractions. It was also available for his personal vendettas and criminal ventures, accompanying him on the drive-by shootings at the "after hours" clubs. Squad members often acted out of their own sadistic impulses as well, so one was safe from their terror. When one of them was inadvertently insulted by the vice president of the Black Students Union at Grove Street College, the Squad retaliated by executing the offender. The murder was never prosecuted.

Big Bob, a Squad member, confided to a former Panther that in the three years he had been in Oakland, the Squad had killed a dozen people. A friend of mine—Betty van Pater, who I had connected with the Panthers to do their bookkeeping—was one of them, he admitted. When I eventually pieced this together it was a blow that began my retreat from the Left and the radicalism I had until then promoted all my life.

At one point, Huey Newton killed young prostitute Kathleen Smith and Los Angeles police officer John Frey. After shooting Smith, he was driven to the Zen Center in Marin, whose guru, Roshi Baker, gave him refuge. From there, he went to the Beverly Hills home of Hollywood producer Bert Schneider (who co-produced the Oscar-winning

pro-North Vietnamese film *Hearts and Minds)*. Later, a film director who had been present described the scene to me: "Huey was sitting on Bert's couch, shoving drugs up his nose, and sniveling, 'Get me more coke. I want some p*ssy.' He whined that it was the first time he had killed someone for reasons that were 'non-political'—which was typical Huey bullsh*t."

I also learned, later on, why Brenda Bay was in tears when I last saw her at the Panther's Learning Center. In a gesture to revolutionary theory, the Panthers frowned on marriages. All the women in the Panthers were to be available for Huey Newton's pleasure. He had merely to summon any of them—which he did, sometimes several at a time. Brenda had been secretly married to Newton's bodyguard, and when she found herself in Newton's bed, she told him about her marriage. Newton wanted her to tell her husband about their affair, because he felt it would be dangerous for his bodyguard to discover it behind his back. When Brenda refused, Newton arranged to have her husband summoned to the penthouse when he and Brenda were in bed. The discovery wrecked the marriage.

An episode involving Bobby Seale revealed the wide latitude the Panthers had come to enjoy in public life. After being beaten by Huey Newton and threatened by Panther Elaine Brown, Seale, the former chairman of the Panthers, had completely disappeared in 1975. Amazingly, no one seemed to care that one of the most prominent political figures in democratic America had simply vanished—not the press, not his political supporters in the Left, not his former followers. It turned out that Seale was in hiding, in fear for his life. A year and a half later, Charles Garry, the Panther lawyer, told me that Seale had fled because of Elaine's threats, and no one knew where he was—not even his mother.

Seale was easily the most public and popular of the Panther leaders, personally known to most of the prominent figures on the left, including his codefendants in the Chicago conspiracy case, Dave Dellinger, Tom Hayden, Jerry Rubin, and Abbie Hoffman, and their lawyer, William Kunstler. In all the time he was missing, not one of these champions of the oppressed raised his voice to ask where Seale was, and thus provide him with some protection—because Seale's persecutors were the Panthers themselves. In the end, because the Panthers had limited influence, Seale survived. But what would have happened if the Panthers, or radicals like them, had had the kind of societal power we in the Left were trying to hand them?

As radicals, we were impatient with order and had contempt for process. We wanted "direct rule" and "revolutionary justice" unconstrained by legalisms and the hierarchies they required. As a result, we had no means to redress the crimes committed by the Panthers or other tribunes of "the people." Looking back, we had no law to govern us other than that of the gang. The injustice of America's radical vanguards was as brutal and final as Stalin's. It was mercifully smaller in scale only because we were unable to undermine America's "bourgeois" society as much as we had hoped.

THE LOVE OF MALICE

Working years later on a history of the Weather Underground for *Rolling Stone*, my longtime collaborator Peter Collier and I interviewed Mark Rudd, who had led the "uprising" at Columbia in 1968 and been purged from the Underground after an effort at bomb-building went awry, killing three members. A large, affable man, Rudd alone among the New Left leaders I have known or interviewed had a basic honesty about himself and was feeling genuine remorse for the wasted and destructive years he had spent in the Weather army. He told me that the bomb that killed the three activists had been intended for a service-club dance at Fort Dix in New Jersey.

The three bombers were SDS veterans; their intended target—young people at a dance—showed just how malevolent the Movement had become. Later, Bernadine Dohrn and Kathy Boudin—who had narrowly escaped the earlier explosion—planted a bomb in a ladies room of the U.S. Capitol building.

Rudd also helped us piece together the bizarre final acts of the Underground, which had initiated a series of purges in its ranks, complete with confessions and recantings. The purist remnant that conducted the purges subsequently joined elements of the Black Liberation Army to form the May 19 Communist Organization—celebrating a date which marked the birthdays of Malcolm X and Ho Chi Minh. The goal of these revolutionaries was to create a "New Afrika" in America's southern states through a campaign of guerrilla war. To finance this war, the group held up a Brink's armored car in Nyack, New Jersey. This led to a gun battle in which three policeman were killed, including the only black officer on the Nyack police force. The perpetrators were given 20-year sentences, ending their political careers.

Other New Left radicals proved less contrite with age. When Bernadine Dohrn surfaced after nearly a decade underground, she was interviewed from jail on the Phil Donahue show. I watched with Jim Mellen, a handsome, square-jawed friend with a subdued personality, as if he nursed some subtle grievance toward life.

Jim's career was a case study in the opportunities that America offered. His father was an alcoholic who had left the family; his mother had worked as a soda-fountain clerk to support them. Jim was bright enough to earn a Ph.D. and win a Fulbright scholarship to Tanzania as an agricultural expert. On his return to America in the late '60s, he dropped his academic career for the revolution. He abandoned his two children at infancy. He marched with the Weathermen in their "Days of Rage" in Chicago, trashing downtown businesses to protest "Amerikan" racism and the "imperialist" war. He became the group's "theoretician," writing their famous declaration of race war: "You Don't Need a Weatherman to Know Which Way the Wind Blows."

Jim got off the revolutionary train during a famous "War Council" held in Flint, Michigan, when Bernadine Dohrn praised Charles Manson and spread her fingers in the infamous "fork salute." "Dig it!" she cried to the assembled warriors. "First they killed those pigs, then they ate dinner in the same room with them. They even shoved a fork into a victim's stomach. Wild!" It was not the nasty rhetoric, but her call to actually begin the war he had only theorized, which caused Jim to quit. Later, he tor-

mented himself with the idea that he was a coward unable to stomach the risks his own ideas invited.

After leaving politics, Jim first made solar heaters for hot tubs, then became a carpenter, a contractor, and finally a developer. By the time we sat down to watch the Donahue show, he had mortgaged the two-story house he had bought with his carpentry earnings to finance the construction of condominiums he had designed and built. With the profits he bought a small plane and was preparing to enter a new career by going to law school at night.

Given his humble origins and outlaw status, Jim's business success demonstrated how rich in opportunities and how politically tolerant the system he had declared war on actually was. Yet somehow this success failed to satisfy the radical hungers that gnawed his soul. On TV, Bernadine was justifying her life as a political terrorist by attacking "Amerikan injustice" in the most lurid terms, picturing the country as a vast concentration camp for minorities and the poor. And Jim was hanging on her every word and shouting encouragement. "Jim," I said, incredulous, "you're still with her! If she went out and bombed the Capitol tomorrow, you'd probably say 'right on.'" He smiled at me with a look of utter self-satisfaction: "Nothing would delight me more."

My former-radical colleague Peter Collier had long maintained that malice played a larger role in the motives of '60s activists than I had been willing to accept. The more I thought about the moral posturing of the Left, the more I saw that its real interest was less in making reforms than in framing indictments. Resentment and retribution were the radical passions.

Marx had once invoked a dictum of Goethe's devil: "Everything that exists deserves to perish." When the Left called for "liberation," what it really wanted was to erase the human slate and begin again. Marxism was a form of idolatry. And the Creator/Destroyer that the Left worshipped was itself.

David Horowitz is now the president of the Center for the Study of Political Culture.

The Legacy of Watergate

The scandal lingers in public life, 25 years later

Andrew Phillips
in Washington

Here we are," says Maurice Lenders with a broad smile and a shrug of the shoulders. "You see—no guns, no microphones." Lenders is an affable Dutchman who is taking a few minutes to show a visitor the scene of the crime. His company, a marketing firm called Urenco Inc., has the distinction—or burden—of occupying Suite 610 in the distinctive building at 2600 Virginia Avenue on the edge of the Potomac River in downtown Washington. It is part of the Watergate complex, a collection of concrete condos and offices that was designed in the 1960s to look futuristic but now seems oddly dated. And Suite 610, a pleasant but bland space, is ground zero of the greatest political scandal of the last half-century. It was there, exactly 25 years ago, in the early hours of June 17, 1972, that police interrupted five men clad in business suits and rubber gloves in the act of breaking into the headquarters of the Democratic party. By the time Watergate had run its course little more than two years later, a president had been forced from office—and modern political culture had been forever transformed.

There is no plaque on the sixth floor of the building on Virginia Avenue to commemorate the break-in. There doesn't need to be. It was said of Sir Christopher Wren, the architect who designed some of London's most historic churches: "If you would see the man's monument, look around." The same could be said of Watergate. The details may have dulled with time (what exactly were the burglars looking for, and who *was* John Ehrlichman anyway?). But even a quarter of a century later, Americans, and others, are still grappling with the fallout from the scandal. More than any other single event, it undermined public confidence in government and set the tone for a culture of confrontation between politicians and the press that endures to this day. It spawned an entire vocabulary of scandal (coverup, smoking gun, Deep Throat, "what did the President know and when did he know it?"). And it gave rise to one of the most tedious of modern political habits: tagging every purported episode of wrongdoing with the suffix "-gate." Americans have endured Koreagate, Travelgate and a dozen more. Argentines, Brazilians, Israelis, South Africans and even Poles have lived through "gates." Canada is not immune: British Columbia's "Bingo-gate" led Premier Mike Harcourt to resign.

In fact, Watergate has fallen on hard times. Victors always write the history books, of course, and for years the reigning view was that it represented an unambiguous triumph for the forces of liberal openness over the Dark Side of political life—occupied by President Richard Nixon and the White House operatives who ordered the Watergate break-in. Nixon, who died in 1994, still has few defenders of his Watergate behavior. And the conspiracy that he and his closest aides embarked on to hush up their knowledge of the crime is beyond question. But after a quarter century the outcome no longer seems so clear, and the shadows over Watergate loom larger. These days, it is most likely to be mentioned in the course of a lament about the culture of scandal and the climate of mistrust that haunts politics. The news media, which once basked in the glow of bringing down a president, now worry that healthy skepticism about people in public life has turned into rabid aggression. In a typical comment, Larry Sabato, a political scientist at the University of Virginia, bemoans the passage from "lapdog journalism to watchdog journalism to junkyard-dog journalism."

The voice on the tape is low, heavy and all-too-familiar. It is early evening on Sept. 7, 1972, and Richard Nixon is in the Oval Office at the White House with his chief of staff, H. R. Haldeman, and aide Alexander Butterfield. The subject is Senator Edward Kennedy, a Democrat for whom Nixon reserved a special loathing, and the President casually orders his aides to plant a spy in the security detail assigned to protect Kennedy—and try to collect dirt on him. "We might just get lucky and catch this son of a bitch," Nixon says. "Ruin him for '76. It's going to be fun."

The tone is vintage Nixon: earthy, brutal, profane. Nothing did him in as much as the tapes of his private conversations that he made throughout the Watergate period with a voice-activated tape recorder. The key question was what he knew about the break-in and the subsequent effort to cover it up, and when he knew it. The tapes showed that

 From *Maclean's* magazine, June 16, 1997, pp. 31-34. © 1997 by Maclean Hunter, Ltd. Reprinted by permission.

he knew much more than he had admitted, and he knew it much earlier. They were key evidence for the investigators who unlocked the conspiracy, and led directly to Nixon's resignation on Aug. 9, 1974. Now they repose in a vault on the ground floor of a modern, antiseptic building run by the U. S. National Archives just outside Washington. The archives' "Nixon Project" holds 44 million pages of documents from his presidency and 3,700 hours of taped conversations. The holdings are so vast that archivists make new finds all the time: the Kennedy exchange was unearthed only in February, and is identified with clinical precision as conversation number 772-15.

The man who first admitted to investigators that Nixon had secretly bugged his own office was Alexander Butterfield, now 71 and retired in San Diego. He was one of Nixon's closest aides, and has lived the past quarter century under the shadow of having taken part in something sinister and shameful. By the time Watergate erupted, Americans had long lost their political virginity; the assassination of John Kennedy, Vietnam and the turmoil of the late 1960s had taken care of that. But listening to Nixon cursing and conspiring on the tapes tore the last veil from the presidency, an office that Americans, no matter their political allegiance, are taught to revere. Arguably, it has never recovered.

Butterfield has thought long and hard about Watergate, and even after 25 years he believes many Americans still fail to grasp that Nixon himself was fully responsible. "It never ceases to amaze me that after all the coverage of Watergate, so many people just don't get it," he says. "They buy his story that he just made an enormous error of judgment, that he shouldn't have come to the aid of these zealous aides who perpetrated this crime. People buy this stuff all the time."

The truth, says Butterfield, is simpler. "Watergate was a result of Richard Nixon and the way he operated—100 per cent. Nixon was the director of all activity in the White House." And, he says: "I don't think anything happened then that couldn't happen again. It could *easily* happen again if you had another person like that in power. The press might smoke it out later, but they couldn't prevent it from happening."

Butterfield is still obsessed by Watergate. Few who were in Nixon's inner circle could escape it as details of conspiracy, perjury, money laundering, wiretapping and deception by people at the highest levels of government poured out. *The Washington Post* led the news media in exposing the White House's attempt to conceal its involvement, turning its reporters Bob Woodward and Carl Bernstein into folk heroes. Some 30 people went to jail, including Haldeman and senior adviser John Ehrlichman, together known as "The Prussians"

Where Are They Now?

The two-year-long Watergate saga, much of it played out in televised hearings, gripped Americans as completely as the O. J. Simpson trial would nearly a quarter-century later—but it carried far more serious implications. As the drama mounted, a host of obscure officials became household names. Where are they now? Several have died, while others have been affected for life by the scandal. An update on key players:

DIED

Richard Nixon, the Republican president whose aides ordered the break-in at the Democratic headquarters in the Watergate complex and who tried to cover up what he knew; in 1994, at 81.
H. R. (Bob) Haldeman, Nixon's chief of staff, who served 18 months in jail on Watergate charges and went on to develop real estate in California; in 1993, at 67.
John Mitchell, Nixon's attorney general, imprisoned 19 months for his part in the coverup; in 1988, at 75.
Sam Ervin, the folksy but shrewd chairman of the Senate Watergate Committee, which investigated the scandal live on television; in 1985, at 88.

John Sirica, the Washington judge who ordered Nixon to give up secret tapes of his Watergate conversations; in 1992, at 88.

STILL AROUND

John Dean, 58, the White House lawyer whose incisive memory as he testified against Nixon was borne out by the Watergate tapes. An investment banker in Beverly Hills, he is suing the authors of *Silent Coup*, a book suggesting he was the real force behind the break-in.
John Ehrlichman, 72, the Nixon adviser who supervised the White House "plumbers" unit, formed to stop media leaks, and served 18 months for a raid on Daniel Ellsberg's psychiatrist. Ellsberg leaked the "Pentagon Papers," a secret study of the Vietnam War. Ehrlichman is a writer based in Atlanta.
Charles Colson, 65, the tough Nixon aide known as a master of dirty tricks, including the Watergate break-in. During seven months in jail, he became a born-again Christian. He is a lay minister in Virginia.
E. Howard Hunt, 78, the former CIA agent who co-ordinated the break-in. After serving 33 months in prison, he became a prolific mystery writer based in Miami.

G. Gordon Liddy, 66, the ex-FBI agent who led the Watergate burglars and did the most time—52 months. He is an arch-rightist radio talk-show host in Washington.
Rose Mary Woods, 79, Nixon's loyal secretary, who never convincingly explained an 18½-minute gap on a crucial Watergate tape she handled. She is retired in Alliance, Ohio.
Ronald Ziegler, 58, Nixon's press secretary who invented the "non-denial denial." He heads the National Association of Chain Drug Stores lobby group and lives in Alexandria, Va.
Bob Woodward, 54, and **Carl Bernstein**, 53, who wrote the best-selling *All the President's Men*, later a movie, about their exposé of Watergate in *The Washington Post*. Woodward is assistant managing editor for investigative news at the *Post*; Bernstein is a high-profile author and magazine writer.
Deep Throat, Woodward and Bernstein's still-unrevealed crucial source, who they said they would never name while he is alive. The latest theory is that he was a senior FBI official.

BERTON WOODWARD
with SHOWWEI CHU in Toronto

for their unflinching loyalty to Nixon. Some are unrepentant. Their poster boy is G. Gordon Liddy, leader of the break-in team who was the only conspirator to refuse to co-operate with prosecutors to the end and served 52 months in prison. Liddy is a star of right-wing talk radio, self-consciously notorious, driving around with a vanity plate that reads H20-GATE and issuing defiant declarations. "I have no regrets whatsoever," he says of Watergate.

Others found God. Charles Colson, a Nixon adviser who specialized in dirty tricks against political opponents and helped set up the break-in team, became a born-again Christian and runs a prison outreach program in Virginia called Prison Fellowships Ministries. Jeb Stuart Magruder, now 62, was deputy director of Nixon's re-election committee and served seven months for conspiracy to obstruct justice. He now lives in Lexington, Ky., where he is senior minister at First Presbyterian Church, a downtown congregation of 1,250 that builds homes for low-income people under the Habitat for Humanity program. He has made a new life for himself, and he says politely but firmly: "I do not want to talk about Watergate."

What Magruder will talk about is his work with the church, which, inevitably, leads back to Watergate. "Going into the ministry was obviously part of putting my life back together, which was a major project," he says. Did he succeed? "As well as anyone can. Nobody's perfect. Theology teaches us that all of us are imperfect. That's why you need a source beyond yourself." Magruder studied the works of Reinhold Niebuhr, the Protestant theologian who wrote about the relationship between power and morality. "Niebuhr understood how humankind was always fighting a battle

between self-interest, pride and their faith. That's what you're doing all the time. Some just don't know it."

Most of the conclusions drawn after Watergate were less lofty. They are enshrined in laws designed to cleanse the American political system, to raise the ethnical bar and ensure such events were never repeated. Some have been ineffectual; others have had consequences that their sponsors never imagined. A campaign finance law was passed in 1974, aimed at breaking the influence of wealthy donors over political parties. It has been undermined by court rulings and weak enforcement, to the point where political funding is more controversial in Washington than it was when Nixon, not Bill Clinton, presided over the guest list for the Lincoln Bedroom.

A law providing for independent counsels to investigate political controversies, and another one setting strict guidelines for ethical behavior in government, may have backfired. Critics say they led to the culture of scandal that has engulfed U.S. politics since Watergate. Instead of ensuring clean government, runs the argument, they became weapons in the hands of political partisans, feeding what analyst Suzanne Garment calls "the great American scandal machine." In her 1992 book, *Scandal: The Culture of Mistrust in American Politics,* Garment described the infrastructure of rules, investigators, special prosecutors and news media as a permanent fixture that feeds off whiffs of wrongdoing and, in turn, needs fresh controversy to keep it going. The seemingly endless scandals dogging President Clinton—including Whitewater and the funding saga that has been dubbed, in time-honored tradition, "Donor-

gate"—bears that out. (One of the nicer ironies of Clinton's woes is that his wife, Hillary Rodham Clinton, served as a junior lawyer on the staff of the House committee that investigated Watergate. Now, the system of prosecutors and ethics laws created in that era is being used to torment the First Couple.)

The media, too, look considerably less heroic than they did in the aftermath of Watergate. Woodward and Bernstein were role models for a generation, updated versions of a classic American type: the loner against the system. It's been mostly downhill since then. These days the talk in U.S. media circles is about the rise of tabloid TV and the pursuit of public figures that too often slides into character assassination. The most widely discussed trend is so-called public or civic journalism. Its proponents are alarmed at public cynicism and disengagement from the political process; instead of focusing on exposing politicians, they stress finding solutions to social problems. Nothing could be further from the post-Watergate ideal of a press determinedly aloof from the political process. The new movement, says Washington media critic Tom Rosenstiel, is "part of the backlash against Watergate."

Watergate lends itself to that kind of musing. It shook the entire American political system. But at bottom, its lessons may not be so complex. Ben Bradlee, the legendary executive editor of *The Washington Post* who piloted the paper through that period, sums up with admirable simplicity the scandal that started in the unlikely surroundings of Suite 610 at the Watergate building. "What's the lesson?" he asks. "Why not the truth? You tell lies at great, great risk. If Nixon hadn't lied, he would have kept on as president. Not so hard to figure out, really."

How the Seventies Changed America

The "loser decade" that at first seemed nothing more than a breathing space between the high drama of the 1960s and whatever was coming next is beginning to reveal itself as a bigger time than we thought

Nicholas Lemann

Nicholas Lemann, a national correspondent for The Atlantic, *is the author of* The Promised Land: The Great Black Migration and How It Changed America, *published by Alfred A. Knopf [1991].*

"That's it," Daniel Patrick Moynihan, then U.S. ambassador to India, wrote to a colleague on the White House staff in 1973 on the subject of some issue of the moment. "Nothing will happen. But then nothing much is going to happen in the 1970s anyway."

Moynihan is a politician famous for his predictions, and this one seemed for a long time to be dead-on. The seventies, even while they were in progress, looked like an unimportant decade, a period of cooling down from the white-hot sixties. You had to go back to the teens to find another decade so lacking in crisp, epigrammatic definition. It only made matters worse for the seventies that the succeeding decade started with a bang. In 1980 the country elected the most conservative President in its history, and it was immediately clear that a new era had dawned. (In general the eighties, unlike the seventies, had a perfect dramatic arc. They peaked in the summer of 1984, with the Los Angeles Olympics and the Republican National

Convention in Dallas, and began to peter out with the Iran-contra scandal in 1986 and the stock market crash in 1987.) It is nearly impossible to engage in magazine-writerly games like discovering "the day the seventies died" or "the spirit of the seventies"; and the style of the seventies—wide ties, sideburns, synthetic fabrics white shoes, disco—is so far interesting largely as something to make fun of.

But somehow the seventies seem to be creeping out of the loser-decade category. Their claim to importance is in the realm of sweeping historical trends, rather than memorable events, though there were some of those too. In the United States today a few basic propositions shape everything: The presidential electorate is conservative and Republican. Geopolitics revolves around a commodity (oil) and a religion (Islam) more than around an ideology (Marxism-Leninism). The national economy is no longer one in which practically every class, region, and industry is upwardly mobile. American culture is essentially individualistic, rather than communitarian, which means that notions like deferred gratification, sacrifice, and sustained national effort

are a very tough sell. Anyone seeking to understand the roots of this situation has to go back to the seventies.

The underestimation of the seventies' importance, especially during the early years of the decade, is easy to forgive because the character of the seventies was substantially shaped at first by spillover from the sixties. Such sixties events as the killings of student protestors at Kent State and Orangeburg, the original Earth Day, the invasion of Cambodia, and a large portion of the war in Vietnam took place in the seventies. Although sixties radicals (cultural and political) spent the early seventies loudly bemoaning the end of the revolution, what was in fact going on was the working of the phenomena of the sixties into the mainstream of American life. Thus the first Nixon administration, which was decried by liberals at the time for being nightmarishly right-wing, was actually more liberal than the Johnson administration in many ways—less hawkish in Vietnam, more free-spending on social programs. The reason wasn't that Richard Nixon was a liberal but that the country as a whole had continued to move steadily to the left throughout the late sixties and early seventies; the political climate of institutions like the U.S. Congress and the boards of directors of big corporations was probably more liberal in 1972 than in any year before or since, and the Democratic party nominated its most liberal presidential candidate ever. Nixon had to go along with the tide.

In New Orleans, my hometown, the hippie movement peaked in 1972 or 1973. Long hair, crash pads, head shops, psychedelic posters, underground newspapers, and other Summer of Love-inspired institutions had been unknown there during the real Summer of Love, which was in 1967. It took even longer, until the middle or late seventies, for those aspects of hippie life that have endured to catch on with the general public. All over the country the likelihood that an average citizen would wear longish hair, smoke marijuana, and openly live with a lover before marriage was probably greater in 1980 than it was in 1970. The sixties' preoccupation with self-discovery became a mass phenomenon only in the seventies, through home-brew psychological therapies like est. In politics the impact of the black enfranchisement that took place in the 1960s barely began to be felt until the mid- to late 1970s. The tremendously influential feminist and gay-liberation movements were, at the dawn of the 1970s, barely under way in Manhattan, their headquarters, and certainly hadn't begun their spread across the whole country. The sixties took a long time for America to digest; the process went on throughout the seventies and even into the eighties.

The epochal event of the seventies as an era in its own right was the Organization of Petroleum Exporting Countries' oil embargo, which lasted for six months in the fall of 1973 and the spring of 1974. Everything that happened in the sixties was predicated on the assumption of economic prosperity and growth; concerns like personal fulfillment and social justice tend to emerge in the middle class only at times when people take it for granted that they'll be able to make a living. For thirty years—ever since the effects of World War II on the economy had begun to kick in—the average American's standard of living had been rising, to a remarkable extent. As the economy grew, indices

like home ownership, automobile ownership, and access to higher education got up to levels unknown anywhere else in the world, and the United States could plausibly claim to have provided a better life materially for its working class than any society ever had. That ended with the OPEC embargo.

While it was going on, the embargo didn't fully register in the national consciousness. The country was absorbed by a different story, the Watergate scandal, which was really another sixties spillover, the final series of battles in the long war between the antiwar liberals and the rough-playing anti-Communists. Richard Nixon, having engaged in dirty tricks against leftish politicians for his whole career, didn't stop doing so as President; he only found new targets, like Daniel Ellsberg and Lawrence O'Brien. This time, however, he lost the Establishment, which was now far more kindly disposed to Nixon's enemies than it had been back in the 1950s. Therefore, the big-time press, the courts, and the Congress undertook the enthralling process of cranking up the deliberate, inexorable machinery of justice, and everybody was glued to the television for a year and a half. The embargo, on the other hand, was a nonvideo-friendly economic story and hence difficult to get hooked on. It pertained to two subcultures that were completely mysterious to most Americans—the oil industry and the Arab world—and it seemed at first to be merely an episode in the ongoing hostilities between Israel and its neighbors. But in retrospect it changed everything, much more than Watergate did.

By causing the price of oil to double, the embargo enriched—and therefore increased the wealth, power, and confidence of—oil-producing areas like Texas, while helping speed the decline of the automobile-producing upper Midwest; the rise of OPEC and the rise of the Sunbelt as a center of population and political influence went together. The embargo ushered in a long period of inflation, the reaction to which dominated the economics and politics of the rest of the decade. It demonstrated that America could now be "pushed around" by countries most us had thought of as minor powers.

Most important of all, the embargo now appears to have been the pivotal moment at which the mass upward economic mobility of American society ended, perhaps forever. Average weekly earnings, adjusted for inflation, peaked in 1973. Productivity—that is, economic output per man-hour—abruptly stopped growing. The nearly universal assumption in the post–World War II United States was that children would do better than their parents. Upward mobility wasn't just a characteristic of the national culture; it was the defining characteristic. As it slowly began to sink in that everybody wasn't going to be moving forward together anymore, the country became more fragmented, more internally rivalrous, and less sure of its mythology.

Richard Nixon resigned as President in August 1974, and the country settled into what appeared to be a quiet, folksy drama of national recuperation. In the White House good old Gerald Ford was succeeded by rural, sincere Jimmy Carter, who was the only President elevated to the office by the voters during the 1970s and so was the decade's emblematic political figure. In hindsight, though, it's impossible to miss a gathering conservative stridency in the politics of the late seventies. In 1976 Ronald Reagan, the retired governor of California, challenged Ford for the Republican presidential nomination. Reagan lost the opening primaries and seemed to be about to drop out of the race when, apparently to the surprise even of his own staff, he won the North Carolina primary in late March.

It is quite clear what caused the Reagan campaign to catch on: He had begun to attack Ford from the right on foreign policy matters. The night before the primary he bought a half-hour of statewide television time to press his case. Reagan's main substantive criticism was of the policy of détente with the Soviet Union, but his two most crowd-pleasing points were his promise, if elected, to fire Henry Kissinger as Secretary of State and his lusty denunciation of the elaborately negotiated treaty to turn nominal control of the Panama Canal over to the Panamanians.

Less than a year earlier Communist forces had finally captured the South Vietnamese capital city of Saigon, as the staff of the American Embassy escaped in a wild scramble into helicopters. The oil embargo had ended, but the price of gasoline had not retreated. The United States appeared to have descended from the pinnacle of power and respect it had occupied at the close of World War II to a small, hounded position, and Reagan had hit on a symbolic way of expressing rage over that change. Most journalistic and academic opinion at the time was fairly cheerful about the course of American foreign policy—we were finally out of Vietnam, and we were getting over our silly Cold War phobia about dealing with China and the Soviet Union—but in the general public obviously the rage Reagan expressed was widely shared.

A couple of years later a conservative political cause even more out of the blue than opposition to the Panama Canal Treaty appeared: the tax revolt. Howard Jarvis, a seventy-five-year-old retired businessman who had been attacking taxation in California pretty much continuously since 1962, got onto the state ballot in 1978 an initiative, Proposition 13, that would substantially cut property taxes. Despite bad press and the strong opposition of most politicians, it passed by a two to one margin.

Proposition 13 was to some extent another aftershock of the OPEC embargo. Inflation causes the value of hard assets to rise. The only substantial hard asset owned by most Americans is their home. As the prices of houses soared in the mid-seventies (causing people to dig deeper to buy housing, which sent the national savings rate plummeting and made real estate prices the great conversation starter in the social life of the middle class), so did property taxes, since they are based on the values of the houses. Hence, resentment over taxation became an issue in waiting.

The influence of Proposition 13 has been so great that it is now difficult to recall that taxes weren't a major concern in national politics before it. Conservative opposition to government focused

on its activities, not on its revenue base, and this put conservatism at a disadvantage, because most government programs are popular. Even before Proposition 13, conservative economic writers like Jude Wanniski and Arthur Laffer were inventing supply-side economics based on the idea that reducing taxes would bring prosperity. With Proposition 13 it was proved—as it has been proved over and over since—that tax cutting was one of the rare voguish policy ideas that turn out to be huge political winners. In switching from arguing against programs to arguing against taxes, conservatism had found another key element of its ascension to power.

The tax revolt wouldn't have worked if the middle class hadn't been receptive to the notion that it was oppressed. This was remarkable in itself, since it had been assumed for decades that the American middle class was, in a world-historical sense, almost uniquely lucky. The emergence of a self-pitying strain in the middle class was in a sense yet another sixties spillover. At the dawn of the sixties, the idea that *anybody* in the United States was oppressed might have seemed absurd. Then blacks, who really were oppressed, were able to make the country see the truth about their situation. But that opened Pandora's box. The eloquent language of group rights that the civil rights movement had invented proved to be quite adaptable, and eventually it was used by college students, feminists, Native Americans, Chicanos, urban blue-collar "white ethnics," and, finally, suburban homeowners.

Meanwhile, the social programs started by Lyndon Johnson gave rise to another new, or long-quiescent, idea, which was that the government was wasting vast sums of money on hare-brained schemes. In some ways the Great Society accomplished its goal of binding the country together, by making the federal government a nationwide provider of such favors as medical care and access to higher education; but in others it contributed to the seventies trend of each group's looking to government to provide it with benefits and being unconcerned with the general good. Especially after the economy turned sour, the middle class began to define

its interests in terms of a rollback of government programs aimed at helping other groups.

As the country was becoming more fragmented, so was its essential social unit, the family. In 1965 only 14.9 percent of the population was single; by 1979 the figure had risen to 20 percent. The divorce rate went from 2.5 per thousand in 1965 to 5.3 per thousand in 1979. The percentage of births that were out of wedlock was 5.3 in 1960 and 16.3 in 1978. The likelihood that married women with young children would work doubled between the mid-sixties and the late seventies. These changes took place for a variety of reasons—feminism, improved birth control, the legalization of abortion, the spread across the country of the sixties youth culture's rejection of traditional mores—but what they added up to was that the nuclear family, consisting of a working husband and a non-working wife, both in their first marriage, and their children, ceased to be so dominant a type of American household during the seventies. Also, people became more likely to organize themselves into communities based on their family status, so that the unmarried often lived in singles apartment complexes and retirees in senior citizens' developments. The overall effect was one of much greater personal freedom, which meant, as it always does, less social cohesion. Tom Wolfe's moniker for the seventies, the Me Decade, caught on because it was probably true that the country had placed relatively more emphasis on individual happiness and relatively less on loyalty to family and nation.

Like a symphony, the seventies finally built up in a crescendo that pulled together all its main themes. This occurred during the second half of 1979. First OPEC engineered the "second oil shock," in which, by holding down production, it got the price for its crude oil (and the price of gasoline at American service stations) to rise by more than 50 percent during the first six months of that year. With the onset of the summer vacation season, the automotive equivalent of the Depression's bank runs began. Everybody considered the possibility of not being able to get gas, panicked, and went off to fill the tank; the result was hours-long lines at gas stations all over the country.

It was a small inconvenience compared with what people in the Communist world and Latin America live through all the time, but the psychological effect was enormous. The summer of 1979 was the only time I can remember when, at the level of ordinary life as opposed to public affairs, things seemed to be out of control. Inflation was well above 10 percent and rising, and suddenly what seemed like a quarter of every day was spent on getting gasoline or thinking about getting gasoline—a task that previously had been completely routine, as it is again now. Black markets sprang up; rumors flew about well-connected people who had secret sources. One day that summer, after an hour's desperate and fruitless search, I ran out of gas on the Central Expressway in Dallas. I left my car sitting primly in the right lane and walked away in the hundred-degree heat; the people driving by looked at me without surprise, no doubt thinking, "Poor bastard, it could have happened to me just as easily."

In July President Carter scheduled a speech on the gas lines, then abruptly canceled it and repaired to Camp David to think deeply for ten days, which seemed like a pale substitute for somehow setting things aright. Aides, cabinet secretaries, intellectuals, religious leaders, tycoons, and other leading citizens were summoned to Carter's aerie to discuss with him what was wrong with the country's soul. On July 15 he made a television address to the nation, which has been enshrined in memory as the "malaise speech," although it didn't use that word. (Carter did, however, talk about "a crisis of confidence . . . that strikes at the very heart and soul and spirit of our national will.")

To reread the speech today is to be struck by its spectacular political ineptitude. Didn't Carter realize that Presidents are not supposed to express doubts publicly or to lecture the American people about their shortcomings? Why couldn't he have just temporarily imposed gas rationing, which would have ended the lines overnight, instead of outlining a vague and immediately forgotten six-point program to promote energy conservation?

His describing the country's loss of confidence did not cause the country to gain confidence, needless to say. And it didn't help matters that upon his return to Washington he demanded letters of resignation from all members of his cabinet and accepted five of them. Carter seemed to be anything but an FDR-like reassuring, ebullient presence; he communicated a sense of wild flailing about as he tried (unsuccessfully) to get the situation under control.

I remember being enormously impressed by Carter's speech at the time because it was a painfully honest and much thought-over attempt to grapple with the main problem of the decade. The American economy had ceased being an expanding pie, and by unfortunate coincidence this had happened just when an ethic of individual freedom as the highest good was spreading throughout the society, which meant people would respond to the changing economic conditions by looking out for themselves. Like most other members of the word-manipulating class whose leading figures had advised Carter at Camp David, I thought there *was* a malaise. What I didn't realize, and Carter obviously didn't either, was that there was a smarter way to play the situation politically. A President could maintain there was nothing wrong with America at all—that it hadn't become less powerful in the world, hadn't reached some kind of hard economic limit, and wasn't in crisis—and, instead of trying to reverse the powerful tide of individualism, ride along with it. At the same time, he could act more forcefully than Carter, especially against inflation, so that he didn't seem weak and ineffectual. All this is exactly what Carter's successor, Ronald Reagan, did.

Actually, Carter himself set in motion the process by which inflation was conquered a few months later, when he gave the chairmanship of the Federal Reserve Board to Paul Volcker, a man willing to put the economy into a severe recession to bring back price stability. But in November fate delivered the *coup de grâce* [to] Carter in the form of the taking hostage of the staff of the American Embassy in Teheran, as a protest against the United States' harboring of Iran's former shah.

As with the malaise speech, what is most difficult to convey today about the hostage crisis is why Carter made what now looks like a huge, obvious error: playing up the crisis so much that it became a national obsession for more than a year. The fundamental problem with hostage taking is that the one sure remedy—refusing to negotiate and thus allowing the hostages to be killed—is politically unacceptable in the democratic media society we live in, at least when the hostages are middle-class sympathetic figures, as they were in Iran.

There isn't any good solution to this problem, but Carter's two successors in the White House demonstrated that it is possible at least to negotiate for the release of hostages in a low-profile way that will cause the press to lose interest and prevent the course of the hostage negotiations from completely defining the Presidency. During the last year of the Carter administration, by contrast, the hostage story absolutely dominated the television news (recall that the ABC show *Nightline* began as a half-hour five-times-a-week update on the hostage situation), and several of the hostages and their families became temporary celebrities. In Carter's defense, even among the many voices criticizing him for appearing weak and vacillating, there was none that I remember willing to say, "Just cut off negotiations and walk away." It was a situation that everyone regarded as terrible but in which there was a strong national consensus supporting the course Carter had chosen.

So ended the seventies. There was still enough of the sixties spillover phenomenon going on so that Carter, who is now regarded (with some affection) as having been too much the good-hearted liberal to maintain a hold on the presidential electorate, could be challenged for renomination by Ted Kennedy on the grounds that he was too conservative. Inflation was raging on; the consumer price index rose by 14.4 percent between May 1979 and May 1980. We were being humiliated by fanatically bitter, pre-modern Muslims whom we had expected to regard us with gratitude because we had helped ease out their dictator even though he was reliably pro-United States. The Soviet empire appeared (probably for the last time ever) to be on the march, having invaded Afghanistan to Carter's evident surprise and disillusionment. We had lost our most recent war. We couldn't pull together as a people. The puissant, unified, prospering America of the late 1940s seemed to be just a fading memory.

I was a reporter for the *Washington Post* during the 1980 presidential campaign, and even on the *Post's* national desk, that legendary nerve center of politics, the idea that the campaign might end with Reagan's being elected President seemed fantastic, right up to the weekend before the election. At first Kennedy looked like a real threat to Carter; remember that up to that point no Kennedy had ever lost a campaign. While the Carter people were disposing of Kennedy, they were rooting for Reagan to win the Republican nomination because he would be such an easy mark.

He was too old, too unserious, and, most of all, too conservative. Look what had happened to Barry Goldwater (a sitting officeholder, at least) only sixteen years earlier, and Reagan was so divisive that a moderate from his own party, John Anderson, was running for President as a third-party candidate. It was not at all clear how much the related issues of inflation and national helplessness were dominating the public's mind. Kennedy, Carter, and Anderson were all, in their own way, selling national healing, that great postsixties obsession; Reagan, and only Reagan, was selling pure strength.

In a sense Reagan's election represents the country's rejection of the idea of a sixties-style solution to the great problems of the seventies—economic stagnation, social fragmentation, and the need for a new world order revolving around relations between the oil-producing Arab world and the West. The idea of a scaled-back America—husbanding its resources, living more modestly, renouncing its restless mobility, withdrawing from full engagement with the politics of every spot on the globe, focusing on issues of internal comity—evidently didn't appeal. Reagan, and the country, had in effect found a satisfying pose to strike in response to the problems of the seventies, but that's different from finding a solution.

Today some of the issues that dominated the seventies have faded away. Reagan and Volcker did beat inflation. The "crisis of confidence" now seems a long-ago memory. But it is striking how early we still seem to be in the process of working out the implications of the oil embargo. We have just fought and won a war against the twin evils of Middle East despotism and interruptions in the oil supply, which began to trouble us in the seventies. We still have not really even begun to figure out how to deal with the cessation of across-the-board income gains, and as a result our domestic politics are still dominated by squabbling over the proper distribution of government's benefits and burdens. During the seventies themselves the new issues that were arising seemed nowhere near as important as those sixties legacies, minority rights and Vietnam and Watergate. But the runt of decades has wound up casting a much longer shadow than anyone imagined.

Unit 6

Unit Selections

Key Points to Consider

❖ Fascism was defeated in 1945, and the more recent collapse of the Soviet Empire effectively discredited communism. What are the threats to peace we are most likely to confront in coming years? What impact will the end of the cold war have on American institutions and politics?

❖ Analyze the article on our "failing schools." Is the author persuasive in rejecting cross-cultural and historical comparisons of performance as invalid? Why or why not?

❖ If, as the essay "American Apartheid? Don't Believe It" contends, the Kerner Commission's prediction that the nation was moving toward two societies, one black and one white, has proven false, why are some people claiming that the problem has gotten worse?

❖ What do you think should be the proper role of the Central Intelligence Agency now that the cold war is over? Should it be abolished altogether? Defend your answer.

 **Links**   **www.dushkin.com/online/**

These sites are annotated on pages 4 and 5.

The cold war dominated American foreign policy for more than four decades, and had a huge impact on domestic affairs as well. It led to a nuclear arms race that produced more than enough explosive power to destroy both the United States and the Soviet Union. Some scientists predicted that an all-out nuclear war might even make the planet uninhabitable. The cold war began in Europe, quickly spread to Asia, and, as time went on, became a global struggle. Some American policymakers tended to blame Moscow for every development that threatened our interests. We maintained a standing army of troops for open warfare and a crawling army of secret agents for covert operations such as toppling governments deemed to be infected by the Communist "conspiracy." National security became the justification for actions that would have been unthinkable before the cold war began. National security also became the justification for intruding into the lives of those citizens suspected of "un-American" activities.

For all its appalling consequences, the cold war did provide a unifying theme of anti-Communism. That theme ended with the collapse of the Soviet Empire. Those who hoped for a new era of peace were soon disappointed as conflicts erupted in the Balkans, Africa, the Middle East, and in various parts of Asia. What obligations, if any, does the United States have in trying to settle disputes in such far-off places? What can justify putting young American lives at risk? Can the United Nations assume a more important role than before? Two articles in this unit deal with such issues. In "America after the Long War," Daniel Deudney and G. John Ikenberry predict that a reordering of our international priorities will have profound effects on domestic institutions and politics. "Our Century . . . and the Next One," by Walter Isaacson, provides a survey of some of the major developments of the twentieth century and suggests that tribalism and threats to the environment are some of the challenges that we will face in the twenty-first century.

The news media periodically trumpet some new study showing how badly American students perform in reading and mathmatics compared with young people in other nations. Individuals and groups often use these alarming statistics to promote special agendas with regard to American education. "The Near-Myth of Our Failing Schools" shows how cross-cultural and historical comparisons of performance can be misleading. Without minimizing what is wrong with our schools, author Peter Schrag argues that they are not doing as badly as many people think. "The dumbest thing we could do," he concludes, "is to scrap what we're doing right."

The Central Intelligence Agency (CIA) was created more than 50 years ago in response to the cold war. It was both an intelligence-gathering organization and one that carried out covert operations against real and imaginary enemies. Along the way it engaged in other activities that were not specified in its charter. Recent revelations about spies in the agency have made it something of a laughingstock. "Can't Anybody Here Play This Game?" argues that these revelations have obscured the larger issue that the CIA is not very effective in the first place. Author Edward Shirley, a former CIA member, calls for long-overdue reforms.

In response to a wave of urban race riots, President Lyndon B. Johnson appointed what became known as the Kerner Commission to study racial issues. The commission's report of 1968 concluded that the nation was "moving towards two societies, one black, one white—separate and unequal." Several much-cited books appeared in the 1990s claiming that every problem defined by the Kerner commission has since grown worse. "American Apartheid? Don't Believe It" denies that this is the case. In the mid-1960s only one in five white Americans had black neighbors, authors Abigail and Stephan Thurnstrom point out, while today the number is three of five. "And five out of six blacks now say they have white neighbors."

During the 1970s, the American government abandoned its long-standing policy of trying to integrate Native Americans into the dominant culture in favor of recognizing tribal sovereignty. In "Revolution in Indian Country," Fergus Bordewich evaluates this new approach and concludes that it has been beneficial overall. At the same time, it has caused generational friction among Native Americans and between them and whites living within tribal enclaves.

The Near-Myth of Our Failing Schools

Ideologically inspired lamentations about the parlous state of American education mask the much more complex truth

by Peter Schrag

In the spring of 1991, as warnings accumulated that America's second-rate schools were dooming the nation to permanent failure in the global economy, systems analysts at Sandia National Laboratories, a federal institution of generally impeccable reputation, compiled a lengthy report showing that the picture in American education was far more complex—and in many respects a great deal less gloomy—than the rhetoric of alarm allowed. But for two years the report—a collection of tables and statistics on everything from dropout rates and SAT scores to college degrees awarded in engineering and other technical fields—was buried by the Department of Energy, which had commissioned it. The document, said James Watkins, George Bush's Secretary of Energy, was "dead wrong," and would be regarded as "a call for complacency at a time when just the opposite is required." It had a small underground cir-

Peter Schrag *writes frequently on education and politics. He is the author of* Paradise Lost: The California Experience and the American Future, *to be published this spring.*

culation, but even after the Clinton Administration finally released it, in 1993,

---

Good news undermines the sense of crisis essential both to liberal demands for more money and to conservative arguments for vouchers and other radical solutions.

---

neither the Sandia data nor similar findings from other sources got much attention. Mixed reports don't make for good headlines, and qualified good news undermines the sense of crisis essential both to liberal demands for more money and to conservative arguments that only vouchers and other radical solutions will do. Good news, even qualified good news, runs counter to the conventional wisdom and undermines almost everybody's agenda of reform.

It was always thus: in the late 1950s, after the launching of *Sputnik*; in the early 1980s, after publication of the fed-

eral report *A Nation at Risk*, which warned that the failures of the nation's schools were about to undermine America's ability to compete economically; in 1989, when President George Bush and the nation's governors initiated what came to be called Goals 2000, pledging to make this country the world leader in education by the year 2000; in 1993, when President Bill Clinton and a Democratic Congress followed that up with legislation to develop voluntary national standards in English, history, science, and other fields; and in 1995–1996, when that same effort collapsed in controversy and dispute over the standards that were produced.

Now, as President Clinton is calling yet again for higher school standards, and for a program of national testing in reading and math, the same assumptions of crisis and failure that have fueled every other recent reform debate are being invoked. The debate is driven once again by our favorite myths: that there was once a golden age, an era when schools maintained rigorous academic standards, when all children learned, when few dropped out and most graduated on time; that sometime in the past generation or so (most commonly pegged to the 1960s) the system began to fall apart under a siege of social promotion, grade inflation, and progressive mush that is leaving America helpless against superior foreign education; and that the large amounts of new money that have gone to the schools in the past generation have largely been wasted. House Speaker Newt Gingrich and the University of California regent Ward Connerly, who spearheaded California's drive against race-based affirmative action, wrote in a recent *New York Times* op-ed piece,

> The education bureaucracy won't concede that, despite spending trillions of dollars on education over the past 30 years, American children are further behind today. It doesn't want to admit that the S.A.T. scores of African-American children, which average 100 points less than the scores of white children, are the direct result of the current [Great Society] policies.

In some places, circumstances, and contexts, some of those criticisms are correct. Many schools are academically flabby, mindless, and laced with an anti-intellectualism sometimes bordering on outright sabotage; some are wastelands of crime, drugs, and despair; many are afflicted by multicultural fashion and politically correct clichés. Some are run by arrogant, rigid bureaucracies or crippled by unions that make it impossible to move any teacher with seniority, let alone fire the bad ones, and classrooms are often without a regular teacher for the first month of school while the seniority system slowly determines who may be assigned where. Many schools don't demand nearly as much as they should. But many others suffer from few of those things, and without a more realistic sense of what is going on—a better understanding of the myths—the country will never get beyond the horror stories and ideological set pieces that seem endlessly to dominate the education debate.

MISLEADING STATISTICS AND COMPARISONS

Among the Sandia findings, many of them corroborated by other studies, are the following: High school completion rates—now roughly 90 percent—and college graduation rates are the highest in history. One in four adult Americans has at least a bachelor's degree—the highest percentage in the world (and the percentage keeps getting higher). A larger percentage of twenty-two-year-olds receive degrees in math, science, or engineering in the United States than in any of the nation's major economic competitors. Although SAT verbal scores declined over the years 1975 to 1990, the decline occurred chiefly because a larger percentage of lower-ranking students (those from the bottom half of their school classes) began taking the test. If the same population that took the SATs in 1975 had taken them this year, the average score would be significantly higher than it was then—and higher than it was in 1990.

Because of reforms instituted in the 1980s, more American high school students than ever before are taking four years of English and at least three years of math and science. Far more are taking and passing Advanced Placement examinations (198,000 in 1978 and 535,000 in 1996). More teachers, for all the flaws in our teacher training-and-reward system, are subject to tough standards for certification and promotion.

To be sure, as the Sandia report recognized, on tests like the Third International Mathematics and Science Study and other international comparisons of academic achievement American students continue to score lower than their peers in Singapore, Taiwan, Japan, Korea, and elsewhere. Whereas parents of high-achieving students in Japan or China worry that their children are not doing well enough and ought to work still harder, among parents of American students who are scoring far less well on the same tests "satisfaction with . . . students' achievement and education remains high and standards remain low," according to a team led by the University of Michigan psychologist Harold W. Stevenson. "Innate ability [not diligence or high expectations] continues to be emphasized by Americans as a basis for achievement." Stevenson's collaborator James Stigler, of the University of California at Los Angeles, has found an academic intensity in Japanese classes that is almost unthinkable in this country.

Many American universities, including even as selective an institution as the University of California, continue to provide remedial courses to their freshmen; a quarter of the students entering UCLA are required to take what used to be called bonehead English, and nearly a third of those entering the University of California system as a whole are.

But as Iris Rotberg, a professor at George Washington University, points out, cross-cultural comparisons of academic achievement are tough to make. Many countries begin specialized education at age fourteen or even earlier, which means that some students have already left school and many others have begun cramming for (in the words of the Sandia report) the "life determining tests . . . that specify their eventual position in the workforce." Many lower-achieving students in Great Britain and other countries have by age seventeen already been tracked into job-training programs or have simply left school and thus are not included in the test samples, making comparisons meaningless. (For example, England and Wales rank near the bottom in international math comparisons of eighth-grade students; in comparisons of twelfth-graders, only six percent of whom in England take math, they rank near the top.) Intense competition in places like Singapore and Japan for good university slots and other rewards that will have consequences for a lifetime must wonderfully concentrate the mind.

The late Albert Shanker, for many years the president of the American Federation of Teachers, argued persuasively that the fierce competition in other countries is hardly an excuse for a U.S. system in which academic success or failure has so few consequences—for either teachers or students—and in which so little fosters intense academic effort. Even the best American students, he argued, do not perform as well as their peers elsewhere. Questions that all college-bound nineteen-year-olds in France or Great Britain are expected to answer would be impossible for most graduating seniors here. But the debate ought to make the complexity and ambiguities of the larger issue obvious enough. Which is better for the student—to have the discipline that intense competition for relatively few college openings brings, or to have ample opportunity?

MISLEADING HISTORICAL COMPARISONS

What is true of cross-cultural comparisons is even more emphatically true of historical ones. Precisely when was the golden age of American education that the conventional wisdom assumes existed? Was it in the early years of this century, when, as the education historian Colin Greer pointed out years ago, "All minority groups, white as well as black, with the exceptions of the English, Scots, Germans, and Scandinavians, were negatively portrayed" in American textbooks; when "Jews, Italians, Chinese and blacks were mean, criminal, immoral, drunken, sly, lazy, and stupid in varying degrees"? Was it in the 1920s, when most students never went beyond the eighth grade, when large numbers of children, especially in the South, never went to school at all from April to November, and when no one had ever heard of any such concept as the dropout rate? Was it in the 1930s and 1940s, when even the more enlightened medical schools had strict quotas for Jews and blacks, and the others systematically excluded them, as did a great many other educational institutions as well? Was it in the 1950s, when the historian Arthur Bestor published *Educational Wastelands: The Retreat From Learning in Our Public Schools* (reissued, significantly, in a new edition in 1985), when Rudolf Flesch's *Why Johnny Can't Read* was long a best seller, and when the schools were thought to be failing because, with the launching of *Sputnik*, the Russians had beaten us into space? Was it in 1963, when Admiral Hyman Rickover published *American Education, a National Failure*?

Consider our contemporary why-Johnny-can't-read arguments. In 1987 Chester Finn and Diane Ravitch, two of the country's most thoughtful conservative school critics, published a set of statistics and related data about what American students don't know about their own history and literature. The book title took the form of a question,

What Do Our 17-Year-Olds Know?, and the answer was unequivocal. "If there were such a thing as a national report card," Finn and Ravitch wrote, "then we would have to say that this nationally representative sample of 11th-grade students earns failing marks in both subjects." But as at least some parents have noticed, and as Gerald Bracey, a prolific debunker of schools-are-failing stories, reported in the journal *Phi Delta Kappan* in March of 1995, students may in fact know more than their parents and grandparents do. In any case, Bracey showed, such complaints are hardly new. In 1943 *The New York Times*, citing findings by the historian Allan Nevins, reported its shock at discovering that

> a large majority of [college] students showed that they had virtually no knowledge of elementary aspects of American history [and] could not identify such names as Abraham Lincoln, Thomas Jefferson, Andrew Jackson, or Theodore Roosevelt. . . . Some students believed that George Washington was president during the War of 1812. . . . St. Louis was placed on the Pacific Ocean, Lake Huron, Lake Erie, the Atlantic Ocean, Ohio River, and almost every place else.

Similarly, the college students described Walt Whitman as a missionary, a pioneer, a colonizer, an unpatriotic writer, a humorist, an English poet, and (not surprising in the days of Paul Whiteman) a band leader. Plus ça change . . .

Chester Finn and like-minded people point to scores on the National Assessment of Educational Progress (NAEP), widely considered to be among the most reliable measures of academic achievement, to show how little progress has been made from the late 1970s to the present, despite the orgy of curricular reforms and the growing amounts of money that have been appropriated for K–12 schools in most states over the past decade. But rarely do these people point to the changing demographics of the American school—the growing proportion of students whose native language is something other than English (now more than 25 percent in California, and nearly half in Los Angeles), and the growing proportion of students from poor or one-parent families. A Rand

analysis of the same NAEP scores, issued in December of 1994, shows that although overall scores for students aged thirteen and seventeen didn't rise much from 1970 to 1990, scores for all ethnic subgroups were up (three percentage points for whites, eleven points for Hispanics, nineteen points for blacks). And although one reason for that change was that the parents were better educated (in 1970, 38 percent of mothers had not finished high school; in 1990 the figure was 17 percent), Rand's researchers concluded that the gains for blacks and Hispanics were larger than any change in family characteristics could explain. Whether the gains were a direct effect or a second-generation effect of the parents' better schooling, public investment, contrary to the conservative critics, had made a difference.

CONTRADICTORY OBJECTIVES

That the same charges now being directed at the schools were leveled a half century ago is hardly reason to ignore them, but it does say something about those myths. Editorials in *The Wall Street Journal*, a newspaper long devoted to the cause of school vouchers, often complain that Americans spend more per pupil in their public schools than the French or the Germans and get less in return. But what goes unmentioned is that the French and the Germans spend more on health and child care, public transportation, and related social services (not counted in their school spending, though it often is part of ours), and that theirs are for the most part still monocultural societies with less social pathology. Nor is it generally recognized that most of the growth in American school spending in the past three decades has gone for special education for the ballooning numbers of students officially considered handicapped or disabled, a designation that hardly existed in the years immediately after the Second World War. The Sandia report estimates that from 1960 to 1988 constant-dollar spending for "regular" students increased by 39 percent per pupil while spending for all students increased by roughly 150 percent. The difference is almost entirely accounted for by special education, which, as the report points out, can have little impact on average performance on national standardized tests. (Among unfunded federal mandates special education, which diverts huge sums from the regular classroom, is certainly one of the most costly.)

Another myth is that Americans really do want schools with high academic standards, and would get them if the education establishment didn't stand in their way.

None of this is meant to deny the system's enormous problems and failures—crime, drugs, arteriosclerotic bureaucracies, self-serving unions, decaying facilities, vocational-education programs a half century out of date—or to suggest that all our students are doing splendidly. Despite the glories of a higher-education system that, even after the sharp tuition increases and the cutbacks in public funding of the past few years, is still the world's most accessible and abundant, Albert Shanker was right: as long as so few real rewards are given for distinction and so few real penalties exacted for failure, the educational process will tend to remain lackadaisical and inefficient. The question is whether Americans will ever tolerate anything more demanding. Equally important, the schools are so riven with contradictory objectives—merit versus inclusion, for example—and so loaded down with extraneous social mandates for everything from drug education and AIDS counseling to diversity training and social awareness (often imposed by the same politicians who complain about school failure) that it's a wonder anyone learns anything. But flat generalizations about crisis and failure, the superiority of foreign schools, or the glorious past will do nothing to solve the problems.

WHO WANTS RIGOR?

Which brings us to yet another myth: that Americans—and parents in particular—really do want schools with high academic standards, and would get them if the education establishment didn't stand in their way. In *Inside American Education* (1993) Thomas Sowell, of the Hoover Institution, listed the usual complaints, from the travesties of sex education and the overemphasis on school sports to the pressure for political correctness in curricula. But if he had ever been to a school-board meeting where someone proposed making it harder for students with bad grades to play football, he'd know that it's not only educationists who foist this stuff on the system. Ross Perot's first great public campaign—for tougher school standards in Texas—wasn't against teachers but against ordinary folks all across Texas. The censors and the enemies of high standards come as often from outside the system as from inside. They may be religious fundamentalists fighting the teaching of evolution or demanding equal time for creationism in science programs, or complaining about witches and secular humanism in reading textbooks and dirty words in novels. They may be gays complaining that Michelangelo and Tchaikovsky are not identified in the history books as homosexual, or black self-esteemers blocking the adoption of updated history texts because they're short on the civilizations of Africa (even though the older texts don't mention them at all). They may be civil-rights groups demanding that *The Adventures of Huckleberry Finn* be taken out of the syllabus because it contains the word "nigger," or opposing tougher standards because they fear that more poor children will fail. Clinton's new proposal for national testing is already under assault from groups that include the Mexican American Legal Defense and Educational Fund and FairTest on the left, and the Christian Coalition and Phyllis Schlafly's Eagle Forum on the right. (The right, Chester Finn has said, doesn't like anything with the word "national" in it; the left doesn't like anything with the word "testing.") In addition, groups all across the spec-

trum have fought over the content and requirements of every form of educational testing, asserting that the SAT is biased against minorities and women, that the (now defunct) California CLAS test was too intrusive into the personal lives of students and their families and didn't focus enough on the basics, that yet another test simply demands too much. And then there are the age-old fights (in and outside the schools) about phonics versus whole language, math facts versus constructivism, progressivism versus drill-and-kill. Of course the school establishment is not an innocent in these things, but it is hardly the only culprit. Virtually every national poll shows that although only a fifth of Americans rate the nation's public schools very highly, some 70 percent of us think that the schools our own children attend are doing just fine—a phenomenon that Finn calls "retail complacency." We could be wrong on either count, or on both, but things are obviously not quite as simple as the rhetoric of failure suggests. Anti-intellectualism is as American as apple pie.

THE WEAK ECONOMIC ARGUMENT

There was a time when American schools were known for their successes: the children of immigrants who made it to City College or Columbia or Harvard and went on to have professional careers. Dropouts and failures simply vanished into the large market for unskilled labor. Now the schools tend to be known for their failures: dropouts, kids who bring guns to school, students who score lower than their counterparts abroad. We forget that we are trying to take children from an unprecedented array of ethnic and cultural backgrounds, many of them speaking little or no English, and educate them all to a level of sophistication never imagined for so large a proportion of any population.

A few years ago our presumed failure to do that was blamed for what was regarded as the nation's slipping competitiveness against the Germans and the Japanese, but now that the business pages—and the front pages, too—are celebrating a triumphant economic recovery, no one credits the schools. The old litany simply continues. In 1995, at yet another "national summit" in Washington on "world-class education for all America's children," business people blithely reiterated that American students were being insufficiently educated for the global economy in which they will have to survive. All assumed that if young people were well enough educated, great jobs would await them; none seemed concerned that since 1979, according to the Bureau of Labor Statistics, real wages have declined for all men except those with more education than four years of college. The business people did not mention that increasing numbers of college graduates were doing jobs that required no college training at all—that, as *Phi Delta Kappan* reported a couple of years ago, the number of college-educated door-to-door salesmen, for example, grew from 57,000 in 1983 to 75,000 in 1990, and the number of bus drivers with bachelor's degrees rose from 99,000 to 166,000. The job market for college graduates has surely improved with the economic recovery, but the boom will not last forever either.

In 1995, when the University of Illinois surveyed its 1994 graduates about whether their college training was being put to good use, nearly 40 percent said they regarded themselves as overqualified. In the early 1990s Sam Ginn, the chairman of Pacific Telesis, went around California talking about how his company had given seventh-grade reading tests to 6,400 applicants for operator positions and only 2,700 had passed. He didn't point out that the jobs paid less than $7.00 an hour, or that since the company had only 700 jobs to offer, there were almost four qualified applicants for every available slot. For such problems a lot of fixes are needed, many of them only remotely connected with the schools.

The Stanford University educationist Larry Cuban may well have been right when he said, "The myth of better schools as the engine for a leaner, stronger economy was a scam from the very beginning." Yet even if he wasn't, economic recovery has changed the basis for argument. It's hard to read without embarrassment a statement like the one from *A Nation at Risk* about how the country must reform its educational system "if only to keep and improve on the slim competitive edge that we still retain in world markets." But the obsolescence of the economic rationale hardly weakens the case for better schools and higher standards, particularly in the inner cities, from which a disproportionate number of the nation's school failures have always come. On the contrary, it returns our attention to the broader case for good public education—the desirability of a liberally educated community, Thomas Jefferson's argument about the importance of an enlightened citizenry, the desperate need to end our cycles of poverty and to apply resources accordingly. But those objectives require a far more realistic appreciation of what we have done in our educational system in the past, what we are doing now, and what we think we want to do. Despite the problems encountered by Goals 2000 and Clinton's national-standards effort, the trend of the past few years—surely a healthy one—has been to find ways to set broad goals and standards, and to free local schools and teachers to accomplish them in their own ways. But those things can be done only if we can see the results without ideological blinders, if the tests and assessments we use really measure what we want to know, and if we have the confidence to support the schools that this society needs. A growing number of people, in the name of world-class standards, would abandon, through vouchers, privatization, and other means, the idea of the common school altogether. Before we do that, we'd better be sure that things are really as bad as we assume. The dumbest thing we could do is scrap what we're doing right.

Can't Anybody Here Play This Game?

The sensational revelations of recent years about the Central Intelligence Agency almost obscure a larger point: the Agency is just no good at what it's supposed to be doing. So writes the author, a former CIA officer, who describes a corrosive culture in which promotion-hungry operatives collect pointless intelligence from worthless foreign agents. Reform, the author warns, may prove impossible

by Edward G. Shirley

The arrest of Aldrich Hazen Ames, a CIA operative turned KGB mole, in February of 1994, fundamentally changed the public perception of the clandestine service of the Central Intelligence Agency. Before Ames only "case officers," operatives who recruit and run foreign agents, knew how dysfunctional the service had become. Since Ames the outside world has learned that much is rotten in the Directorate of Operations—the official name of the clandestine service, known to insiders simply as the DO. Yet the senators and congressmen who oversee the DO, the journalists who report on it, and the civilian directors who run it have failed to understand and to confront the service's real problems. Even among CIA analysts who work in the Directorate of Intelligence, the overt, think-tank side of the house, few have grasped the extent of the DO's decrepitude.

Politically charged, usually lurid stories of CIA misconduct have deflected

---

Edward G. Shirley *is a pseudonymous former case officer in the CIA's Directorate of Operations. He is the author of* Know Thine Enemy: A Spy's Journey Into Revolutionary Iran *(1997).*

attention from telling questions about U.S. intelligence. Journalists level charges of Agency involvement in Latino drug-smuggling rings. The American wife of a Central American guerrilla accuses the DO of complicity in torture and murder. Female case officers sue their male bosses for sexual discrimination.

All these affairs have blackened the Agency's image. None advances the debate on whether the clandestine service actually spies well. Protected by secrecy, by a disciplined and obedient bureaucracy, and by the average outsider's basic ignorance of and fascination with espionage, the leadership of the DO has pre-empted and stalled pressure for Agency reform.

In 1985 I joined the Directorate of Operations. A devout cold warrior, I had no qualms about espionage or covert action against the Soviet Union and in defense of America's national interests. I was proud and eager when the Near East Division chose me to join its ranks. I had dreamed for years of applying my academic training in Islamic history to the DO's Middle Eastern mission.

Twelve years later I retain an appreciation for espionage—for those rare moments when a case officer contributes

to his nation's defense. But I have long since lost my pride in the DO, which has evolved into a sorry blend of Monty Python and Big Brother. I resigned in 1993.

When current and former case officers gather, their conversations inevitably converge: they wonder whether the DO has irretrievably fallen apart. A few years ago I asked a former colleague who had served in Moscow whether she had ever successfully explained the DO's problems to an outsider. "No, never," she replied. "I've given up trying. You have to explain so much you get lost in the details, or you just sound like a whiny, unpatriotic left-winger."

The CIA, with a certain fanfare, recently celebrated its fiftieth anniversary. The Agency wants the American public, and especially Congress, to believe that its men and women won the Cold War, along the way had a few problems, and yet are now rising to the challenges of the twenty-first century. In front of the intelligence-oversight committees in Congress senior Agency officials repeat the CIA's new mission statement about battling terrorism, drugs, the proliferation of nuclear, biological, and chemical weapons, and rogue regimes in Iran, Iraq, Libya, Sudan, and North Korea. With the Ames fiasco receding, some current and retired CIA officials are asserting that if Congress and the press would only back off, the professionals would once again get the job done.

One feature of a closed society is that it lies to itself as readily as it lies to outsiders. Writing as "X" in his 1947 assessment of the Soviet Union, the diplomat George F. Kennan borrowed from Gibbon's *Decline and Fall of the Roman Empire*; the passage applies equally to the CIA's present-day Directorate of Operations.

> From enthusiasm to imposture the step is perilous and slippery; the demon of Socrates affords a memorable instance of how a wise man may deceive himself, how a good man may deceive others, how the conscience may slumber in a mixed and middle state between self-illusion and voluntary fraud.

The sad truth about the CIA—what the Ames debacle didn't reveal—is that the DO has for years been running an espionage charade in most countries, deceiving itself and others about the value of its recruited agents and intelligence production. The ugliest DO secret is how the clandestine service encourages decent case officers, gradually and naturally, to evolve into liars about their contribution to America's security. By 1985, the year Ames volunteered to spy for the KGB, the vast majority of the CIA's foreign agents were mediocre assets at best, put on the payroll because case officers needed high recruitment numbers to get promoted. Long before the Soviet Union collapsed, recruitment and intelligence fraud—the natural product of an insular spy world—had stripped the DO of its integrity and its competence.

Younger operatives are resigning in droves, because they have given up hope of reform. The attrition was sufficient to provoke an investigation by the inspector general in 1996. Though the inspector general's office did a poor job of questioning young case officers who had resigned, the final report doesn't deny the increasing resignation rate among the best and the brightest who entered

the DO during the Reagan years. Nearly three quarters of the case officers from my 1985 junior-officer class have quit the service. When my class entered, we were told that the DO had the lowest attrition rate—under five percent—in the U.S. government. Though this figure was no doubt inaccurate—a normal and healthy rate of attrition in any bureaucracy should be higher—it does reflect the DO's credo that officers don't quit the clandestine service unless they are flawed. Within the DO and in front of Congress senior officials downplay the rising resignation rate and even deny that the directorate's younger officers—let alone its best ones—are abandoning ship.

But the senior officers themselves know the truth. As early as 1988 a senior CIA official responsible for the Directorate of Operations' budget and personnel visited stations and bases worldwide, discreetly asking young case officers why so many good young officers were quitting. The official wanted to know whether junior officers would be willing to participate in a round-table discussion with the deputy director of operations, the boss of the clandestine service. The senior official, not a case officer herself, didn't realize that she was asking case officers to commit professional suicide. The round-table discussion never took place.

A DYSFUNCTIONAL FAMILY

Americans were shocked by the DO's nine-year failure to catch Ames, a hard-drinking, free-spending KGB mole inside the Soviet-East Europe Division. How could the DO have entrusted its premier agents—probably the best Soviet agents the CIA ever had—to a counterintelligence case officer with such evident flaws? Unlike the usual agent chaff that case officers recruit in order to get promotions, these Soviet agents were the real thing. Treason and his spending habits aside, the truth is that Ames was not much different from many of his peers. He was disgruntled and he drank too much. He disliked recruiting foreign agents and he did it poorly. He distrusted most of his colleagues, particularly those more senior.

He was stalled in his career as a mid-level officer (a GS-14), slightly higher in grade than the average retiring case officer.

Not a single Iran-desk chief could speak Persian. Not a single Near East division chief knew Arabic, Persian, or Turkish.

Before the collapse of the Soviet Union moving in the cocktail-party circuit was the primary, often the only, way a case officer could rub shoulders with Communist "hard targets"—foreigners who were extremely difficult to approach, let alone develop and recruit. In seeking to press the flesh, many officers drank too much. More important, many case officers—and Ames was one of them—chafed at the recruitment game, the desperate socializing in search of a foreigner who could be written up as a promising "developmental." Case officers grow cynical in such a world—and they've been living in one since the 1960s. Before he volunteered his services to the Soviets, Ames amused himself in Mexico City by privately critiquing the station's case officers and their numerous recruited agents, who produced very little intelligence. Contrary to the common, outsider view of him, Ames was attentive to both operational details and intelligence reports. He discovered before most of his peers did that one of the most renowned case officers working in the Latin American division was a corrupt fraud, who inflated or invented most of his agents and probably pocketed some agents' pay in diamonds. Though dismissed from the service, the case officer was never jailed. On his spacious balcony in a high-rise above Mexico City, Ames often passed evenings with friends wryly belittling the DO's contributions to America's defense.

Deeply troubled and venal, Ames slipped across that space between dissent and treason, believing it was all a charade. Given his free-spending ways, the Agency should of course have found him sooner. But spotting Ames psychologically, or by questioning his peers, would have been very difficult. In the CIA family there are many dysfunctional members.

Peeling away the layers of the Agency's mystique—by learning how to read agents' files, acquiring familiarity with operational details, gaining access to "restricted-handling" cases—can take years. One thing, however, did not take me long to learn: there was a severe discrepancy between the reputations of most senior officers and their talents. Sterling exceptions aside, the average senior officer rose through the hierarchy without ever learning much about the language, culture, or politics of the countries in which he served. The good case officers in my junior-officer class hunted vainly for mentors like Richard Helms, Paul Henze, and Robert Ames—renowned case officers from the past who knew their languages and their countries well. Not a single Iran-desk chief during the eight years that I worked on Iran could speak or read Persian. Not a single Near East Division chief knew Arabic, Persian, or Turkish, and only one could get along even in French. One Near East officer, sent during the Iran-contra affair to assess and debrief Manucher Ghorbanifar, the slick and savvy Iranian middleman between the Ayatollah Khomeini's regime and the Americans and Israelis, spoke no Persian and had no background in the Middle East. He repeatedly had to ask Ghorbanifar to spell the names of well-known senior Iranian officials.

At the Agency's espionage-training school ("The Farm") at Camp Peary, near Williamsburg, Virginia, instructors regularly told trainees that cultural distinctions did not matter, that an operation was an operation regardless of the target. Whether Arab, German, Turkish, Brazilian, Persian, Russian, Pakistani, or French, targets were (as Duane Clarridge, a Europe Division and counterterrorism-center chief, baldly put it) "all the same." "An op is an op," a favorite mantra of English-only case officers, is one of the DO's most self-defeating conceits.

Of all the clandestine service's Cold War missions, no task was more mys-

tique-building, but at the same time more illusory, than the recruiting of Soviet agents. The No. 1 operational directive of every case officer was to recruit KGB officials, Soviet military-intelligence officers, and Soviet diplomats, but this essentially amounted to little more than paper-shuffling between CIA headquarters, in Langley, Virginia, and case officers in the field. Real recruitment was more often than not a sheer fluke. According to Soviet-East Europe Division officers, the best agents Ames killed were all "walk-ins," who had volunteered their services to the United States. Handling walk-ins is no mean feat, and CIA case officers have often handled sensitive walk-ins exceptionally well. But "recruiting" walk-ins has little to do with the protracted "recruitment cycle"—the spotting, assessing, developing, and recruiting of foreigners worldwide—on which the DO has built its budget and espirit de corps.

The CIA's clandestine service encourages decent case officers, gradually and naturally, to evolve into liars.

During the Cold War, DO managers in the field wanted young case officers to telephone, out of the blue, Soviet officials with whom they had no plausible reason to be in touch. The lucky case officers who made it past the telephoning and the awkward encounters were encouraged to socialize as intensely as possible. They were to ignore the constant advice of KGB defectors who warned that if a case officer met a Soviet citizen, he should simply say hello, offer a business card with a home telephone number, and then say good-bye. If the Soviet wanted to defect or to work in place against the Communist system, he would send a message. KGB defectors argued that the active development of Soviets would only draw the attention of Soviet counterintelligence, and would amplify a Soviet embassy's or consulate's normal paranoia. Yet the CIA persisted. The DO's mystique and pride,

not to mention its jobs and budget, were at stake.

Terrible DO failures occurred in the 1980s and 1990s in Latin America, Africa, Europe, and the Middle East. Not just in the Soviet Union did the CIA lose numerous agents. An organization whose motto is the verse from the Gospel of John "And ye shall know the truth and the truth shall make you free" had grown sloppy, developing a lackadaisical appreciation of the distinction between fact and fiction. Some good agents, and many mediocre or worthless ones, died for their case officers' mistakes; in an environment in which poor-quality agents routinely got inflated into first-rate ones, case officers frequently put agents who really didn't know much into harm's way.

A LIARS' PARADISE

From 1947 through the early 1960s it was good to be a case officer. Almost everyone feared the Soviet Union; Communists in league with the USSR were everywhere. Except for the United States, the world was poor. More important, Washington knew very little about the postwar world for which it had reluctantly become responsible. The communications and transportation revolutions had not yet taken place. Relatively few Americans traveled abroad. Slow-moving diplomatic pouches, not arduously encrypted and decrypted cables, were the primary means of contact between Washington and the field. Diplomats and spies were often at the forefront in obtaining and analyzing information. A U.S. embassy official in Moscow could write a telegram about the Soviet soul, as Kennan did, that would actually be passed around among White House Cabinet members. What today might seem self-evident, or academic, was then exotic and classified.

The CIA sent its case officers out to gather all the information they could, and in most countries outside the Communist bloc they found the locals receptive. Enlisting the support of the Germans, the French, or the Japanese in the face of a common enemy was not Mission Impossible. An overwhelming mutual interest, not money, brought American case officers and otherwise prickly foreigners together. Many, if not most, of the Agency's finest intelligence-producing sources were unpaid. In the first two decades of the Agency's existence, when the DO evolved out of the covert-action-oriented Office of Policy Coordination and the espionage-oriented Office of Special Operations, recruiting spies was not a head-counting game. According to one old Agency hand, "We would never have tolerated . . . bragging about lining up ducks [recruitments], as if clandestine intelligence were some kind of assembly line."

The Directorate of Operations (or, as it was then euphemistically known, the Directorate of Plans) was a clubbish group of men. Even after the huge expansion of the clandestine service, during the early 1950s (more new employees were hired then than during the Vietnam War), graduates of prestigious colleges and universities predominated. Washington's Metropolitan and Alibi Clubs perhaps had as many operational discussions within their walls as did Agency headquarters. Senior officers ranked and promoted their juniors in a highly subjective manner. This old-boy system had its problems. But racking up recruitments, good or bad, did not necessarily get an officer promoted. In the 1950s and early 1960s the CIA's top leaders—men like Allen Dulles, Frank Wisner, Richard Bissell, Tracy Barnes, and Desmond Fitzgerald—were profoundly devoted to covert action. Covert action (orchestrating coups, anti-Communist insurgencies, academic conferences, labor unions, political parties, publishing houses, and shipping companies) required considerable manpower, and it drew the intellectual crème de la crème. It compelled a higher degree of intellectual curiosity, accomplishment, and operational savoir faire than did espionage ("espionage" referring specifically to the recruitment of foreign intelligence agents). With so many talented officers working in covert action, and with most of the foreigners involved being friendly collaborators and not "recruited" assets, the DO could scarcely base promotions on the number of recruitments a case officer made each year.

After the Bay of Pigs fiasco, covert action became politically riskier. More important, press revelations during the 1960s and 1970s about various CIA maneuvers of dubious legality and wisdom, followed by several bouts of congressional investigation, helped to sully the Agency's covert-action credentials. Though covert action continued worldwide in the 1970s, it employed less manpower. Inside the CIA working on covert action no longer had the same prestige, and was becoming a slower track for promotions.

By the time Stansfield Turner became Jimmy Carter's director of central intelligence, in 1977, the decades-old tug-of-war inside the Agency between covert action and espionage was over. Henceforth covert action would be only an avocation. Espionage was the area in which case officers could better manage their destinies.

Sometime in the late 1960s and early 1970s recruiting became the case officer's categorical imperative. The Vietnam War helped to propel the change. Before the war espionage was a cause; Vietnam turned it into a business. The CIA was in competition and collusion with the Pentagon in the acquisition and dissemination of intelligence about South Vietnam, North Vietnam, Cambodia, and Laos. As the war intensified, CIA chiefs in Saigon demanded a minimum of 300 intelligence reports a month from their station. Local agents of highly dubious value were continually added to the roster and the payroll in order to meet this unrealistic objective.

Confronted with an expanding war, Langley significantly enlarged the case-officer corps. Now far fewer new officers came from the nation's elite schools. The growing anti-war movement on eastern college campuses deprived the Agency of the long-cherished "P" (professor) factor in its discreet, highly successful university recruiting networks. Scandals involving domestic mail interception, wiretaps, and surveillance activities by the CIA, reported by Seymour M. Hersh in *The New York Times* in 1974, finished off CIA-university relations.

The war combined and accelerated three factors highly corrosive of the clandestine service: a surplus of easily recruited "sources"; poor quality control on intelligence reports; and falling admission standards for case officers. Though there were CIA operatives and analysts who realized (and steadfastly advised Washington policymakers) in the late 1960s that America's war in Vietnam was lost, Southeast Asia became, bureaucratically, a liars' paradise, where aggressive, self-promoting case officers quickly got ahead.

THE NUMBERS RACKET

As the Soviets expanded the Cold War geographically in the 1960s and 1970s, the CIA significantly increased the size and number of its stations and bases throughout Africa and Latin America. In the Third World working for the CIA was a rite of passage for many men (Third World agents were and are almost all men). For Latin Americans, Arabs, and Africans, association with the Agency could be highly respectable and reasonably well paid. The CIA was the little guy's conduit to the cabal that ruled the world. Third World targets were usually inexpensive and relatively easy for the DO to recruit and run, and their "flap" potential was far less than that of agents operating against our sensitive First World allies.

With most of the Third World seen as a legitimate Cold War arena, case officers worldwide could go after local diplomatic or military representatives. Even if the CIA was not in fact interested in recruiting a given official of a given Third World country (admittedly, a rare circumstance during the Cold War), a case officer could still chase the target and label him an "access agent," who might conceivably lead to a more promising, usually Soviet, recruit. With the entire Third World "on the screen," recruitment possibilities for the average case officer increased enormously. One of my former chiefs of station once remarked about a Soviet case, "Isn't it amusing to contemplate the hundreds—God knows—of African access agents we've recruited over the years when the Russians are among the world's worst racists?" All told, the CIA recruited thousands of people from the Third World.

The Civil Service Reform Act of 1978, with its enthusiasm for "objective criteria" in "performance appraisal systems," further solidified the DO's head-counting ethic. Though the act didn't technically apply to the Agency (Langley is in theory exempt from civil-service regulations), in spirit it did. The business-school philosophy of "management by objective" officially became de rigueur throughout the DO. (The current harassment problems of the IRS probably also stem from this quantitative philosophy run amok.)

As the CIA got larger, bureaucratic standards were formalized. The power of DO promotion panels eclipsed the old patronage system. The organization needed a common criterion for "objectively" judging the case-officer corps. To a considerable extent the American ethic of judging all people equally and the American fondness for translating merit into numbers gave rise to the practice of agent head-counting on case-officer evaluations.

To most people at the time, the annual head count—how many agents have you recruited?—seemed an efficient, progressive idea. Quickly, however, a rather raw reckoning of numbers took hold. By the early 1980s Africa, Near East, and Latin America Division case officers dominated the DO because recruitments in their regions were relatively easy. By the time I entered the service, senior officers regularly counseled young Soviet and Europe Division case officers to have at least one "recruitment tour" in Africa or the Middle East early in their careers, in order to avoid being forgotten by the promotion panels. At The Farm senior Africa Division officers tried to enlist trainees by bragging that operatives in their division racked up more recruitments, and thus were promoted more quickly, than those in any other division. Not once did I meet a senior Africa Division officer who extolled the quality of the intelligence reports produced by the division's vast roster of agents.

Overseas in the 1980s and 1990s my junior-officer class encountered DO managers offering $3,000 bonuses for "scalps" provided by Christmas or Easter. Bottles of champagne were awarded to case officers who generated the most intelligence reports. The winners usually scored twenty or thirty reports a month. In 1989 many of my colleagues were stunned to receive a cable from a division chief who had spent his career chasing Soviets. He recommended one "high quality" recruitment *per year* for each case officer in his division. This cable came on the heels of a worldwide headquarters cable announcing that *all* our Cuban agents had probably been double agents. The competition realized long ago how desperate America's case officers are for scalps. They have been happy to provide them.

In 1993 CIA Director James Woolsey sent a cable to all stations and bases encouraging case officers and their managers to push for quality, not quantity, in their recruitments and intelligence production. To an extent Woolsey knew that there was a recruitment problem in the DO. That same year, however, the DO issued new performance-evaluation guidelines for young case officers, who are responsible for the vast majority of all DO recruitments, re-emphasizing the centrality of recruitments in the promotion process. Officers in the field didn't have to read between the lines: the numbers game continued. Woolsey never knew that the DO had betrayed his good intentions.

By the time I resigned, in 1993, the DO had introduced the "Asset Validation System" for assessing foreign recruits. The DO billed the AVS as a means to prevent the recruitment and running of double agents and tired Cold War leftovers. The AVS did not officially attempt to root out "cheap recruitments." However, in the early 1990s a number of scandals in which star case officers were caught fabricating agents and intelligence reports gave reform-minded case officers hope that the DO might finally rein in the promotion-by-recruitment system. We all knew that these aggressive officers had merely pushed accepted standards of exaggeration and deceit a little too far.

This hope has proved naive. Although some senior officers will now quietly admit that there has been a numbers game, they usually complain that the 1980s generation of case officers gave rise to the problem, which they and the AVS are now solving. However, the AVS—dubbed "agent scrubbing" by *The Washington Post* and often credited as a reform initiated by John Deutch (in fact William Webster began the program; Robert Gates and James Woolsey significantly expanded it)—has not really affected the recruitment game. Case officers must now write a few more cables for each recruitment—a little extra paperwork in order to gain a seal of approval. Officers can even avoid doing the paperwork altogether: in the ever-growing paper flow between headquarters and the field, AVS requirements can easily disappear for years into a bureaucratic black hole. The recruitment of mediocre, if not entirely worthless, access agents continues.

Case officers have learned that they can recruit a worthless agent and later have the agent scrubbed without damage to their careers. Close questioning of recruitments in the DO remains uncommon. A case officer can recruit eight assets in Geneva, move on to his next tour in Paris, have all eight Geneva-based agents scrubbed, and still receive glowing evaluations from the Paris chief of station.

The AVS also does nothing to verify the value of information from the foreign agents who produce clandestine intelligence and who are the *raison d'être* of espionage. Standards for judging a source's intelligence production are so low that a case officer can easily believe, or pretend to believe, that the most routine contact is a first-rate "intel" developmental. With "forward-leaning" (that is, optimistic) cable traffic papering his way, an ambitious case officer can turn a friendly low-level telephone-company official into a sensitive penetration of a foreign nation's telecommunications industry. Once headquarters certifies a developmental's intelligence reports, the case officer knows that the developmental's recruitment will probably be approved. Clever case officers can also easily "push" the facts and opinions available in open-source news, or mirror classified State Department telegrams, to make a developmental or an agent seem like an adequate intelligence producer. Pushing the news and mirroring State have, regrettably, become second nature inside the DO, particularly among aggressive officers who know the system. And once poor intelligence becomes acceptable, the rule of the lowest common denominator takes hold, and cheap intel and agents inevitably become the standard.

The Agency knows that DO soft reporting on State Department issues often draws the ire of U.S. diplomats. Foreign Service officers who have access to clandestine-intelligence reports have long known that the CIA is poaching on their terrain. And as any Agency analyst will admit, the State Department and overseas representatives of the U.S. Treasury have generally provided the finest official commentary on politics and economics. Clandestine information from paid agents is by no means inherently superior to information from unpaid sources, as outsiders usually presume. Whether the subject is NATO expansion, democracy in Russia, Toulouse's Airbus versus Seattle's Boeing, the U.S. trade embargo against Iran, or the future course of South Africa, Kazakhstan, or Croatia, it has been diplomats and their contacts—not case officers and their agents—who have usually proved to be the U.S. government's most knowledgeable sources. But State reporting is not, like Agency reporting, appetizingly packaged in bite-size morsels. Diplomatic telegrams do not benefit from the boldly printed, highly classified code words that adorn Agency products. Bureaucratically inept, politically timid, and cash-starved, the State Department has rarely tried to take on Langley—a rich and tough bureaucratic power—for the DO's recruitment antics and shoddy reporting.

When I was in the service, I regularly encountered DO bosses who encouraged their case officers to put information gained from State cover work into CIA intelligence channels. When they couldn't duplicate State sources, case officers tried to borrow or to steal them, thereby putting U.S. diplomats in the awkward position of having to explain to their foreign counterparts why the U.S. government sometimes sends two "diplomats" asking the same questions.

Though case officers deserve most of the blame for debasing American espionage, they could not have done it alone. Analysts in the CIA's Directorate of Intelligence, who are the primary consum-ers and judges of foreign-intelligence reporting, share the responsibility. Like case officers, the analysts generally don't have the necessary languages, academic preparation, or in-country experience in their areas of supposed expertise. Ever since Robert Gates, as deputy director of intelligence, reorganized the Directorate of Intelligence in the early 1980s, it has been rare for an analyst to spend more than a few years working on one country. Promotions, especially promotions to managerial grades, come more quickly to generalists who have covered several areas. Sitting in six-by-six, usually windowless, cubicles, and confronted daily with demands for short-order "finished" intelligence, analysts rarely have the desire to sacrifice their careers by slowly building the skills that give uncommon insight into foreign countries.

TOO MANY SPOOKS— TOO FEW SPIES

Agent scrubbing has not yet advanced an answer to the question that has bedeviled the Directorate of Operations: How do you rank and promote the entire cadre of DO case officers when valuable recruitments are so few in number and so difficult to obtain? The exact number of case officers is classified, but U.S. press reports of approximately 2,000 are not far off the mark. In some U.S. embassies and consulates CIA case officers outnumber diplomats who report on political and economic affairs. The number of developmentals and agents necessary to keep junior and mid-level case officers busy is large: demand creates supply.

An honest discussion of recruitments, intelligence production, and promotions would cast doubt on Agency operations and careers since at least the 1970s. The DO's future, or at least its staffing levels and current management, would also be called into question. And case officers would have to confess to themselves and to Congress that the chances of success in agent recruitment today are even worse than they were in the past.

The much trumpeted challenges of the twenty-first century, unlike those of the Cold War era, are not worldwide struggles that define, galvanize, and divide nations. The Chinese may well become a serious menace, but they are not inspiring or funding radical anti-Western guerrilla movements and political parties in the Third World. China and the rogue states—Iran, Iraq, Libya, Sudan, North Korea—have embassies and consulates worldwide, offering the DO, in theory, numerous targets, but the CIA has had little success in recruiting these countries' diplomats and intelligence officers. With rare exceptions, intelligence coups against rogue states, terrorists, and the Chinese come from volunteers.

Only a handful of people in Paris, Bonn, or New Delhi have, for example, exploitable access to resident Iranian officials and scientists; the odds that a case officer could locate, let alone recruit, an Iranian source are poor. Just meeting an interesting Iranian without the host country's assistance or knowledge is extremely difficult. If the French, the Germans, or the Indians were to become hostile to U.S. espionage operations, CIA case officers would have only a remote chance of doing anything worthwhile. And with the Soviet threat gone, Europeans have become noticeably more hostile to CIA officers operating on European soil. The Western Europeans now regularly exchange information among themselves about the CIA. The French, the Germans, and the Austrians recently fired warning shots by seeking the removal of case officers who failed to understand the new post-Cold War ground rules. National pride and differing national interests (the European Union, for instance, has consistently downplayed Iran's nefarious behavior in order to maintain commercial ties with Iran) have severely restricted Agency operations in Europe and elsewhere.

Current DO operations against America's toughest Middle Eastern foes—Iran and Iraq—have essentially devolved into "cold pitches," in which case officers with little biographical or psychological information on their targets, whom in many cases they have never even met before, "pitch" a clandestine relationship with the CIA in exchange for money. This approach can occasionally work, but it is neither a particularly clever nor a thoughtful way to get foreigners to risk their lives for the United States. When the approach does work, however, such quick hits read well on case-officer performance evaluations.

GLASNOST?

Spying is the second-oldest profession. Irrespective of Langley's incompetence, or American doubts about covert action, spying in some form will continue. The intelligence debate is not about whether we should spy but about how we can spy well. If Washington could find reliable sources of information on Iran's Ministry of Intelligence, local Shi'ite opposition in the oil-rich regions of Saudi Arabia, or Communist China's military general staff, America would be safer for the effort. All these "human intelligence" targets are extraordinarily difficult to reach, but if the DO were an organization with long-range plans and talented personnel, it might have a chance.

No senior officer was fired for the Ames debacle. No one was fired for any of the flaps and fiascoes of the past ten years.

The window of opportunity for reform that was inadvertently opened by the Ames case is now closing. In Washington, where elected and appointed officials remonstrate with the CIA's functionaries but rarely fire them, the DO's senior officers suspect that if they take a few blows, make a few cosmetic reforms, and hang tight, they will outlast their critics. Not a single senior officer was fired for the Ames debacle. No one was fired for any of the strictly operational flaps and fiascoes of the past ten years (case officers dismissed because of the highly politicized Iran-contra and Guatemalan human-rights affairs don't count). Some of the perpetrators have ended up with senior-service promotions and distinguished-intelligence medals.

Reforming the CIA is a herculean task. The unforgiving law of bureau-

cratic rot—first-rate people usually associate with and advance other first-rate people, but second choose third, and third choose fourth—has come brutally into play in the CIA's closed society. First-rate people are now few and far between. How does one reform an institution in which the guiding 10 percent are arguably the institution's most disingenuous, least qualified officials? How does a director of central intelligence who comes from outside the CIA look down from his seventh-floor perch and separate capable people from the incompetent? No outsider, no matter how savvy, can navigate successfully inside the DO without case officers to guide him.

Closed societies are by definition impervious to most forms of outside discipline and oversight, and an espionage service must to a large and unhealthy extent be a closed society. First-rate or third, case officers and agents must be camouflaged and protected.

Outsiders cannot save the Directorate of Operations from itself unless they hold it accountable for all its failures and deficiencies. The junior and mid-level case officers who are considering leaving the organization need to see some sign that outsiders will no longer tolerate sham or bungled operations. At a minimum, the President, the CIA director, and Congress's intelligence-oversight committees must ensure that the Agency's inspector general and counterintelligence investigations are accurate and fair. The inspector general's office has often oscillated between blatant collusion with the DO and anti-DO grandstanding before Congress. And counterintelligence reports by the DO's various staffs and divisions usually fall victim to back-room machinations that keep even useless senior officers relatively unblemished and consistently unpunished.

Though inspector general and counterintelligence reports have rarely been tough on the DO, they have almost always been too tough for senior case officers to swallow. When surprisingly scathing inspector general or counterintelligence investigations do not lead to the dismissal of senior officers guilty of gross incompetence, good officers resign or fall silent.

Firing the old guard will not by itself change the culture of the clandestine

service. As in any bureaucracy, senior functionaries have progeny. Even good case officers inevitably make debilitating compromises if they are working in a bad system. First-rate operatives who know they've collected little truly meaningful intelligence over the years can nevertheless idealize the Directorate of Operations, the myth and methods of clandestine intelligence becoming inseparable from their identities, honor, and family life. Only a complete overhaul of the service that would drastically reduce the number of veteran case officers has a chance of saving the clandestine service. In order to reform U.S. espionage, outsiders must use the only sure leverage they have for safely prying open the clandestine service: DO intelligence reports. The director and the intelligence-oversight committees, or the outside experts they appoint, can review the intelligence production of selected officers, operational desks, staffs, centers, and divisions. Though a case officer may recruit a highly valuable agent who produces no intelligence reporting (for example, a code clerk at a foreign embassy), all non-covert-action recruitments are meant to lead, eventually, to intelligence production. If outside experts compare open-source, classified non-Agency, and DO information on a subject, they can find out whether the DO is lying to itself and others. This will take time and energy, of course.

With a cadre of good case officers as his eyes, ears, and hands, the CIA director might have a chance to overcome the DO's problems. He may discover, however, that the bureaucracy has irretrievably broken down. In that case he, or Congress, should consider what only a few years ago would have been unthinkable: rebuilding the clandestine service from scratch. America's national security would not be compromised by temporarily shutting down the DO. A Directorate of Operations that produces mostly mediocre intelligence and egregiously stupid coup d'état schemes against, for example, Saddam Hussein harms the United States abroad.

If the Agency were truly intent on reform, the Directorate of Operations would abolish most of its diplomat-spy positions and replace them with "non-official cover" officers, who operate outside an embassy or consulate, usually as businessmen or consultants. NOCs are far from the elite of the clandestine service, and typical non-official covers are usually weak and small-scale, given the growing and understandable reluctance of U.S. businesses to provide Langley with any help in this regard. Nonetheless, only NOCs and NOC-directed agent networks can plausibly penetrate terrorist groups, arms-merchants' networks, and scientific associations, institutes, and corporations potentially involved in nuclear, chemical, and biological weapons production. Unlike inside case officers, with their flimsy diplomatic covers, NOCs can quietly enter and exit countries, meet foreigners, and pass through foreign internal-security checks without setting off alarms. Deploying mostly NOCs overseas would also subvert the numbers game. NOCs work without diplomatic immunity: contemplating jail or worse, they would more scrupulously evaluate the intelligence benefits of a prospective espionage operation.

Senior inside officers, who have no intention of superannuating themselves and their protégés, will disparage the value of non-official cover in the DO's future, keeping NOCs an obedient sideshow. NOCs, who are locked into the closed world of the clandestine service more tightly than inside officers are, won't complain. The better NOCs, of course, have already done what most of

their better diplomat-spy colleagues have done: they've resigned or retired.

If there were no entrenched bureaucracy tirelessly challenging reform, rebuilding the clandestine service would be much easier. Bringing in graduates of America's leading colleges and universities and multilingual Americans who have lived abroad—our finest pool of intelligence talent—is not an impossible task. More than any other country, the United States can draw on a multiethnic, polyglot society for its intelligence service. Congress in particular bears special responsibility for guaranteeing the reform of the clandestine service. It alone has the financial authority to force changes inside the DO. After the scandals of the 1970s Congress wisely chose to exercise its right under the 1947 National Security Act to oversee the CIA more closely. Unfortunately, the oversight committees have become more often Langley's sympathetic partners than its demanding judges. Trafficking in executive-branch "secrets" is habit-forming, and congressmen and their staffers aren't immune to the allure and patriotism of being players in America's covert efforts. Especially Republicans, who generally admire the Directorate of Operations for its stealthy, anti-Communist, realpolitik image, should be more parsimonious with their favor. Congress's recent decision to drop the "whistle blower" provision from the 1998 intelligence authorization bill, which would

have protected Agency employees who notify Congress of CIA wrongdoing, was a serious mistake. Capitol Hill needs more and sharper eyes inside the DO, not fewer.

Last July, George Tenet, the newly confirmed CIA director, appointed Jack Downing to be the new head of the clandestine service. A good linguist, an ex-Marine, and a member of the DO's old guard, Downing is described by a case officer who worked with him as "a consensus candidate, entirely acceptable to the DO dons" who run the DO in coordination with the deputy director of operations. In his worldwide "hello" cable to the troops, Downing wrote that the DO was still suffering from serious problems and required continuing reform. His Marine Corps candor is certainly a step in the right direction, but as every case officer who has developed a foreigner knows, words are cheap—particularly when coming from senior DO officers. But Downing deserves the benefit of the doubt. Tenet and Congress's intelligence-oversight committees should ensure, however, that the doubt is reasonable and fleeting.

It would be a shameful irony if America allowed the clandestine service, which once tried so enthusiastically to fight the Cold War, to fall victim to a closed society of its own making. Good case officers, who really have been on the front lines of America's defense, deserve better: the right to be proud, once again, of their dark profession.

American Apartheid? Don't Believe It.

By Abigail Thernstrom And Stephan Thernstrom

Thirty years old and still going strong: that is the remarkable story of the Kerner Commission report, issued on March 1, 1968. The nation was "moving towards two societies, one black, one white—separate and unequal," it declared. In subsequent years its ominous prediction became a civil rights mantra. But while the report is generally viewed as the authoritative word on race relations, in fact it was close to worthless in 1968, and events since have proved just how wrong it was.

The National Advisory Commission on Civil Disorders, as the Kerner Commission was officially known, was created by President Lyndon B. Johnson in the wake of the wave of terrible urban riots that began in 1965. The commission, chaired by Illinois Gov. Otto Kerner, was to explain the racial violence in which almost 300 Americans died (with another 8,000 injured), and to propose a solution. It failed on both counts.

THE USUAL SUSPECT

Not that the riots were easy to explain. The commission fingered what has become the usual suspect, white racism. But not with much conviction, since the phrase appears in the executive summary and nowhere else. In truth, however, the causes of the violence remain obscure to this day.

Detroit was the city hardest hit (2,500 stores destroyed, 43 citizens killed, 7,200 arrested), but preriot Detroit was hardly a vast slum, a tinderbox ready to explode. The auto industry was booming; the black unemployment rate was a minuscule 3.4%; the black home-ownership rate was the highest in the country; and the income of the typical black family was a mere 6% below the white average. In Los Angeles, too, the economy was humming along nicely; indeed, in 1964 the National Urban League had rated L.A. the best city in the country for blacks. In contrast, serious rioting never developed in the South, where life for blacks was unquestionably harder and meaner.

The Kerner Commission warned of inevitable further violence—the consequence of ever-blacker cities ringed by white suburbs. It was a grim but mesmerizing fantasy.

The riots came and went mysteriously. Nevertheless, the commission warned of inevitable further violence—the consequence of ever-blacker cities ringed by white suburbs. That vision of American apartheid was the central prediction of the report: separate lives in separate places, rampant inequality and growing racial hostility.

It was a grim but mesmerizing fantasy. In 1968 only one of the nation's top 20 cities—Washington, D.C.—was majority-black, and the Second Great Migration of southern blacks to the North was already petering out. Thus, in the next two decades, only three more cities (Baltimore, Detroit and New Orleans) became more than 50% black. Later, in the 1980s, the black proportion of the population actually shrank in Chicago, Los Angeles, San Francisco and Washington, D.C., while remaining constant in Houston, San Antonio, San Diego and Seattle. In addition, the list of the nation's largest cities changed over time, and among those that grew most rapidly, most—Phoenix, San Diego, San Jose—had very small black populations.

In fact, Kerner and his colleagues had closed their eyes to two stories. In 1965—three years before the report—immigration law had been radically rewritten, with the result that a flood of Asians and Hispanics soon changed much of the urban landscape. Today, Hispanics outnumber blacks in Los Angeles and five other top-20 cities, while more Asians than blacks live in San Diego, San Francisco and San Jose.

The prediction of black cities and white suburbs was also way off. By 1970 blacks were again on the move—this time away from the cities in which they were allegedly stuck. It was a third "great migration," almost totally ignored in the literature on race, but in fact much more dramatic than that precipitated by World War II.

Between 1970 and 1995, seven million blacks moved to the suburbs—compared with the 4.4 million who had left the South after 1940. In these 2½ decades, as the white suburban population grew 63%, the black suburban population increased three times as fast—by 193%. Today, one-third of all blacks live in suburbia, twice the proportion 25 years ago. These suburbs are generally racially mixed.

The typical neighborhood within our central cities has become more integrated as well—an exceedingly well-kept secret in most discussions of race. "The majority of . . . African-Americans are as segregated now as they were at the height of the civil rights movement in the 1960s," declared Rep. John Lewis (D., Ga.) in 1994. But in fact, by every measure the level of residential segregation is down. In 1964, only one in five white Americans had any black neighbors; today the figure is three out of five. And five out of six blacks now say they have white neighbors. By 1990, the typical black resident of a metropolitan area lived in a census "block group" that was only 60% black.

Residential concentrations 60% black—low by historical standards—may still appear much too segregated. But name a group whose members are randomly distributed across the residential landscape. In Massachusetts, Jews tend to gravitate to Brookline, Armenian-Americans to Fall River, Cambodian-Americans to Lowell, Hispanics to Lawrence and so forth. Surveys find that blacks want to live in "integrated" neighborhoods, but not neighborhoods in which their numbers are proportional to their presence in the American population as a whole, 12.7%. "Integration," the surveys suggest, means roughly half black, a figure not so far from the current average of 60%. Of course, residential tastes are not fixed, and if blacks come to feel more welcome by whites, their definition of an ideal neighborhood may change.

'QUIET RIOTS'

Ten years ago, on the 20th anniversary of the Kerner Commission Report, 14 notable scholars released a volume that spoke of ongoing "quiet riots"—"even more destructive of human life than the violence riots of 20 years ago." Conditions unchanged, perhaps even worse: this has become the mantra of civil rights spokesmen and too many scholars. In a much-cited 1993 book entitled "American Apartheid: Segregation and the Making of the Underclass," authors Douglas S. Massey and Nancy A. Denton claim that "almost every problem defined by the Kerner Commission has become worse." Andrew Hacker's 1992 bestseller, "Two Nations: Black and White, Separate, Hostile, Unequal," was in much the same vein.

Thirty years later, its time to bury the Kerner Commission report. It's had a sad but influential life. How about a new, less gloomy but more realistic message: "Much progress, much still to do."

Ms. Thernstrom and Mr. Thernstrom are the authors of "America in Black and White: One Nation Indivisible" (Simon & Schuster, 1997).

Revolution in Indian Country

After centuries of conflict over their rights and powers, Indian tribes now increasingly make and enforce their own laws, often answerable to no one in the United States government. Is this the rebirth of their ancient independence or a new kind of legalized segregation?

Fergus M. Bordewich

Fergus M. Bordewich's book Killing the White Man's Indian *was published in 1996 by Doubleday. He is also the author of* Cathay: A Journey in Search of Old China.

Micki's Cafe is, in its modest way, a bulwark against the encroachment of modern history and a symbol, amid the declining fortunes of prairie America, of the kind of gritty (and perhaps foolhardy) determination that in more self-confident times used to be called the frontier spirit. To Micki Hutchinson, the problem in the winter of 1991 seemed as plain as the grid of streets that white homesteaders had optimistically laid out in 1910, on the naked South Dakota prairie, to create the town of Isabel in the middle of what they were told was no longer the reservation of the Cheyenne River Sioux Tribe. It was not difficult for Hutchinson to decide what to do when the leaders of the tribal government ordered her to purchase a $250 tribal liquor license: She ignored them.

"They have no right to tell me what to do. I'm not Indian!" Hutchinson told me a year and a half later. She and other

white business people had by then challenged the tribe's right to tax them in both tribal court and federal district court and had lost. The marks of prolonged tension showed on her tanned, angular, wary face. "If this were Indian land, it would make sense. But we're a non-Indian town. This is all homestead land, and the tribe was paid for it. I can't vote in tribal elections or on anything else that happens on the reservation. What they're talking about is taxation without representation."

When I visited, everyone in Isabel still remembered the screech of the warning siren that someone had set off on the morning of March 27, 1991, when the tribal police reached the edge of town, as if their arrival were some kind of natural disaster, like a tornado or fire. The convoy of gold-painted prowl cars rolled in from the prairie and then, when they came abreast of the café, swung sideways across the road. Thirty-eight tribal policemen surrounded the yellow brick building. The tribe's police chief, Marvin LeCompte, told Hutchinson that she was in contempt of tribal court. Officers ordered the morning breakfast crowd away from

their fried eggs and coffee. Then they went back into the pine-paneled bar and confiscated Hutchinson's stock of beer and liquor—"contraband," as LeCompte described it—and drove off with it to the tribal government's offices at Eagle Butte.

A few days before I met Hutchinson, I had interviewed Gregg J. Bourland, the youthful chairman of the Cheyenne River Sioux Tribe. Bourland is widely reckoned to be one of the most effective tribal chairmen in the region and, with a degree in business from the state college in Spearfish, also one of the best educated. "Let them talk about taxation without representation," Bourland told me dismissively. "We're not a state. We're a separate nation, and the only way you can be represented in it is to be a member of the tribe. And they can't do that. They're not Indians. These folks are trespassers. They are within reservation boundaries, and they will follow reservation law. They've now had one hundred years with no tribal authority over them out here. Well, that's over."

More than Micki Hutchinson or than any of the other angry whites in their declining prairie hamlets, it was

Bourland who understood that what was at stake was much more than small-town politics. The tax, the ostentatious convoy, and the lawsuit were part of a much larger political drama that was unfolding across the inland archipelago of reservations that make up modern Indian Country. They symbolized the reshaping of the American West, indeed of the United States itself. By the 1990s, almost unnoticed by the American public or media, a generation of legislation and court actions had profoundly remade Indian Country, canonizing ideas about tribal autonomy that would have shocked the lawmakers who a century before had seen the destruction of the reservations as the salvation of the American Indian. If Bourland was right, Micki Hutchinson and the white residents of Isabel were living in a sovereign tribal state. They were tolerated guests with an uncertain future.

Until the 1870s, reservations were established throughout the Dakota Territory and other parts of the West with the promise that they would be reserved in perpetuity for the Indians' exclusive use. Those promises were broken almost everywhere when reservations were opened to homesteading at the end of the century, usually with only perfunctory consultation with the tribes or none at all. As I listened to Gregg Bourland, it was easy to sympathize with the tribe's striving for some kind of control over forces that were felt to have invaded their land and undermined their culture. Bourland justified the tax as a means both to raise revenue for the tribe and to control alcohol consumption on a reservation where more than 60 percent of the adults were unemployed and 53 percent were active alcoholics.

But promises that had been made a century ago to the ancestors of settlers like Micki Hutchinson were now being broken too. From the 1880s until the 1930s, the cornerstone of federal Indian policy had been the popular program known as allotment, the systematic breaking up of most of the nation's reservations into private holdings. In its day allotment seemed the perfect panacea to resolve at a single stroke the perennial problems of white settlers' insatiable desire for new land and Indi-

ans' growing dependency on the federal government. Sen. Henry L. Dawes, the idealistic architect of the Allotment Act of 1881, which set the pattern for a generation of similar legislation, ringingly proclaimed that as a result of allotment, the Indian "shall be one of us, contributing his share to all that goes to make up the strength and glory of citizenship in the United States."

The means of the Indian's salvation was to be the family farm, which most people of the time had been taught to regard as the ultimate repository of American individualism and the democratic spirit. Each Indian allottee would receive 160 acres of land and eventual United States citizenship, along with money for seed, tools, and livestock. The "excess," or leftover, land would be offered for sale to white settlers, who would be free to form their own municipal governments. The promise of the allotment policy was twofold: that the nation would integrate Indians into white society and that non-Indian settlers would never be subject to tribal regimes.

At the time, the Commissioner of Indian Affairs dismissed notions of separate Indian nationality as mere sentimentality: "It is perfectly clear to my mind that the treaties never contemplated the un-American and absurd idea of a separate nationality in our midst, with power as they may choose to organize a government of their own." To maintain such a view, the commissioner added, was to acknowledge a foreign sovereignty upon American soil, "a theory utterly repugnant to the spirit and genius of our laws, and wholly unwarranted by the Constitution of the United States."

As I left Isabel, I wondered who really was the victim here and who the victimizer. Behind that nagging question lurked still more difficult ones that occupied me for many months, from one end of the United States to the other, in the course of researching what was to become *Killing the White Man's Indian,* an investigation into the political and cultural transformation of modern Indian Country. Are Native Americans so fundamentally different from other Americans that they occupy a special category to which con-

ventional American values and laws should not apply? Or are they simply one more American group, whose special pleading is further evidence that the United States has become a balkanized tangle of ghettos and ethnic enclaves? Do we discriminate against Indians by failing to blend them more effectively into the national mainstream? Or is the very notion of "mainstreaming" Indians so inherently racist that it should not even be contemplated as a component of national policy? Are Indian reservations and the way of life they preserve a precious national resource that must be maintained without the taint of contact with white America? Or is tribal self-determination creating a new form of segregation that merely freezes decayed tribal cultures like ghettoized versions of Colonial Williamsburg? Who, ultimately, are Indians in the 1990s? What are they to other Americans, and the others to them?

Killing the White Man's Indian represented a return to familiar country. As a youth in the 1950s and early 1960s, I often accompanied my mother, who was the executive director of the Association on American Indian Affairs, in her travels around reservations, part of her tireless effort to prod the federal government into improving tribal economies, education, health care, and law and order. Vivid experiences were plentiful: participating in a nightlong peyote rite in a tepee on the Montana prairie; a journey by pirogue deep into the Louisiana bayous to meet with a forgotten band of Houmas who wanted Washington to take notice of their existence; walking the Little Bighorn Battlefield with an aged Cheyenne who, as a small boy, had witnessed the annihilation of Custer's command. Poverty shaded almost every experience. Staying with friends often meant wind fingering its way through gaps in the walls, a cheese and bologna sandwich for dinner, sleeping three or four in a bed with broken springs. It seemed there was always someone talking about an uncle who, drunk, had frozen to death on a lonely road or about a cousin already pregnant at sixteen. More generally those years left me with a sense of the tremendous diversity of the lives and communities that lay submerged within the catchall label of "Indians" and a recognition that Native Americans were not mere vestiges of a mythic past but modern men and women struggling to solve twentieth-century problems.

In the course of four years' research on my book, I visited reservations from upstate New York to southern California and from Mississippi to Washington State, meeting with tribal leaders, ranchers, farmers, educators, and hundreds of ordinary men and women, both Indian and white. In Michigan I sailed Lake Superior with waterborne Chippewa police, searching for poachers on tribal fisheries in the lake. In Oregon I hiked the Cascades with professional foresters from the Warm Springs Tribe, which with its several hydroelectric dams and thriving timber industry is one of Indian Country's great success stories. I sweated with a group of recovering Navajo alcoholics in a traditional sweat lodge in the New Mexico desert. I also spent many a night in dust-blown reservation towns where, as an old South Dakota song puts it, "There's nothing much to do except walk up and down." In a few places, as a result of childhood connections, I was welcomed as a friend. More frequently I met with suspicion rooted in the widespread belief that curiosity like mine was just a form of exploitation and that whites are incapable of writing about Indians with objectivity and honesty.

My original intention had been to use the lives of several men and women whom I had known in the 1950s as a microcosm and through them to chart the changes that had been wrought in Indian Country during the intervening years. But I soon realized that such a focus would be far too narrow, for it had become clear to me that a virtual revolution was under way that was challenging the worn-out theology of Indians as losers and victims and was transforming tribes into powers to be reckoned with for years to come. It encompassed virtually every aspect of Indian life, from the revival of moribund tribal cultures and traditional religions to the development of aggressive tribal governments determined to remake the relationship between tribes and the United States.

The ferment was not unalloyed, however. Alongside inspired idealism, I also found ethnic chauvinism, a crippling instinct to mistake isolation for independence, and a habit of interpreting present-day reality through the warping lens of the past.

In the 1970s, in a reversal of long-standing policies based on the conviction that Indians must be either persuaded or compelled to integrate themselves into mainstream America, the United States enshrined the concept of tribal sovereignty at the center of its policy toward the nation's more than three hundred tribes. In the watershed words of Richard Nixon, federal policy would henceforth be guided "by Indian acts and Indian decisions" and would be designed to "assure the Indian that he can assume control of his own life without being separated from the tribal group."

In 1975 the Indian Self-Determination and Education Assistance Act amplified this principle, calling for a "transition from Federal domination of programs for and services to Indians to effective and meaningful participation by the Indian people." This has been reflected in a national commitment to the strengthening of tribal governments and to more comprehensive tribal authority over reservation lands. More ambiguously, it has also led to the increasing development of a new sphere of political power that rivals, or at least claims to rival, that of the states and the national government and for which there is no foundation in the Constitution. In the mid-1990s I found tribal officials invoking "sovereign right" in debates over everything from highway maintenance and fishing quotas to law and order, toxic-waste disposal, and the transfer of federal services to tribal administrations, not to mention the rapid proliferation of tribally run gambling operations. Reflecting the sentiments of many tribal leaders, Tim Giago, the publisher of *Indian Country Today,* the most widely read Indian newspaper in the United States, likened state legislation that affects Indians to "letting France make laws that also become law in Italy."

To people like Micki Hutchinson, it often seemed that Indians were playing an entirely new game, and that no one but the Indians understood the rules. In Connecticut, and elsewhere, tribes were exploiting a principle of sovereignty unknown to the average American in order to build casinos that sucked colossal sums of money from neighboring regions. New Mexicans found that they were equally helpless in the face of the Mescalero Apaches' determination to establish a nuclear-waste facility on their reservation outside Alamogordo. In Wisconsin and in Washington State, recurrent violence had accompanied the judicially mandated enlargement of Indian fishing rights in accordance with nineteenth-century treaties. In Nevada farmers found themselves on the brink of failure as the Paiutes of Pyramid Lake gained political leverage over the watershed of the Truckee River.

In some states Indian demands for the return of sacred lands posed significant threats to local economies, including, most prominently, the Black Hills region of South Dakota. Nor was science exempt. Tribal claims on ancestral bones and artifacts were depleting many of the most valuable anthropological collections in the country.

Strangely enough, these conflicts—widespread, often bitter, and with profound ramifications for American institutions—seemed to be happening beyond the ken of most Americans, for whom Indians largely remain a people of myth and fantasy. Like no other inhabitants of the United States, Indians have nourished our imagination, weaving in us a complex skein of guilt, envy, and contempt; yet when we imagine we see "the Indian," we often see little more than the distorted reflection of our own fears, fancies, and unhappy longings. This was vividly brought home to me on a visit to the reservation of the two-hundred-member Campo Band of Mission Indians, in the arid hills an hour's drive east of San Diego. This reservation landscape is a profoundly discouraging one. It offers nothing to comfort the eye, produces nothing of value, and provides almost nothing to sustain life as it is enjoyed by most Americans today. The single resource that the Campos possess is wasteland. In 1987 the band learned that the city of San Diego had named the reservation as one of several potential dump sites for the city's refuse.

"We just need this one little thing to get us started," the band's chairman, Ralph Goff, told me as we walked through the redshank and yucca and ocher sand where the first trenches had been cut for the new landfill. "With it we can create our own destiny." Goff, a formidably built man with little formal education, grew up in the 1940s, when the only work available was as a cowhand or day laborer for whites. When there was no work, people went hungry. "You just had to wait until there was some more food." In the 1960s most of the unskilled jobs disappeared, and nearly every Campo family went on welfare. "We needed it, but it really wrecked us as people. It created idleness. People didn't have to do anything in order to get money."

If the Campos have their way, by the end of the decade daily freight trains will be carrying loads of municipal waste to a three-hundred-acre site on a hilltop at the southern end of the reservation. For the privilege of leasing the band's land, a waste-management firm will pay the Campos between two and five million dollars a year. Goff argued that the dump would put an end to the band's dependence on federal largess. It would create jobs for every adult Campo who is willing to work, provide long-term investment capital for the band, supply money for full college scholarships for every school-age member of the band, and finance new homes for the families that now live in substandard housing. The dump would, in short, give the Campos financial independence for the first time in their modern history.

The landfill would be one of the most technically advanced in the United States; to regulate it, the Campos enacted an environmental code more stringent than the State of California's. Nevertheless, the dump generated fierce opposition in towns near the reservation, where thousands of non-Indians live. Geologists hired by the dump's opponents have suggested, but not proved, that seepage from the dump might contaminate the water supply of ranches beyond the reservation bound-

ary. Environmentalists accused the band of irresponsibility toward the earth and charged that the Campos had been targeted in an "assault" on reservations by "renegade" waste-dumping companies. A bill was even introduced in the California legislature that would have made it a crime to deliver waste to the Campo landfill. Goff shrugged away the protests. "It's a sovereignty issue. It's our land, and we'll do what we want to with it."

"How can you say that the economic development of two hundred people is more important than the health and welfare of all the people in the surrounding area?" an angry and frustrated rancher, whose land lay just off the reservation, asked me. "It's hard making a living here. The fissures will carry that stuff right through here. We'll have all that stuff in our water and blowing down on us off the hills. If our water is spoiled, then everything's spoiled."

There were predictable elements to her rage: the instinctive resistance of most Americans to any kind of waste dump anywhere near their homes and the distress of many white Americans when they realize the implications of tribal sovereignty for the first time and find themselves subject to the will of a government in which they have no say. But there was something more, a sort of moral perplexity at Indians' having failed to behave according to expectation, an imputation that they were guilty of self-interest. Revealingly, I thought, on the wall of the rancher's trailer there was a poster decorated with Indian motifs. Entitled "Chief Seattle Speaks," it began, in words that are becoming as familiar to American schoolchildren as those of the Gettysburg Address once were: "How can you buy or sell the sky, the warmth of the land?" Here, in sight of the dump, the so-called testament of Chief Seattle was a reproach to the Campos, an argument rooted in what the rancher presumably believed to be Indians' profoundest values. "Before all this I had this ideal about Indian people and all they've been through," she told me. "I used to think they had this special feeling about the land."

More than any other single document, Seattle's twelve-hundred-word "testament" lends support to the increas-

ingly common belief that to "real" Indians any disruption or commercialization of the earth's natural order is a kind of sacrilege and that the most moral, the most truly "Indian" relationship with the land is a kind of poetic passivity. Having been translated into dozens of languages and widely reproduced in school texts, the "testament" has attained a prophetic stature among environmentalists: In 1993 Greenpeace used it as the introduction to a scarifying report on toxic dumping, calling it "the most beautiful and profound statement on the environment ever made." Unfortunately, like much literature that purports to reveal the real nature of the Indians, the "testament" is basically a fiction. Seattle was indeed a historical figure, a slave-owning chief of the Duwamishes who sold land to the United States in the mid-1850s and welcomed the protection of the federal government against his local enemies. However, the "testament," as it is known to most Americans, was created from notes allegedly made thirty years after the fact by a white doctor who claimed to have been present when Seattle spoke, and which then were extravagantly embroidered by a well-meaning Texas scriptwriter by the name of Ted Perry as narration for a 1972 film on the environment, produced by the Southern Baptist Radio and Television Commission. How is it, I wondered, that Americans have so readily embraced such a spurious text, not only as a sacred screed of the ecology movement but also as a central document of "traditional" Native American culture?

Increasingly it became clear to me that to be able to describe the realities of modern Indian life and politics, I would have to strip away the myths that whites have spun around Native Americans ever since Columbus arbitrarily divided the peoples he encountered into noble Arawaks and savage Caribs, conflating European fantasies with presumed native reality and initiating a tradition that would eventually include Montesquieu, Locke, Hobbes, and Rousseau, as well as a vivid popular literature stretching from *The Last of the Mohicans* to *Dances With Wolves*. Untamable savage, child of nature, steward of the earth, the white man's ultimate victim:

each age has imagined its own mythic version of what the historian Robert F. Berkhofer, Jr., termed the "white man's Indian."

Typically the Denver *Post* could declare, not long ago, in an editorial attacking the University of Arizona for a plan to build an observatory atop an allegedly sacred mountain: "At stake is the very survival of American Indian cultures. If these sacred places are destroyed, then the rituals unique to those places no longer will be performed and many tribes simply may cease to exist as distinct peoples." Such logic implies both that only Native Americans who profess to live like pre-Columbians are true Indians and that Indians are essentially hopeless and helpless and on the brink of extinction. Apparently it never occurred to the paper's editorialist that the religion of the great majority of Indians is not in fact some mystical form of traditionalism but a thriving Christianity.

In keeping with our essentially mythic approach to the history of Indians and whites, Americans were generally taught until a generation or so ago to view their national story as a soaring arc of unbroken successes, in which the defeat of the Indians reflected the inevitable and indeed spiritual triumph of civilization over barbarism. More recently, but not so differently, numerous revisionist works like Kirkpatrick Sale's *The Conquest of Paradise: Christopher Columbus and the Columbian Legacy* and Richard Drinnon's *Facing West: The Metaphysics of Indian-Hating and Empire Building* have tended to portray the settlement of North America as a prolonged story of unredeemed tragedy and failure, in which the destruction of the Indians stands as proof of a fundamental ruthlessness at the heart of American civilization. Such beliefs have steadily percolated into the wider culture—to be embodied in New Age Westerns like *Dances With Wolves* and popular books like the best-selling *Indian Givers: How the Indians of the Americas Transformed the World,* which purports to show how practically every aspect of modern life from potatoes to democracy derives

from the generosity of American Indians—and into the consciences of journalists, clergy, and others who shape public opinion.

On the whole the complex and intricate relationship between whites and Indians has been presented as one of irreconcilable conflict between conqueror and victim, corruption and innocence, Euro-American "materialism" and native "spirituality." The real story, of course, is an often contradictory one, disfigured by periods of harsh discrimination and occasional acts of genocide but also marked by considerable Indian pragmatism and adaptability as well as by the persistent, if sometimes shortsighted, idealism of whites determined to protect Indians from annihilation and find some place for them in mainstream America.

For instance, in contradiction of the notion that Indians were innocent of even the most elementary business sense, it was clear during negotiations over the Black Hills in the 1870s that Sioux leaders had a perfectly good grasp of finance and that indeed they were determined to drive the best bargain they could. "The Black Hills are the house of Gold for our Indians," Chief Little Bear said at the time. "If a man owns anything, of course he wants to make something out of it to get rich on." Another chief, Spotted Tail, added: "I want to live on the interest of my money. The amount must be so large as to support us." Similarly, in contrast with the popular belief that the United States government was committed to a policy of exterminating the Indian (no such policy ever existed, in fact), Senator Dawes publicly described the history of Indians in the United States as one "of spoliation, of wars, and of humiliation," and he firmly stated that the Indian should be treated "as an individual, and not as an insoluble substance that the civilization of this country has been unable, hitherto, to digest."

Indeed, the impulse behind the allotment of tribal lands and the national commitment to Indians was dramatically (and, with the benefit of hindsight, poignantly) acted out in a rite of citizenship that after 1887 was staged at Timber Lake, in the heart of the Cheyenne

River Sioux country, and at many other places in the freshly allotted lands of other tribes. In the presence of representatives of the federal government, new allottees stood resplendent in the feathers and buckskins of a bygone age. One by one, each man stepped out of a tepee and shot an arrow to symbolize the life he was leaving behind. He then put his hands on a plow and accepted a purse that indicated that he was to save what he earned. Finally, holding the American flag, the Indian repeated these words: "Forasmuch as the President has said that I am worthy to be a citizen of the United States, I now promise this flag that I will give my hands, my head, and my heart to the doing of all that will make me a true American citizen." It was the culminating, transformative moment of which Senator Dawes had dreamed.

It is true enough, however, that, as so often in Indian history, reality failed to live up to good intentions. Unscrupulous speculators soon infested the allotted reservations, offering worthless securities and credit in return for land. Within a few years it was found that of those who had received patents to their land at Cheyenne River, 95 percent had sold or mortgaged their properties. When the Allotment Act was passed in 1881, there were 155 million acres of Indian land in the United States. By the time allotment was finally brought to a halt in 1934, Indian Country had shrunk by nearly 70 percent to 48 million acres, and two-thirds of Indians either were completely landless or did not have enough land left to make a living from it. In the mid-1990s Indian Country as a whole is still a daunting and impoverished landscape whose inhabitants are twice as likely as other Americans to be murdered or commit suicide, three times as likely to die in an automobile accident, and five times as likely to die from cirrhosis of the liver. On some reservations unemployment surpasses 80 percent, and 50 percent of young Indians drop out of high school, despite progressively increased access to education.

Is the tribal-sovereignty movement a panacea for otherwise intractable social problems? In the cultural sphere, at least, its importance cannot be underestimated. "Our people live in a limbo culture that is not quite Indian and not quite white either," said Dennis Hastings, surrounded by books, gazing out toward the Iowa plains through the window of the sky blue trailer where he lives in a cow pasture. Hastings, a burly former Marine and the tribal historian of the Omaha Nation, which is in northeastern Nebraska, has almost single-handedly led an effort to recover tribal history as a foundation for community renewal that is probably unmatched by any other small tribe in the United States. "It's like living in a house without a foundation. You can't go back to the old buffalo days, stop speaking English and just use our own language, and ignore whites and everything in white culture. If we did that, we'd become stuck in history, become dinosaurs."

Teasing small grants and the help of volunteer scholars from institutions around the country, Hastings has initiated an oral-history project to collect memories of fading tribal traditions. "We go into each family, get an anthropologist to record everything right from how you wake up in the morning," he said. Hundreds of historic photographs of early reservation life have been collected and deposited with the State Historical Society, in Lincoln. A friendly scholar from the University of Indiana recovered a trove of forgotten Omaha songs recorded in the 1920s on wax cylinders. Another at the University of New Mexico undertook a collective genealogy that would trace the lineage of more than five thousand Omahas back to the eighteenth century. Hastings explained, "Until now everything was oral. Some people knew the names of their ancestors, and some knew nothing at all. There was a loss of connection with the past. Now people can come back and find out who their ancestors were." In sharp contrast with the combative chauvinism of some tribes, the Omahas invited scientists from the University of Nebraska and the Smithsonian Institution to examine repatriated skeletons to see what they could discover about the lives of their ancestors. In 1989, astonishing perhaps even themselves, tribal leaders brought home Waxthe'xe, the True Omaha, the sacred cottonwood

pole that is the living embodiment of the Omaha people, which had lain for a hundred years in Harvard's Peabody Museum; at the July powwow that year, weeping hundreds bent to touch it as if it were the true cross or the ark of the covenant.

"We want the benefits of modern society," Hastings told me in his nasal Midwestern drawl. "But America is still dangerous for us. The question is then, How do we take the science that America used against us and make it work for us? The answer is, we try to build on the past. It's like a puzzle. First you see where the culture broke and fragmented. Then you try to build on it where people have been practicing it all along. Then people start to think in a healthy way about what they were in the past. If you can get each person to be proud of himself, little by little, you can get the whole tribe to become proud. We're going to dream big and be consistent with that dream."

In its broadest sense the tribal sovereignty movement is demonstrating that the more than three hundred Indian tribes in the lower forty-eight states (more than five hundred if you count Alaskan native groups) are distinct communities, each with its unique history, traditions, and political environment, for whom a single one-size-fits-all federal policy will no longer suffice. Greater autonomy will surely enable well-governed and economically self-sufficient tribes—mostly those located near big cities and those with valuable natural resources—to manage their own development in imaginative ways. For many others, however, far from airports and interstate highways, populated by ill-trained workers and governed, in some cases, by politicians who do not abide by the most basic democratic rules, the future is much less assured.

There is nothing abstract about such concerns in Timber Lake, South Dakota, which lies a short drive east from Isabel across the rolling plains of the Cheyenne River Sioux Reservation. Like Isabel, Timber Lake has been battered by the general decline of a region that is hemorrhaging jobs and people. Timber Lake is one of the rela-

tively lucky places, kept alive by the presence of the Dewey County offices, the rural electric co-op, the central school, and a cheese factory. Even so, one hundred of the six hundred people who lived there a decade ago have moved away to places with better prospects and more hope. Isabel's population has dropped by half, to three hundred. Trail City has shrunk from three hundred and fifty to thirty, Firesteel to a single general store, and Landeau has disappeared completely. Entire towns have lost their doctors, banks, and schools. From a certain angle of vision, Sioux demands for the restoration of the reservation to its original nineteenth-century limits are simply an anticlimax.

The people of Timber Lake—the mechanics, the teachers, the co-op clerks, the men who work at the grain elevator, the retired farmers—are the human fruit of allotment, the flesh-and-blood culmination of the cultural blending that Senator Dawes envisioned. "Everyone here has relatives who are Indian," said Steve Aberle, a local attorney whose Russian-German father married into the Ducheneaux, a prominent clan of Cheyenne River Sioux. Aberle, who is thirty-five, is one-eighth Sioux; he is a voting member of the tribe and served for two and a half years as chairman of the tribal police commission. Nevertheless he shares the uneasiness of non-Indians who feel themselves slipping toward a kind of second-class citizenship within the reservation's boundaries. "It would be better to be in a situation where everybody works together and deals with people as people, but it's hard to do that when people know they pay taxes but are excluded from benefits and services," Aberle told me. "When my grandparents came from Russia, the United States government told them that they would be full citizens if they moved out here. Now I see people being told that they can't even take part in a government that wants to regulate them. Something is inherently wrong when you can't be a citizen where you live because of your race. It just doesn't fit with the traditional notion of being a U.S. citizen. At some point there has to be a collision between the notion of tribal sovereignty and the notion of being United States citizens. Anytime you have a group not represented in the political process they will be discriminated against. There's going to be more and more friction. It's going to hurt these communities. People start looking for jobs elsewhere."

The Sioux were the victims of nineteenth-century social engineering that decimated their reservation. But the descendants of the adventurous emigrants who settled the land are also the victims of an unexpected historical prank, the trick of the disappearing and now magically reappearing reservation. Reasonably enough, the rhetoric of tribal sovereignty asks for tribes a degree of self-government that is taken for granted by other Americans. However, the achievement of a sovereignty that drives away taxpayers, consumers, and enterprise may be at best but a Pyrrhic victory over withered communities that beg for cooperation and innovation to survive at all.

With little debate outside the parochial circles of Indian affairs, a generation of policymaking has jettisoned the long-standing American ideal of racial unity as a positive good and replaced it with a doctrine that, seen from a more critical angle, seems disturbingly like an idealized form of segregation, a fact apparently invisible to a nation that has become accustomed to looking at Indians only through the twin lenses of romance and guilt and in an era that has made a secular religion of passionate ethnicity. Much of the thinking that underlies tribal sovereignty seems to presuppose that cultural purity can and ought to be preserved, as if Indian bloodlines, economies, and histories were not already inextricably enmeshed with those of white, Hispanic, and black Americans.

Such concerns will be further exacerbated in the years to come as Indian identity grows increasingly ambiguous. Virtually all Indians are moving along a continuum of biological fusion with other American populations. "A point will be reached . . . when it will no longer make sense to define American Indians in generic terms [but] only as tribal members or as people of Indian ancestry or ethnicity," writes Russell Thornton, a Cherokee anthropologist and demographer at the University of Southern California, in *American Indian Holocaust and Survival,* a study of fluctuations in native populations. Statistically, according to Thornton, Indians are marrying outside their ethnic group at a faster rate than any other Americans. More than 50 percent of Indians are already married to non-Indians, and Congress has estimated that by the year 2080 less than 8 percent of Native Americans will have one-half or more Indian blood.

How much ethnic blending can occur before Indians finally cease to be Indians? The question is sure to loom ever larger for coming generations, as the United States increasingly finds itself in "government-to-government" relationships with tribes that are becoming less "Indian" by the decade. Within two or three generations the nation will possess hundreds of "tribes" that may consist of the great-great-grandchildren of Indians but whose native heritage consists mainly of autonomous governments and special privileges that are denied to other Americans.

Insofar as there is a political solution to the Indian future, I have come to believe that it lies in the rejection of policies that lead to segregation and in acknowledgment of the fact that the racially and ethnically variegated peoples whom we call "Indian" share not only common blood but also a common history and a common future with other Americans. The past generation has seen the development of a national consensus on a number of aspects of the nation's history that were long obscured by racism or shame; there is, for instance, little dispute today among Americans of any ethnic background over the meaning of slavery or of the internment of Japanese-Americans during the Second World War. There is as yet no such consensus, however, with respect to the shared history of Indians and whites, who both still tend to see the past as a collision of irreconcilable opposites and competing martyrdoms.

That history was not only one of wars, removals, and death but also one of calculated compromises, mutual accommodation, and deliberately chosen risks, a story of Indian communities and individuals continually remaking themselves in order to survive. To see change as failure, as some kind of cultural corruption, is to condemn Indians to solitary confinement in a prison of myth that whites invented for them in the first place. Self-determination gives Indian tribes the ability to manage the speed and style of integration but not the power to stop it, at least for long. Integration may well mean the eventual diminishing of conventional notions of "tribal identity," but it must also bring many new individual opportunities, along with membership in the larger human community. "People and their cultures perish in isolation, but they are born or reborn in contact with other men and women, with man and woman of another culture, another creed, another race," the Mexican novelist Carlos Fuentes has written. Tribes will survive, if anything, as stronger entities than they have been for many generations. The question is whether they will attempt to survive as isolated islands or as vital communities that recognize a commonality of interest and destiny with other Americans.

America After the Long War

"Nothing is inevitable in politics, but there is evidence that the domestic order forged by the cold war is coming apart, ushering in a period of political disarray and posing daunting new challenges for parties and presidents. This decay and the tasks it implies will increasingly define the fault lines in American politics."

Daniel Deudney and G. John Ikenberry

Daniel Deudney is an assistant professor of social sciences at the University of Pennsylvania and author of the forthcoming book, Pax Atomica: Planetary Geopolitics and Republicanism.

G. John Ikenberry is an associate professor of political science at the University of Pennsylvania and author of After Victory: Power, Social Purpose, and the Recreation of Order After Major War.

There is universal recognition that the end of the cold war marks the close of one era and the beginning of another. The collapse of the Soviet threat promises both improved global security and a hefty worldwide peace dividend. American politics without the cold war, however, may not be so benign—the end of the East-West conflict holds deeper implications for the American polity than has been recognized.

Despite the widespread expectation that relations between the Western democracies would be disrupted with the end of the cold war, it is the case that relations within those democracies have been more profoundly disturbed. At the moment of victory of Western institutions over their rivals, Western polities are disioriented and dispirited, and Western leaders have unprecedentedly low approval ratings. While the domestic disarray in the West does not begin to approach that in the former Yugoslavia and Soviet Union, it is surprising and reveals a darker legacy of the cold war era.

The aftershocks of the cold war's end have been slower to register in the United States than in front-line countries, but the effects are already visible and growing. The war's end weighed heavily in the reelection bid of George Bush, the quintessential cold war president whose foreign policy accomplishments could not prevent a precipitous drop in popularity from an unprecedented high to electoral defeat in less than a year. Domestic political coalitions have begun to unravel, seen most dramatically in the strongest third party presidential showing since 1912 in the 1992 presidential election. The dramatic Republican capture of both houses of Congress in the 1994 midterm elections underscores the volatility of post–cold war American politics. Public support for American involvement in the world is waning—particularly in areas of foreign aid, military involvement, and United Nations support. Unlike the Soviet threat, which stimulated national unity, the emerging politics of global trade and finance pit region against region, and class against class.

The diplomatic historian John Lewis Gaddis has dubbed the cold war era "the long peace": the lengthiest period of general peace in Europe in modern times. But from the American public's standpoint, it has been "the long war." Since the late 1930s, the United States has sustained a nearly continuous military mobilization for global war, an effort that has profoundly shaped and changed the country. In the flush of triumph and optimism, it is easy to overlook the key historical fact that the great half-century struggle with fascism and communism made it easier—perhaps even possible—to cope with a wide array of domestic problems. Mobilization during the long war set a new mold for relations between the state and society, between the institutions of government, and between the parties, and it reshaped the national identity.

Foreign struggle had great domestic benefits for the United States. Mobilization for global conflict required a "social bargain" that effectively modernized and democratized American institutions. It is easy to forget that before World War II, the American political system had reached an impasse in responding to the demands of industrialization and state building. The permanency and pervasiveness of international conflict, beginning in the 1940s, required and enabled the United States to build a strong modern state, manage an industrial economy, reduce social inequalities, and foster national cohesion. It was the fascist and communist challenges from abroad that stimulated the progressive development of American capitalism.

The cold war's end forces us to ask a fundamental question about the future of American politics: can the accidental social bargain be sustained in the absence of a global external challenge?

The end of the cold war threatens to unravel these accomplishments and return the United States to the impasses of the 1920s and 1930s. If modernization and democratization were accidental side effects of this struggle, then it may be beyond the capacity of the American polity to sustain this institutional legacy. As the social bargain unravels, it will have to be rewoven. The tasks ahead are not simply manipulation of the budget, but reconstitution of the underlying domestic consensus on an activist state, social welfare provisions, and the political bases of national identity. This reweaving will be inextricably connected to the redefi-

nition and reordering of the parties and the presidency. The future holds not a return to mythical or halcyon normalcy, but rather a potentially divisive struggle over the basic principles of the American political and economic order.

PREWAR DOMESTIC DILEMMAS

To understand the domestic impact of the cold war, it is necessary to recall the underlying trajectories and dilemmas of American political development before permanent global engagement. Since the middle of the nineteenth century, American institutions, like those in other major countries such as Germany, Japan, and Russia, have had to cope with and adapt to the manifold imperatives of spreading industrialization. Industrialization brought with it capitalist cycles of boom and bust, which generated demands for elaborate and powerful mechanisms for state intervention and management of the economy. In addition, the emergence of a mass urban working class produced the "social problem" and the attendant need for a social "safety net" of labor laws, unemployment insurance, retirement income, and welfare provisions. Finally industrial societies tended to become much more occupationally and socially stratified while at the same time more densely linked and integrated, thus generating the need for new forms of national identity and cohesion.

In the United States, efforts to cope with these dilemmas ran against the grain of the American system. America was better equipped to deal with these problems than countries with feudal social and autocratic political systems—such as Germany, Russia, and Japan, where violent revolution ensued. But the twin pillars of the American political system—individualism and limited government—imposed formidable political constraints. In the late nineteenth and early twentieth centuries, the populist and progressive reform movements met with only modest success in mobilizing sufficient political power to restructure American institutions.

In the decade immediately before World War II, however, the United States

was mired in economic collapse and political impasse. Although the populist-progressive coalition had a working majority entrenched opposition to modern state building had blocked important institutional change. By the mid-1930s, when the first New Deal programs had lost momentum, America suffered from chronic economic stagnation, class warfare, and political disarray. Despite the magnitude of the problems and the breadth of the awareness that change was necessary the decentralized American political system hindered the mobilization of necessary political power to restructure core American social, political, and economic institutions. Without external pressures, these features of the American regime impeded the emergence of a modern state and the realization of progressive social goals set in the industrial era.

THE COLD WAR ORDER

The domestic political order of the United States has been profoundly altered by a half century of global engagement. Beginning with rearmament in anticipation of World War II, intensifying during the struggle with the Axis powers, and routinized with the four decades of cold war, American political development took a new direction. America's rise to global engagement required major institutional innovation that broke through the impasse of political development and accomplished much of the progressive agenda. Fifty years of global engagement produced changes in four domestic areas: the strength of the state, economic management, social equity and welfare, and national identity. The United States, in effect, reaped the benefits of such change without mobilizing a national political consensus for domestic modernization. The long war forged a social bargain, but it was an accidental one.

War and state building have been intimately connected throughout history, and the United States is no exception. From the Declaration of Independence to the beginning of World War II, war played a crucial role in the expansion of central state power. The need for a sufficiently strong central government to fend off European economic and military predations was a decisive factor in the ratification of the Constitution. During the Civil War the strength of the central government grew with the establishment of the federal banking system, conscription, direct taxation of individuals, the transcontinental railroad, and the Homestead Act; the war also saw the strengthening of the presidency within the national government. The demands of War World I led to further expansion of the powers and resources of the central government. In each case, the return to prewar normalcy was marked by the partial dismantlement of war-born institutions and powers—but much remained.

In the twentieth century America's struggle to maintain a global balance of power greatly altered the domestic balance of power. The demands of war enhanced the power and prestige of the central government at the expense of the states. Within the federal government, the power of the executive grew at the expense of the judicial and legislative branches. As leader of the free world and sole commander-in-chief of nuclear forces with global reach, the American presidency gained an almost monarchical aura.

Permanent global engagement also generated requirements for centralized economic management. In the conditions of total war, it was politically possible for the federal government to effectively manage labor and capital in pursuit of maximum economic output. As war raged abroad, the fear of class struggles at home gave way to an administered peace. After World War II, the actual system of wage and price controls was ended, but the techniques of Keynesian macroeconomic management and a commitment to federal responsibility for full employment were maintained. During the postwar struggle, direct federal involvement tended to concentrate in key technological sectors. In the cases of atomic energy, aeronautics, and space, the federal government called whole industries into existence and dramatically quickened the pace of innovation. During the 1950s, measures such as the expansion of the federal highway system and the science and education system were justified as national defense measures.

The cold war's impact on equity, class, and social welfare was equally significant, if less direct. The expansion of the defense budget and related manpower requirements led to programs and institutions that advanced social equity and mobility. Veterans' benefits, especially the G.I. Bill, opened the door to the middle class for millions of Americans. The post-Sputnik commitment to improve education further broadened social opportunity. Moreover, the initial success of radical integration in the armed services gave impetus to racial integration in American society.

American sensitivity to social and class issues was heightened by the distinctive nature of the Soviet Union and communism. Unlike the Japanese and German threats, the communist challenge contained an ideological commitment to build a "workers' paradise" as well as a great power military threat. In this context, especially in the 1950s and 1960s, the performance of American capitalism in meeting social goals such as full employment, health care, and adequate housing had international ideological importance. At the same time, the communist threat delegitimized radical programs and comprehensive agendas for change. Ironically, the struggle with Soviet communism aided American capitalism in overcoming many of the flaws and instabilities present in the 1930s.

Finally, the mobilization of the American polity to a semipermanent war footing strengthened American national identity. This unifying threat helped overcome the extreme centrifugal tendencies of American society rooted in ethnic and sectional differences and the ideological heritage of individualism. The long war was especially important in integrating the South and the West into the national economy and society. Moreover, the fact that the United States was the leader of the "free world" and advancing itself as a model for people elsewhere infused American citizens and leaders with a sense of high purpose and responsibility with domestic as well as international consequences.

The net result of this half century of global struggle was the forging of a social bargain that met many progressive goals but did not depend on the establishment of a domestic progressive consensus. The cold war was neither always necessary nor always strongly felt. The effect of this competition was greatest between the late-1930s and the mid-1960s, and had already begun to wane in subsequent decades. Domestic constituencies for progressive change existed, but the cold war gave them a decisive boost. Because of this conflict, American institutions are more modern—more centralized, more democratic, and more cohesive.

THE DEMISE OF ORDER?

The cold war's end forces us to ask a fundamental question about the future of American politics: can the accidental social bargain be sustained in the absence of a global external challenge? Nothing is inevitable in politics, but there is evidence that the domestic order forged by the cold war is coming apart, ushering in a period of political disarray and posing daunting new challenges for parties and presidents. This decay and the tasks it implies will increasingly define the fault lines in American politics. Trouble ahead is visible in four areas.

First, power at the center of the political system is weakening. At the federal level the power of the presidency is eroding. Presidential authority is greatest in foreign and military policy. Without foreign threats, the salience of the presidency wanes. Outside foreign and military policy, the presumption of presidential preeminence is lacking, and many strong domestic groups and interests impede action. Similarly the overall importance of the federal government is in decline. Even if the size of the federal government remains large because of spending on domestic social programs, its political complexion will change.

Second, the ability to justify federal support for technological innovation and industrial development will decline, and state capacities for economic management could weaken. Without the cold war threat it will be necessary to justify industrial policies supporting promising future technologies on their own merits. National security agencies such as the

Defense Advanced Research Projects Agency have played a comparable role to Japan's Ministry for International Trade and Investment in stimulating high-tech development, but they lack an explicit mandate to help the civilian sector despite their long record of technological stimulus. American industrial policy debate must move into the open political arena where the cacophony of competing corporate, sectional, and ideological divisions weakens the chances for their survival. Without the cloak of national security secrecy, decisions on technology funding become more contentious and difficult to resolve.

Third, the cold war's end will make the achievement of domestic social equity and welfare more difficult, and will thereby reinvigorate class division and conflict. In the absence of a major foreign military threat, the size of the military will continue to decline, thus shrinking this vehicle for social mobility. Moreover, no longer faced with an ideological challenge to capitalism, the political costs of severe social inequity decline. Domestic concern for social equity will be further eroded as the relevant standard of comparison shifts to third world countries teeming with cheap labor, blighted by severe class inequity and bereft of rudimentary social programs. The American welfare state, already under fiscal pressure and lacking a strong constituency, is further weakened by the changing international environment.

Finally, the end of the long war will tend to erode national political cohesion, thus allowing ethnic and sectional differences to dominate politics. With the triumph of capitalism and the spread of liberal democracy, the distinctiveness of the United States as a "free" people will be diminished. If, as many argue, we are shifting from an age of geopolitics to geoeconomics, then national unity and cohesiveness are likely to weaken as deep sectional economic differences rooted in geography assert themselves. Also, the centrifugal tendencies in American culture will increasingly lack a national counterbalance, thereby eroding a common collective identity.

Is this bleak picture the entire story? Skeptics might raise several doubts. The

social bargain, though accidental in origin, may have achieved sufficient momentum and constituency to endure absent the conditions that generated it. Institutions tend to persist and create their own constituencies. Whatever the ultimate merits of this view, it is probably true that institutional inertia will slow the decay. But it is unlikely to prevent it, especially in an era of extreme fiscal limits.

Another possibility is that a new foreign threat will arise to reinvigorate the institutions of the long war. The most likely candidates are China, Japan, Germany or a united Europe. All are capitalist states and potential economic rivals, but aside from China they are also strong security allies of the United States. Although conflict among capitalist states may increase, the lines of conflict are not as clear-cut and alliances across national lines are as likely as those between them. Barring the unlikely degeneration of intracapitalist conflict into military confrontation, these conflicts are not likely to evoke measures of the sort needed to underpin the unraveling social bargain.

PRESIDENTS AND PARTIES

The end of the long war is also likely to significantly alter the balance of power between the parties and their ability to capture the White House. Since the 1940s, the Republican Party has dominated presidential politics, in large measure because of its stance toward the communist threat. When faced with an ominous foreign threat, the president's job description asked him to be "tough but responsible," something at which the Republicans excel. To be president during the cold war was to be the leader of the Western alliance—the man with the finger on the button—and candidates were judged accordingly. The first post–cold war presidential election in 1992 provides evidence of a new political pattern.

Republicans must find new ways to unify themselves. Political commentator George Will has tellingly observed that the Democrats are the party of government, but it is equally true that the Republicans—at least when in comes to

foreign policy—are the party of the state. Although opposed to a strong state in domestic affairs, the Republicans have been the most vigorous advocates of the national security establishment. With a consistently smaller bloc of registered voters, the Republicans captured the White House in seven of eleven races. In all seven victories (Eisenhower twice, Nixon twice, Reagan twice, and Bush once) the Republicans were clearly positioned to the right on issues of anticommunism. The Republican presidential candidates lost in 1948, 1960, and 1976 when Democrats appeared to be at least, if not more, anticommunist than the Republican candidates. (The anomaly of 1964 resulted from the fact that Johnson, a hawkish Texas Democrat, was strongly anticommunist, while Goldwater seemed threateningly irresponsible.) For the Republican Party, anticommunism in the postwar era served to rally supporters in much the same way that the ghost of Herbert Hoover and the Great Depression worked for the Democrats and "waving the bloody shirt" worked for the Republicans after the Civil War.

The 1992 presidential election marked the first defeat of an incumbent elected Republican president since Hoover, and it revealed the contours of a fundamentally new post–cold war political landscape. Like previous Republican presidents, Bush's strong suit was foreign and military affairs. He believed that victory in the Persian Gulf War would sustain his electoral support, but found that the popular impact of this episode quickly faded. Saddam Hussein may have looked like Hitler, but the American people were able to see that he represented an altogether different caliber of threat. Without a strong foreign threat, the presidential election turned on domestic issues that had long been overshadowed.

Taking the traditional Republican line, Bush hammered away on the issue of seasoned judgment and foreign policy experience, but with little consequence. The plausibility of Ross Perot as a presidential candidate was made possible by the fact that the public did not assess him with the old cold war standard—as a man who could calmly lead through crises in the shadow of nuclear war. That

Perot's legendary volatility and his long record of gun-slinging hypernationalism were hardly mentioned, let alone disqualifying, revealed just how little the American public remembered the standards by which it had so carefully judged previous candidates.

Republican liabilities were Democratic opportunities. Questions about Bill Clinton's character and military service record were much debated, but they did not have the impact they might have had in previous elections. Furthermore, Clinton was able to largely ignore foreign and military policy during the campaign without political cost.

The long war's end has opened a fissure in the Republican Party on foreign affairs that has yet to be fully explored. With the end of the cold war, the Republicans have lost an electoral trump card. More important, the party contains radically opposing impulses on foreign policy. One powerful impulse is inward looking and suspicious of the federal government. The new era has released a torrent of latent Republican isolationism and antistatism. During the cold war, even the most ardent antigovernment conservatives saw a strong central government as a crucial counterbalance to the menace of international communism. With the demise of the Soviet Union, conservatives increasingly see Washington as the "Evil Empire." The Oklahoma City bombing this April brought to public prominence a current in far-right thinking that is far more paranoid of federal power and foreign entanglement than perhaps at any time in American history. The intense fear of totalitarianism that was cultivated on the right during the cold war seems not to have ended, but to have been displaced toward the institutions of government and anything seen as foreign. This impulse is a more strident echo of the pre-cold war isolationism of the Republican Midwest and West that was exemplified by Senator Robert Taft of Ohio.

At the same time, a strong opposing impulse in Republican foreign policy thought is also evident. Over the last 50 years there has been a decisive shift in the American business community away from the inward-looking, Midwestern-centered capitalism of "Main Street" toward globally oriented, multinational, and outward-looking free traders. It is revealing that the most active support for NAFTA and the most recent GATT trade round came from the mainstream business community. It is difficult, therefore, to see how the free trade global village of business elites can be squared with nationalist, nativist, and protectionist factions.

THE BEGINNING OF THE NEW POLITICS

Many of these dynamics are already evident in the Clinton era. In the aftermath of the long war, the powers of the presidency, public expectations about the post, and the tasks commanding attention are being transformed.

The office of the presidency is ill-designed for achieving a domestic agenda. The powers of the office are not interchangeable: institutions created to do one thing cannot easily do another. The instruments assembled to wage global war against the Soviet Union do not readily lend themselves to cleaning up the environment, providing health care, or controlling street crime. There will be a strong temptation to view domestic problems through lenses left over from the cold war—declaring a "war on drugs" or proclaiming environmental degradation a national security threat. Doing so reflects the greater ease with which resources can be mobilized, consensus achieved, and powers deployed when national security is at stake. Unfortunately the national security rationale does not travel well. As the gridlock over energy policy in the 1970s demonstrated, it is difficult to resolve complex domestic problems even when they can be credibly linked with traditional national security concerns.

These constraints were vividly revealed during the first two years of the Clinton administration. Clinton came to office believing that he had a strong mandate to address the country's health care crisis. Following the long war pattern, Clinton cast the problem as one of "health care security" and sought a major expansion of the federal role in this area. Despite the high priority he attached to this issue and the control of both houses of Congress by the Democratic Party, Clinton's health care reform program was completely stymied.

The long war has also left expectations about the president and standards for measuring his performance in office; these will weigh heavily on future presidencies, with important ramifications for the legitimacy of the political system. During the cold war the president was first and foremost expected to be a successful leader of the anticommunist alliance. A central ingredient in a successful presidency during that era was the ability to display the toughness, resolve, and judgment on the grave issues at play on the world stage. If the public continues to judge presidencies by these wartime standards, presidents will appear chronically deficient. The combination of presidential incapacity and public expectation is likely to fuel the growing sense that political institutions are unresponsive to public demands.

Future presidents will also find themselves at an impasse in conducting foreign affairs. Given the way the office is structured and the difficulty in making major headway in dealing with domestic problems, it will be natural for post–cold war presidents to turn to foreign affairs—however strong their desire to focus on domestic policy. It is here that a president can operate as the spokesman for the nation, thus setting himself above the partisan struggles of mere politicians. But in this area presidents will also face frustration. The American public is now less concerned about foreign events and much less willing to pay the costs for international leadership. Fearful of diminishing its standing, the military has grown increasingly unwilling to see force used and suffer casualties, unless backed by overwhelming public support and core national security interests. With these constraints, the lofty trappings of presidential leadership are increasingly meaningless.

This pattern is present in the Clinton administration. Despite having been elected to refocus the power of the presidency on domestic problems, Clinton has been drawn into the foreign arena. In part this was inevitable, given the expectations and commitments the United

States has around the world. The continuing crisis in Bosnia and Herzegovina clearly reveals the new political terrain. As leader of NATO and advocate of an expanded UN role in peacekeeping, the United States was looked on to orchestrate a solution to the problem, thus prompting Clinton to focus extensively on it. But the antipathy of the American public to seeing its soldiers killed in battle meant that the threats and promises of the United States were empty. As a result, not only the credibility of the United States but the prestige and authority of the Clinton administration were badly tarnished. The post–cold war environment appears to offer few opportunities to act boldly and effectively, especially with military force. Indeed, many of the trouble spots beckoning American military intervention look like quagmires and promise to frustrate presidential initiative and divide public sentiment.

ERASING THE POLITICAL DEFICIT

Without the overriding mission of the long war, American politics is undergoing fundamental change. Even if the contours of this new era are undefined, the American political system is losing important and underappreciated sources of progressive modernization. The cold war forged and nurtured many central American institutions. As this period fades into history, there is reason to worry about the ability of America's parties and presidents to build coalitions and form a consensus around the management of a modern society and economy.

The current debate about the prospects for domestic renewal overlooks this deep-seated problem that strikes at the heart of the American polity. In effect, what the United States faces is yet another deficit—this one political. The American political system has enjoyed the benefits of public institutions whose formation did not require an explicit consensus on their behalf. Now American politics must confront the gap between the institutions it has come to depend on and the political support that undergirds them. The challenge for presidents and other would-be political leaders in the years ahead is to find ways to legitimate and build support for an activist state and a progressive political agenda without the easy rationale of an external threat. A new social bargain must be found. Only then will the long war really give way to a long peace.

Our Century . . . and the Next One

By Walter Isaacson

As centuries go, this has been one of the most amazing: inspiring, at times horrifying, always fascinating. Sure, the 15th was pretty wild, with the Renaissance and Spanish Inquisition in full flower, Gutenberg building his printing press, Copernicus beginning to contemplate the solar system and Columbus spreading the culture of Europe to the Americas. And of course there was the 1st century, which if only for the life and death of Jesus may have had the most impact of any. Socrates and Plato made the 5th century B.C. also rather remarkable. But we who live in the 20th can probably get away with the claim that ours has been one of the top four or five of recorded history.

Let's take stock for a moment. To name just a few random things we did in a hundred years: we split the atom, invented jazz and rock, launched airplanes and landed on the moon, concocted a general theory of relativity, devised the transistor and figured out how to etch millions of them on tiny microchips, discovered penicillin and the structure of DNA, fought down fascism and communism, bombed Guernica and painted the bombing of Guernica, developed cinema and television, built highways and wired the world. Not to mention the peripherals these produced, such as sitcoms and cable channels, "800" numbers and Websites, shopping malls and leisure time, existentialism and modernism, Oprah and Imus. Initials spread like graffiti: NATO, IBM, ABM, UN, WPA, NBA, NFL, CIA, CNN, PLO, IPO, IRA, IMF, TGIF. And against all odds, we avoided blowing ourselves up.

All this produced some memorable players. Look around. There's Lenin ar-

> *"As centuries go, this has been one of the most amazing: inspiring, at times horrifying, always fascinating."*

riving at the Finland Station and Gandhi marching to the sea to make salt. Winston Churchill with his cigar, Louis Armstrong with his horn, Charlie Chaplin with his cane. Rosa Parks staying seated on her bus and a kid standing in front of a tank near Tiananmen Square. Einstein is in his study, and the Beatles are on *The Ed Sullivan Show*.

In this special issue, the first of five in which we'll pick and profile the 100 most influential players of this century, we start with the category of leaders, politicians and revolutionaries. Future issues will look at artists and entertainers, business titans, scientists and thinkers, then heroes and inspirations. By the end of 1999 we plan to sum it all up with, among other things, a choice of the Person of the Century. It's not a simple task, but it helps to start by looking at what the great themes of this century have been.

Rarely does a century dawn so clearly and cleanly. In 1900 Freud published *The Interpretation of Dreams*,

ending the Victorian era. Her Majesty, as if on cue, died the following January, after a 63-year reign. Her empire included one-quarter of the earth's population, but the Boer War in South Africa was signaling the end of the colonial era. In China, the Boxer Rebellion heralded the awakening of a new giant. In America, cars were replacing horses, 42% of workers were in farming (today it's 2%), and the average life-span was about 50 (today it's around 75).

The tape recorder was unveiled in 1900 at the Paris Exposition, to which visitors flocked to be scandalized by Rodin's non-Victorian statues, and Kodak introduced the Brownie camera, an apt symbol of a century in which technology would at first seem magical, then become simple, cheap and personal. The Scholastic Aptitude Test was born that year, permitting a power shift from an aristocracy to a meritocracy. The Wright brothers went to Kitty Hawk to try out their gliders. Lenin, 30, published his first newspaper calling for revolution in Russia. Churchill, 25, was elected to the House of Commons. J. P. Morgan began working with a young executive named Charles Schwab to buy out Andrew Carnegie and conglomerate U.S. Steel, by far the biggest business in the world. And the German physicist Max Planck made one of the discoveries that would shape the century: that atoms emit radiations of energy in bursts he called quanta.

From these seeds was born a century that can be summed up and labeled in a handful of ways:

From *Time*, April 13, 1998, pp. 70-75. © 1998 by Time Inc. Magazine Company. Reprinted by permission.

THE CENTURY OF FREEDOM

If you had to pick a two-word summation, it would be: freedom won. It beat back the two totalitarian alternatives that arose to challenge it, fascism and communism. By the 1990s, the ideals developed by centuries of philosophers from Plato to Locke to Mill to Jefferson—individual rights, civil liberties, personal freedoms and democratic participation in the choice of leaders—finally held sway over more than half the world's population.

THE CENTURY OF CAPITALISM

Democracy can exist without capitalism, and capitalism without democracy, but probably not for very long. Political and economic freedom tend to go together. Early in the century, Theodore Roosevelt laid the foundation for a government-guided free market, one that encouraged individual initiative while protecting people against cartels and the colder faces of capitalism. His cousin Franklin confronted capitalism's greatest challenge, the Great Depression, by following these principles. Half a world away, Lenin laid the groundwork for a command economy, and his successor, Stalin, showed how brutal it could be. They ended up on the ash heap of history. Although capitalism will continue to face challenges, internally and externally, it is now the economic structure for most societies around the world.

THE ELECTRONIC CENTURY

A defining event actually occurred three years before the century began: the discovery of the electron by British physicist J. J. Thomson. Along with Planck's 1900 theory of quantum physics, this discovery led to the first weapon of mass destruction, which helped hasten the end of the Second World War and became the defining reality of the cold war. Alan Turing harnessed electronics to devise the first digital computers. Five

centuries earlier, Gutenberg's printing press had cut the cost of transmitting information by a factor of a thousand. That paved the way for the Reformation by allowing individuals to have their own Bibles, and for the progress of individual liberties, which became inevitable once information and ideas flowed freely. The transistor and the microchip have cut the cost of transmitting information by a factor of more than a million. The result has been a transition from an industrial age to an information age.

THE GLOBAL CENTURY

Human society over the millenniums has evolved from villages to city-states to empires to nation-states. In this century, everything became global. Much of the first half was dominated by the death spasms of an international order that for 400 years was based on the shifting alliances of European nation-states, but this time the resulting wars were world wars. Now not only are military issues global, so are economic and even cultural ones. People everywhere are threatened by weapons anywhere, they produce and consume in a single networked economy, and increasingly they have access to the same movies and music and ideas.

THE MASS-MARKET CENTURY

Yet another defining event of the century came in 1913, when Henry Ford opened his assembly line. Ordinary people could now afford a Model T (choice of color: black). Products were mass-produced and mass-marketed, with all the centralization and conformity that entails. Television sets and toothpaste, magazines and movies, shows and shoes: they were distributed or broadcast, in cookie-cutter form, from central facilities to millions of people. In reaction, a modernist mix of anarchy, existential despair and rebellion against conformity motivated art, music, literature, fashion and even behavior for much of the century.

THE GENOCIDAL CENTURY

Then there was the dark side. Amid the glories of the century lurked some of history's worst horrors: Stalin's collectivization, Hitler's Holocaust, Mao's Cultural Revolution, Pol Pot's killing fields, Idi Amin's rampages. We try to personalize the blame, as if it were the fault of just a few madmen, but in fact it was whole societies, including advanced ones like Germany, that embraced or tolerated madness. What they had in common was that they sought totalitarian solutions rather than freedom. Theologians have to answer the question of why God allows evil. Rationalists have one almost as difficult: Why doesn't progress make civilizations more civilized?

THE AMERICAN CENTURY

That's what TIME's founder Henry Luce called it in a 1941 essay. He was using the phrase to exhort his compatriots to prepare for war, to engage in the struggle for freedom. They did, yet again. And they won. Some countries base their foreign policy on realism or its Prussian-accented cousin, real-politik: a cold and careful calculation of strategic interests. America is unique in that it is equally motivated by idealism. Whether it is the fight against fascism or communism, or even misconceived interventions like Vietnam, America's mission is to further not only its interests but also its values. And that idealist streak is a source of its global influence, even more than its battleships. As became clear when the Iron Curtain collapsed in 1989, America's clout in the world comes not just from its military might but from the power and appeal of its values. Which is why it did, indeed, turn out to be an American Century.

So what will the next century be? The reams of guesses made in the next two years are destined to be digitally retrieved decades hence and read with a smirk. But let's take that risk, peer into the haze and slap a few labels on the postmillennial period:

In the digital realm, the Next Big Advance will be voice recognition. The rudiments are already here but in primitive form. Ask a computer to "recognize speech," and it is likely to think you want it to "wreck a nice beach." But in a decade or so we'll be able to chat away and machines will soak it all in. Microchips will be truly embedded in our lives when we can talk to them. Not only to our computers; we'll also be able to chat with our automobile navigation systems, telephone consoles, browsers, thermostats, VCRs, microwaves and any other devices we want to boss around.

That will open the way to the next phase of the digital age: artificial intelligence. By our providing so many thoughts and preferences to our machines each day, they'll accumulate enough information about how we think so that they'll be able to mimic our minds and act as our agents. Scary, huh? But potentially quite useful. At least until they decide they don't need us anymore and start building even smarter machines they can boss around.

The law powering the digital age up until now has been Gordon Moore's: that microchips will double in power and halve in price every 18 months or so. Bill Gates rules because early on he acted on the assumption that computing power—the capacity of microprocessors and memory chips—would become nearly free; his company kept churning out more and more lines of complex software to make use of this cheap bounty. The law that will power the next few decades is that bandwidth (the capacity of fiber-optic and other pipelines to carry digital communications) will become nearly free.

Along with the recent advances in digital switching and storage technologies, this means a future in which all forms of content—movies, music, shows, books, data, magazines, newspapers, your aunt's recipes and home videos—will be instantly available anywhere on demand. Anyone will be able to be a producer of any content; you'll be able to create a movie or magazine, make it available to the world and charge for it, just like Time Warner!

The result will be a transition from a mass-market world to a personalized one. Instead of centralized factories and studios that distribute or broadcast the same product to millions, technology is already allowing products to be tailored to each user. You can subscribe to news

sources that serve up only topics and opinions that fit your fancy. Everything from shoes to steel can be customized

---

"We'll encode our dreams and vanities and hubris. We'll clone ourselves, we'll custom-design our kids ... The challenges will be not scientific but moral."

---

to meet individual wishes. What does that mean for the modernist revolt against conformity that dominated art and literature? Postmodernism, with its sense of irony, is more amused by connections and historical hyperlinks.

The digital revolution that burns so brightly today is likely to pale in comparison to the revolution in biotechnology that is just beginning. Physicist Stephen Hawking, speaking at the White House last month on science in the next millennium, pointed out that for the past 10,000 years there has been no significant change in our human DNA. But over the next hundred years, we will be able and tempted to tinker. No doubt we'll make some improvements and some mistakes. We'll encode our dreams and vanities and hubris. We'll clone ourselves, we'll custom-design our kids. By playing Dr. Frankenstein, we'll have the chance to make miracles or monsters. The challenges will be not scientific but moral.

In the political realm, democratic capitalism, having defeated the twin foes of fascism and communism, is likely to face three others. The first is tribalism, as in Bosnia. This is, of course, nothing new. But democracies are often maladroit at dealing with minorities that seek group empowerment. The second challenge will be fundamentalism. Capitalism can be cold, consumption oriented and spiritless, alienating those who feel repelled by its modernity and its materialist values. Some will respond by embracing tradi-

tional religions or New Age spirituality, but there is also likely to be, especially in the Islamic world, a more fierce religious challenge that rejects individual liberties as well as the materialism that comes with capitalism. Finally, there is the radical environmentalism of the Green movements, which could start seeming less radical and more urgent if the quest for economic growth that is inherent in capitalism continues to threaten the health of the planet. To counter this, humans will have to become the first species to learn how to control its own population growth.

Among the few things certain about the next century is that it will be wired, networked and global. Because national borders will be unable to block the flow of information and innovation, the societies that thrive will be those that are comfortable with openness and with the free flow of services, goods and ideas.

By these standards, the U.S. is rather well positioned. Ever since the days of the colonial pamphleteers, we've been comfortable with the cacophony that comes from freedom of information. We're used to being multicultural, and though we're constantly struggling with the consequences, we don't Balkanize because of it. Our disputes, such as those over affirmative action, may be divisive, but we have the political and constitutional means to resolve them peacefully.

But like other nations, the U.S. will have to adapt to a new century. With a global economy that will be increasingly knowledge based, we will no longer be able to permit unequal educational opportunities. Schools will need to be open to competition and subjected to standards so that we avoid creating a two-tiered society. We also must realize, as both Theodore and Franklin Roosevelt did, that capitalism can be efficient but it can also be cold. America's social fabric is strong when it weaves together rewards for individual initiative and neighborly compassion for all members of the community. The ultimate goal of democracy and freedom, after all, is not to pursue material abundance but to nurture the dignity and values of each individual. That is the fundamental story of this century, and if we're lucky and wise, it will be the story of the next one.

We encourage you to photocopy and use this page as a tool to assess how the articles in **Annual Editions** expand on the information in your textbook. By reflecting on the articles you will gain enhanced text information. You can also access this useful form on our Web site at **http://www.dushkin.annualeditions.com/**.

NAME: _____ DATE: _____

TITLE AND NUMBER OF ARTICLE: _____

BRIEFLY STATE THE MAIN IDEA OF THIS ARTICLE: _____

LIST THREE IMPORTANT FACTS THAT THE AUTHOR USES TO SUPPORT THE MAIN IDEA:

WHAT INFORMATION OR IDEAS DISCUSSED IN THIS ARTICLE ARE ALSO DISCUSSED IN YOUR TEXTBOOK OR OTHER READINGS THAT YOU HAVE DONE? LIST THE TEXTBOOK CHAPTERS AND PAGE NUMBERS:

LIST ANY EXAMPLES OF BIAS OR FAULTY REASONING THAT YOU FOUND IN THE ARTICLE:

LIST ANY NEW TERMS/CONCEPTS THAT WERE DISCUSSED IN THE ARTICLE, AND WRITE A SHORT DEFINITION:

ANNUAL EDITIONS revisions depend on two major opinion sources: one is our Advisory Board, listed in the front of this volume, which works with us in scanning the thousands of articles published in the public press each year; the other is you—the person actually using the book. Please help us and the users of the next edition by completing the prepaid article rating form on this page and returning it to us. Thank you for your help!

ANNUAL EDITIONS: American History, Volume II, 15/E

ARTICLE RATING FORM

Here is an opportunity for you to have direct input into the next revision of this volume. We would like you to rate each of the 41 articles listed below, using the following scale:

1. **Excellent: should definitely be retained**
2. **Above average: should probably be retained**
3. **Below average: should probably be deleted**
4. **Poor: should definitely be deleted**

Your ratings will play a vital part in the next revision. So please mail this prepaid form to us just as soon as you complete it. Thanks for your help!

We Want Your Advice

RATING

ARTICLE

1. The New View of Reconstruction
2. Miriam Leslie: Belle of the Boardroom
3. The First Chapter of Children's Rights
4. The Stolen Election
5. 'The Chinese Must Go'
6. The Nickel and Dime Empire
7. Iron John in the Gilded Age
8. Terrorism Revisited
9. Electing the President, 1896
10. The Meaning of '98
11. Our First Southeast Asian War
12. How We Lived
13. Theodore Roosevelt
14. Woodrow Wilson, Politician
15. The Burden of Taxation
16. The Fate of Leo Frank
17. Margaret Sanger
18. Alcohol in American History
19. F. Scott Fitzgerald
20. When White Hoods Were in Flower
21. Bang! Went the Doors of Every Bank in America
22. A Monumental Man

RATING

ARTICLE

23. Eleanor Roosevelt
24. Home Front
25. Our Greatest Land Battle
26. The Biggest Decision: Why We Had to Drop the Atomic Bomb
27. The G.I. Bill
28. Baseball's Noble Experiment
29. From Plan to Practice: The Context and Consequences of the Marshall Plan
30. Echoes of a Distant War
31. Sputnik
32. Martin Luther King's Half-Forgotten Dream
33. Scenes from the '60s: One Radical's Story
34. The Legacy of Watergate
35. How the Seventies Changed America
36. The Near-Myth of Our Failing Schools
37. Can't Anybody Here Play This Game?
38. American Apartheid? Don't Believe It
39. Revolution in Indian Country
40. America after the Long War
41. Our Century . . . and the Next One

(Continued on next page)

ANNUAL EDITIONS: AMERICAN HISTORY, Volume II, 15th Edition

BUSINESS REPLY MAIL
FIRST-CLASS MAIL PERMIT NO. 84 GUILFORD CT

POSTAGE WILL BE PAID BY ADDRESSEE

Dushkin/McGraw-Hill
Sluice Dock
Guilford, CT 06437-9989

ABOUT YOU

Name _____ Date _____

Are you a teacher? ☐   A student? ☐
Your school's name _____

Department _____

Address _____ City _____ State _____ Zip _____

School telephone # _____

YOUR COMMENTS ARE IMPORTANT TO US !

Please fill in the following information:
For which course did you use this book?
_____

Did you use a text with this *ANNUAL EDITION*? ☐ yes ☐ no
What was the title of the text?
_____

What are your general reactions to the *Annual Editions* concept?
_____

Have you read any particular articles recently that you think should be included in the next edition?
_____

Are there any articles you feel should be replaced in the next edition? Why?
_____

Are there any World Wide Web sites you feel should be included in the next edition? Please annotate.
_____

May we contact you for editorial input? ☐ yes ☐ no
May we quote your comments? ☐ yes ☐ no